T0192655

Securing Office 365

Masterminding MDM and Compliance in the Cloud

Matthew Katzer

Apress®

Securing Office 365

Matthew Katzer
Hillsboro, OR, USA

ISBN-13 (pbk): 978-1-4842-4229-2 ISBN-13 (electronic): 978-1-4842-4230-8
https://doi.org/10.1007/978-1-4842-4230-8

Library of Congress Control Number: 2018966697

Copyright © 2018 by Matthew Katzer

This work is subject to copyright. All rights are reserved by the Publisher, whether the whole or part of the material is concerned, specifically the rights of translation, reprinting, reuse of illustrations, recitation, broadcasting, reproduction on microfilms or in any other physical way, and transmission or information storage and retrieval, electronic adaptation, computer software, or by similar or dissimilar methodology now known or hereafter developed.

Trademarked names, logos, and images may appear in this book. Rather than use a trademark symbol with every occurrence of a trademarked name, logo, or image we use the names, logos, and images only in an editorial fashion and to the benefit of the trademark owner, with no intention of infringement of the trademark.

The use in this publication of trade names, trademarks, service marks, and similar terms, even if they are not identified as such, is not to be taken as an expression of opinion as to whether or not they are subject to proprietary rights.

While the advice and information in this book are believed to be true and accurate at the date of publication, neither the authors nor the editors nor the publisher can accept any legal responsibility for any errors or omissions that may be made. The publisher makes no warranty, express or implied, with respect to the material contained herein.

Managing Director, Apress Media LLC: Welmoed Spahr
Acquisitions Editor: Joan Murray
Development Editor: Laura Berendson
Coordinating Editor: Nancy Chen

Cover designed by eStudioCalamar

Cover image designed by Freepik (www.freepik.com)

Distributed to the book trade worldwide by Springer Science+Business Media New York, 233 Spring Street, 6th Floor, New York, NY 10013. Phone 1-800-SPRINGER, fax (201) 348-4505, e-mail orders-ny@springer-sbm.com, or visit www.springeronline.com. Apress Media, LLC is a California LLC and the sole member (owner) is Springer Science + Business Media Finance Inc (SSBM Finance Inc). SSBM Finance Inc is a Delaware corporation.

For information on translations, please e-mail rights@apress.com, or visit www.apress.com/rights-permissions.

Apress titles may be purchased in bulk for academic, corporate, or promotional use. eBook versions and licenses are also available for most titles. For more information, reference our Print and eBook Bulk Sales web page at www.apress.com/bulk-sales.

Any source code or other supplementary material referenced by the author in this book is available to readers on GitHub via the book's product page, located at www.apress.com/9781484242292. For more detailed information, please visit www.apress.com/source-code.

Printed on acid-free paper

To Barbara—my friend, business partner, soul mate, and wife to whom I owe so much; I could never have written this book without your love and support.

Table of Contents

About the Author

 **Matthew Katzer** is the CEO and president of KAMIND IT, a direct Tier 1 Microsoft Gold Partner, and author of the best-selling cloud book *Office 365: Managing and Migrating Your Business in the Cloud* (Apress, 2013) as well as *Moving to Office 365* (Apress, 2015). He is an active member of many technical community organizations and local business communities.

Matt's focus on cloud solutions started in 2008, as he was looking at ways that businesses could grow quickly while still reducing operating costs. His interest in security began while working in Intel's security division.

Matt holds a BSEE from the University of Michigan and an Executive MBA from the University of Oregon. His greatest satisfaction comes from helping customers and others become more competitive by scaling their businesses in an increasingly technology-driven world.

About the Technical Review

Unlike most technical reviews, this one took a team approach, leveraging the talents of the internal team at KAMIND IT. This book lays out a collective and strategic security road map for businesses using Office 365. It brings together hard-earned "notes from the field" that the team at KAMIND IT has generated to help educate our clients as we support their goals for migrating to a secure environment based on Microsoft Office 365. Also, many customers attended KAMIND IT's Microsoft Cloud Immersion Experience training and gave feedback and suggestions to further clarify how Office 365 security can be easily implemented.

Acknowledgments

I want to thank all of my customers who have spurred me on to write this book and have encouraged me to share what I have learned. To my editors, who kept me going even when it seemed impossible, I owe a special debt of gratitude: Nancy Chen, Joan Murray, and Gwenan Spearing. Thank you all.

A special mention must also be made to Justin Slagle, our Microsoft business development manager; Matt Soseman, security architect at Microsoft; and the countless support staff at Microsoft who have helped steer me in the right direction.

Robin Robins of Technology Marketing Toolkit has inspired me in so many ways, and I want to thank her for the countless opportunities she has opened up for me. Her support has been invaluable.

I also want to acknowledge my core team at KAMIND IT, which allowed me the time to write this book, especially Chris Speigel and Barbara Dawson. Your teamwork amazes me!

Brian Geraths, photographer extraordinaire, has also helped me in many ways. Thank you, Brian.

Last but by no means least, my wife, Barbara—I owe her so much for her encouragement and support.

Without the assistance of all these individuals and companies, this book would never have been written.

Introduction

I started writing this book in 2016. At that time, the European Union had just released the new requirements for data privacy. Businesses were being breached, and millions of data records were being stolen and sold. Large organizations such as Sony, Target, and Equifax had millions of records of information stolen and sold on the dark web. Privacy was in turmoil. Some online search companies were selling millions of records of information for revenue. I was concerned and wanted to help businesses that use Office 365 do so in a secure manner.

Fresh off of coauthoring two security books, I personally felt that there were no reasons for having data breaches on Office 365. I researched the problem and discovered that the issue was directly related to the Office 365 subscriptions that the users purchased and their configurations. I also discovered that there was a secondary problem: users and most IT professionals did not know how to configure Office 365 in a secure manner. So, my goal with this book was to produce a practical security guide that could be used by businesses and IT companies in the Office 365 community.

Office 365 is a cloud-based service based on familiar software that you know—the Microsoft Office suite. It simply works, and you don't have to give up your intellectual property to use the service. Microsoft is adamant that the customer owns the data; Microsoft is only a custodian of the customer data, with a shared responsibility with the client. This is important. Not all cloud solutions are this forthright. My customers who use Office 365 have significantly reduced their IT service costs and their concerns in the areas of data security, compliance, and discovery. They reduce their IT costs because my company helps them choose the correct Office 365 licenses and helps them manage the security and logs.

This is a critical book of knowledge based on tried-and-true methods to deploy the services for Office 365. Office 365 is a secure service. The challenge was to write a book on a complex subject about security configurations in Office 365 and Azure cloud services and structure the book in such a way that any user could deploy Office 365/Azure securely. In some ways, I consider this a living book about security for Office 365. Not only does it cover the security of today, but given the changing nature of the tech world, the content will expand and evolve with newer tips and techniques through the blog at `www.kamind.com/blog`.

The problem has been how to present the information in a roadmap form that will help you build a secure solution for your company on Office 365. To do this I decided to use the Microsoft 365 E5 subscription along with an Azure Cloud Solution Provider (CSP) subscription and walk through the configuration process.

Chapter 1, "Why Security and Compliance?"

Security and compliance need to be a way of life as business becomes more digital. We need to look at the tools and how we run our businesses to determine how best to manage and secure them. The goal of the chief information security officer (CISO) and business owners is to protect and secure assets to increase business value. Security, Office 365, and Azure are all complex topics. I found the best way to describe this is to use one of the Microsoft simplified roadmaps that shows the security products and how they interoperate with each other. This chapter is an overview of the different security technologies and gives you the background. At the end of this chapter, you will have an understanding of the path we will follow on Office 365 and Azure security configuration.

Chapter 2, "Azure and Office 365 Security"

Office 365 and Azure are complex. As an Office 365 administrator, you need to configure the Office 365 portion of security but also the Azure security services. In this chapter, we build out the Azure data collection portals and the dashboards that are used to monitor and collect data. The information services we configure are Log Analytics Services, Azure Security Center and Office 365 Admin and Compliance Center. As part of this chapter, we link Cloud App Security to start the data collection from Office 365 and the device endpoints. Security is about information collection and analysis. In this chapter, you will see how to set up the Office 365 Security & Compliance Center and Azure Security Center. At the end of this chapter, you will have configured the key cloud data collection services.

Chapter 3, "Microsoft Secure Score"

Security is a difficult topic to address with moving threats. How do you tell whether you need to do more (or even if you have done enough)? In this chapter, you will take a deep dive into your security score and the measures that you can use to configure your Office

365 tenant and Windows 10 Security Center. This chapter talks about the security metrics and how to measure against them. At the end of the chapter, you will have a Microsoft security score (composed of Windows 10 and Office 365) that can be used to manage your security profile and threats against your business in the cloud.

Chapter 4, "Deploying Identity Management with EMS"

In this chapter, you will expand your learning by looking into the Enterprise Mobility Suite (EMS) from the viewpoint of identity management and information protection. Identity is how you manage information about the users and information protection is how you manage a user's access to protect corporate data. These tools are important in the management of Office 365 and Azure. At the end of this chapter, you will have configured the necessary components required to set up Azure information protection services from the Microsoft 365 E5 suite. You will have configured a base line identity Management and Information protection services in Azure. The Azure integration is a key service that you can use to manage your digital assets.

Chapter 5, "Mobile Device Management with EMS"

How do you manage user devices in the enterprise today? The answer is with Windows Information Protection (WIP), Mobile Device Management (MDM) and Mobile Applications Management (MAM). This chapter walks you through the configuration of MAM, WIP and MDM to manage your environment for Office 365 and Azure. At the end of this chapter, you will have a configured solution for both MAM, WIP and MDM to manage your corporate data. This chapter concludes with some helpful suggestions on the management of the mobile applications in your environment.

Chapter 6, "Using Office 365 Compliance Center"

Office 365 has a set of tools that are preconfigured for the compliance management of Office 365 through the Office 365 Security & Compliance Center. Office 365 includes a complete eDiscovery capability that offers all compliance managers the tools necessary to perform search discovery requests to meet the new regulation requirements. You are left with a "cookbook" on the deployment of the eDiscovery center and how to perform keyword searches across Exchange, OneDrive, and SharePoint.

Chapter 7, "Step-by-Step Migration"

The secret to a successful deployment to Office 365 is picking the correct plan that supports your business. Another key is the planning and purchase process. Once you select a plan, your primary consideration must be to ensure that the migration process is seamless for your organization. This chapter describes the basic purchase choices. It concludes with information about pre-deployment, deployment, and post-deployment.

Chapter 8, "Managing Office 365"

This chapter describes the different administration centers in Office 365 and the most common tools that you will use to administer Office 365. Depending on your Office 365 plan, there are 15 possible administration centers that are used to manage Office 365 and Azure. This chapter focuses on the primary administration portals for your business. The chapter closes with showing you how to use PowerShell to manage your Office 365 tenant.

I want to share with you what I've learned over the years so that you can benefit from my mistakes. I've been fortunate in that my company is a Microsoft direct Tier 1 Cloud Solution Provider, Cloud Champion, and a multi-year Microsoft Partner award winner. We've learned a lot as an early cloud adopter and want to share our experience. I wanted to write the book with a combination of the "why" and the "how-to" so business owners, Corporate Security Officers and IT Managers will have a roadmap to protect your company's digital assets. Good luck in your journey with the Microsoft Intelligent cloud!

CHAPTER 1

Why Security and Compliance?

Whenever IT managers hear the terms *security*, *compliance*, and *audit*, they tend to run and hide. Executive management fears the cost and additional regulations required. In fact, all levels of management are concerned. People think, does the government have access to my information? Are there federal regulations from the Department of Homeland Security to address? Has my company been sued? Executives and IT managers assume compliance and security mean nonplanned budget expenses.

The challenge that we all have is that we do not know what we do not know. It may sound trite, but this is the way people operate. Therefore, we need to change and adapt to a new security mind-set.

Today, all of us have a responsibility to manage information in a secure way. We are the custodians of information. Our role is to manage and protect not only our employees and fellow co-workers' information but also that of our clients and vendors. This is the new security and compliance mind-set I'm talking about. Many times, we abdicate this duty and do not realize the impact that we have on the users and businesses we support.

This book addresses the issues of security and compliance with Office 365. For us to reach the same destination together, we need to have a common understanding of the problem and the potential solutions that are available. In this book, you will learn how to use Office 365 security services to defend your organization from internal and external threats.

The purpose of this book is to provide you with the necessary tools and information to secure your Office 365 services. There are many solutions that you can use, but there are also many different ways you use those services. My goal is to assist you with additional information that you can use to manage your Office 365 services—in the most secure manner possible. On this journey together, we'll look at the threats we're facing in the current environment. Our first task as a team is to understand the threats and the Office 365 tools that can be used to combat the threats.

© Matthew Katzer 2018
M. Katzer, *Securing Office 365*, https://doi.org/10.1007/978-1-4842-4230-8_1

Security and Hackers

We all need to change the way that we look at security and how we handle threats. Before we can understand the threats, we need to take a step back and look at the industry as a whole and what is driving this new imperative. Security threats are everywhere.

> *"There are two kinds of companies: those who've been hacked and those who don't know they've been hacked."*

> —James Comey, Former Director, FBI

To understand hackers (also known as *bad actors*) today, you need to understand that they are after information in all forms for the sole purpose of selling the information. When an organization is hacked (such as Equifax), the attacker first tries to get into the organization by any means. The bad actor uses phishing attacks or overt trojans on USB memory stick (One of the classic trojans intrusions is to randomly drop a number of USB drives on the side walk in front of a building you want to penetrate. Statistically 1 out of 5 people will pick up the USB memory stick and plug it into their work computer to see what is on the USB memory stick and infect their system with a trojan). Once the hacker is in an organization, the bad actor goes quiet, and there is little detectable movement. The bad actor slowly probes the organization for weaknesses with the sole purpose of understanding the organization. The bad actor covertly learns the organizational structure and begins to understand the business practices and how to subvert them. This is what happens to all organizations, and you can see the results with large data breaches such as Sony and Target. The organizations do not even know their security has been breached.

Compliance and Security Are a Mind-Set

Vigilant companies must protect their environment with methodical planning and security best practices. Security and compliance audits are simple to achieve and do not break the bank. How you service these compliance audits is simply planning for them. This is where Office 365 is a must-have tool. Office 365 makes compliance audits simple because the compliance tools are built into Office 365. When you look at compliance, Microsoft cloud products are far simpler to use and easier to deploy than other methods. For years, Microsoft has been under the scrutiny of the Department of Justice (DOJ) and Federal Trade Commission (FTC) for many of its business practices in early 2000. This oversight has driven Microsoft to develop a common set of software-as-a-service (SaaS) products that are focused on business security.

Microsoft has developed products to address a fundamental business need, that is, to address internal compliance requirements. Today, these products form the basis of the Microsoft threat detection road map (see Figure 1-1).

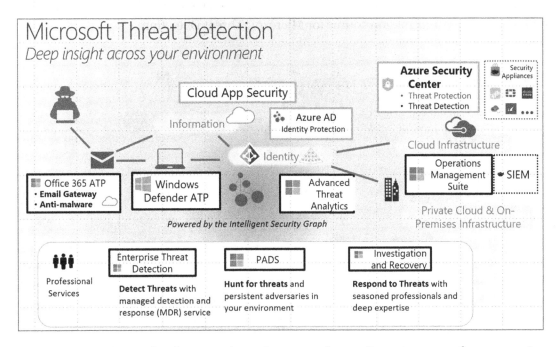

Figure 1-1. *Microsoft cybersecurity reference—threat detection map (courtesy of Microsoft)*

It is also ironic that the pressures that Microsoft faced in years past are now the pressures that we all face in our businesses. That is, how can we create full transparency and information controls in our business practices? As I said, to start we need to change our mind-set. It is all about security and the road map that we use to get to our destination.

Note   Office 365 security/compliance is a large topic. To simplify the view for new users, the approach I will take in this book is to look at Office 365 as an application that runs in Azure. Looking at this from the book's perspective, Azure provides identity services/management for Office 365. So, this book is about using Azure identity services to manage Office 365 security and configuring those services. I will not go into Azure in much detail, unless it helps clarify Office 365.

3

The Microsoft cybersecurity road map shown in Figure 1-1 ties all the Microsoft cloud services together. Before you can truly understand this road map, you need to understand where the data comes from and how it is collected. This is where the Intelligent Security Graph shown in Figure 1-2 comes into play. The Intelligent Security Graph is the base information source for Microsoft Threat Detection.

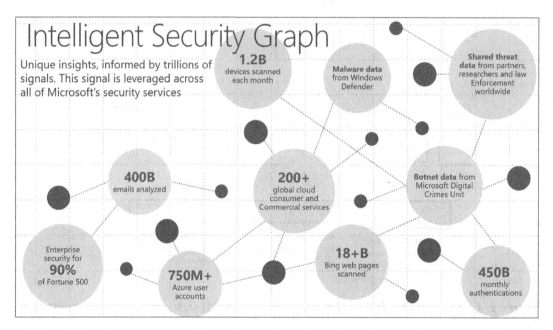

Figure 1-2. *Intelligent security graph (courtesy of Microsoft)*

Note   Not on Office 365 yet and wondering what to do next? Chapter 7 covers how to migrate to Office 365.

All new security models for preventing attacks comes down to the analysis of information. Microsoft published the Intelligent Security Graph as the basis of its security backbone. It is the collection of information from billions of devices and data from endpoints around the world. This information is analyzed to look at the user usage of Microsoft programs and at different attacks by bad actors. The data shows trends of attacks, which provides Microsoft with the necessary responses. In other words, this data allows the analytic tools to detect a bad actor and take the appropriate actions to combat the threat. The different Microsoft technologies such as Windows 10 Defender and Windows 10 Advanced Threat Protection (WATP) deploy these defenses automatically to the connected devices. WATP uses new behavioral analysis to defend the desktop and is included in the office 365 subscriptions for Windows 10 E5.

The simplest example of the impact of information collected in the Intelligent Security Graph is to look at the Office 365 login process. You have probably run into the situation where you try to log in to Office 365 in your browser and get prompted to try again. You know that the password is correct and cannot understand why you can't log into the service.

When you look under the hood and you review the data collected in the Intelligent Security Graph, you will begin to understand that Microsoft looks not only at the location where you are logging into the service but also at how you logged into the service. The way you type your password or login ID is an important action. The pause between letters and how long you wait before you press Enter are other forms of identification. If I look at myself, for instance, my right hand types faster than my left hand. This tracking maps to a unique behavior and a predictable pattern. This is one of my "digital characters." In this AI-enabled world, everything is collected and analyzed to determine whether it's really you or a bad actor. If the Office 365 security mechanism classifies you as a bad actor, you need to provide some additional level of authentication to ensure you are who you say you are. In Figure 1-3, the learner builds a pattern for your account. The patterns are unique (albeit not 100 percent trustworthy) and provide a level of guarantee that you are indeed the correct person for the account.

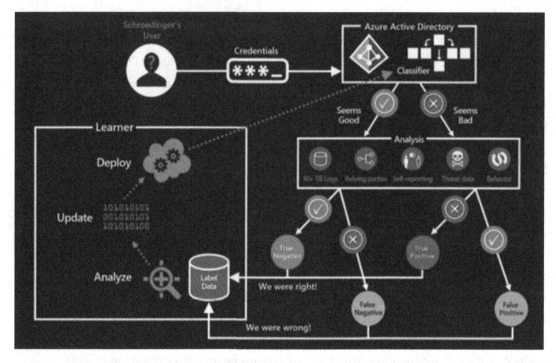

Figure 1-3. *Login processing for Office 365 (courtesy of Microsoft)*

As another example, say you use Microsoft security services to manage your account. You can link additional information about you to your account such as cell phone, e-mail address, office phone number, and answers to those pesky security questions. Any information like this is linked into the multifactor authentication (MFA) service and is integrated with Azure Identity Protection (more about this in Chapter 4). Combine this new security information along with a customized Office 365 portal and compute devices that are "joined to Azure Active Directory" and you have a secure compute environment. The integrated security of Office 365 is further enhanced with your credentials and user identity protection.

As a side note, look at your neighbors' homes as you drive home from work. Do you see homes with alarm signs on them? Are the homes well-lit or dark? If you are a bad actor, which home would you pick to break into? Which home would give you the best opportunity as a thief? Would you pick the well-lit home with the alarm sign on it or the dark house with few lights on and no posted alarm sign? Your Office 365 organization is very much like your home. What are the tools that you need to look at to make it so the bad actors look somewhere else? What changes do you need to make in your business processes and basic configuration so that the environment is much more difficult to clone? Do you have a universal cloud-based signature (like Crossware, https://www.crossware.co.nz) that signs all e-mail from all devices in the same way so you can easily tell whether your e-mail has been spoofed? You need to approach your SaaS security from this mind-set—assume that you could be breached and put tools in place to make it difficult for the bad actors to impersonate you.

You can add internal security controls with Azure privilege identity to control access to the Office 365 tenant by your administrators. Figure 1-4 shows my home page login for Office 365, and it is different from the generic home page login for Office 365. This difference is important for the simple reason that the bad actors do not expect it.

Figure 1-4. *Customized login portal for Office 365*

Changing your home login screen for Office 365 helps your employees recognize when something is not quite right. The bad actors send out millions of e-mails in an attempt to break into a company, so if you change the default look (like putting the alarm sign outside of your house), you also make it difficult for the bad actors to penetrate the company. When your users receive a phishing e-mail and someone clicks the bait (yes, there will be one person who will click the link in the e-mail no matter how much training you do), they know that the company's front door is different (because you have trained them) and so do not try to log in to the phishing site with their credentials.

This is a simple thing to do to make your digital home harder to breach than your neighbors' homes. If you make this simple change, you will have completed the following:

- Deployed custom login screens to help users detect phishing attacks

- Deployed multifactor authentication (using cell phones and a non-Office 365 e-mail account)

- Deployed Azure privilege identity to manage the security aspects for your administrative user account

These items are simple to complete. These capabilities (and others) exist within the Office 365 security license. Once you add these capabilities, you have drastically improved the security of your Office 365 service, and in the process you have made your company less susceptible to attacks by bad actors. Remember, security is a mind-set. The way I approach security is to review weekly (and sometimes daily and hourly) the accounts that my organization manages for security. On these accounts we deploy the Microsoft 365 Enterprise E5 suite (a combination of Office E5, Enterprise Mobility Suite [EMS] E5, and Windows 10 E5 security software). This allows us to handle both proactive and reactive security. During my weekly review session, I look at the security of the Office 365 organization. I review a set of key reports that cover the health of the behavior of the employees. These behavior reports flag actions based on incorrect privacy data releases or bad actors impersonating users in the organization.

A key component of an organization's security strategy is to continuously review the employee behaviors, looking for ways to educate employees to improve security and looking for ways to address any data leaks by bad actors. In fact, a review of the security policy by the computer information security officer (CISO) and of any privacy issues by the data protection officer (DPO) is crucial for a business's long-term survival. Typically, I look at the following reports to get an understanding of the security of the business:

- Cloud App security (CAS) dashboard, showing the dashboard access

- Service assurance status of the Office 365 and Azure tenants

- Azure Advanced Threat Protection security dashboard and reports

- Windows Security Center for Windows Advanced Threat Protection (WATP)

- Microsoft Secure Score value

In Chapter 2, we will build the baseline reporting structure and detail of the reports that you need to review. After you set up and enable some basic Azure services, in Chapter 3 you will look at your Microsoft Secure Score for your cloud-based services and make changes to improve that score. You will use the Microsoft Secure Score for both Office 365 and Windows 10 E5 Advanced Threat Protection.

Note   The DPO is the person responsible for the data management and privacy policies in the company. This is different than the compliance officer. The compliance officer looks for governance activity, such as related to a FINRA or SEC policy. The DPO looks for data privacy violations. In small organizations, these are the same person. Under the new data protection laws (in the European Union and California), all companies (no matter how small) must have a DPO role assigned.

In another example, Figure 1-5 shows the Azure Advanced Threat Protection analytics (see `https://portal.atp.azure.com`) to detect patterns of access. This is the new model for security. (The old model for security consisted of bloated data scanners looking at known bad program signatures.) The new model is an AI-based machine learning or deep learning model that looks at behaviors and characteristics. When you look at the data from the Microsoft Intelligent Threat Graph, the information that is detected across the user base is integrated into the different security tools. The new model incorporates behavior analysis of the data access and threat modeling of systems activities on desktop and mobile devices.

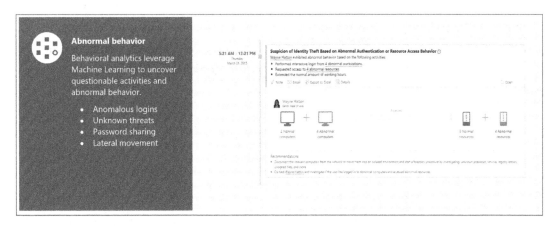

Figure 1-5. *Advanced Threat Protection a dashboard for on-premises/ Azure endpoints*

Detection today looks at how applications work and how users use the applications. This combination of data and usage collection develops an operational profile for the users. As an example, let's look at Microsoft Word, which is a fancy text editor. It does not run administrator scripts or look at permissions (or change user permissions and access). You would not expect Word to invoke an administrator application that changes a user's password or performs other administrative functions. The next-generation security software operates in this manner. It analyzes the applications (on a Mac or PC) and logs (or blocks) the nonstandard behavior when it is detected.

In addition, we are not faced with just security for the sake of security; we are also faced with new requirements on how governments expect us to manage our employees and customers' information. Security is a broad topic, and Office 365 contains hundreds of product codes. This book is based on the configuration of a specific security suite called Microsoft 365 Enterprise E5.

To simplify the process, you will use the Microsoft 365 Enterprise E5 subscription as a base for all configurations. To continue on our security journey, you will need to deploy a Microsoft 365 E5 subscription and an Azure subscription. Azure Cloud Service Provider (CSP) subscriptions are nothing more than a payment commitment through a Microsoft cloud partner.

My goal in this chapter is to expose you to the different aspects of security in Office 365 and slowly help you configure your Office 365 and Azure security service. To get started on this journey, let's look at the European regulation—the General Data Protection Regulation (GDPR)—that will have a major impact on how you manage personal information. Office 365 is designed around privacy. But for privacy to work, you need to conform to the new and upcoming regulations. The U.S. version of GDPR is coming. In fact, California has recently passed the California Consumer Privacy Act (CCPA), and many states are about to clone the same law. We all need to change our view about security and data privacy. Let's take a quick look at the GDPR and then step through some Office 365 security features.

General Data Protection Regulation and Privacy Policies

Information security is an ever-changing landscape. As a compliance officer (or IT manager), you must constantly be aware of changes in the laws and regulations. The EU GDPR law will have a dramatic impact on everyone who manages any IT activity. We will all need to change our business processes and software compliance tools to ensure that our organizations will conform (see Figure 1-6).

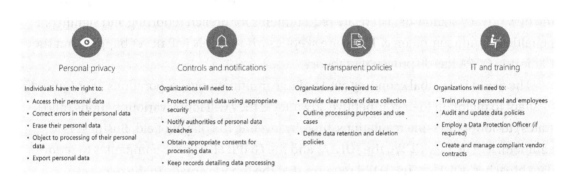

Figure 1-6. *EU GDPR overview (courtesy of Microsoft)*

All IT managers and compliance officers need to recognize that there will be a significant change starting in 2018 that will affect personal privacy and how we as both businesses and consumers need to understand our responsibilities under the European Union General Data Protection Regulation. The law was introduced in May 2016 and became fully enforceable in May 2018. The GDPR put in place privacy policies, strengthening data protection controls and making breach notification procedures highly transparent. Breaking the GDPR rules can generate fines of 20 million euros or 4 percent of the worldwide revenue of the corporation—there are no business exemptions. California, in June 28, 2018, enacted the California Consumer Privacy Act. The CCPA, like the GDPR, has stiff fines. If the CCPA was in effect when the Target breach occurred a few years ago, Target's fines would have been $5 billion.

The impact for business is significant. The GDPR puts in place transparent policies for data management. This policy is a requirement for all entities that have a business transaction with the EU and all entities that consume EU information. Why should you care if your business operates only in the United States? The answer is simple: if your business transacts or allows any product or service to be purchased or consumed in a country that is covered under the GDPR, you have no choice but to conform. Again, the penalties are severe. The GDPR measures the fines in a percent of the gross sales of the organization. The California CCPA measure fines per data record. In both regulations, the fines are extreme.

Office 365 is a foundational service that is designed to meet the GDPR requirements. Office 365 with Azure services collects information for audit and analysis for millions of endpoints. What each of us needs to do next is to look at our organization and discuss how we need to change our business processes and business practices to conform to the new regulations. This is important because these standards will take over worldwide as the new privacy standards. There are requirements for breach reporting and significant penalties for noncompliance. There are skeptics who say this will never happen, but the California CCPA has disproven that theory.

The world is a global economy, and as large multinational corporations are required to adapt to maintain their competitive advantage, they will lobby various nations (and states) to adopt the same regulations, thereby leveling the playing field. Business is competitive. The new CCPA, the HIPAA, and the GDPR all require companies to report data breaches quickly. The GDPR requires that the report is made to the relevant supervisory authority no later than 72 hours after the data breach occurs (note this is not business hours).

The GDPR is applicable to businesses of all sizes—both large and small. Its basis is all about how personal data is managed for employees, contractors, and customers. The regulation is broad. Some data is processed under the GDPR, and some data is not managed under the GDPR. Looking at the GDPR in detail, there are four tenets to the regulations that all organizations need to address.

- Personal privacy and individual rights to access collected information

- Controls and notifications that an organization must deploy under new regulations

- Transparent policies with data management

- IT training and responsibilities for the organization collected data

Getting back to Office 365 and your own company, you need to look at the changes you need to adopt to conform to the GDPR and other regulations. This will allow you to be competitive and transparent in your business practices. Where and how does Office 365 come into play? The Microsoft road map is designed to implement security processes that conform to the GDPR practices. When you look at products like Enterprise Mobility Suite or Advanced Threat Protection, you are looking at tools that help organizations conform to the new global regulations. The GDPR includes any data, images, or analytics that can be linked to any person. Organizations must look at the four tenets of security shown in Figure 1-7 and implement the necessary policies. Organizations must take organizational and technical measures that manage the data for the appropriate security of the data. Article 28 of the GDPR specifically talks about the processor that manipulates the data on behalf of the customer. The responsibility is shared between the controller and the processor. As compliance officers, we are custodians for our users' information, and we need to understand what we need to do to conform. Let's consider each of these areas for a better idea as to the requirements and see how the Microsoft cybersecurity road map can help us conform to these requirements.

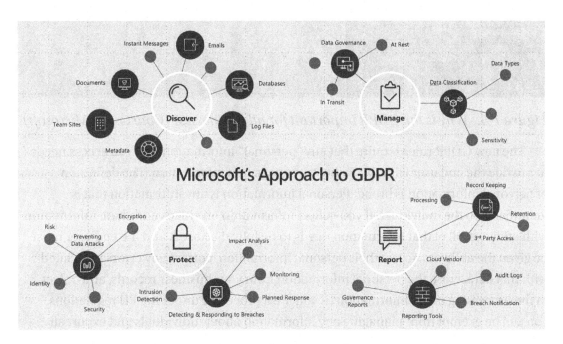

Figure 1-7. *Microsoft approach to implementing the GDPR regulation changes (courtesy of Microsoft)*

Personal Privacy and Individual Rights

Personal privacy rights require you to implement Office 365 Advanced Data Governance (ADG). The ADG capabilities are part of the Microsoft 365 E5 license that we are using in this book. The new data protection laws are about how we managed personal privacy. To manage personal privacy, you need to also manage the different cloud-based apps that are installed in the environment using tools like Cloud App Security. Everything is about personal data protection and the services used to manage personal information (see Figure 1-8).

GDPR: Not just Europe.

The GDPR applies more broadly than many people think. The law imposes new rules on companies, government agencies, non-profits, and other organizations that offer goods and services to people in EU or that collect and analyze data tied to EU residents—no matter where they are in the world.

GDPR is applicable to organizations of all sizes and all industries.

It all comes down to personal data.

GDPR analysis begins with understanding what data exists and where it resides. The GDPR regulates the collection, storage, use, and sharing of "personal data."

Personal data is defined very broadly under the GDPR as any data that relates to an identified or identifiable natural person. Data can reside in:

- Customer databases
- Feedback forms filled out by customers
- Email content
- Photos
- CCTV footage
- Loyalty program records
- HR databases

Figure 1-8. *Why is the GDPR important for all businesses? (Courtesy of Microsoft)*

The new GDPR rules require that any "personal" information that you access needs to provide the end user with the ability to manage that information. The definition of personal information is broad. Personal information is any information that is identifiable to the individual. If you collect information on videos and share information with affiliates, all of that information needs to be fully disclosed, and the end user must be given the ability to access their personal information, correct any errors associated with that data, erase the personal information from your business records, and object to the processing of the information (if you are a processor under the EU regulations, you can be exempt from managing any information about individuals and export all information that you have collected on them).

Note   Some people think that in the United States they are not subject to personal data protection laws. However, because of the GDPR, there has been an increase in audits and fines associated with all sorts of data privacy violations. Check out `https://ocrportal.hhs.gov/ocr/breach/breach_report.jsf`.

As a business manager, you need to seriously look at how you manage personal data and what controls you have on that data. If you are a multinational company that does business in the European Union, you are subject to data regulations—even if you are based in the United States. The privacy laws (worldwide, not just in the United States) are changing, and the data breach laws and the penalties for noncompliance are significant. One of the new features that Google is providing in the European Union to comply with the GDPR is the ability to destroy all information collected in Gmail accounts and the Chrome browser. This capability is slowly being introduced in the United States.

Note   Organizations tend to collect much more personal information than what is needed to complete a job or support customers. For example, IT service companies do not need to know the sex, home address (unless you support computers in the home), or any personal characteristics of the people we support—and we should not know their home phone numbers. As a business, unless we have a business reason to collect information, we do not want or care to have any personal information. Too many times we collect personal information for no apparent reason. Everyone should look at the information they collect in their businesses and ask the question—is there a business reason for the information? If there is no business reason, then remove the information from your systems.

Controls and Notifications

The management of personal information is only one aspect of the new privacy laws. Other requirements are based on the type of data maintained. There is a fine line between personal information and health-related information, for example. The fines for data breaches and security are significant, and you need to use different data storage and encryption methods for the data that you retain. There is a requirement to notify "supervisory" authorities (local, state, federal and international agencies) when a data breach occurs. You need to get permission to process personal data, and you need to keep detailed records (with no time limitations) on how you process the data. Figure 1-9 shows the data visibility that you need to have in your company to meet the GDPR requirements.

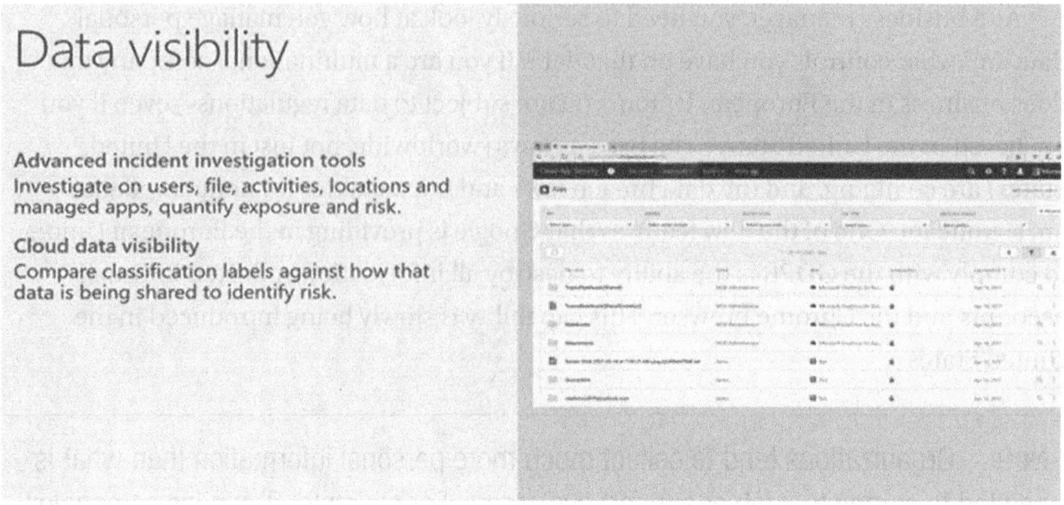

Figure 1-9. Data access visibility (courtesy of Microsoft)

The GDPR requires different rules for data controllers and for data processors. As an IT manager, you are required to manage the audit logs and security associated with different data types. In some cases, you will be the data processor, and in other cases you will be the data controller. In either case, how you manage, supervise, and review access to information is critical. How you use the different tools to manage this service (such as Compliance Manager in the Microsoft Security and Trust center to managed GDPR compliance) reduces your business liability as well as your personal liability.

Note   *Data processors* are entities that receive data from data controllers and process personal information (security lookup, credit references, etc.). Under the GDPR regulations, the management of the data is a shared responsibility. *Data controllers* control the personal information. In this case, this is the Office 365 service.

Transparent Privacy Policies with Data Management

The latest federal laws require notification of the usage of private information, but the laws are so broad that no one really understands what is going on. What the GDPR has done is simplify the requirements. The GDPR has defined organizations that process information and organizations that supply information. The California CCPA does something similar. Under the GDPR, all data controllers and data processors are required to provide a clear statement (which needs to be approved by regulators) about data collection and what type of data is collected. There are also requirements on data processing as well as a full audit process for the data (what has been done, what was changed) and the data retention policy associated with that information and audit logs. In other words, you need a 100 percent transparent policy in how data is used, who it is shared with, and why. Along with this is a new requirement that the personal data can be deleted at any time if requested by the individual. This is also part of the California CCPA. As IT managers and CISOs, we need to look to the future and expect that personal information (from consumers, business associates, employees) management regulation will be more stringent; therefore, we need to develop the processes and learn to use the tools with Microsoft Security and Compliance center to address these new requirements.

IT Training and Responsibilities

All types of security require training. You need to establish the necessary process rules and train the IT personnel to manage the information according to the regulations. It is imperative that information is managed properly. GDRP requires that every company have a data protection officer (DPO) who has the responsibility to manage the information. The regulation also provides methods of contact and requirements for the users who have access to personal information.

Organizations will need to train individual who have access to personal information under the new GDPR privacy requirements. There needs to be a full audit of information access. In addition, vendors that transact against data from a data collector must be fully complaint with the GDRP requirements.

GDPR Next Steps

As the Corporate Information Security Officer (CISO), my role has just expanded to the DPO role in addition to my traditional compliance role. It is no longer acceptable to use older tools that no longer meet the new data regulations. As the CISO, I need to be proactive and look at how to minimize my organization's risk. The GDPR is a wake-up call on data management. The call to action for all of us is to reduce the amount of personal information that we collect and to implement additional management tools to manage our employees' and client information. Information management is the key to managing our business securely.

Microsoft Trusted Cloud

Office 365 services are built on a secure public platform from the ground up. The implementation is a partnership with Microsoft and its customers (see Microsoft Cloud Security for Enterprise Architects at `https://www.microsoft.com/en-us/download/48121`) and is built from Microsoft's Trusted Cloud principles (see Figure 1-10).

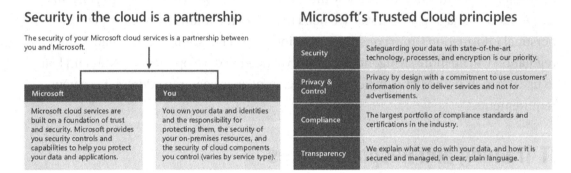

Figure 1-10. *Microsoft Cloud Security for Enterprise Architects (courtesy of Microsoft)*

The Microsoft threat detection road map (shown in Figure 1-1) shows the different capabilities that are in the Microsoft Office 365/Azure offering. Regardless of the security services that are built around Office 365 and other Microsoft SaaS services, the data owner is the customer. Microsoft acts as a custodian for the customer data and continuously looks at how the data is accessed (and not what's in the data) and who is accessing the data. Since Microsoft does not own the customer data but is acting as a custodian, the responsibilities are different. The difference is that this is a partnership between Microsoft and the client who owns the data. When you look at the changes in the regulatory landscape over data privacy, Microsoft's management of the data—as the custodian—is aligned. Likewise, as an IT manager or a CISO, you must also accept that you are the custodian of your company data and accept that shared responsibility with Microsoft. From this viewpoint, when you look at security in the Microsoft cloud, you should be concerned with these five questions:

- Do you know who is accessing your data?

- Can you grant access to your data based on risk in real time?

- Can you find and react to a breach?

   – Can you protect your data on devices, in the cloud, and in transit?

   – Is security integrated into a user's day-to-day activities with little effort?

These are just a few of the questions that you need to be asking your IT staff to ensure that you have the different solutions in place to address the security needs of your organization. Looking back at the Microsoft threat detection road map, there are a key set of services that are designed around the fundamental capabilities of the Microsoft cloud.

   – Exchange e-mail gateway/anti-malware services called Office 365 Advance Threat Protection (ATP)

   – Windows Defender with Advance Threat Protection (WATP)

   – Cloud App Security (CAS)

   – Azure AD Identity Protection

   – Azure Security Center

   – Azure Advance Threat Protection

   – Log Analytics workspace

   – Mobile Application Management, Windows Information Protection and Mobile Device Management

Most data breaches originate from some form of identity management breach. This type of breach is either because of incorrect permissions or a bad actor getting access to a user identity through various phishing means. The goal of the Office 365 security services is to provide detection and remediation of data breaches; Office 365 also uses the information gained to be proactive in managing the services. The Office 365 security services are designed to look at the behavior of the user based on the user role. These services are a combination of different service offerings and are described next.

Exchange E-mail Gateway/Advanced Threat Protection

Office 365 Advanced Threat Protection protects users from unsafe e-mail attachments and message URLs. The service can work in Office 365, work stand-alone, or in a hybrid environment when the e-mail services are routed through Office 365. ATP processes all URLs and e-mails that are sent to the user's mailbox. These URLs are examined in real time and blocks access to bad sites and code. ATP also deals with dynamic threats.

Dynamic threats are when the links in the e-mail are valid when initially processed by the service and later turn bad because of delayed execution payload. Figure 1-11 is an example of the ATP service executing on a delayed payload link.

Office 365 ATP also validates attachments. Office 365 ATP not only looks for unsafe links but also looks for unsafe attachments and will block them from the user's mailbox. The user can still override the unsafe attachments, so no data is lost in the case of mischaracterization.

The Office 365 ATP service is included as part of the Microsoft 365 E5 license and is optional with all other 365 services. As a matter of recourse, I recommend that all clients include this license with their Office 365 service. In fact, my organization requires that any customer that we provide security support must purchase this license.

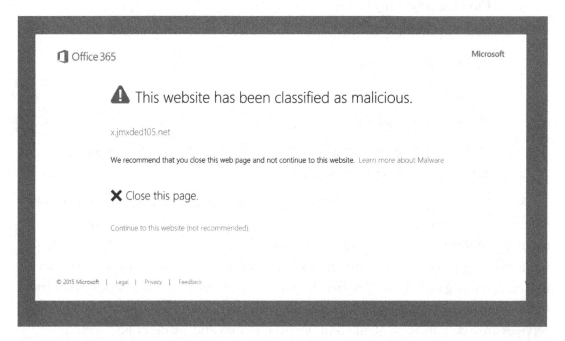

Figure 1-11. *Office 365 Advanced Threat Protection trigger on a malware-based URL*

Windows 10 Defender Advanced Threat Protection

Windows 10 Defender Advanced Threat Protection (`https://securitycenter.windows.com`) is the next generation of behavioral threat and deep learning tool. This tool is included in the Microsoft 365 E5 security suite and is an optional tool of other Office 365 subscriptions (such as Windows 10 E5 subscription). Windows Defender Advance Threat

Protection not only blocks malicious activity but also provides postbreach detection, investigation, and response to ongoing attempts.

Figure 1-12 shows a trigger on one of the alerts from Windows 10 Defender Advanced Threat Protection. In this example, a malicious activity was detected in a Word application. The Windows 10 Defender Advanced Threat Protection monitoring service detected and blocked the malicious activity. In this case, this attack was a kernel attack. Traditional antivirus software would not have caught this activity because traditional antivirus is siginiture based. This attack was detected by the Windows Defender Advance Threat Protection AI behavioral change monitoring.

Figure 1-12. *Windows Defender Advanced Threat Protection trigger in Word (courtesy of Microsoft)*

Another feature of Windows Defender Advanced Threat Protection is the historical analysis of various attacks on the user (see Figure 1-13). In this case, you can see a complete history of the users, the machines for which a user has logged in to the Office 365 and other services, and what type of behavioral problems were detected.

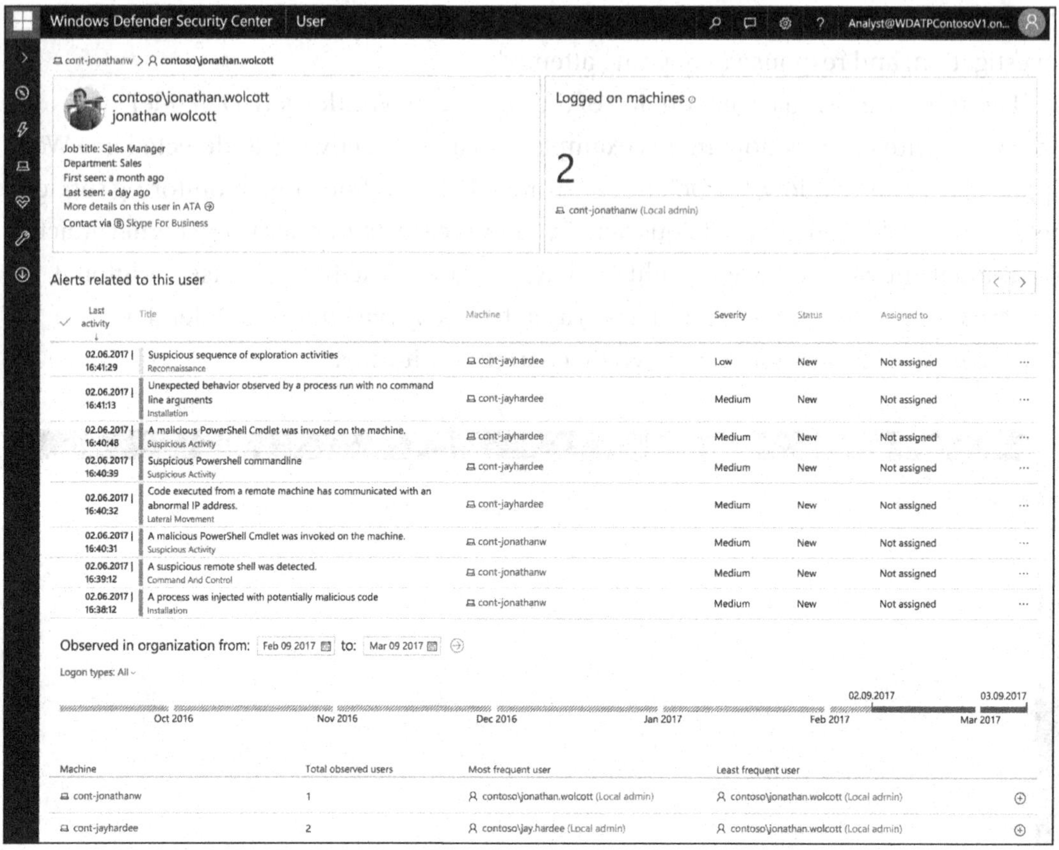

Figure 1-13. *Windows Defender ATP: historical analysis (courtesy of Microsoft)*

Windows Defender is built into the core of Windows 10 operating systems. In other words, it is not a third-party add-on, and it is integrated with the Microsoft intelligent security graph. Simply, this means that when a breach is detected in the various endpoints, Windows Defender ATP (the Windows 10 that includes the Windows E5 with Advance Threat Protection extensions) begins to monitor and block malicious activity in all connected endpoints.

As you deploy Windows Advanced Threat Protection in this book, you will also collect Windows Telemetry data. Windows Telemetry, when used with Windows Advanced Threat Protection, will give you the ability to identity lateral attacks that the bad actors use to penetrate your environment.

A *lateral attack* is an attack used to breach the defenses in a company. The bad actor looks for a weak entry point (such as a Mac with an out-of-date version of OS X or a 3-year-old BIOS). The bad actor breaches the system, and the help-desk folks try to remotely address the problem. The bad actors use the information from the help-desk access to attack other systems in the network. Windows 10 Defender ATP and Azure ATP help protect and identify this threat.

Cloud App Security

Cloud App Security (CAS) is a key component in the ongoing identification of security breaches. There are new apps released daily with new features and exploits, and users do not know whether an app is valid when they install it. They just download the cloud application and try the service and then uninstall the application. This is where malicious services will creep into the enterprise environment and exploit the user credentials and supply personal data to third-party services. Under the new data privacy laws, this is a data breach.

What Cloud App Security does is to detect the activity of users either from agents running on the local machine (agent-based) or via access to the firewall and other security appliances (agent-less) in the environment. Cloud App Security provides visibility into the user desktop activities, controls for sanctioned apps, deep integration with Office 365, integration with Microsoft intelligent graph to improve detection, remediation, and proactive management (see Figure 1-14).

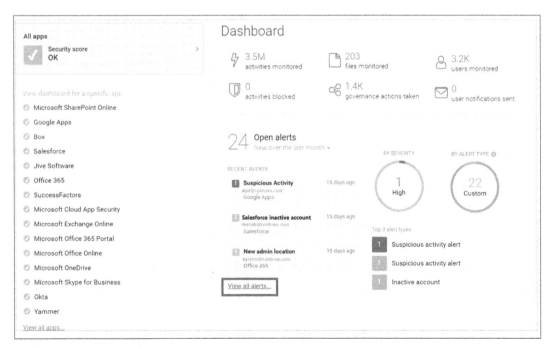

Figure 1-14. *Cloud App Security dashboard (courtesy of Microsoft)*

When Cloud App Security (CAS) is deployed, you have access to analytics on user behavior. You have the tools to block activities and remediate problems. CAS supports detections for ransomware, access to subscriptions, and access to unauthorized data. This is a key tool that is used for compliance and data governance and is included as part of the Microsoft 365 E5 subscription.

There have been numerous situations where I had to review the logs of different activities to understand potential threats in SaaS-based environments. Cloud App Security is a must-have tool for security analysis.

Azure Identity Protection

Cloud App Security provides the tools to better understand the behavioral side of the user and provides the tools for remediation. There is another side of security management, and this is the Azure Identity Protection management. Azure Identity Protection allows you to detect potential vulnerabilities affecting your organization's identities, configure automated responses to detected suspicious actions, and investigate suspicious incidents and take appropriate action to resolve them. The vast number of security breaches take effect when a user identity is stolen. The issue is knowing what to do to identify risk-based activities so you can track the activity and take appropriate action—leveraging the different ways to authenticate a person who is accessing your systems.

Note   Nothing is absolute. The closest you can get to true security is to make the access composed of three different types of information. This includes something you have (like a smartphone), something you are (like fingerprints or biometric), and something you know (like a password). These three pieces of information comprise true security.

The approach that Azure Identity Protection uses is to classify users into three different risk categories: high, medium, and low. The AIP configuration allows you to take specific action based on the risk. As an example, a high-risk user could have their password automatically reset at the next login or be forced to use multifactor authentication) to log in. Azure Identity Protection uses two types of security (something you have and something you know). The Azure Identity Protection dashboard shows the users and how they access different activities (see Figure 1-15).

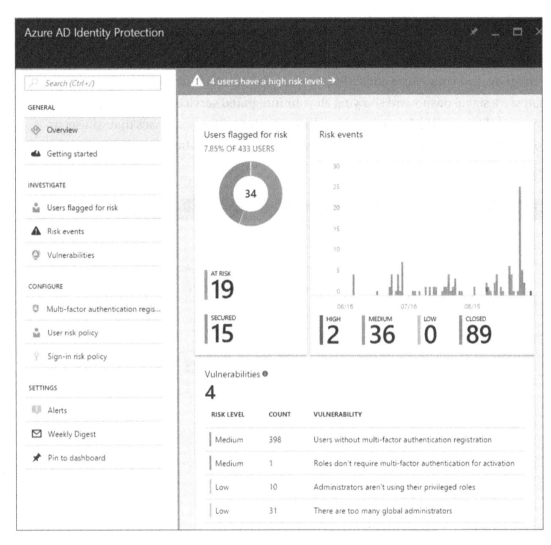

Figure 1-15. *Azure Identity Protection dashboard (courtesy of Microsoft)*

Figure 1-15 shows users who are at high risk. In this case, you have policies in place to act on when users are flagged for risk events and vulnerabilities. These are reports such as "Users flagged for risk," "Risk events," and "Vulnerabilities." Risk events could include logging in from multiple addresses, logging in from nontrusted locations, or logging in from devices that are not registered with the Azure identity suite. These policy settings can enable multifactor authentication, password reset, and a reduction in access to different areas of Office 365. The goal of the Azure Identity Protection service is to mitigate risk while managing a user's credentials. Integrate into this the Azure threat protection's DNS detection services and you have significantly strengthened the security capability of your deployment.

Azure Security Center

Azure Security Center is an Azure service that assists you in monitoring and analyzing threats against your Azure and Office 365 infrastructure. In the Security Center, you can see a signal dashboard showing all your integrated services and the status of these services (Figure 1-16). You can also see the threats and the responses that you set up to counter the threats. The policies that you put in place are integrated into a single management policy.

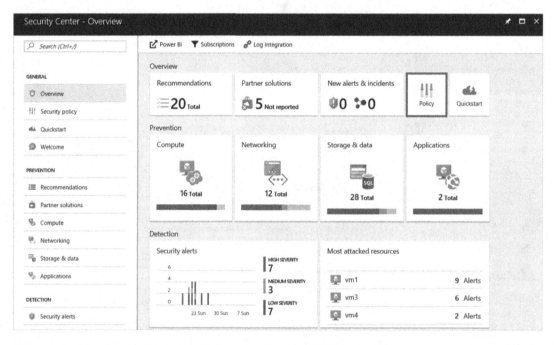

Figure 1-16. *Azure Security Center (courtesy of Microsoft)*

When you think about security, you need to think of incident response and the processes that you have in place to address an incident. Typically, there are five phases with an incident: detect, assess, diagnose, stabilize, and close. The Azure Security Center has been designed around these five basic steps. The Security Center assists you in the management of the incident by giving you the necessary information to address the event.

Cloud based Advanced Threat Protection for endpoints

Advanced Threat Protection (previously called Advanced Threat Analytics) is about detecting threats using behavior analytics in your enterprise. What is unique about Azure ATP is it uses self-learning to build a behavior profile that represents your organization. Azure ATP is deployed on your domain controller and integrates into the Windows Security Center. The detection tool supports Windows desktops, Windows servers, Linux servers. The simplest example is to look at how your organization uses multiple devices to access information. When you access information from multiple sources, using multiple tools, this creates a blind spot in the organization on data management and user behavior. What happens is that you leave backdoors open for bad actors to gain access to your credentials. This opens the door for data breaches. Keep in mind that in this post-GDPR world, those breaches will need to be reported within 72 hours of the event.

This self-learning approach is used to dynamically create a threat profile in your organization while reducing the noise of the information collected. The Azure ATP tool is different than the Office 365/Azure privileged identity feature. Azure ATP is a self-learning tool that looks at the behavior of entities in your organization and helps you make decisions on the best way to handle security management in a deterministic fashion. Figure 1-17 shows the typical deployment for this tool on Azure or on-site servers.

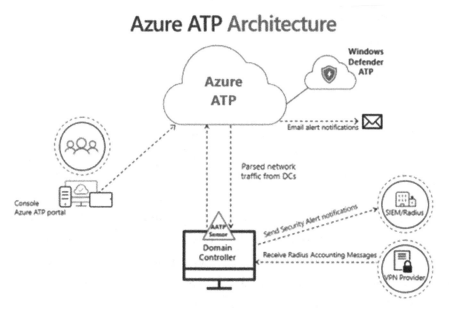

Figure 1-17. *Advanced Threat Protection Data Mapping*

Note   I mention EU GDPR a lot in this chapter, and I am sure you are wondering why you should care about a European law if you are in the United States. The simple answer is that a U.S. version of the GDPR is slowly making its way through Congress. So, eventually there will be a GDPR-like law in the United States. So, from an IT perspective, we need to look at our business processes and start making changes now. The GDPR is a wake-up call for the United States, and California has already responded with the CCPA.

Azure Log Analytics Suite

Log Analytics is a Microsoft cloud service that allows you to manage any instance of a cloud or on-premises services. Log Analytics can manage on-premises systems, AWS deployment, private clouds, and Azure deployments in multiple networks. Log Analytics allows you to configure the different service "blades" (or groups) to give you a more detailed view of your infrastructure. To get you started, Log Analytics provides four logical data groups for information organization in the management plugin in the Log Analytics Azure dashboard.

- Search and analyze data logs

- Manage alert rules

- Manage usage and cost

- Customize data views for work process automation

These are the basic configuration blades that are set up to add to Log Analytics. However, there are additional services that can easily be configured (see Figure 1-18). Typically, I recommend configuring the Office 365 services, the health agents, and the Windows telemetry devices. Depending on your infrastructure, you can deploy the data collection agents on your on-premises services or add them to different environments, such as your Windows servers hosted in a private data center. Accessing many of the new features for Azure security and monitoring is simple; just add an Azure CSP subscription to the environment. Once you have added the subscription, the Azure interface is enabled for the optional services.

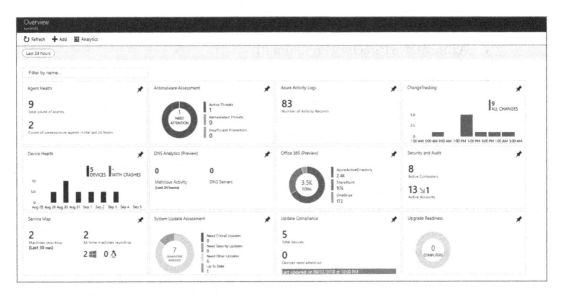

Figure 1-18. *Azure Log Analytics*

Mobile Device Management and the Enterprise Mobility + Security Suite

Mobile Device Management (MDM), Mobile Application Management, Windows Information Protection and the Enterprise Mobile + Security (EMS) suite are core components of the Microsoft security strategy. The main component of the EMS strategy is the Azure identity feature and how this relates to mobile device deployment. I have dedicated Chapter 5 to Mobile Application Management(MAM), Windows Information Protection (WIP) and Mobile Device Management (MDM). There are simple deployments (MAM/WIP) and compliance deployments (full MDM). In Chapter 5, I will go through the details of how to deploy this in your organization. MDM is managed from the intune dashboard Azure.

In the deployments of MAM/WIP/MDM, EMS is the core component. EMS provides you with the user identity glue that you use to tie the different components together. EMS is a combination of products under the branding of EMS/E3 and EMS/E5. The components are listed here:

- Enterprise Mobility + Security E5

  - Azure Active Directory Premium P2

  - Microsoft Cloud App Security

  - Azure Information Protection Premium P2

- Enterprise Mobility + Security E3 (included in E5)

    - Azure Active Directory Premium P1

    - Microsoft6 Advance Threat Analytics

    - Microsoft Intune

    - Azure Information Premium P1

This security combination comprises the core offering with Office 365, and Microsoft offers different suites that are composed of a mix of these products (see Figure 1-19). Depending on the base product you are using, you can easily add different products to your Office 365 subscription. Figure 1-20 shows a good representation of the offerings. The prices listed are subject to change.

Figure 1-19. *Enterprise Mobility + Security suite with an EMS/E5 configuration*

The subscription that I am using in this book is the Microsoft 365 E5 suite. This subscription is composed of the following components: Windows 10 E5, Office 365 E5, and EMS E5. These three components will give you the maximum configuration of Office 365 for your environment. As you read this chapter and deploy some of the advanced security features, you will deploy a Microsoft 365 E5 security suite. This will give you the capabilities that are needed to manage access and information.

		Business Essentials $5 or Business Premium $12.50	Microsoft 365 Business $20	Office 365 Enterprise E3 $20	Microsoft 365 Enterprise E3 $32	Office 365 Enterprise E5 $35	Microsoft 365 Enterprise E5 $57	Price
Security	Advanced Threat Protection	Add-on	Add-on	Add-on	Add-on	Included	Included	$2
	Advanced Security Management	Add-on	Add-on	Add-on	Add-on	Included	Included	$3
	Advanced Compliance	Add-on	Add-on	Add-on	Add-on	Included	Included	$8
	Threat Intelligence	Add-on	Add-on	Add-on	Add-on	Included	Included	$8
Analytics	MyAnalytics	Add-on	Add-on	Add-on	Add-on	Included	Included	$4
	Power BI Pro	Add-on	Add-on	Add-on	Add-on	Included	Included	$10
Voice	PSTN Conferencing	Add-on	Add-on	Add-on	Add-on	Included	Included	$4
	Cloud PBX	N/A	N/A	Add-on	Add-on	Included	Included	$8
	PSTN Calling (US Only)	N/A	N/A	Add-on Cloud PBX Required	Add-on Cloud PBX Required	Add-on	Add-on	$12/$24**

Figure 1-20. *Office 365 and Microsoft 365 security product mix and add-ons for different subscription types*

Microsoft Secure Score

Compliance and security go hand in hand. One of the tools that I will discuss in detail in Chapter 3 is Microsoft Secure Score. This tool allows the CISO to deploy an Office 365 and Windows solution with the best-known methods compared to peer organizations. The Microsoft Secure Score is not the end-all strategy solution for security. The security score is another tool the CISO will use to verify the Office 365 tenant and Windows 10 configuration. If you follow the recommendations, you can configure your Office 365 tenant to a known baseline for your industry (https://securescore.office.com/; see Figure 1-21) because Secure Score rates your Office 365 tenant against the other Office 365 companies in your industry.

Figure 1-21. Microsoft Secure Score (https://securescore.office.com)

Microsoft Secure Score is a key tool that the CISO will use to verify that the Office 365 tenant has been configured correctly. This tool continuously analyzes the 365 configurations (updated nightly) and looks for security configuration problems. The tool is a key component in the compliance officer toolbox. In Chapter 3, you will look at the best-known methods for configuring your Office 365 tenant, and the Microsoft Secure Score is the tool that you will use to complete this analysis.

Typical Security Offerings

The typical offerings of the security products for Office 365 vary, depending on a partner's capability and focus. As a CISO, you need to look at the business requirements to see what the needs of the organization are. A typical security package is composed of the following components:

- Basic-level security (usually notifications and data mining on the dark web)

- Midrange package (these usually are reports of a predictive nature)

- High-end package (this is where the real work begins and includes threat modeling)

As a CISO, you will be looking at either the midrange package or the high end. Which one you pick is determined by your staff capabilities. Smaller organizations will typically select a higher-end package. Established organizations with a well-defined process will select a midrange package. Where does your organization fit in? It depends on your business process and how you view security. The low-end packages make sense only if you already have deployed many of the capabilities discussed in this book. If you have not deployed security packages like the ones I have discussed and you consider security as "not" important, then you have a fundamental business problem. In the past 20 years, there are hundreds of fast-growing businesses that are now defunct because they lost their competitive advantage and intellectual property due to cyber-theft.

Let's take a quick look at a typical security offering (Figure 1-22). In these security classes, you have three different mixes depending on the needs of the CISO. The shield package provides the basic monitoring package.

KAMIND IT Security Offerings

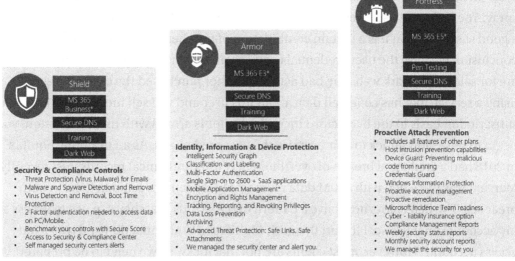

Figure 1-22. *Office 365 security product mixes (courtesy of KAMIND IT)*

The basic monitoring package assumes that the organization has the necessary security structure in place. This is an incremental addition to an organization. Most organizations select the middle package. This way they have the best of both worlds: active detection and predictive monitoring of potential threats. The third package is a proactive package that leverages the predictive package to take corrective action on the organization. Which package should you use? Again, this depends on the capabilities of the organization. If you lack infrastructure and resources, choose the higher-end packages. If you have an individual who can monitor what is going on in your organization, then select the middle package. Looking at the security plans offered earlier, we have 3 different plans, and each of the plans are composed of a cyber security early warning detection system. The Shield, Armor and Fortress security plans include dark web monitoring. The reason for this, is that dark web monitoring provides and early warning on potential compromised of information breaches in a business. When a user account is compromised this gives teh bad actor an additional insight into potential security holes in the organization. These security holes are where data breaches occur. There is a company called idagent (www.idagent.com) that specializes collecting data that is for sale on the dark web. Any security operations center uses this data to look for potential data breaches. When a user credentials is discovered in the dark web, the impact to a security team is significant. What is the bad actors will try different combinations of passwords (based on the information for sale in the dark web) in an attempt to get access to the user accounts? This approach is known as password spray. You know the user credentials, but you do not have their passwords, but you have a good suspicion that it is a certain combination of numbers and letters. You draw this conclusion because the user credentials have been breached a number of times and they are for sale on the dark web. The bad actor has either purchased the credentials, or is using a service that has collected data about this user and will sell the information on a subscription basis to the bad actor. Once a bad actor is armed with the information, you begin to see a slow attack to compromise the user credentials. As an example, Equifax in 2018 had a credential breach of over 146M accounts and finical records. Just recently Marriott was breached with 500M data records. My credentials happen to be in both breaches. The bad actors now have a pattern of passwords that they can use to access my accounts. In my case, I thwart this with Multifactor authentication and restricted access accounts. However, most clients are not that lucky, so we need to be prepared. Cybercrime is a profit-making business that sells our digital assets. Dark web monitoring is key to a healthy cybersecurity program.

The security packages are described in the following sections.

Shield: Basic Monitoring

The Shield class of products is designed to provide basic monitoring services to any client. Companies that have a process-oriented infrastructure will use these packages to augment additional security service offerings. Companies that use MobileIron, a third-party antivirus package, will use this product. Most vendors will have an offering that looks like this. This basic package offers enough security products to provide basic monitoring, but if you are being targeted or are in a high-risk industry, you need to look at a higher-end offering.

Armor: Predictive Security Class

The Armor class will typically include predictive monitoring. In this case, I am referring to the configuration of services that can show you trends and analysis on your infrastructure. Data is collected from different endpoints (including Microsoft's intelligent cloud) and presented in a series of dashboards that the IT manager/CISO can review to make business decisions. Data is collected and analyzed, and reports are generated. Companies that use this class of product have an existing IT staff that has experience in remediation and analysis of the company's data. Basically, you have data being presented in a logical fashion where knowledgeable individuals can decide on the appropriate changes to the infrastructure.

Fortress: Proactive Security Class

The third class of products you typically see are the proactive security products. In this case, the example is the Fortress class. This is the high-end product with different types of security offerings targeted at high-risk industries. High-risk industries are defense contractors, financial businesses with compliance requirements, and any organization that manages large amounts of personal data. Products in this class include two distinct offerings: predictive analysis and proactive management. In this case, you need to have the skills to read the reports and make decisions on the different data that is being collected. The vendor that provides this service will proactively make changes in your security infrastructure to keep the bad actors out of the organization and protect the organization data.

As you look at different security products, you need to look at the offerings in respect to Office 365 because you want to use an integrated service offering. Table 1-1 shows the different options of the security products and how they overlap with Microsoft's threat detection road map discussed earlier.

Table 1-1. *Office 365 Security Product Feature Comparison (Courtesy of KAMIND IT)*

Security Feature	Shield	Armor	Fortress
Advanced Threat Analytics			✓
Azure Active Directory Premium P1	✓	✓	✓
Azure Active Directory Premium P2			✓
Azure Information Protection Plan 1	✓	✓	✓
Azure Information Protection Premium P2			✓
Compliance Scanning			✓
Cloud Backup			✓
Dark Web Data Monitoring	✓	✓	✓
Delve Analytics			✓
Document Classification		✓	✓
Exchange Online Advanced Threat Protection		✓	✓
Microsoft Azure Multi-Factor Authentication	✓	✓	✓
Microsoft Cloud App Security			✓
Microsoft Intune and MDM	✓	✓	✓
Azure Security Monitoring via OMS		✓	✓
Organization MyAnalytics		✓	✓
Office 365 Advanced eDiscovery			✓
Office 365 Advanced Security Management		✓	✓
Office 365 Threat Intelligence			✓
Open DNS	✓	✓	✓
Predictive Reporting			✓
Proactive Management			✓
Remediation			✓
Rights Management	✓	✓	✓
Sentinel AI Software		✓	
Threat Reporting		✓	✓
Windows Defender AI - ATP (Win 10-E5)			✓

It is important to look at product positioning and at what you are doing internally to make sure that you are aligned with the business. As you look at different product offerings, you need to step back and look at the services that are available in Office 365 and Azure. My goal in this book is to provide you with a good introduction to the various elements of Office 365—from a security perspective—and allow you to use those services as it makes sense for your business. There are two key security dashboards in Office 365 that you need to manage. These are the Security & Compliance Center dashboard and the Azure Advanced Threat Protection dashboard.

Secure & Compliance Center

I've discussed all the different components of Office 365 security. The one place where all the information is tied together is the Security & Compliance Center (see Figure 1-23). The Security & Compliance Center dashboard is the center for analysis of Office 365 on a day-to-day basis. The process that all CISOs go through with Office 365 is the same, as outlined here:

1.   Work with the Microsoft partner to purchase an Azure CSP subscription and Microsoft 365 E5 licenses.

2.   Configure Azure security services (see Chapter 2).

3.   Configure Secure Score (see Chapter 3).

4.   Deploy Cloud App Security (see Chapter 3).

5.   Deploy Privilege Identity Management (see Chapter 4).

6.   Deploy Azure Identity Protection (see Chapter 4).

7.   Deploy Azure Information Management/Protection (see Chapter 4).

8.   Deploy Mobility Application Management (see Chapter 5).

9.   Deploy Mobile Device Management (see Chapter 5).

10.   Manage Compliance (see Chapter 6).

Once you have the necessary dashboards configured, the issue is to manage the alerts and the day-to-day activity for your organization. The three classes of security products discussed earlier are examples of different types of third-party offerings to assist you in the management of the compliance and security activity. The CISO will do the following on a scheduled basis:

1.   Manage the day-to-day activity through the Security & Compliance Center. Look for alerts and breaches.

2.   Resolve alert notices, and focus attention on Cloud App Security (CAS).

3. On a weekly basis, check the Microsoft Security Score for changes once you set your baseline.

4. On a weekly basis, check the Compliance Manager score in the security and trust center.

Those are the CISO security responsibilities on an ongoing basis. To access the Security & Compliance Center, log in to Office 365, and click the Security & Compliance icon (see Figure 1-23).

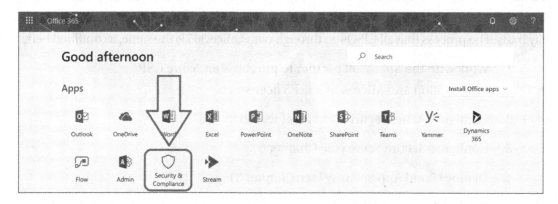

Figure 1-23. *Accessing the Security & Compliance Center for the first time*

If you are new to Office 365, you may notice that your tenant is not configured with all the features shown in Figure 1-23. The reason for this is that you have the incorrect subscription. To enable all the features in the Office 365 Security & Compliance Center, you need to purchase the Microsoft 365 E5 subscription for your account. This will give you the complete set of rights to manage and set the permissions for your Office 365 tenant.

Once you have the complete set of permissions, you can enable the different features for the organization. This way you can define the necessary business processes required to grow your organization. Note I said grow. Businesses that use Office 365 are growing businesses because Microsoft has designed the solution to allow your business to scale. All the features that I described earlier are available to you as an administrator.

I have been asked many times what the best way to proceed is when configuring Office 365 as a secure environment. I have many different tech notes, but the bottom line is to read and configure the services outlined in this book. This will get you started in the correct direction. The best business practice I have discovered is to build the capabilities into Office 365 on the first day. This way the organization can change and grow. If you are proactive and use this approach (as all CISOs should be doing), you will be setting your company up for a secure experience with Office 365. Keep in mind the steps you need to follow that I discussed earlier. Use Secure Score to start, review the configuration in the Security & Compliance Center (see Figure 1-24), and monitor the organization.

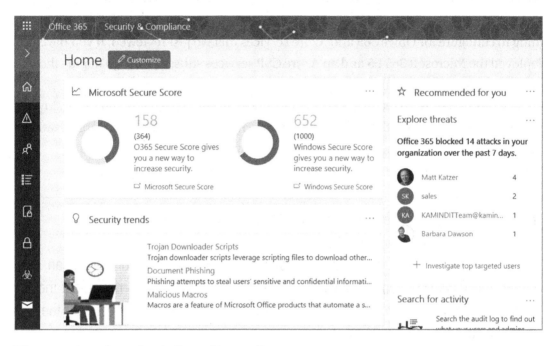

Figure 1-24. *Security & Compliance Center*

Summary

This chapter gave you an overview of the security features in Office 365. My approach was to show you the possibilities that exist and explore what you can do with Office 365. Our road map (refer to Figure 1-1) is the Microsoft threat detection road map. Everything that you do in Office 365 are choices you make as the custodian for your company's data and your customers' information. We all need to be vigilant on our responsibilities.

I wanted this book to be a useful guide to IT managers on what they need to configure and do to manage an Office 365 environment, so I wrote the chapters from a CISO's perspective. I wanted to give you insight into the capabilities of Office 365 and open your mind up to the possibilities in managing a secured environment. As we walk through the chapters in the book, I will expose you to the configuration of Microsoft Secure Score (configurations for your industry), monitoring techniques on handling the Security & Compliance Center, and configuration of Office 365 and Azure services.

This will lead us into the management of privilege information and risk analysis of our users, and we will end up with Mobile Application and Mobile and Mobile Device Management. Once we reach this point, we will walk through the configuration of the Mobile Device Management to see how you can lock down your environment. The goal of chapter 1 was to give you an overview of what is coming in the next chapters. We are going to configure for Office 365 and Azure services that we just reviewed. If you have not deployed the Microsoft 365 E5 and an Azure CSP services subscription, go deploy those subscriptions before we proceed.

The processes discussed in the chapter revolved around the GDPR and CCPA. My goal was to provide you with the necessary information to ensure that your organization has the fundamental business processes and security processes to meet the data protection and privacy requirements.

Note   Before you proceed, you will need to purchase Microsoft 365 E5 and an Azure CSP subscription. To fully understand the concepts in this book, you must have these subscriptions deployed on your administrator account. You can deploy these subscriptions from your current partner. If you are worried about the long-term commitment for Office 365, check out `www.kamind.com/csp` for the different subscription offerings.

Next Steps

I have assumed that your Office 365 environment is fully set up and you are using the service. If you are not on Office 365, refer to Chapter 7 and migrate your company to Office 365. (You can also refer to my previous book, *Moving to Office 365*). The chapters in this book are written based on the assumption that you are have Office 365 and are looking for a better way to securely manage it. As we proceed through the book, we will deploy Office 365 and Azure services based on the deployment of the Microsoft 365 E5 subscription and an Azure Cloud Solution Provider (CSP) consumption subscription for Azure. If you do not have these subscriptions, please acquire them as soon as possible.

Reference Links

There is a lot of information about Office 365 on the Web—the issue is finding the right site. The information contained in this chapter is a combination of my experience performing deployments and of support information published by third parties.

Microsoft Azure Architecture Center

- `https://docs.microsoft.com/en-us/azure/architecture/`

Microsoft Cloud Security for Enterprise Architects

- `https://www.microsoft.com/en-us/download/48121`

Microsoft Cloud Storage for Enterprise Architects

- `https://www.microsoft.com/en-us/download/details.aspx?id=49552`

US Department of Health and Human Services—Breach Notification Site

- `https://ocrportal.hhs.gov/ocr/breach/breach_report.jsf`

CHAPTER 2

Azure and Office 365 Security

In the previous chapter, I gave you an overview of the different services available in Office 365. The chapter then gave you a series of steps CIOSs should do to start using Office 365 securely. Those steps were the roadmap to our successful build out of our security services. In this chapter, you will begin to implement your baseline Azure and Office 365 security services. By the end of this chapter, you will have a baseline security configuration in place for Azure with monitoring and appropriate security services for Office 365. The configuration discussed in this chapter is the baseline for all future services deployed in the following chapters, so you'll want to follow along in your Office 365 and Azure tenant. This chapters builds your security foundation and lays the keys at your feet - the keys to build that successful cyber defense for your company.

CISOs have a responsibility to deploy the necessary detection tools to process and analyze threats in client environments. Your job as a security specialist is to protect the user identities and company information. You manage the Security Operations Center (SOC) and protect the organization against all threats. The objective is to prevent the exploit of data by a bad actor.

Figure 2-1 shows an exploit. In this case, there is a trojan that was in a client PST mail archive file. The Windows Advanced Threat Protection tool (which is AI-based) detected and remediated the threat. As you can see, the tools of today provide a deep analysis of where the action took place and how to remediate the problem. The tools you deploy in your enterprise must have the capability to detect, respond to, investigate, and resolve threats.

© Matthew Katzer 2018
M. Katzer, *Securing Office 365*, https://doi.org/10.1007/978-1-4842-4230-8_2

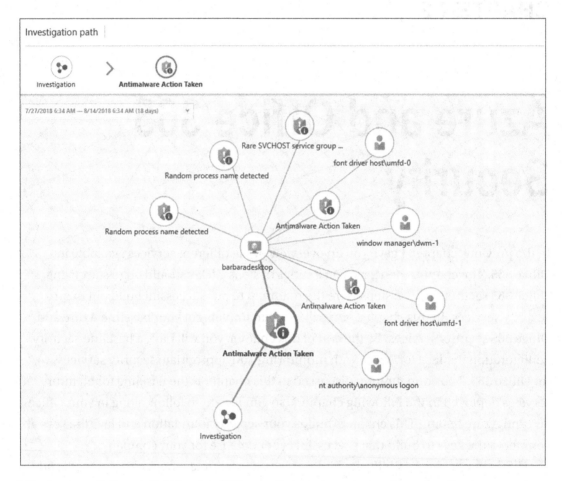

Figure 2-1. *Microsoft Advanced Threat Protection, Azure Security Center*

This chapter is about configuring the Azure, Office 365, and Windows 10 tools that are necessary to build your organization's security capabilities to manage your infrastructure. The size of your network does not matter. The tools must be able to protect, detect, defend against, and remediate all the threats in your infrastructure. Why does this work across all business sizes? Well, we all have the same problem. There is a bad actor who is trying to access our information in our network and we must stop the breach and the bad actors use the same tools and techniques across all companies - large and small.

The capabilities of detection and response with Office 365 are based on the data that is collected from billions of endpoints. Microsoft has created the Threat Intelligence Graph shown in Figure 2-2, which shows information being collected and analyzed.

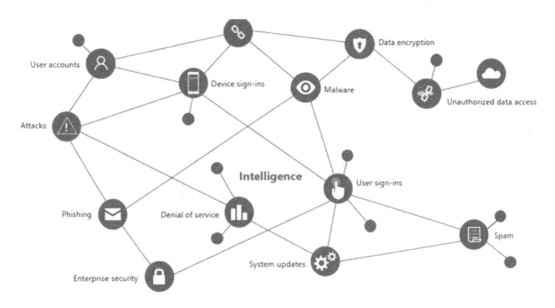

Figure 2-2. *Microsoft threat intelligence information collected (courtesy of Microsoft)*

An organization is no longer an individual entity as it was in the past. Today, we are all connected in one form or another. We all share information and have a common goal of protecting our businesses. Organizations that choose to provide information to Microsoft can leverage the results of the analysis in their own environments. You could argue against information being shared (nobody likes the fact that Google data mines our e-mail and web activity for targeted ads), but security information is different. Security information is about protecting our computing environments from bad actors, and the information that we are sharing is the telemetry data from our systems. This way, the security prevention tools can analyze threats and make a determination-based defense.

The Intelligent Threat Graph collects information from many organizations and endpoints, with billions of them collecting trillions of pieces of data. The threat vectors are analyzed, and the result is a unified threat response. As the CISO, you have the responsibility to configure your security services to have the best possible defenses in this new world. Threats today are AI based and are based on machine learning, with a new technology called *deep learning* (a preventive approach to threat analysis). The bad actors are also using the same type of AI services that we use to defend ourselves, the bad actors use the AI services to build targeted attacks against organizations. The attacks today are swift and massively penetrating. Gone are the days when you could wait to deploy security pack updates (or not deploy security services) or not install OS patches. Old hardware with Intel processor hacks and older machine BIOS hacks has created a landscape that is open for attackers. Today, IT services not only include help-desk and network operating center (NOC) services but also must include a security operations center (SOC), where threats are activity detected and analyzed and preventative processes are put in place to stop the bad actors before they enter an organization. Cybersecurity requires a financial and resource investment, but the threats are real, and you need to aggressively defend your company. Today, you need to look at the threats and understand that you need to protect your computing environment. As the CISO, you are the custodian for your company information, and you have a responsibility to protect it. Looking at this from an Office 365/Azure perspective, take a look at Microsoft's threat protection road map, which is shown in Figure 2-3 (see `https://cloudblogs.` `microsoft.com/microsoftsecure/`).

Security is integrated in the Microsoft cloud. The subscriptions we are using in this book are the Microsoft 365 E5 subscriptions. These Office 365 security subscriptions have the necessary components in Office 365, Azure, and the next-generation Windows 10 Defender AI software. The security services in Azure are related to the Office 365 subscription that we are using. The best way to look at this is through the Microsoft threat protection road map. As a CSO, you need to understand the threat landscape of the cloud service that you are using. Once you have a grounded understanding, you can configure your environment to be protected from the bad actors who are trying to exploit it.

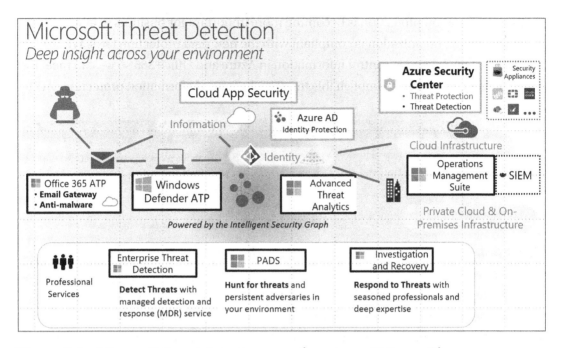

Figure 2-3. Microsoft threat detection map (courtesy of Microsoft)

Office 365 and Azure is a trusted cloud. The *trusted cloud* (see `https://www.microsoft.com/en-us/research/project/trusted-cloud/`) philosophy that is the underlining premise of the Microsoft cloud is that "no one should be able to access customer data without permission." This approach has been further strengthened by the countless number of governmental standards (including the recent GDPR and the California CCPA) and regulations. When we look at the Office 365 and Azure services, the underlining principle is data security. Earlier we discussed building a security baseline for our cyber defenses. One of our first challenges is to collect data so we can use the data to defend against the cyber attacks.

When you add all the collected data in your environment, you have a 360-degree view. You will be able to look at the data, analyze the alerts, and take proactive actions. This is the new norm and the only way you can actively analyze and detect threats. Along with data protection from external threats, we must learn to classify information in our enterprise against known threats. In Figure 2-4, we label documents to allow us to better take care of the information in our enterprise.

Data information protection is becoming more important for business to label documents so the organization is compliant with the new data protection laws. We are building the capabilities to control information in Azure and Office 365 so we can meet the new data regulation. We accomplish this through the Azure Information protection (AIP).

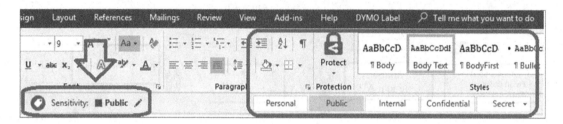

Figure 2-4. *Azure information protection with document classification*

The security level that we will configure in this chapter will be used to develop a security benchmark score (security score), so you can compare your organization against other companies in the same market segment. There are two subscriptions that we are using to configure the services in this chapter (and book), this is the Azure Cloud Solution Provider (CSP) subscription and the 365 Microsoft 365 E5 security suite subscription (see Figure 2-5). The Microsoft 365 security suite contains the primary security components that are necessary for a smooth operation of your 365 (and Azure) security services.

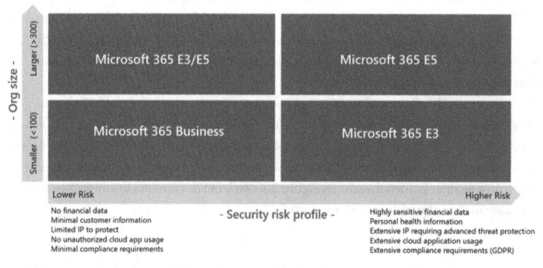

Figure 2-5. *Microsoft security subscriptions (courtesy of Microsoft)*

This chapter covers two parts of a security configuration of Office 365 and Azure. In the first half of the chapter, you will learn how to configure the Azure security services. This is the necessary monitoring and management component to your Office 365 installation. In the second half of this chapter, you will learn how to configure the necessary security components of the Office 365 Security & Compliance Center. The Office 365 Security & Compliance Center is used to monitor the activity of users to ensure that you have policies in place that meet the necessary standards of the government entities that you are subject to. Both Azure and Office 365 configurations are required for the successful management of Office 365.

The Microsoft 365 E5 and Azure CSP subscriptions will give you the best security footprint possible. You will need both of these subscriptions to successfully configure your Office 365 tenant and Azure security services. Before we get started, let's walk through the components of the Microsoft 365 security suites.

Note   The services that you are configuring in this chapter (and in later chapters) are based on using the Microsoft 365 suite known as Microsoft 365 E5. Your organization must purchase at least one Microsoft 365 E5 subscription and have an active CSP Azure subscription. If you do not have these two subscriptions in your Office 365 tenant, you will not be able to configure the services described in the following chapters.

Microsoft 365 Security and Azure Subscriptions

Figure 2-5 showed three different security suites: Microsoft 365 Business, Microsoft 365 E3, and Microsoft 365 E5. Each of the security subscriptions has different features that are targeted to different customers in different market segments. In all these cases, you will have a combination of subscription types in your business. For smaller organizations with fewer than 300 employees, you will have a mix of all of the 4 different types of security suites. The mix will be based on the organization roles. C-level executives will have Microsoft 365 E5 deployed. Office workers will deploy either the Microsoft 365 E5 or E3 subscription. Individuals in an organization who travel should deploy Microsoft 365 E5.

There is also a production worker subscription, known as the *front-line worker*. This is the Microsoft 365 F1 (front-line workers) who are doing the factory floor or production work.

This subscription mix provides the organization with a cost-effective way to manage the day-to-day activity and reduce the organization's risk of data breaches. These security suites give your organization coverage with a security solution that reduces risk. My philosophy on subscriptions comes down to organization risk and data breach remediation. An organization with a bigger risk should move to Microsoft 365 E5. User roles with less risk should use the smaller subscription types. However, in all cases, you will need to monitor the Azure and Office 365 security service logs to determine the best approach to mitigating risk. Failure to report will result in fines under the current and upcoming laws (see Figure 2-6 and `https://ocrportal.hhs.gov/ocr/breach/breach_report.jsf`).

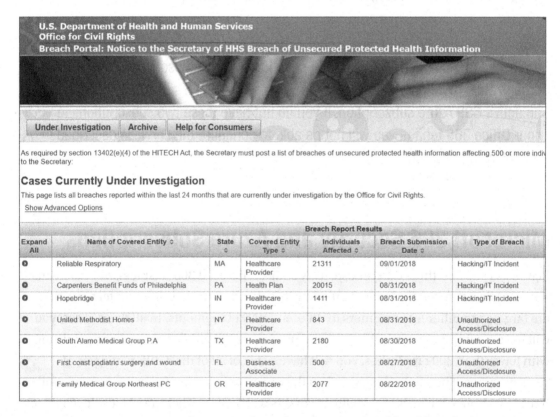

Figure 2-6. *Latest reported security breaches for protected health information*

Let's look at the different security subscription suites in Office 365. These subscriptions are targeted at three classes of workers.

- *Microsoft 365 Enterprise E5*: C-level and at-risk employees

- *Microsoft 365 Enterprise E3*: Office workers

- *Microsoft 365 Business*: Office workers at businesses with fewer than 300 users

- *Microsoft 365 F1*: Front-line workers who use KIOSK

The security subscriptions will not stop all types of threats. As the CISO, you will need to have rules on which devices are to be allowed in the organization, how the devices are managed, and different levels of authentication. Personal devices that are allowed in the organization are usually managed under Mobile Application Management (MAM). Corporate owned devices are managed under Mobile Device Management. Once a device is managed, the user identity is managed with the device. Typically, organizations have two levels of authentication to validate a user's identity and the user's access to the resources of the organization.

The Microsoft 365 suites are a combination of an Office 365 subscription and the appropriate security subscriptions. As an example, Microsoft 365 E3 consists of EMS E3 (with Intune for mobile device management), Office E3, and Windows 10 Enterprise. In addition, Microsoft adds security and configuration software that is unique for the Microsoft 365 suite. Let's look at each of these Microsoft 365 security suites to get a better understanding of the capabilities.

Microsoft 365 Enterprise E5

Microsoft 365 E5 is the Microsoft enterprise security suite package (Figure 2-7). This version of the suite contains all the different product options associated with the different subscriptions, such as Office 365 E5 and Enterprise Mobility and Windows 10 E5. The security software included in the Microsoft 365 E5 is crucial to protecting the business. The mobile device management (part of the EMS suite) allows the business to lock down employees personal devices (as well as corporate), and includes the next generation AI detection tools for all endpoints (part of the Windows 10 E5 subscription). There is a fundamental change that has occurred with the latest security threats. It relates to the quote from former FBI director James Comey when he stated that there are two types of companies, those that have been compromised and those that do not know that they have been compromised. The Microsoft 365 E5 suite was designed to address the active threat to business on data loss based on the assumption that the business has already been breached.

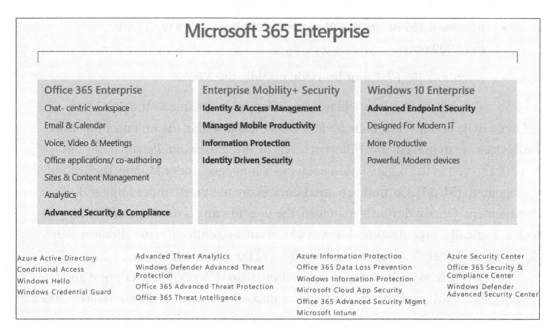

Figure 2-7. *Microsoft view of the security suites (courtesy of Microsoft)*

When you look at security today, you are looking at security from two different perspectives. You are designing for resilience and quick recovery, and you are assuming that your network has been compromised. When you look at network security being compromised, you are detecting the compromise and killing the breach along the chain. In this case, you are looking at where the threat came from, what it modified, and what credentials it used, along the event trail and how you can prevent this in the future.

This approach is considerably different than the approach of earlier years. The mentality previously was designed infrastructure as not to fail, with a security posture of preventing every possible attack, but those days are long gone. The bad actors today deploy tools with machine learning capabilities with one objective: to breach the corporate data networks. This approach leads to a different level of protection, one that is different than in the past. The new attacks today are called Advanced Persistent Threats (APT). The APT attacks are continuous and designed to breach all security tools and defenses. The APT attacks are adaptive and are AI based.

You must think differently than in the past. Today, you need to deploy the correct subscriptions to protect and defend your company. The Microsoft 365 E5 suite is designed to give you the maximum level of protection in your environment, and you need to place a proactive security service on top of the subscription to manage your infrastructure. The tools you deploy must not only protect business information, but they also must detect the new generation of APT attacks.

What Does Microsoft 365 E5 Contain?

The Microsoft 365 E5 suite contains all the software components that are part of Office 365 E5, EMS E5, and Windows 10 E5. Figure 2-8 shows the difference between the two different enterprise security suites. The main difference is the level of the security functions for the enterprise subscription. As an example, Office 365 and CAS are key services that the enterprise needs to manage and are included in the Microsoft E5. One of the key features in the subscriptions is the Advanced Threat Protection services that are included. The Advanced Threat Protection services (3 different versions) are included Microsoft 365 E5.

	Microsoft 365 Enterprise E3	Microsoft 365 Enterprise E5
Device management		
Securely manage data on Windows, macOS, iOS, & Android, Intune	•	•
Self-service PC deployment with Windows Autopilot	•	•
Fine Tuned User Experience, and Windows Analytics Device Health	•	•
Advanced Security Features		
Advanced Threat Analytics, Win Defender Antivirus, Device Guard	•	•
Windows Information Protection, BitLocker & Azure Information P1	•	•
Office 365 Advanced Threat Protection, Office 365 Threat Intelligence		•
Preservation, Compliance & Archiving capabilities w/ backup		•
Windows Defender Advanced Threat Protection		•
Advanced eDiscovery, Lockbox, Advanced Data Governance		•
Azure Information Protection P2		•
Microsoft Cloud App Security, Office 365 Cloud App Security		•
Document storage		
Office document versioning and history	•	•
File storage and sharing with 5TB per user	•	•
Document co-authoring and offline sync	•	•

Figure 2-8. *Microsoft view of the security suites (courtesy of Microsoft)*

Who Do You Deploy This To?

Typically, you will deploy a mix of the different subscription types depending on your business needs. As an example, you would deploy Microsoft 365 E5 to the C suite, IT staff, compliance officers, sales personnel, and the financial users. Microsoft 365 E5 should also be deployed to anyone who is deemed at risk, when there is not a better alternative. Microsoft 365 E5 will be deployed with Microsoft 365 E3.

Microsoft 365 Enterprise E3

What is the difference between Microsoft 365 Enterprise E3 and Microsoft Enterprise E5? It is security. Microsoft Enterprise E3 has fewer security options included with the service than Microsoft 365 E5. There are some additional differences, aligned with the differences between Office 365 E3 and Office 365 E5. The differences are with audio team conferencing and Power BI/My Analytics. These three applications are not part of the Microsoft 365 Enterprise E3 subscription. Microsoft designed the Microsoft 365 Enterprise suite to address two types of workers: those who are at risk and those who are at less risk. At-risk employees need to be at the Microsoft 365 Enterprise E5 level. If your organization has fewer than 300 users, you have a different option; you can deploy Microsoft 365 Business. There are some limitations to this, but it is a good substitution if you have deployed at least one Microsoft 365 E5 subscription. When we deploy Microsoft 365 E3, we also add to the subscription Office 365 Advance Threat and Windows 10 E5. We mix the subscriptions types with additional subscriptions to improve security. Looking at this from a cost point of view, Microsoft 365 E3 is 32 (USD) and adding Office 365 ATP is 2, and the Windows 10 E5 is 11. The combination is 45 versus the Microsoft 365 E5 price at $57. Our new subscription does not have all of the features of the MS 365 E5, but has the key security features that all businesses need. The point of this is that you can add to any of the security suites with additional security based on the business needs. I will discuss this in more detail in the "Microsoft 365 Business" section.

Microsoft 365 Enterprise F1

There is another type of worker in a corporate environment. This is the production worker. The production worker typically does not have a PC and uses a personal cell phone. Any business communications is via email or a shared KIOSK on the production floor. The Microsoft 365 F1 subscription is designed for the production worker. The applications are all web based. The kiosk devices have digital licenses for Windows 10 Enterprise.

The functionality is like Microsoft 365 E3 but with web-only capabilities. This subscription is targeted at the production floor and other user accounts and leverages the Mobile Device Management or Mobile Application Management capability; therefore, the enterprise has an MDM/MAM deployment. The production workers can be anywhere. They are the field service employees or workers at nurses stations. The common thread is that these people are using corporate assets and the corporate data must be protected. To secure the enterprise, you need to manage the information on the device with capabilities to wipe corporate data from the user device to protect corporate assets. In Figure 2-9, I have configured an iOS device for the F1 user subscription to be managed and have blocked the user's ability to back up corporate data to an iCloud account. I have also blocked the user's ability to cut and paste to third-party applications.

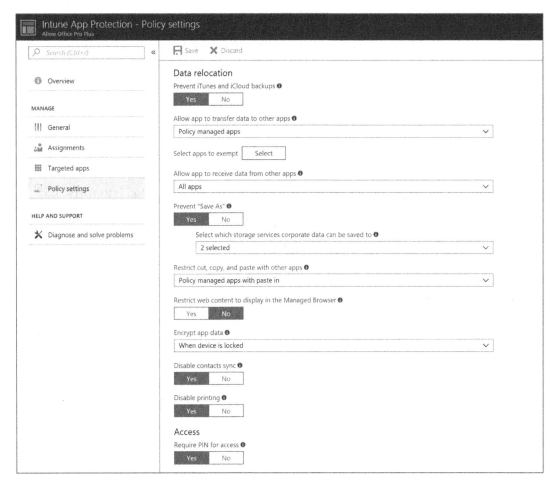

Figure 2-9. *iOS configuration in an F1 subscription that blocks data from being copied to a noncorporate account*

Microsoft 365 Business

The final suite option to cover is Microsoft 365 Business. Microsoft 365 Business is designed to support organizations with fewer than 300 users. It is similar to Microsoft 365 Enterprise E3, but there are some differences.

– Designed for Windows 10 Pro users

– Wizard-based, easy to configure (no hands-on IT with autopilot)

– Limited MDM/MAM support; not a full deployment like Microsoft 365 Enterprise E3

– Limited security, but focused on addressing data breaches

– No integrated compliance manager

Microsoft 365 Business addresses most of the needs of users using Office 365 for organizations with fewer than 300 employees. I do recommend that you deploy a mix of subscriptions, just like with the Microsoft 365 E5 subscription suite. One of the nice features in the Microsoft 365 Business are the wizards for deployment. The Microsoft 365 Business wizard sets up a MAM deployment (Figure 2-10). The MAM wizard makes it very easy to protect corporate data (we discuss Mobile Application Management in Chapter 5). The focus here is to show you where the necessary configuration is located for Microsoft 365 Business. In this book, we are using the Microsoft 365 Enterprise E5. One last note on how we deploy Microsoft 365 Business. Similar to the Microsoft 365 E3, we deploy additional security with the Microsoft 365 Business. The Microsoft 365 Business includes Office 365 ATP, so we only need to add the Windows 10 E5 Advance Threat Protection. The additional $11 expense improves the threat remediation of the Microsoft 365 Business devices significantly.

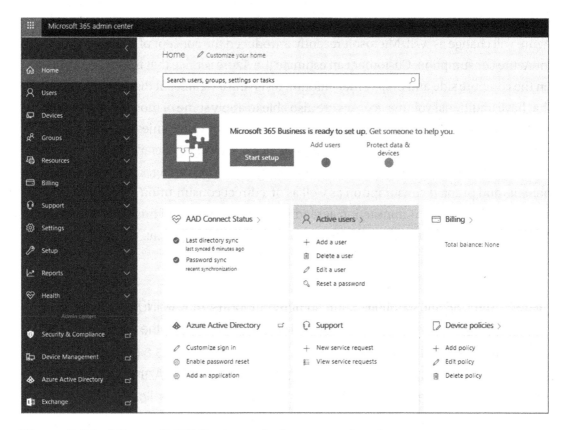

Figure 2-10. *Microsoft 365 Business deployment wizard*

Azure CSP Subscription

All cloud services are consumption-based. Consumption-based subscriptions are estimated subscriptions for billing, with credits or additional charges if under-billed. Like Office 365 subscriptions, once you have used the service, you have consumed the resource. The key to consumption-based billing is a good estimate based on previous usage patterns. You estimate what you are planning to spend, and you are charged a fee for actual spending. There are different ways to get an exact invoice that is predictable, but the costs associated are variable. Microsoft Azure operates this way. There are different types of Microsoft Azure cloud subscriptions, but all of the subscriptions are variable based on your consumption. You either prepay the subscription (like filling your tank with gas) or commit to prepaying and are billed an estimated amount in advance. It does not matter if you have a CSP agreement, enterprise agreement (EA), or direct billing (credit card). You are ultimately billed for actual usage.

As Azure starts to outpace other forms of cloud computing, the payment model for Azure will change as well. Microsoft recently introduced the concept of a prepay option for Azure consumption. Customer can estimate the Azure service that they will consume on the compute side and prepay that amount, receiving a significant discount. Companies that have traditional volume licenses are also able to apply some of those licenses in the hybrid-use license model and receive additional discounts. Companies are now able to leverage the licenses and prepaid consumption to get a lower predictable cost.

CSP is another type of agreement that offers the same advantages of hybrid-use benefits and prepaid consumption as well as of a direct consumption agreement. A CSP agreement is a payment transaction agreement. The usefulness of this type agreement with Azure is significant. When you have a CSP subscription, you can use any service because there is a promise to pay for the services.

Note   The CSP subscriptions come in different forms. At KAMIND IT, our initial CSP subscriptions are prepaid, usually $100. As you consume the Azure services, we invoice you for the consumed service and treat the $100 as a prepaid gas tank. In KAMIND IT's case, we assist the customer in managing the Azure consumption. The client can actively manage the Azure consumption and our licenses that are being used for the Microsoft service in real time.

Flat price IT Services

Office 365 subscriptions have also introduced a trend called a flat price IT service. I bring this up because there is a change that is happening for how you use and deploy IT services. Typically, IT services were deployed as *break fix*. This means when something is broken, you call the IT service provider, and the equipment is fixed. Over time, this changed to a managed service provider. There was only a slight difference, in that the managed service provider was paid a flat monthly fee; however, much work was declared out of scope and was billed per project, or like break fix work. The problem with these two approaches is that even though the work was positioned as a flat fee, in essence it was not a flat fee but a variable project for increment billing.

This is changing. Today, you have the concept of an outsourced IT department. In this model, you calculate your IT budget that you are planning to use and add fixed-rate services that cover all break fix and project events. In this model, the outsourced IT organization is incentivized to make sure everything just works so there is no call associated from the clients. This managed IT department approach creates different levels of service need, and these needs are added as fixed monthly services. This way, the monthly cost is predictable and is always the same. As an example, if an organization has an agreement with a managed service provider to provide a level of help-desk service, these services typically do not come with security management services. Support cost today are in two different cost centers: traditional support services (help desk etc) and new security services. Both cost structures are usually a flat monthly fee with no additional costs associated with them.

Security management services are a separate option that allows an organization to contract out security services and management in Office 365 at a fixed cost. Typically, these services are on a three-year agreement, with a fixed-price add-on. As an example, you could have the following:

- Desktop and 24/7 help-desk services (with on-site remediation) per device

- Proactive security management service and breach resolution

- Office 365 subscription and Azure consumption

Why did I bring this up at this point? The issue is one that we all face. How do we hire or contract out for the IT expertise to manage the security in our organization? There are limits as to what we can do and how we can manage those different environments. There are two different levels of support services - help desk and security services. These services are different. Businesses today need to find a partner to work for security as well as support. This model is known as a *partnership model*, which is now becoming the mainstream model for IT services support.

Note   The best example of the partnership model is through an organization called the20 at www.the20.com. This model has a group of service providers that are providing fixed-rate support on a national basis with a U.S.-based help desk. This is a different approach than traditional MSP or break fix IT but seems to be catching steam throughout the industry. This model allows the client to have a predictable IT cost.

Azure Security Configuration

Earlier we talked about the different Azure subscriptions. In this book, we are using an Azure CSP subscription that is configured in our environment. Once the Azure subscription and the Microsoft 365 E5 subscriptions are in place, you are ready to go! The next activity is to build out Azure Security Center. Azure Security Center is the central point for security management and monitoring that you need to manage the Office 365 and Azure services.

Microsoft Azure is the location where users' identities are managed. In Office 365, we refer to this as the Azure User Identity Management services. As an example, when you create an account in Office 365, that account information is managed in Azure. When you run directory sync services, those credentials and directory information are replicated from Office 365 and the user information in the on-site Active Directory. Information from the on-site Active Directory, including user workstations and desktops, is synced into Azure. Most companies when they configure Office 365 don't realiz that the Azure security services are in place and forget about them.

Figure 2-11 shows the end game for the Azure security configuration. Adding security services to Office 365 is not complex; you just need to follow the build recipe like we do when we deploy new clients on Office 365. The build that we will walk through in this chapter is a key component for our security deployment later in this book.

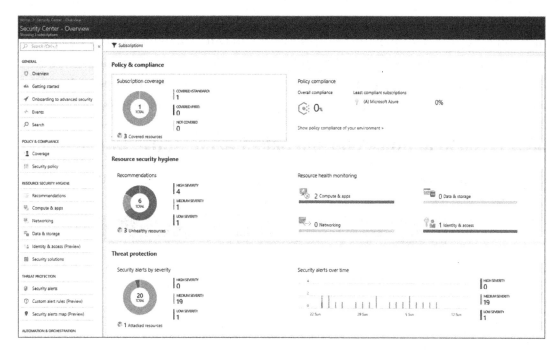

Figure 2-11. *Azure Security Center built out for Office 365 management*

Note   At this point, you need to have a trial of Microsoft 365 E5 and a valid Azure subscription. If you are lacking either of these two subscriptions, you will not be able to configure the Azure Security Center or the Azure logs necessary to integrate Office 365 and Azure.

Building Out the Azure Security Services

So, you have just purchased Office 365 Microsoft 365 E5 and added this to your 365 tenant. You have to verify that you have a Microsoft 365 E5 subscription in the tenant and have assigned the licenses to the user account. Later in this book, you will build out additional Azure security sites, and these sites will give you access to Secure Score, `https://securitycenter.windows.com`, and the Intune management center, discussed in Chapter 5.

There are shortcuts to setting up the Azure tenant, but our purpose here is to make sure you have access to all of the features associated with your subscription. At this point, you have logged into Office 365 and verified your domain. (If you do not know what we are referring to, then quickly jump to Chapter 7.) Follow the steps outlined in the next sections to set up the Azure tenant and link it to your Office 365 subscription.

Step 1: Log in to Office 365 and Select Azure Active Directory

Select Azure Active Directory in the Office 365 admin center (see Figure 2-12).

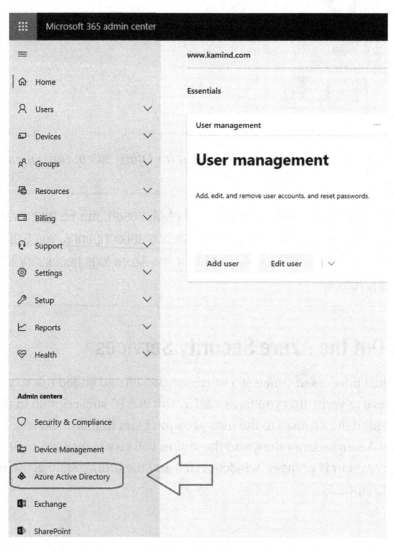

Figure 2-12. *Accessing the Azure Security Center in Office 365*

Step 2: Select Azure Active Directory

Once you have selected the Azure active directory, select `portal.azure.com` in the Azure Active Directory portal. This is where you will be able to manage your user access credentials in Azure/Office 365 (see Figure 2-13). You will be directed to the main Azure portal. The account we are using in this example is a global admin account.

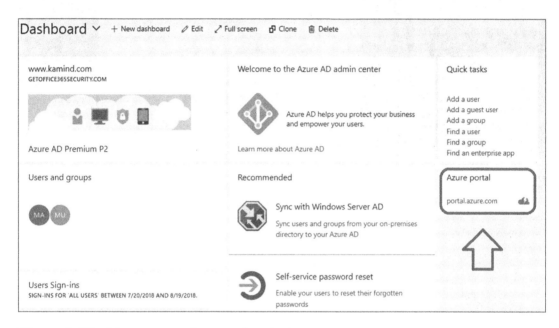

Figure 2-13. *No access to Azure subscription*

Step 3: Create a Resource in the Azure Portal

Click "Create a resource" (see Figure 2-14) and then click Management Tools (see Figure 2-15). You are going to create a Log Analytics logging resource. This resource will collect all of the log information from Office 365/Azure.

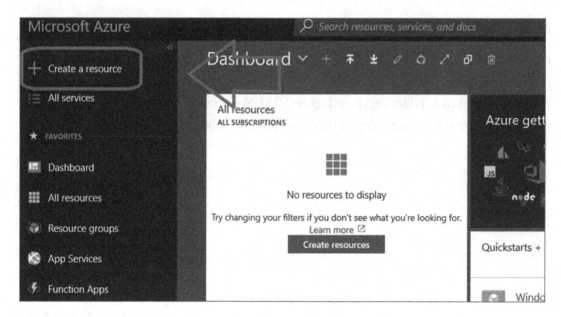

Figure 2-14. *Adding an Azure resource*

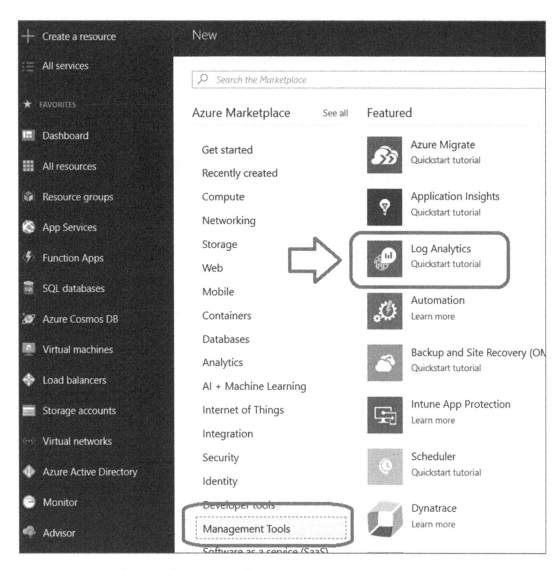

Figure 2-15. *Selecting the Log Analytics resource*

Step 4: Set Up the Log Analytics Resource

Once you have selected the Log Analytics resource, fill in the information and select the correct Azure subscription (see Figure 2-16). Label the subscription as shown in the figure and click OK.

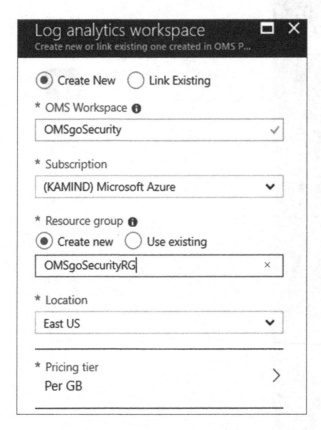

Figure 2-16. *Setting up the Log Analytics resource*

After you click OK, the resource will be set up. Azure will validate the resource and provide a status (see Figure 2-17). Once the resource has been validated, you are ready to assign data to the resource. Click OK to move to the next step.

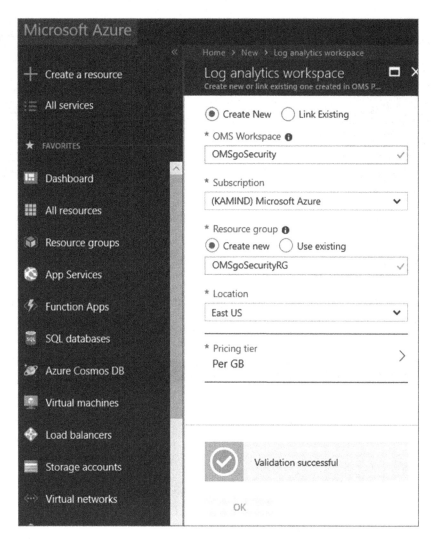

Figure 2-17. *Validation of resource after clicking OK*

Step 5: Setting up Log Analytics

Select the dashboard, and then select Log Analytics (called OMSgoSecurity here). If the new resource does not appear, then refresh the browser (see Figure 2-18). Select the OMSgoSecurity resource.

Figure 2-18. *Resource showing up on the Azure dashboard after a refresh*

Step 6: Configure Log Analytics

Once you have selected Log Analytics, select the Azure activity logs and connect the resources to Office 365 (see Figure 2-19).

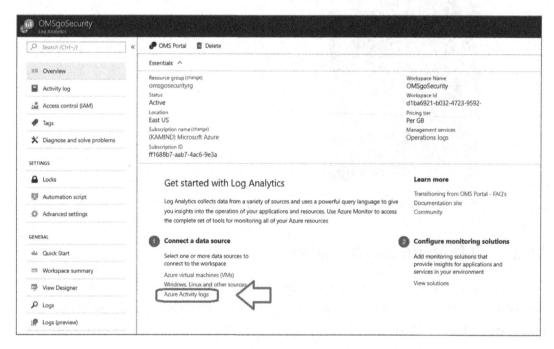

Figure 2-19. *Configuration of the OMS resource with Office 365*

You'll now want to connect both the Microsoft Azure resource and the Access to Azure Active Directory resource. Select a resource and then click *Connect*; do this for both resources (see Figure 2-20).

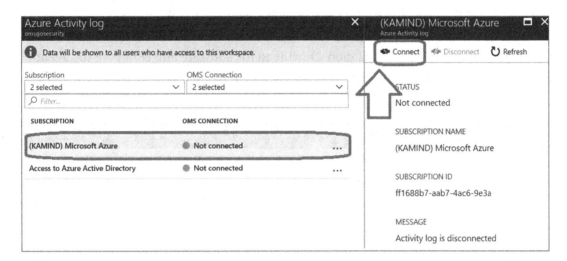

Figure 2-20. *Connecting the logs to the Azure and Active Directory resources*

After you select the resource and click *Connect,* the data will start to be recorded in the Log Analytics resource for analysis. The connected resource will change from gray to green (see Figure 2-21). Set up both the Microsoft Azure resource and the Access to Azure Active Directory resource. Select the resource and then click *Connect* for each resource.

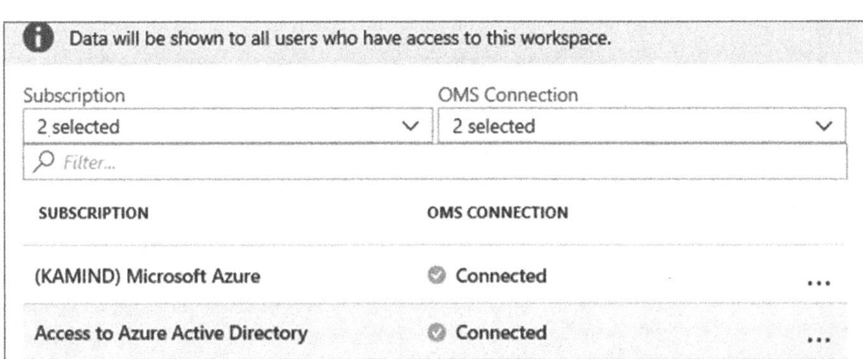

Figure 2-21. *Connected resources showing status*

Step 7: Deploy the Windows Collection Agent on Desktop System

Return to the Log Analytics home screen and click "Advanced settings" (see Figure 2-22). Select "Advanced settings." For the Connected Sources option, select Windows Servers (see Figure 2-23). This will give you the download agent for the Windows server and the Windows client. Install the agent on the Windows server and Windows clients. The download agent is an easy installation. Download the software and configure the agent with the workspace ID and primary key. Do not regenerate the key.

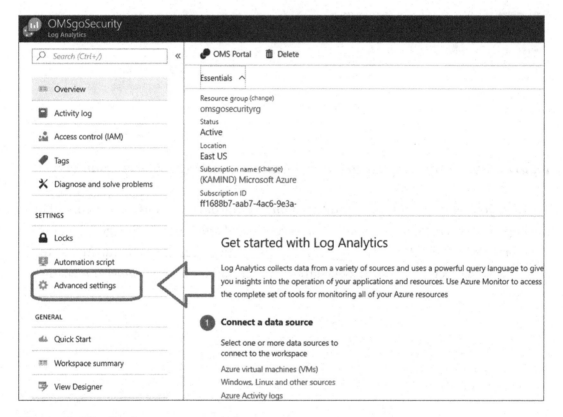

Figure 2-22. *Setting up connected sources*

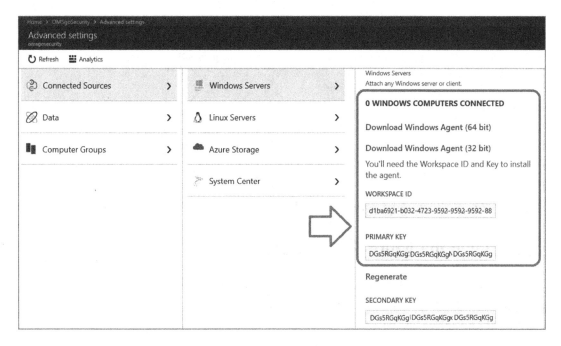

Figure 2-23. *Downloading the agent*

There are additional services that you can connect to Log Analytics. Each service has different capabilities. In some cases, you will need to download multiple agents. The interesting agent to install on the servers is the service map agent (see Figure 2-24).

Note   The Advanced settings are where you connect all of the different data sources for the security analysis. If you have Active Directory syncing in place, the Active Directory accounts are integrated into Log Analytics in the advanced settings. While you are here, take a look at the different data collection items. From a security viewpoint, you will want to connect as many logs as you can.

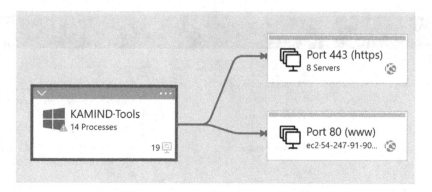

Figure 2-24. *Service map agents installed on KAMIND IT tools server*

Step 8: Load the Azure Security Center

After the service agents are installed on the different Windows client and Windows/ Linux servers, the next step is to enable the Azure Security Center. Return to the main dashboard and select Security Center to load the dashboard (see Figure 2-25).

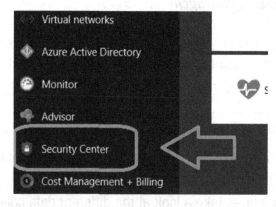

Figure 2-25. *Accessing the Security Center*

Once the dashboard builds out, you will start the configuration of the security subscriptions. Log Analytics supplies data to the Security Center, as shown in Figure 2-26.

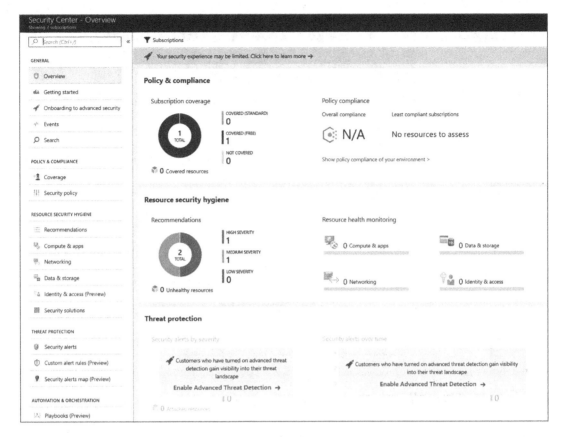

Figure 2-26. *Security Center build-out, first-time access*

Step 9: Upgrade the Azure Security Center

You will link the Log Analytics data to the Security Center so the Security Center can process the data collected. As you add more clients and servers, the data will be processed by the Security Center. The Security Center also allows you to upgrade to the full data collection capabilities. To upgrade, select "Onboarding to advance security" and click "Apply Standard plan" (see Figure 2-27).

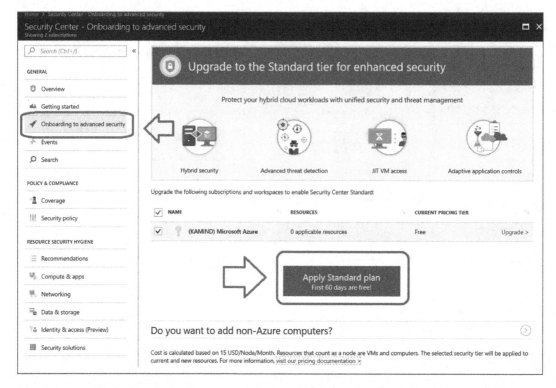

Figure 2-27. *Upgrading the security data analysis plan from free to Standard*

Once the Security Center is configured, you need to set up some additional configurations for collecting data and enabling the security subscriptions associated with the Microsoft 365 E5 subscription.

Step 10: Change the Data Configuration

The next step is to configure the alerts for the Security Center and enable the data retention. In this case, you will modify the Log Analytics data retention capability and set up the notification alerts for the Azure CSP subscription. Returning to the security dashboard, select "*Security policy*" (under Policy & Compliance) in the Security Center. Once you select the security policy, you need to edit the Log Analytics subscription and change the data collection to "*All events.*"

Select the *security policy*, again and edit the Microsoft CSP subscription (see Figure 2-28). In this case, change the logging to full, and set up notification alerts to the subscription owners.

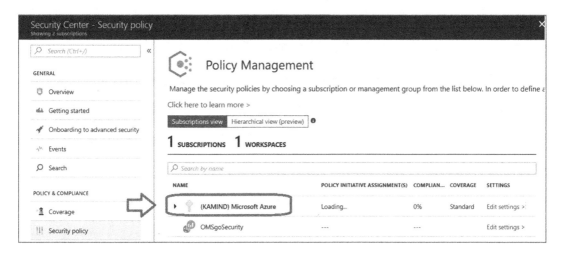

Figure 2-28. *Enabling logging in the Azure CSP subscription*

Data Collection Options

Select the first subscription in the center (the one with the key) and select *edit settings*. You will change the parameters in all three categories (Data Collection, Email notifications, and Pricing tier). In this case, I set up auto provisioning, as shown in Figure 2-29. Once this option is enabled, you have a second option to set up the default workspace configuration. It is important that you select the workspace where to send the collected information. You want to use the same workspace you created earlier. This will ensure that all of the data that is collected is logged in one place.

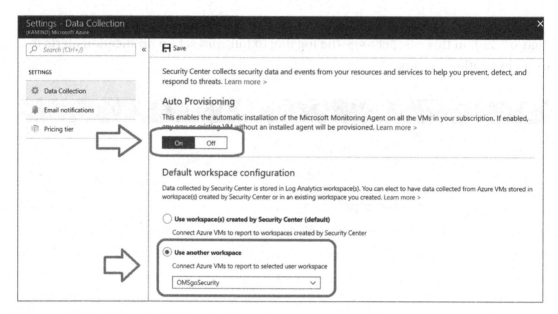

Figure 2-29. *Changing the security options*

The workspace allows you to group all of the log data together for security analysis. The workspace you created earlier will be used throughout the book for data collection. Once you have selected these options, click *Save*. You will be prompted to reconfigure the monitored VMs. Click *Yes* when prompted.

E-mail Notifications

You can set up e-mail notifications for your subscriptions. You need to select the e-mail address that you will use in your tenant to centralize all notifications. In this case, I'm using the account o365Admin for all notifications in Azure (see Figure 2-30). In 365 I have added an e-mail forwarder to our ticket systems, so when a notification is generated, a ticket is issued. Also, enable alerts and select "Send email also to the subscription owners."

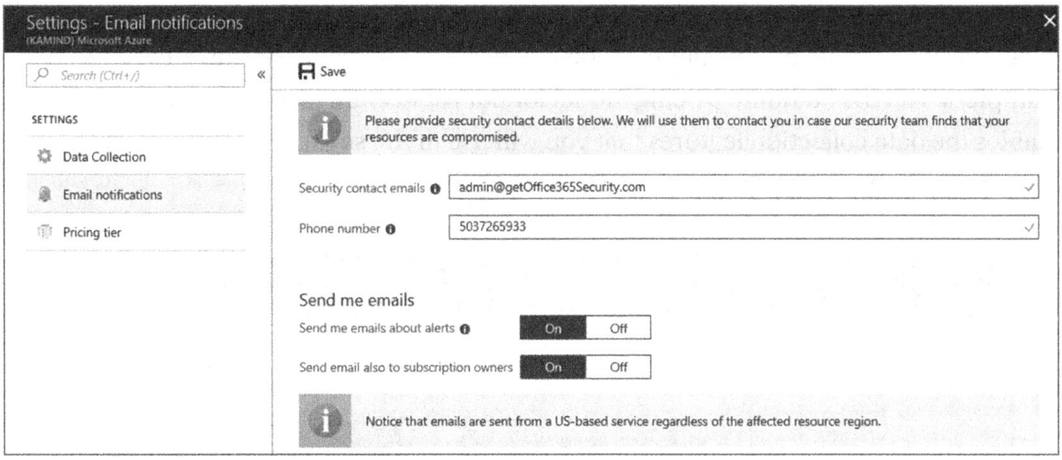

Figure 2-30. *Setting the e-mail notification*

The next step is to configure the alerts for the Security Center and enable the data retention. In this case, you will learn how to modify the Log Analytics data retention capability and set up the notification alerts for the Azure CSP subscription. Returning to the security dashboard, select "Security policy" (under Policy & Compliance) in the Security Center. Once you select the security policy, you need to edit the Log Analytics subscription and change the data collection to "All events."

Configuring Log Analytics: Payment Tier

Once you have configured the resource where the data will be logged, the next step is to configure Log Analytics. In Figure 2-31, select the account and edit the settings.

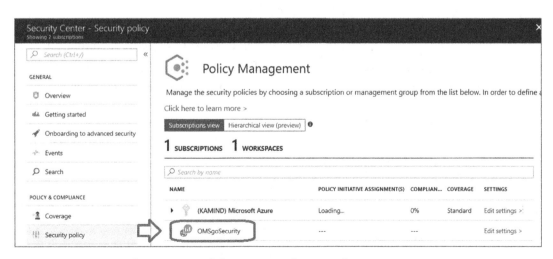

Figure 2-31. *Configuration of the Log Analytics subscription*

There are two options that need to be set: the pricing tier and the data collection. Select the appropriate pricing tier that you will use in your Security Center. For this example, select the Standard pricing model for data collection (see Figure 2-32). This enables the data collection features that you will use in the security analysis. Bear in mind that we have a 60-day trial of the Security Center.

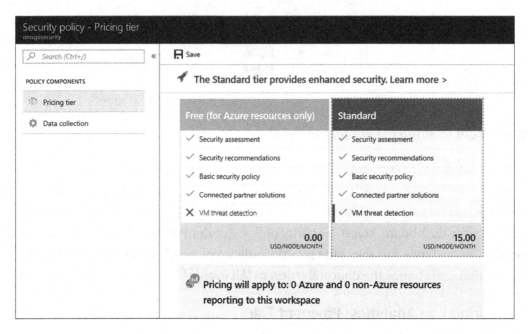

Figure 2-32. *Selecting the security mode payment plan: 60-day trial*

Configuring Log Analytics: Data Collection

Once you have set up the pricing tier, the final step is the set up the data collection. You have four options. For the policy, select All Events (see Figure 2-33) and then click Save. In our case, we are collecting all log events, because later we will be enabling Windows 10 telemetric data to be collected.

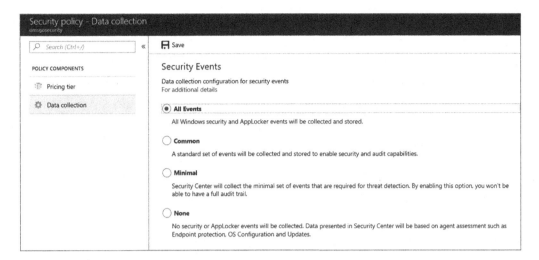

Figure 2-33. *Collecting all data for Log Analytics*

Step 11: Adding Azure Active Directory Identity Monitoring

In this step, you have to enable the different security solutions that you have in your environment. We started our configuration using Microsoft 365 E5, and Microsoft 365 E5 enables a variety of security options for data management (see Figure 2-34).

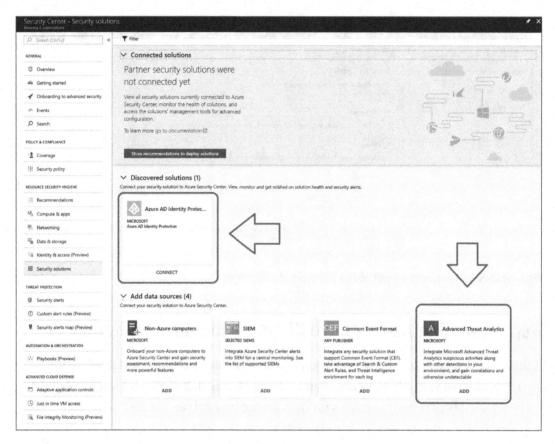

Figure 2-34. *Enabling additional security options*

The next step is to configure the security options for Azure Security Center. There are five security options you can select. (Your screen may look different as Microsoft adds new security solutions to your Azure tenant.) The two security options we are using here are Azure AD Identity provider and Advanced Threat Protection (for Active Directory implementations).

Note   The Advanced Threat Protection subscription is a service that Microsoft provides with the EMS or Microsoft 365 Enterprise suite subscription. This is a critical subscription for your environment for the management of Active Directory, workstations and servers. If you have a hybrid environment, you must deploy this subscription. This subscription/service is being renamed to Azure Advanced Threat Protection and is at `https://portal.atp.azure.com`. The old name was Advanced Threat Analytics. If you see the old name, just think of the new name.

Deploying Azure AD Identity Protection

The Azure Security Center will process the different security options, and if they are already configured or need to be connected to your service, you will see the Connect option. In the case of the two subscriptions that we selected, one is connected, and the other is not. We will walk through the configuration options of both of these subscriptions. First, click *Connect* on the Integrate Azure AD Identity Protection screen (see Figure 2-35).

Figure 2-35. *Enabling Azure Active Directory Identity Protection*

Once you have selected the subscription, the next step is to map the data to the Log Analytics subscription being used for security data. In this case, select the Log Analytics workspace (this is the workspace we created at the beginning of this chapter) that you are using to manage all log events and then click *Connect* to add the workspace to your environment.

Linking the subscription is extremely critical to the management of Office 365 and Azure identity protection. What you are doing at this step is pulling the information from the security subsystems about data breach attempts into your environment. This includes the following:

- Leaked credentials

- Impossible travel locations (logging in from China at the same time you access from Portland)

- Signing in from an anonymous IP address (individuals hiding their locations)

- Sign-ins from an IP address where there is known ID theft (kiosk locations, etc.)

You have linked the Azure Identity Protection into the Security Center for data management, and you have set up the alerts from the Azure Identity security management to the security dashboard.

Step 12: Adding Azure Advanced Threat Protection (optional)

The final security solution we are adding is the Azure Advance Threat Protection. Azure ATP requires an on premise AD that is linked to Office365/Azure via AD Connect. If you do not have an Active Directory environment (either in Azure or on-site) and AD Connect service running, then you can skip this step. Once you have configured the service, the service will generate alerts about data breaches and lateral attacks on your network (see Figure 2-36).

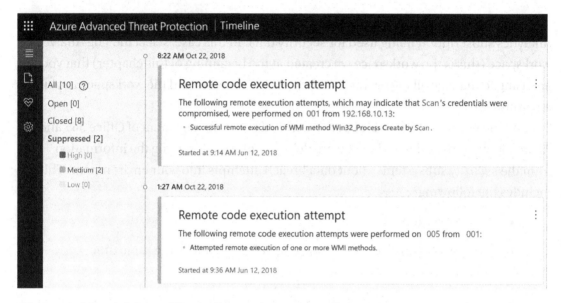

Figure 2-36.   *Advance Threat Protection at portal.atp.azure.com*

There are two components to Advance Threat Protection, the Windows Security Center device ATP component (which we have already configured), and the configuration of the Azure ATP security center at portal.atp.azure.com. The Azure ATP security center downloads an agent to the domain controllers in your network to process information from your active directory and integrate the information into Azure security services.The configuration is an easy process, just follow the steps outlined below.

1. Enter the on-premise domain administrator account and password.

2. Download the agent and install on all of the domain controllers.

3. Configure the weekly reports.

Advanced Threat Protection is an important service in detecting data breaches. This service is important because it provides you with a deep inspection of threats and remediation of those threats. The ATP service provides the following:

- Detection of lateral account breaches

- Passwords exposed in clear text

- Modification of sensitive groups in Active Directory

There is never enough security. You need to enable all of the reporting and data processing for your environment. After you review the different logs and capabilities, you will discover trends, and if they are perpetuated by a bad actor, you can block them. As an example, now that you have the security logs enabled, you can access the logs through Azure Active Directory and see the attempts to breach the Office 365/Azure environment (see Figure 2-37).

IP address	Location	Failure reason
13.93.216.68	San Jose, California, US	Invalid username or password or Invalid on-premise username or password.
13.91.61.249	San Jose, California, US	Invalid username or password or Invalid on-premise username or password.
13.64.196.27	San Jose, California, US	Invalid username or password or Invalid on-premise username or password.
13.93.233.42	San Jose, California, US	Invalid username or password or Invalid on-premise username or password.
13.93.216.68	San Jose, California, US	Invalid username or password or Invalid on-premise username or password.
13.64.196.27	San Jose, California, US	Invalid username or password or Invalid on-premise username or password.
13.91.61.249	San Jose, California, US	Invalid username or password or Invalid on-premise username or password.
117.24.36.159	Baogaizhen, Fujian, CN	Account is locked because user tried to sign in too many times with an incorrect user ID or pa
117.24.36.159	Baogaizhen, Fujian, CN	Account is locked because user tried to sign in too many times with an incorrect user ID or pa
117.24.36.159	Baogaizhen, Fujian, CN	Account is locked because user tried to sign in too many times with an incorrect user ID or pa
117.24.36.159	Baogaizhen, Fujian, CN	Account is locked because user tried to sign in too many times with an incorrect user ID or pa
117.24.36.159	Baogaizhen, Fujian, CN	Account is locked because user tried to sign in too many times with an incorrect user ID or pa
117.24.36.159	Baogaizhen, Fujian, CN	Account is locked because user tried to sign in too many times with an incorrect user ID or pa
117.24.36.159	Baogaizhen, Fujian, CN	Account is locked because user tried to sign in too many times with an incorrect user ID or pa
117.24.36.159	Baogaizhen, Fujian, CN	Account is locked because user tried to sign in too many times with an incorrect user ID or pa
117.24.36.159	Baogaizhen, Fujian, CN	Account is locked because user tried to sign in too many times with an incorrect user ID or pa
117.24.36.159	Baogaizhen, Fujian, CN	Account is locked because user tried to sign in too many times with an incorrect user ID or pa
117.24.36.159	Baogaizhen, Fujian, CN	Account is locked because user tried to sign in too many times with an incorrect user ID or pa
117.24.36.159	Baogaizhen, Fujian, CN	Account is locked because user tried to sign in too many times with an incorrect user ID or pa
104.209.35.177	San Jose, California, US	Invalid username or password or Invalid on-premise username or password.
117.24.36.159	Baogaizhen, Fujian, CN	Account is locked because user tried to sign in too many times with an incorrect user ID or pa
40.118.211.172	San Jose, California, US	Invalid username or password or Invalid on-premise username or password.
117.24.36.159	Baogaizhen, Fujian, CN	Account is locked because user tried to sign in too many times with an incorrect user ID or pa
117.24.36.159	Baogaizhen, Fujian, CN	Account is locked because user tried to sign in too many times with an incorrect user ID or pa
13.64.196.27	San Jose, California, US	Invalid username or password or Invalid on-premise username or password.
117.24.36.159	Baogaizhen, Fujian, CN	Account is locked because user tried to sign in too many times with an incorrect user ID or pa

Figure 2-37. *Login attempts to Office 365 account*

Azure Security Services Checklist

Congratulations, you have completed the Azure security configuration. Before moving on, let's review what we have configured for our Azure security services. In later chapters, we will build on the Azure security service and extend our security converge. At this point, you have completed the following 11 steps:

1. Purchase a Microsoft 365 E5 subscription and an Azure CSP services subscription.

2. Create the Log Analytics resource.

3. Connect the Log Analytics resource to Active Directory and Office 365.

4. Deploy the Microsoft monitoring agents.

5. Connect the data sources to the Log Analytics subscriptions.

6. Deploy the Azure service map agents in your servers.

7. Extend the Azure Security Center with a standard log data collection.

8. Link the Log Analytics resource to the Azure Security Center.

9. Configure notifications.

10. Link Azure Identity to the Azure Security Center.

11. Deploy Advanced Threat Protection (portal.atp.azure.com)

At this point, the Azure security services are enabled and functioning. You will be receiving alerts from the security subsystems based on actions in the environment (see Figure 2-38). These alerts are sent to the e-mail notification address that you added.

Figure 2-38. *Azure Security Center security alert*

Office 365 Security & Compliance Center

You have completed the major security setup for the Azure Security Center. This center manages the Office 365 identities and security attacks against your infrastructure. There is an additional security center that will need to be configured: the Office 365 Security & Compliance Center.

To access the Security & Compliance Center, log in to Office 365 and select the administration portal. In the administration portal, select the Security & Compliance Center located (see Figure 2-39). This will redirect you to the location `https://protection.office.com`.

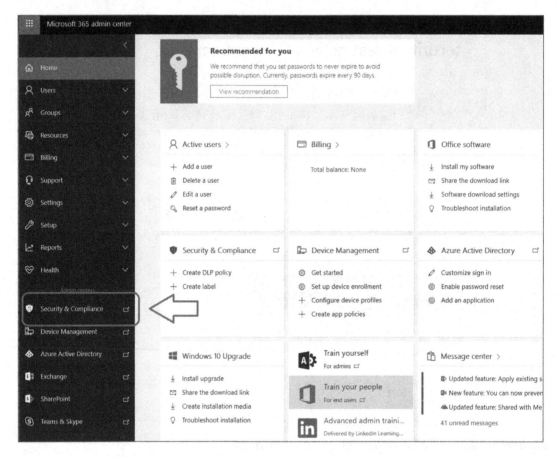

Figure 2-39. *Accessing the Office 365 Security & Compliance Center*

The Security & Compliance Center is used to do the following:

- Enforce data policy for activities with Office 365

- Set up the Secure Score measurements (see Chapter 3)

- Configure data privacy

- Manage the threat management dashboard

- Manage the cloud data policies on data access

- Perform eDiscovery tasks

In Chapter 6, you will configure the compliance settings based on the business needs. The security and compliance settings need to link up to the Compliance Manager configuration in the Microsoft service's Trust Center. This is where you will set the configuration for the GDPR, NIST-800-35 for federal government contractors, and other security and compliance requirements.

The only configuration that we will set up at this time is the audit logs. The audit logs will need to be enabled because of privacy issues. To enable the audit logs, select "Search & investigation" and then "Audit log search" (see Figure 2-40).

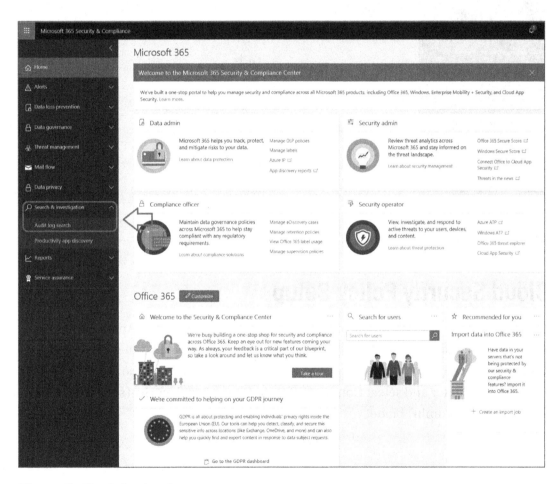

Figure 2-40. Selecting logs

Once you have selected the audit log search, turn on auditing (Figure 2-41). This will start the data collection of specific changes to the Office 365 subscriptions and users. Typically, I set up the audit logs for 720 days (2 years) to recover events.

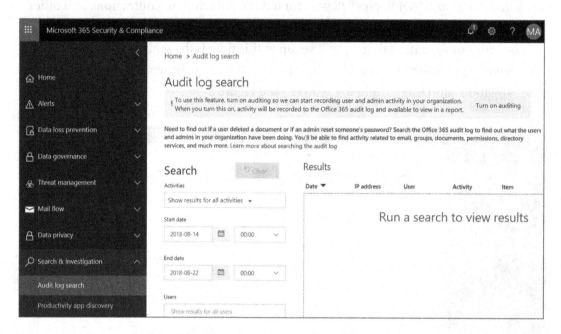

Figure 2-41. *Enabling audit log search*

Cloud Security Policy Setup

There is one last step that you need to complete, which is the Cloud Application Security service setup. I will discuss the details of the service later, but for now I will show how to enable the service and start collecting data. Return to the Security & Compliance Center and select Connect Office to Cloud App Security (see Figure 2-42) in the "Security admin" blade.

Figure 2-42. *Connecting to Cloud App Security CAS*

Cloud App Security gives you additional alert management on users (and bad actors) who are accessing your Office 365 environment (and your on site server if you have integrated the security center ATP agenda and data collectors). This link will direct you to the security portal at `https://getoffice365security.portal.cloudappsecurity.com`. The initial dashboard will show no connected applications. What you need to do is to link the Office 365 and Azure accounts. In Figure 2-43, click the plus sign and then select the connected applications that you want to integrate to Office 365. The integration that you will be completing links the internal audit logs of the connected apps into the Office 365 CAS security services.

Figure 2-43. *Accessing CAS for the first time*

When you click the plus sign, add the selected applications that you are using in your Office 365 tenant (see Figure 2-44). In our case, we are using Office 365 and Azure. So, you will select those two applications and integrate them into the CAS service.

Figure 2-44. *Setting up CAS applications for security monitoring*

Once you have selected a service, just select the green Connec button. For third-party services, you will need the administrator accounts for access. You will want to add the Azure service and the Office 365 service to link them to CAS (see Figure 2-45).

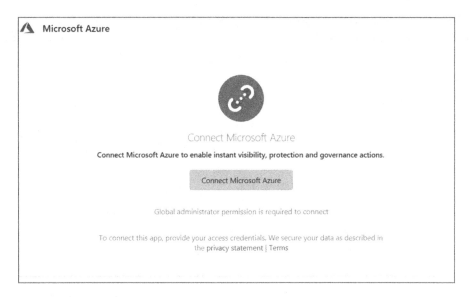

Figure 2-45. *Linking Azure services to CAS*

Once you click Connect, the CAS service will begin to scan the users and data. If the service is connected properly, it will display a green connected check mark. If there is an error, then you will need to troubleshoot (do not use trial subscriptions; otherwise, the service will fail).

Once you have added the services, they should look similar to Figure 2-46. At this point, you have completed the CAS integration.

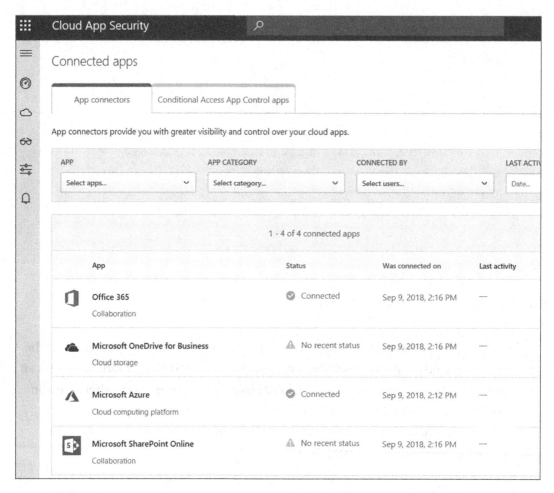

Figure 2-46. *CAS status board after services are added*

Once you have deployed CAS, take a moment to exam the templates of the services. CAS is a great tool to use when you are setting up data alert conditions as different resources access your tenant. CAS is the tool you use to monitor and review data access in your Office 365 tenant. Figure 2-47 is an example of the data tracking that is available in CAS. Most of the rules are enabled once CAS is connected to a data source.

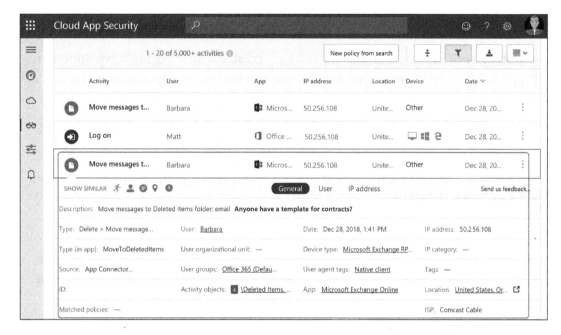

Figure 2-47. *CAS detailed log- see* $http://www.portal.clouappsecurity.com$

However if you want more detailed alerts, review the template and add the additional alerts that you with to use to monitor access. Keep in mind that as you deploy Windows Advance Threat Protection, the data reported by the agents in Windows 10 version 1809 and Windows server 2019 acts like a security SIEM (Security Information and Event Management). If you add the necessary logs from the firewall and other SNMP devices, you have uploaded the same capabilities that you would find in any commercial SIEM (such as splunk).

Summary

This chapter focused on setting up Azure security services so you can use the Azure configuration you just built to deploy a set of measurement scores to see how you are doing. The focus in this chapter was to set up the services. Feel free to explore the rest of the service configuration to see the additional features. I wanted the basic integration to be completed so we can begin to collect data. One of the last configuration changes we made was to enable detailed logging of the Office 365 security activities and to connect up CAS. With these features being enabled, you now have a full security logging data collection service in place that you can use for the rest of the Office 365/Azure security services.

Next Steps

The ground work has been completed. You have created a data logging subscription to collect data in Azure for review in log Analytics. You have linked the Office 365 tenant into azure and set up Office 365 logging and the initial set up of Cloud App Security CAS. Our next step is to deploy Microsoft Secure Score and configure Windows Secure Sore by deploying Windows 10 Advance Threat protection. If you have not deployed Office 365, you should stop and read Chapter 7 before you continue.

Reference Links

There is a lot of information about Office 365 and the new Microsoft 365 security suites. The issue is finding the right site. The information contained in this chapter is a combination of my experience doing deployments and of support information that has been published by third parties.

KAMIND IT Security and Managed Services

- https://www.kamind.com/csp/

Microsoft 365 Business

- https://docs.microsoft.com/en-us/microsoft-365/business/

Microsoft 365 Enterprise

- https://docs.microsoft.com/en-us/microsoft-365/enterprise/

CloudBuild: Microsoft Distributed and Caching Build Service

- https://www.microsoft.com/en-us/research/wp-content/
  uploads/2016/06/q_signed-2.pdf

Microsoft Secure Blog

- https://cloudblogs.microsoft.com/microsoftsecure/

Microsoft Trusted Cloud

- https://www.microsoft.com/en-us/research/project/trusted-cloud/

Microsoft Threat Protection

- https://www.microsoft.com/en-us/security/threat-protection

Microsoft Cybersecurity Reference Architecture

- https://cloudblogs.microsoft.com/microsoftsecure/2018/06/06/
  cybersecurity-reference-architecture-security-for-a-hybrid-enterprise/

CHAPTER 3

Microsoft Secure Score

You are the corporate information security officer (CISO), responsible for managing activities in the United States and in the European Union. As part of your role, you are the data production officer (DPO) under GDPR, and you are also the Compliance Manager under your corporate responsibilities. Your company has made the strategic decision to purchase Office 365 and integrate the on site active directory into Office 365 Azure services. The problem is where do you begin. You have spoken with a number of Microsoft partners and they point to two areas: Azure security services and Microsoft Secure Score. You are worried about phishing attacks and the next generation of worms that are AI based. You are using an older version of anti virus that is signature based. Your security tools are out of date and you need to look at the problem from a new perspective. What do you do next? The answer is simple - deploy Microsoft Secure Score!

Ninety-five percent of penetration attacks begin with a phishing attack. The bad actors data mine LinkedIn and other social media sites to find information about a target using an approach that is no different than what most companies use for marketing programs. The bad actors start to develop a relationship and become trusted. How does a bad actor become trusted? They start to imitate your friends and contacts through phishing and spoof attacks and then breach your network.

What is a CISO to do? The simple answer: you'll want to configure the Security & Compliance Center (see Figure 3-1) to provide early notification and access and deploy Microsoft Secure Score.

© Matthew Katzer 2018
M. Katzer, *Securing Office 365*, https://doi.org/10.1007/978-1-4842-4230-8_3

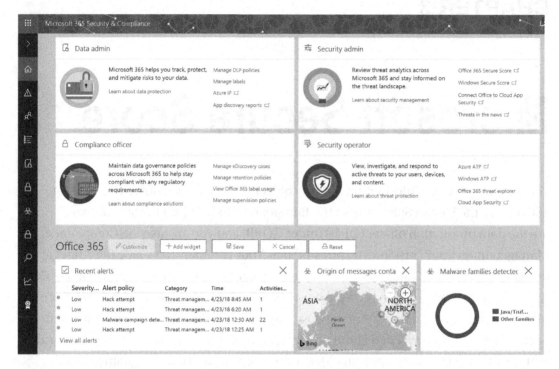

Figure 3-1. *Office 365 Security & Compliance Center*

There is so much to do. The EU new regulation- GDPR, requires you start a security training and proactively manage your cloud and on-site resources. Account breaches start with users. As a CISO, your job is to educate workers and put in place the necessary monitoring and analysis tools to keep your enterprise safe. You need to deploy additional security tools, such as multifactor authentication to control credentials and Windows 10 E5 Advanced Threat Protection (see Figure 3-2) to actively manage and protect your companies resources. The new Windows 10 E5 Advance Threat Protection (WATP) give you a deep understanding of the scope of the problem. Before you were worried about how to detect data breaches from emails, now you have the tools to look at data breaches real time and take proactive steps to block the breaches.

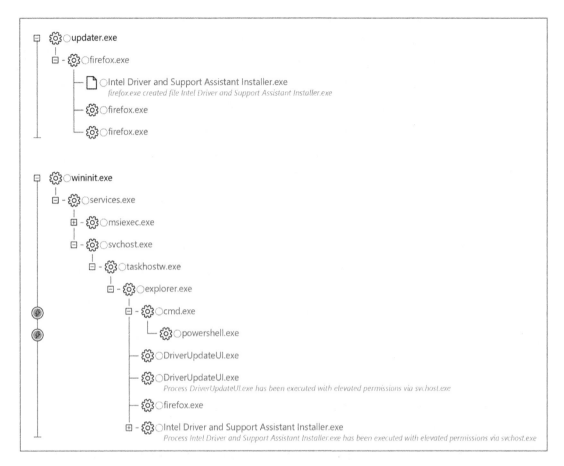

Figure 3-2. *Walking through an alert*

Security can no longer be an afterthought. Microsoft refers to this constant vigilance as *intelligent security.* As a CISO, you need to be configuring user identify and access, protecting corporate information, constantly looking at threats (predicting and responding to problems), and managing the overall security. Along with this, is the impact to your business environment that the latest changes in compliance (such as the GDPR and the CCPA) can have on Intelligent security (see Figure 3-3).

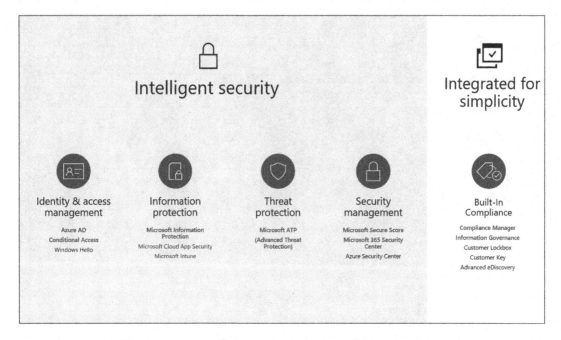

Figure 3-3. *Intelligent security (courtesy of Microsoft)*

As I've said repeatedly, security is a landscape in flux. As attacks become more vicious, we as custodians for our company information need to change our policies and approaches. Traditionally, IT has been a service and support organization. Because of data threats, support organizations need to change and adopt new policies for audit and security management. One trend that we are seeing is the addition of a security operations center (SOC) to the help desk. Typically, IT services do not include all three branches: the help desk, the network operations center (NOC), and the security operations center (SOC). Today, SOCs enlist predictive tools to spot and analyze trends, and include machine learning, behavior analysis of users, and deep learning.

Deep learning is one of the latest tools added to security suites and involves the analysis of large data sets. It is likened to a neural network resembling the human mind, and is capable of analyzing all sets of data. To be a successful CISO, you need to deploy the tools that will provide the necessary protection and analysis of the threats your company is facing.

Note   Deep learning is used to develop neural networks, which are a key component in next-generation AI tools. Deep learning software is self-learning and is used to drive automobiles, analyze legal cases, and install threat detection/remediation software. If you look at Windows Advance Threat Protection (part of the Windows 10 E5 solution), you will see an implementation of neural network or deep learning model.

There is an ongoing war between companies and bad actors. To win, you need to constantly look at new tools and integrated solutions. The best-in-class solutions all offer different tools. Your challenge is finding the necessary tools to win the battle (Figure 3-4).

Identity & access management	Information protection	Threat protection	Security management	Built-In Compliance
CA based on device-risk	Classify, label, & protect across O365	Azure ATP GA	Microsoft Secure Score	GDPR sensitive data type
Passwordless Sign in (FIDO)	Secure file sharing to anyone, on any device	Automatic investigation & remediation in WDATP	Security Graph API	Compliance Manager
		Win 7/8.1 Support for WDATP		
		Attack Simulator		

Figure 3-4. *Product-focused solutions (courtesy of Microsoft)*

The third step is to analyze the data, draw conclusions, and provide a set of recommendations with a timeframe for implementation. The tools are constantly changing, with more options for configuration and analysis. As compliance becomes more part of our business activities, we need to deal with the risk of devices, users' access, and identity management. The question that we ask ourselves is how can we configure the environment and set up the necessary components that we require to be successful in our deployment? Where do we start, and how do we proceed?

This is where Microsoft Secure Score and Microsoft Compliance Manager come into play. Microsoft Secure Score gives you a comparison metric based on other businesses your size in the same market (see Figure 3-5). Microsoft Compliance Manager extends

Microsoft Secure Score and gives you a grade for how you are doing according to the compliance guidelines in your organization. In addition, Microsoft Secure Score compares how you are doing against other members in the same industry. This way you can accurately compare yourself against other organizations to see if you are doing enough.

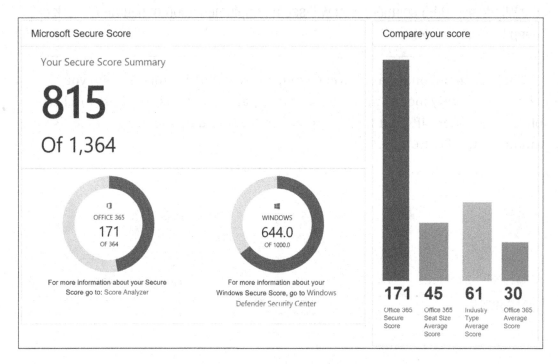

Figure 3-5. *Microsoft Secure Score*

Secure Score is a feature in the Office 365 Compliance Security Center and is available to all users who have an Office 365 subscription. The purpose of Microsoft Secure Score is to get you headed in the correct direction, with a measurement that can be used to see if you have improved your security posture. The Microsoft Secure score is designed so you can measure your deployment so you can improve upon it.

There is a lot of work required to set up your 365 tenants to be monitored and analyzed under Microsoft Secure Score. Each of the Security Centers has a different function associated with it. After you set up the security scoring, the next step is to configure Mobile Device Management and Mobile Application Management for Office 365 (see Chapter 5). Once you complete the MDM/MAM setup, you have a secure environment. The setup order is important, though. Each Security Center feeds on the previous one to provide you with a 360-degree view of the security process.

The goal of this chapter is to provide you with the tools necessary to manage your Office 365 tenant in a secure way. At the end of this chapter, you will have Secure Score and Compliance Manager configured and set up to record information for your security process. As part of this process, you want to record your security score at the start of the process so you can see the impact to the changes that you make on your Office 365 account. The Microsoft Secure Score is composed of two scores when this book was published. The Microsoft Secure Score includes the Office 365 Secure Score and the Windows Secure Score. Let's get started in building out our Microsoft Secure Score and enable the security implementation tracking.

Note   Before you proceed, you will want to purchase the following Office 365 subscriptions for your account: Microsoft 365 E5 and an Azure $100 CSP subscription. To fully understand the concepts in this book, you must have these subscriptions deployed on your administrator account. You can deploy these subscriptions from your current Microsoft partner. If you are worried about the long-term commitment of Office 365, check out `www.kamind.com/csp` for the different subscription offerings.

Security & Compliance Center

You are the CISO. Your Managed IT Department (MID) outsource has provisioned you with the Microsoft 365 E5 subscription and has set up your 365 account with an Azure CSP subscription. You are set up as the contributor of the CSP subscription for your Azure deployment. The first place you should go is the Security & Compliance Center. Log in at `https://portal.office.com` (see Figure 3-6) and click Security & Compliance.

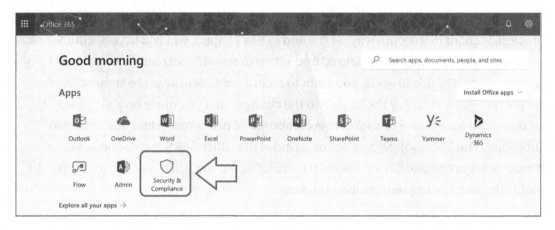

Figure 3-6. *Office 365 admin screen with Security & Compliance link*

Note The IT support industry is changing. There are three types of outsourced IT organizations in the United States: break fix (you call them and they fix things for you), Managed Service Provider (MSP) (these are companies that provide you with a managed services plan and have a limited scope of work to do), and Managed IT Department (MID). The vendor that supplies you MID services becomes the vendor that helps your business move to the next level. The MID organization is your strategic advisor. This is very much like they are in your office and they take care of issues and problems associated with the activities of the IT organization.

The Security & Compliance Center is a data aggregation dashboard for all the Office 365 services. The dashboard is highly configurable, based on the user's desired outlook. The default dashboard will show some key security areas: Data admin, Security admin, Compliance officer, and Security operator. In Figure 3-7, we set the dashboard with information about the GDPR.

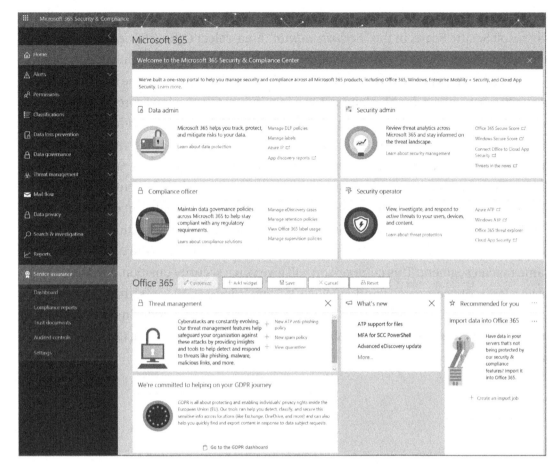

Figure 3-7. *Security & Compliance Center*

At this point you may be wondering as to why we are scoring our configuration and this has to do with Office 365 security. The *Microsoft Security Score* contains baseline configuration data of companies in the same market segment. In essence, we are measuring ourselves against our competitors. The objective is to set up a baseline measurement that we can use to compare our Office 365/Azure tenant implementation to other organizations. As new threats emerge, the security posture changes and our baseline number will change. We can see the impact of changes and take appropriate actions to improve our security posture. This is why Microsoft Secure Score is important to us and our company. A low score means higher risk. A higher score is implying lower risk. Our discussion on compliance (later in this chapter) will also look at the Microsoft Compliance Score to see how we are doing in compliance and see areas where we need to improve. The security and compliance scores provide us with meaningful metrics to assist us in managing our business in the Microsoft Intelligent cloud.

The security score is critical to managing our cloud security posture. To access the Microsoft Secure Score, in the "*Security admin*" area, select *Office 365 Secure Score*. This will redirect you to the Microsoft Secure Score dashboard (which includes Office 365 Secure Score and Windows Secure Score, see Figure 3-8). We will be looking at both security score settings in this chapter. Keep in mind that the secure score settings are a comparison of the different configurations of Office 365 combined with the threat intelligence from the Microsoft security graph. The score is a weighted value based on the importance of the security control and the impact of the control to various threats. If an Office 365 tenant is attacked by a bad actor and the attack is thwarted by a control setting, then this control setting will have a higher value than a different control

The security score is a weighted value that compares the configuration of your Office 365 and Windows 10 deployment as compared to other companies the same size in the same market segment. This comparison will give you a security position. If you find you have a low score compared to other Office 365 and Windows 10 users, then you need to seriously look at your configuration and see what changes you need to make. A low score means that you have a higher probability of penetration by a bad actor. On the other hand, a high score means you have less likely of a penetration.

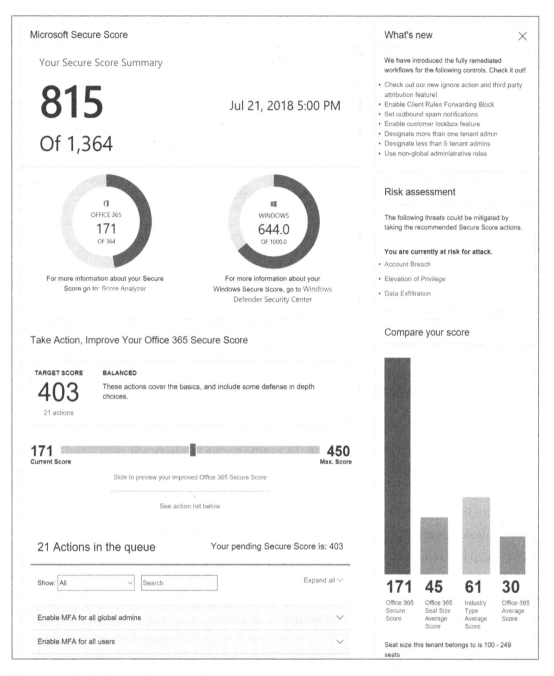

Figure 3-8. *Microsoft Secure Score administration center*

Note   The Microsoft Secure Score is only a number that gives you a *probability* of penetration. This does not mean you should set the number to be the maximum value. On the contrary, you need to look at the controls and determine what makes business sense for your organization. Typically smaller companies will have a lower score and larger companies with a security department will have a higher score. In all cases, you need to continuously monitor the events and take actions as necessary.

Secure Score Overview

Secure Score is composed of two parts: Office 365 Secure Score and the Windows Secure Score from the Windows Security Center (`https://securitycenter.windows.com`). Before you can start using the Microsoft Secure Score, you will need to deploy Windows Security Center Advanced Threat Protection (part of Windows 10 E5).

Deploying the Windows Security Center

The subscriptions that we have deployed in our test organization are the Microsoft 365 E5 and Azure CSP subscriptions. One of the components in Microsoft 365 E5 is the Advanced Threat Protection upgrade for Windows Defender. This is the next-generation end-client threat protection agent. The agent is linked to the larger Microsoft threat brain (called the *threat intelligence graph*) and is able to protect against endpoint threats (servers, desktops and non Microsoft endpoints). The desktop agents are AI-based and deploy deep learning methodologies that you find in neural networks.

The Microsoft 365 E5 subscription includes the Windows 10 E5 subscription which is a digital licenses upgrade to Windows 10 pro systems to Windows 10 Enterprise (no code changes to upgrade subscriptions). This upgrade includes the next-generation Advanced Threat Protection. This software is a key threat protection tool that is used to defend the endpoint from attacks and is a crucial tool in the defenses of your network by bad actors. The following steps will configure the Windows Security Center to be used by your Office 365 tenant. The account you are using must be configured with this subscription as a global administrator and cannot be configured with partner-delegated admin rights.

Installing Windows Advanced Threat Protection

The Windows Security Center score is based on the data collected from the Windows 10 desktops and evaluates the desktop configurations. The Windows Security Center (`https://securitycenter.windows.com`) requires a work account (aka Office 365 account) with global administration access. The Windows Advanced Threat Protection Security Center gives the administrator an integrated view of the Windows desktop and key Office 365 services. Information is presented in the Security Center dashboard. The dashboard status changes all the time depending on what is happening on the client (see Figure 3-9).

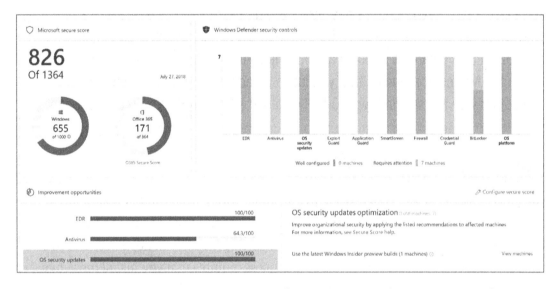

Figure 3-9. *Secure Score admin center in* `https://securitycenter.windows.com`

The installation process for Advanced Threat Protection is straightforward as outlined below.

1. Make sure your account is provisioned with a Microsoft 365 E5 subscription.

2. Log in with a global admin account (and not a delegated admin) to Office 365.

3. Log into `https://securitycenter.windows.com` and follow the steps outlined next.

The detailed steps to set up Windows 10 ATP are outlined next. There is additional software that you will need to deploy to the desktop to enable Windows analytics and to collect data for Azure security services. The Azure security deployment and the Windows 10 analytics are used to address security issues on clients and the actions of bad actors. We deployed the Azure Security Center (in the previous chapter) first so we could enable the additional security monitoring of the Windows Security Center and the Azure security monitoring services. If you have not configured your Azure security services (described in Chapter 2), please return to that chapter and configure them now.

Note   To access a free trial of Windows Defender Advanced Threat Protection, go to `https://www.microsoft.com/en-us/WindowsForBusiness/windows-atp`. Before you start the free trial, make sure you are logged into the Office 365 tenant as a global admin. The free trial will be added to your 365 tenant.   Microsoft requests that you log in a second time to verify your account. The other way to use Windows 10 ATP is to use a Microsoft 365 E5 subscription.

Step 1: Log In to securitycenter.windows.com

The first step is to log into Office 365 with the global admin account that is configured with the Microsoft 365 E5 subscription. Open a new tab on your browser and log in to `https://securitycenter.windows.com`. When you log in, you will need to create your security tenant (see Figure 3-10). The setup process requires that you install the active agents on all Windows 10 systems that have the Windows 10 E5 subscription. Windows 10 Build 1803 or later is required to use the next-generation software. After you log in to the Security Center, you will set up the monitoring agents. Click Next and follow the wizard.

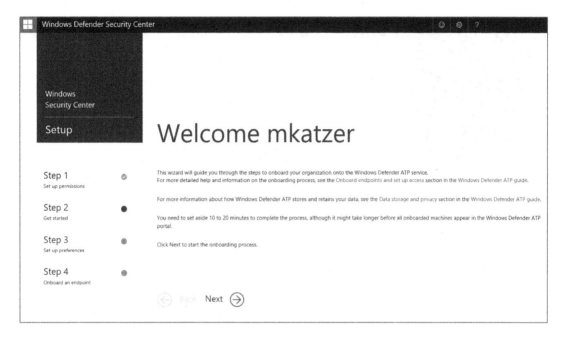

Figure 3-10. *Setup Windows Defender Security Center*

Step 2: Set Up the Data Repository

You need to select the data repository for either the United States or Europe (Figure 3-11). Additional countries will come online eventually. The repository is subject to local laws, and both repositories are GDPR compliant.

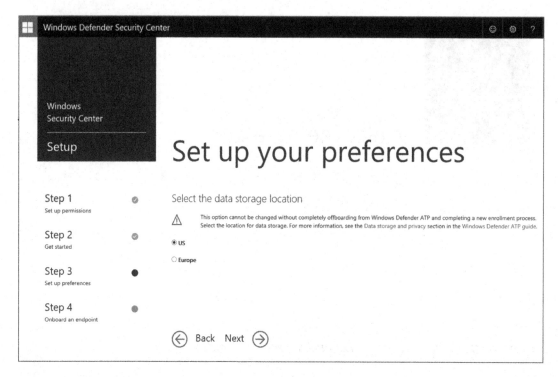

Figure 3-11. *Setting up the data center location preference*

Step 3: Set Up Data Retention Preferences

The next screen (Figure 3-12) defines how long data will be maintained in the repository. I recommend that you select 180 days. However, be aware that if you have a system that is in the repository and you decide to rename the system, you will have the old systems and the new system. The repository systems' names are unique, and the data sets are not merged. Later, I will show you a set of systems in the repository that have the same name. If you are deploying Windows 10 ATP in a new environment, make sure the systems are named correctly before you deploy the agents and the data collection tools.

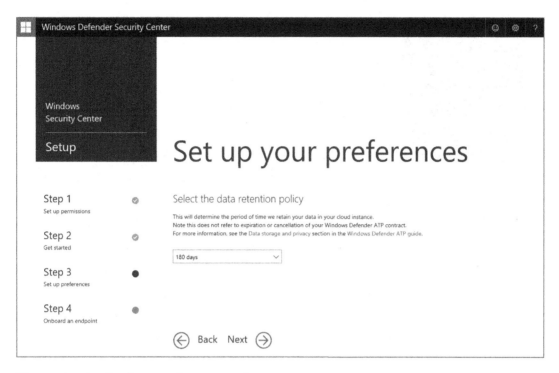

Figure 3-12. *Setting up data retention*

Step 4: Set Up the Organization's Data Size

The next screen (Figure 3-13) sets up the unique characteristics of the organization. Currently, this is the size of the repository.

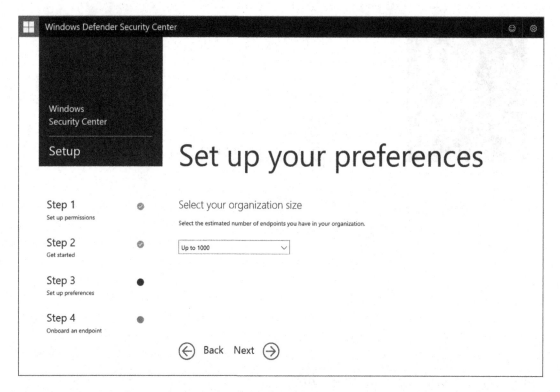

Figure 3-13. *Defining the organization's size*

Step 5: Identify the Organization Type

The next screen (Figure 3-14) is used to define the organization type. There are two locations where this information is maintained: in the Windows Security Center and the Office 365 Security & Compliance Center. This information is crucial for Secure Score operation. The configuration in step 3 allows you to compare how you run your organization against other companies. This allows Microsoft to identify potential threats that target companies in your market segment. Remember, the secure score is not just a reflection of your own configuration. It is also how your Office 365/Azure configuration tacks up against external threats and other organizations.

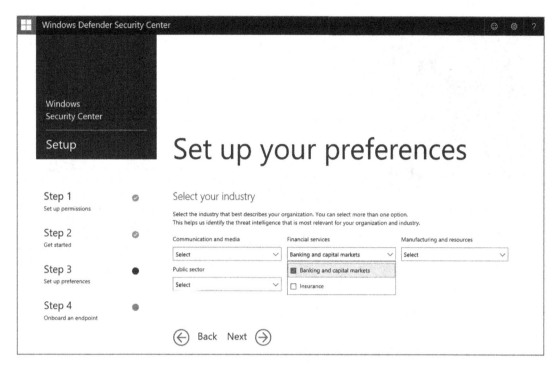

Figure 3-14. *Identifying your organization's market segment*

Step 6: Click Preview and Set Up the Cloud Instance

Advance the wizard through the next two steps to set up the preview (click Yes for new features) and to enable the cloud instance. The cloud instance (the data repository, etc.) will take anywhere from 5 to 20 mins to create depending on the organization size (Figure 3-15).

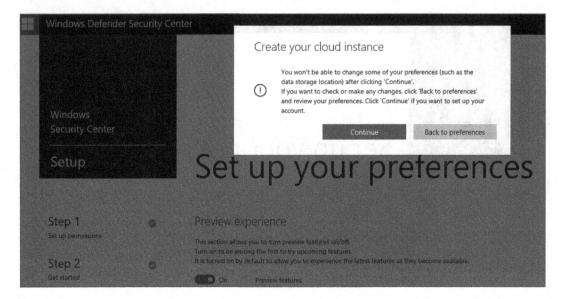

Figure 3-15. *Creating the cloud instance for Security Center*

Step 7: Download the Client Software

The next step is to download the client software endpoint and upgrade Windows Defender to ATP with the next-generation detection software (Figure 3-16). At this point, you have all the components necessary to start collecting information for a Windows secure score. As a reminder, make sure you have already renamed the system to the production name. Windows Security cannot tell if the system is the same and will not merge data or delete data form a systems that does not report status.

Figure 3-16. *Installing the desktop agent*

Step 8: Download the Client Software for Azure Log Analytics

In Chapter 2, we configured the Azure security services and Log Analytics. At this point, we need to download the Log Analytics agent to install on the Windows 10 desktops. In Chapter 2, you configured the Azure dashboard and already placed the Log analytics workspace on your dashboard. Select the *Log Analytics* workspace agent (see Figure 3-17).

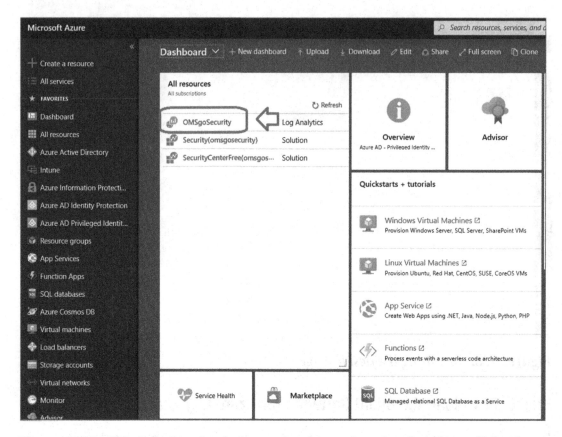

Figure 3-17. *Select the Log Analytics workspace to download and install the data collection agent*

After you have selected the Log Analytics workspace in the Azure dashboard, click *"Advanced settings"* and then select *Connected Sources*. Then click *Windows Servers* to access the monitoring agent. Even though you are installing desktops, the agent on the server and Windows 10 clients are the same (see Figure 3-18).

Figure 3-18. *Downloading the data collection agents for Windows connected devices*

You can also download the same agent for all Windows and non-Windows devices. Data collection for analyzing threats is key to deploying Office 365. If you do not install the data collection agents, you will not have visibility into the threats against your system. As an example, you now have the ability to look at systems' configuration and performance and take appropriate actions. One of the new threats that is emerging is crypto-jacking. *Crypto-jacking* takes over a system using the computer's resources. If your systems have been operating slowly for no apparent reason, then deploy the monitoring agents to see what is happening in your systems through the Log Analytics dashboard.

Note   The Log Analytics monitoring agent supports Windows and non-Windows devices. If you have not looked at the connected services, take the time now to examine what needs to be done to connect the rest of your monitoring services to Office 365 and Azure. To manage your cloud-based services, you will need to install the monitoring agents.

After you have downloaded and installed the agent, move on to step 9 and configure the Windows 10 analytics environment with the commercial ID.

Step 9: Configure the Windows 10 Environment

The final step is to configure the data collection agents on the Windows 10 devices. This is the Windows 10 commercial ID. The commercial ID collects information on the Windows 10 device and uploads the data to Log Analytics and Microsoft. The commercial ID is enabled when the *"Update compliance"* blade is enabled in the Log Analytics portal. If you did not record the commercial ID in Chapter 2, refer to the section *"Retrieving the Commercial ID for Windows 10 Devices"* later in this chapter. The commercial ID allows you to collect data about your Windows 10 clients for security analysis. Because this data may contain business information, the service is disabled and will need to be enabled by the IT department or your end users. To deploy the commercial ID, you need to add the Intune blade to your Azure portal. The steps to add the Intune portal are listed below.

1. In the azure portal (portal.azure.com) select favorites (next option located under create a resource on left hand menu)

2. Scroll down to Intune service

3. Select the Intune service – click on the star so it is yellow. This will add Intune to the favorites on the left hand menu.

4. Select Intune (it will be at the bottom of list, unless already added).

Once you have added the service, select Intune, then *Device configuration*, then *create profile* (see Figure 3-19). Select the plus sign to create a profile. The profile we will create is called *Deploy Commercial ID*. Before you proceed to the next section, make sure you have the Windows 10 Commercial ID. The process to retrieve the Commercial ID is described later in this chapter in the section called ***Retrieving the Commercial ID for Windows 10 Devices***. The Commercial ID is where the windows devices (Server 2016, Windows 10 and later and versions) will report telemetry data collected from the devices. Windows Advance Threat Protection services use telemetry data to pinpoint threats in your enterprise and to detect lateral security attacks with stolen credentials. Commercial ID telemetry data is crucial for a threat prevention and is a key part of an active defense against bad actors.

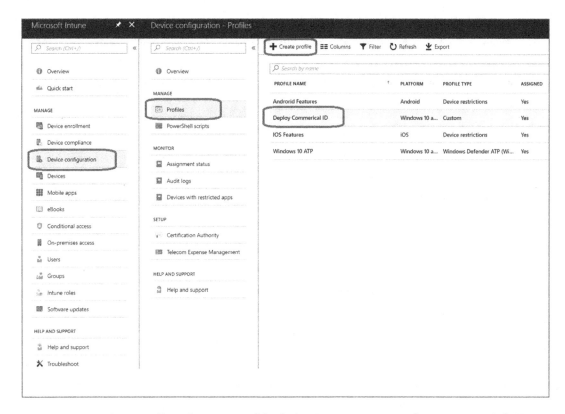

Figure 3-19. *Expanding the Intune blade in Azure to set up the commercial ID deployment*

Once you have the Commercial ID, there are three ways to deploy it. You can deploy it with Group Policy, Local Policy, or EMS deployment (version 1803 or later). In the following steps, we will use Local Policy to configure the Commercial ID. If you want to configure the commercial ID data collection on the local systems, see "Deploying the Commercial ID on Windows 10 Devices" later in this chapter. In this case, we will configure the Commercial ID deployment via the MDM wizard (MDM is covered in detail in Chapter 5).

The approach we are using here is to deploy the Commercial ID via the MDM/ MAM capabilities that are part of the Microsoft 365 E5 license. In the Azure dashboard, select the Intune blade and device configuration. Create a new profile for Windows 10 (see Figure 3-20).

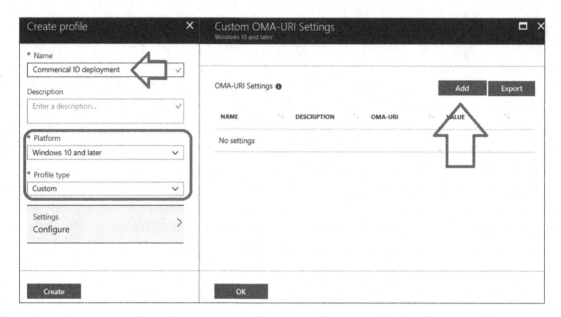

Figure 3-20. *Creating the custom deployment for a registry update to a Windows 10 device*

Select "Create profile" to create a new profile for deployment. Make sure you have selected Windows 10 and later and Custom profile. Once you have set up this information, you can add the deployment information to Windows 10 (see Figure 3-21).

Figure 3-21. *Enabling the Commercial ID via the MDM deployment*

The information that you need to add for the row is the following:

- *Name*: Windows 10 Systems – Telemetry

- *Description*: Enable Commercial ID

- *OMA-URI*: ./Vendor/MSFT/Policy/Config/System/AllowTelemetry

- *Data Type*: Integer

- *Value*: 1

The last step is to make sure you have assigned this deployment to a security group for deployment to the Windows 10 devices (see Figure 3-22). Once you have configured any MDM feature, you will need to assign the deployment to the different groups. In our case, we assign this to a test group for deployment (more in Chapter 5 about this configuration).

If you are not ready to deploy MDM and want to test the data collection, refer to the section called "Deploying the Commercial ID on Windows 10 Devices" later in this chapter. This section will walk you through the same steps, but each system will be deployed individually.

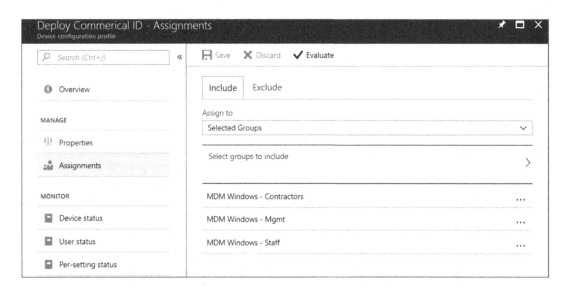

Figure 3-22. *Assigning the Commercial ID deployment to three different deployment groups*

Step 10: Verify the Windows 10 ATP Deployment

The configuration of Windows 10 ATP is complete. We have set up the Windows Security Center and deployed the necessary data collection tools on our systems. These tools include the following:

- ATP agent for Security Center

- Microsoft Monitoring Agent for data collection

- Commercial ID for detailed systems analysis

To make sure that our systems have been deployed, go to the `https://securitycenter.windows.com` and verify the systems are listed in the dashboard. Log in to the Security Center and select the machine icon. This should look similar to Figure 3-23.

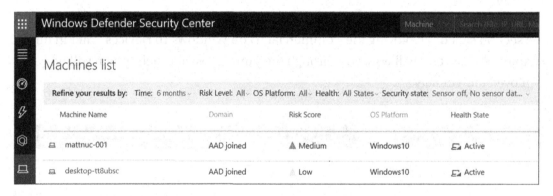

Figure 3-23. *Machines deployed with ATP*

Reviewing Windows Security Center Settings

Once the data starts flowing into the Security Center (it takes 24 hours for a complete data snapshot), you can examine the configuration of the Windows devices and determine what changes need to be made to raise the Windows Security Score. In Figure 3-24, we have selected the Application Guard to see the configuration of the desktop. The Windows Secure Score will show the areas that need to be addressed to raise the score. In this case, the Applications Guard is only 33 percent deployed. To address this, we need to enable the attack surface reduction rules, set controlled folder access (used to control ransomware), and use Windows Defender next generation AI versus a legacy third-party product).

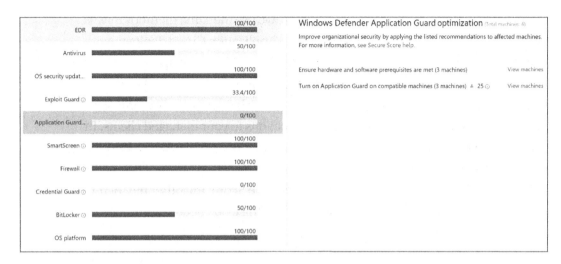

Figure 3-24. *Expanding the security score for Application Guard*

When you select the Application Guard card icon, you will see some areas highlighted (see Figure 3-25). In each of these cases, you need to look at the configuration and determine what features your business wants to enable and what features you do not have enable for a secured environment. Earlier, we used MDM to configure telemetry for the desktop clients. We can also do the same with Application Guard. Application Guard helps isolates enterprise-defined untrusted sites. This protects the company and blocks employees from accessing those sites.

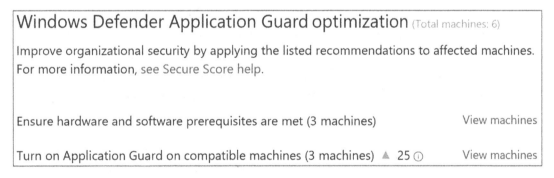

Figure 3-25. *Detailed look at the Application Guard deployment recommendation*

To configure the Application Guard feature, we use the same methods that we used earlier. We configure the OMA-URI for the Application Guard deployment (see `https://docs.microsoft.com/en-us/windows/client-management/mdm/windowsdefenderapplicationguard-csp`). Once this is deployed, our Windows Secure Score will increase with the new policy. Later in this chapter, you will examine how you configure the OMA-URI settings to push notifications to your managed clients. In Chapter 5, I will discuss these settings and others in more detail when talking about the MDM/MAM configuration.

So far, we have configured the Windows Secure Score; the other half of the problem is the Office 365 Secure Score. Let's move to the Office 365 Secure Score and configure the services so we can review the security positioning of our Office 365 environment.

Note   There are many different philosophies on what to configure or not to configure. My best advice is to look at each feature and independently make a decision to deploy or not to deploy. If you leave the defaults without understanding why they are in place, your configuration may not be as secure as needed and you have drastically effected the end user experience in a negative way.

Office 365 Secure Score

We spent a considerable amount of time building out the Windows Secure Score. We also introduced the configuration of the device using Intune MDM for device management (OMA extensions). The next step is to look at the Office 365 security score. If you made changes in the Security Center, those changes will impact the security score (see Figure 3-26). At this time, let's examine the Office 365 Secure Score.

Figure 3-26. *Microsoft Secure Score, via the Office 365 security admin center*

The Office 365 Secure Score is easy to configure; there is little setup required to collect the information. The Office 365 information is collected in your tenant based on your configuration of the different Office 365 services. There are three components that make up the security score. These are your Office 365 configuration, your organization size, and your market segment. Keep in mind that the security score values are recommendations. You will need to look at each of the recommendations to see the impact on your business. In some cases, there is no impact. In other cases, there could be a significant impact on the organization productivity. The goal of Microsoft Secure Score is to set up a configuration that meets your security needs. Do not try to max out the configuration. You want to select the configuration that makes sense for your business.

Comparison Score

What is the comparison score? I have had many discussions with Microsoft over the years on the features of the Microsoft Secure Score. The comparison provides a look into your target market and your company size and the typical configuration of the 365 tenants. This gives you an idea of what you are doing and what your fellow competitors are doing. This is important because bad actors look to target certain industries with different types of attacks. If your industry is banking, it is common that the attack will take on a form that is recognized by your fellow workers as a valid e-mail. In this case, the score gives you a metric to show that you need to be better to reduce your risk. Microsoft has extended the Microsoft Secure Score with threat intelligence, so if you are in a targeted industry that is exposed to certain types of threats and you turn the defenses off, your Microsoft Secure Score will be impacted.

There are three components to the Microsoft Secure Score comparison in Office 365: location, industry, and Office 365 user account. Microsoft Secure Score gives you a comparison against this metric. To set up your industry, go to the *Microsoft Security & Compliance Center*. Select *Service Assurance* and then *Settings*. Select your location and organization size and save the data (Figure 3-27).

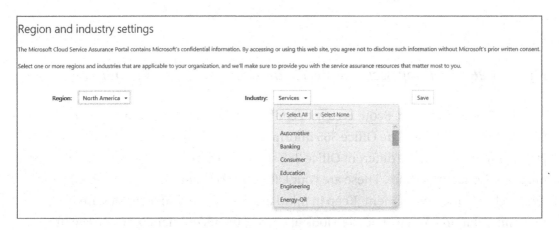

Figure 3-27. *Setting the organization information*

Once you set the organization size, in a few hours, your score will be adjusted based on your competitors. This will give you a good idea to the configuration of your environment compared to others in your industry. As an example, looking at our security score, we show a range of 171, and our industry is at a level of 45 for the same size and type of company (Figure 3-28). In our case, this number may look good, but it is far below our metric.

Figure 3-28. Comparison settings

Note   Secure Score is nothing more than the gamification of security. We all are competitive in one way or another. What we are doing here is getting a target so we can improve. Remember, what is measured can be improved, and what is tracked exponentially improves. In our case, we want to raise our security score.

Microsoft Secure Score Target

Once you have selected your business type and configured the region where your business is located, Microsoft will begin calculating your Office 365 Secure Score. In the Security & Compliance Center, look for the "Security admin" section (shown in Figure 3-29). Click Office 365 Secure Score.

Figure 3-29. *Accessing the Office 365 Secure Score*

Review the configuration of the Microsoft Secure Score and review your comparison. Select the target you are looking to achieve. In our case, the target score is 407 (see Figure 3-30). To set a target score, you simple move the slider based on your business needs. Once you move the slider, the next step is to configure the services.

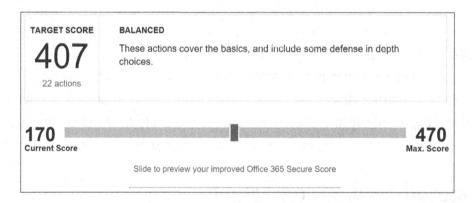

Figure 3-30. *Setting the target*

Once you set the target, all that is needed is to look at the actions necessary to adjust the score. In our case, there are 22 actions that we need to complete. The filter on the actions is extremely useful to separate the easy configuration changes from the more difficult configuration changes. Many of the changes will require you to use PowerShell (see Chapter 7 for an overview) to configure your Microsoft Secure Score.

When you set up the task list, filter out the easy-to-do tasks (Figure 3-31), and let's walk through the configuration. If this is the first time you are using Microsoft Secure Score, set the user impact to Low, and filter the list.

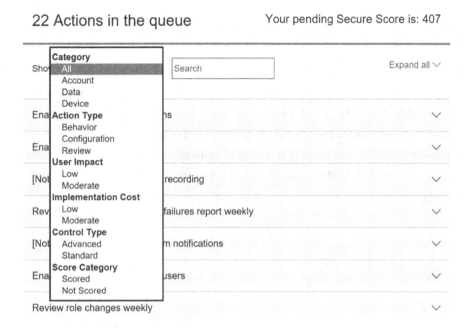

Figure 3-31. *Filtering the easy-to-do tasks*

As an example, our list has the following:

- Enable MFA for global admins

- Enabling audit data recording

- Review signings after multiple failures report weekly

- Set outbound SPMA notification

- Enable mailbox auditing for all users

- Review role changes weekly

- Enable information rights management

- User audit data

- Do not use transport rule to external domains

In the list of tasks that we need to compete, some of these tasks require reviewing reports and others require configuring a specific function. If you expand the action items and add up the score, this would add about 15 points to our score, which would place us at 295 security scores, which is less than 120 points away from our target of 407.

Increasing the Microsoft Secure Score

Looking at the security score recommendation, let's walk through the process of one item to give you a feel for the necessary complexity. If you expand the "enable MFA" item, you can see that there are specific tasks associated with enabling MFA (see Figure 3-32). Each score contains three pieces of information: an overview of the service, security threat information if the service is not implemented, and implementation instructions for the specific service. In this case, the goal is to reduce the threat of a breach by stolen credentials.

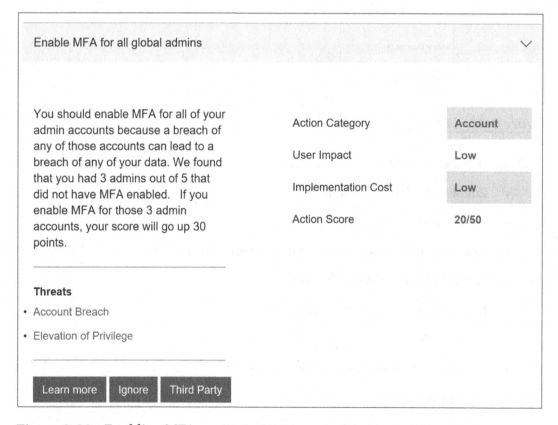

Figure 3-32. *Enabling MFA*

Implementation is easy; just click the "Learn more" button, and Microsoft Secure Score will walk you through the process to enable the specific feature. You can read the explanation and click Launch Now to configure the services that you will be using (see Figure 3-33).

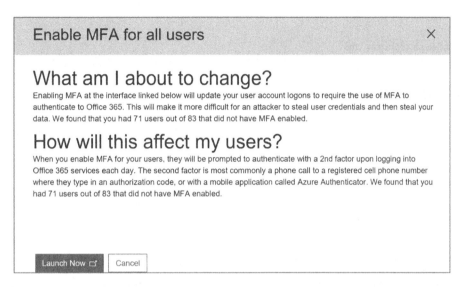

Figure 3-33. *Configuring MFA*

After you configure the MFA function to increase the score, walk through the renaming options to configure the services. The benefit is that your Office 365 tenant will have a secured configuration. Will this block all bad actors? We hope so! What Microsoft Secure Score does is make your data more difficult to compromise. So, the bad actors will be blocked the majority of the time. MFA raises the bar and forces the bad actors to look elsewhere. This is no different from homes that are well-lit and have barking dogs versus home that are quiet and not well-lit. Bad actors will go for the homes that look like they are easy to break into. You need to think of your Office 365 tenant in the same manner. Raise the security level and direct the bad actors to other homes.

Score Analyzer and Next Steps

The impact of the changes can be readily seen in 24 hours. In our example, we enabled MFA on all users, configured the "Lock box" option, adjusted the transport rules for mail forwarded, and reviewed the Azure security logs. These actions move our security score from 170 to xxx (see Figure 3-34). To see the impact of your changes, look at the Score Analyzer tab and click "Compare scores." This will show you the changes that you made and the impact they have on your Office 365 account.

Figure 3-34. Comparison measurement of Secure Score over time

Microsoft Secure Score is designed to be constantly evaluating the configuration of your Office 365 tenant. The evaluation happens at least once a day. The best practice is to make changes in the areas where there is the least impact on your users. In the areas where there is impact (such as setting up MFA) and configuration of the application ID, these changes need to be rolled out more slowly.

Note   Microsoft Secure Score is a set of baseline numbers that give you a recommendation on how your Office 365 tenant should be configured. As a CISO, you need to look at the reports generated in the Security Center and evaluate your business risk. Microsoft Secure Score is a tool that dynamically adjusts your score based on your Office 365 and Windows configuration and compares this to the risk associated to your business in a specific target market. The Microsoft Secure Score is design to assist you in building a solution that has less vulnerabilities. However, if a bad actor has targeted the organization, there is a high probability of penetration by the bad actor.

Compliance Manager

Microsoft introduced a new tool for Office 365 administrators and compliance officers called Compliance Manager, located at https://servicetrust.microsoft. com. Compliance Manager provides you with an assessment of your configuration of Office 365 as compared to the assessment analysis that you use to look at your business. Compliance Manager evaluates your response and scores you according to governmental standards. The most common analysis is the impact of the GDPR on the business. As an example, if we look at the securing data in the public network and what the requirements are under the GDPR, the Compliance Manager allows us to assign a resource that is responsible for the management and implementation of that function. When we successfully complete the task, we are scored (see Figure 3-35).

Figure 3-35. *Compliance Manager*

I do not want to lose sight as to what the problem is and what the regulations are trying to correct. The new regulations are putting in place a set of universal standards to safeguard personal information. The new compliance regulation is all about personal data and data privacy, and we are the custodians for personal information in our organizations. The best definition (which is being mainstreamed as the personal data standard) is from Article 4 of the GDPR regulation.

> *'Personal data' means any information relating to an identified or identifiable natural person ('data subject'); an identifiable natural person is one who can be identified, directly or indirectly, in particular by reference to an identifier such as a name, an identification number, location data, an online identifier or to one or more factors specific to the physical, physiological, genetic, mental, economic, cultural or social identity of that natural person.* [1]

---

[1] From: http://eur-lex.europa.eu/legal-content/EN/TXT/PDF/?uri=CELEX:32016R0679&from=EN

The difference between Secure Score and Compliance Manager is technical implementation versus business process implementation. Compliance Manager is about the business processes being compliant with the different governmental entities. The score that is used in Compliance Manager is a relative weight of the importance of the activity when you look at the overall requirements. In the case of the GDPR, we are looking at changes in how we store and manage information. When you are audited by a governmental agency, the audit looks at who is responsible for the implementation of the various regulations in your business.

So far, we just looked at the EU GDPR requirements. Let's look at the NIST 800-53 requirements. These are the requirements for U.S. federal contractors. If your business receives federal funds, you are required to be compliant with the NIST-800-53 standard.

If we look at Compliance Manager with the NIST 800-53 requirements for federal contractors, we have a similar set of controls for the management of the activities that would be associated with an audit. As an example, at KAMIND IT, we have customers with NIST audit requirements for breaches and remediation (see Figure 3-36). What we need to do is ensure that the documents that we generate for breach analysis are documented in our clients' Compliance Manager tenant.

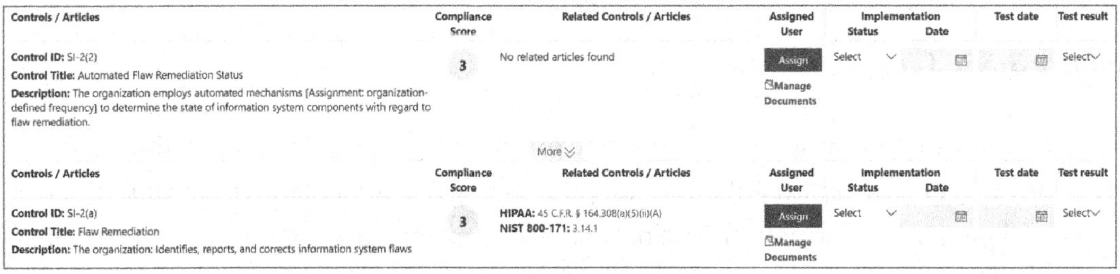

Figure 3-36. Remediation under NIST 800-53

When an auditor approaches an organization, the organization must show that it has implemented the necessary processes and controls and that it has the necessary documentation and checklist assigned to complete the activity. If the organization does not show the necessary controls and documents to support the audit request, the organization is fined.

Note   Compliance Manager supports the EU regulation GDRPR and NIST 800-35 for federal contractors. The next change we will see is the implementation of the California Consumer Privacy Act (CCPA). CCPA also includes fines.

The fines for noncompliance can be large and even close businesses. In the case of the European Union, the fines start at 20 million euros. In the United States, it depends on the agency, but it is not uncommon to have fines of $10,000 per incident with forfeiture of the government contracts.

This is why Compliance Manager is extremely important to your business. If you are subject to any state, federal, or international regulation, you must manage the information from a legality point. For all other businesses, you need to look at the regulations (GDPR and NIST 800-53) and use the same process to manage your internal activity. When the CCPA becomes more widespread, this is the tool you will use to ensure that your organization is complaint.

The purpose of Compliance Manager is to provide you with a set of checklists, where your business can assign resources to resolve the different compliance needs. If this is the first time you have been exposed to the compliance requirements, you need to make sure your business meets the necessary compliance standards. Figure 3-37 shows an update with the status of the different regulations and your internal business process changes.

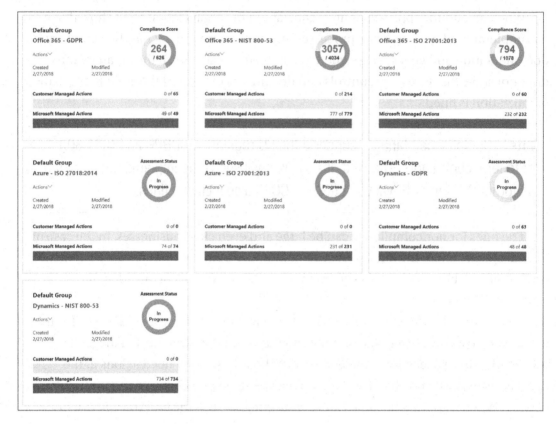

Figure 3-37. Compliance Manager

Compliance is a big topic. My objective here was to introduce you to the service trust center and the configuration necessary to manage your Office 365 tenant. Compliance is all about business processes and changes. Just like with Secure Score, we have a compliance score.

Next Steps

We use Compliance Manager as a check list when we audit a customer for GDPR compliance and NIST 800-53 compliance. This is the check list that your organization needs to implement. All companies should do what is necessary to be NIST 800-53 compliant. If we add into this the change under California's CCPA, our businesses will fundamentally change. What are the steps that you need to follow to implement the necessary changes in your organization? I have outlined some typical questions that you need to ask.

Step 1: Review Your Business

The first step is to determine what regulations you are subject to and what actions you need to implement (this is where Compliance Manager really helps). There are a number of categories for Compliance Manager. The common ones are : NIST 800-53 and the GDPR. One of the nice features of the Compliance Manager is the cross matching of the different compliance category. As an example, if you filled out the audit requirements for NIST 800-35, this would cross reference the task to other regulations. This cross reference allows an organization to look at multiple regulations and fill a number of requirements where there is overlap. The common question you need to ask are the following:

- GDPR

    - Do you have customers from the European Union?

    - Do you supply product or services to EU entities (people and/or businesses)?

- NIST

    - Do you have a federally funded contract for products or services?

    - Do you supply products or services to a vendor that is a government contractor?

- CCPA (use the NIST compliance tool)

    - Do you have customers in California?

    - Do you supply products or services to vendors in California?

    - Is your state passing a law similar to CCPA?

Step 2: Engage with a Licensing/Compliance Partner

Compliance Manager does a good job of helping you with the requirements of compliance. However, you may need a facilitator to provide you with accountability to make sure you are doing the work correctly. Compliance is about record-keeping an inventory assessment. Assign owners to the various regulations, and manage the activity like you would any other project. Set start dates and define a time line for implementation.

The goal of this type of engagement is to identify the compliance gap and who owns the gaps. Bear in mind that everything needs an owner, and everything must be tracked to make progress.

When you engage a Microsoft Partner, they will generate a document that is composed of a series of questions and build out a document (see Figure 3-38) that addresses the different areas. A GDPR assessment is composed of 191 questions and can take 40 to 160 hours to complete depending on the size of the organization and complexity of the problem.

Customer: <Customer Name>

ID	Question	Answer	Reviewer Notes
Discover			
D.1: Search for and identify personal data			**Reviewer Notes**
	Recommended Responder(s): Chief Information Security Officer (CISO), Data Protection Officer (DPO), IT Leadership		
D1.0	Can the organization generally identify all locations where personal data is stored across the enterprise, including on internal servers or cloud storage, as well as those hosted by any third-party providers?	<Enter Yes/No/N/A>	Organization is working on such capacity and is in progress
	Does the organization have:		
D1.1	The ability to locate all instances of personal data pertaining to a given data subject?	<Enter Yes/No/N/A>	
D1.2	A formal process in place to search for personal data in a consistent and timely manner?	<Enter Yes/No/N/A>	
D1.3	Technology in place for personnel to use a single search to return all instances of personal data for a given data subject?	<Enter Yes/No/N/A>	

***Figure 3-38.** Partner data collection form for Compliance Manager (courtesy of Microsoft)*

Once you have completed the compliance management process, Compliance Manager can assist you to make sure the data is kept up-to-date. This will help an organization meet the compliance needs. However, this is not a one-time action. It is a continuous process.

Step 3: Complete the Assessment

There is no way to get around this; you will need to complete the assessment and generate your business compliance score. The deliverable in the compliance score is the detailed process document that your organization needs to execute against for the different areas.

Other Configurations

Microsoft Secure Score is a powerful way to build out your Office 365 configuration and Azure configuration. This section contains some miscellaneous helpful hints on where to find and configure certain information required in Microsoft Secure Score. The techniques to deploy the configurations to the desktops are covered in the Mobile Device Management (Chapter 5).

Retrieving the Commercial ID for Windows 10 Devices

A commercial ID is the ID used to organize information that is shared with Microsoft. This information consists of diagnostic data. The diagnostic data is extremely useful for the care and health of your Office 365 environment. The data collected is used to assist Microsoft in better supporting our environment. Retrieving the commercial ID for Office 365 and Azure joint systems is a two-step process. In Chapter 2, we configured the Windows Update Management compliance blade for Log Analytics (see Figure 3-39).

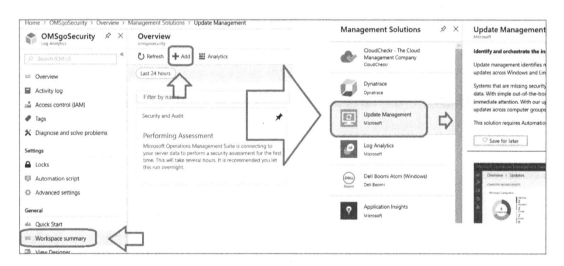

Figure 3-39. *Adding Update Management to the Log Analytics blade*

The commercial ID is used to collect information for Windows 10 desktop devices and supply the information to Microsoft. In this way, Microsoft can advise on the upgrade readiness. The second use of the commercial ID is to collect information that we can use in our security analysis of the workstation and the external threats form bad actors.

What we are doing from a security perspective is adding the Windows information from the desktops (and servers) and linking the information with the Active Directory and Office 365 information to build a full, 360-degree view of the security profile of the user. When we add Windows 10 Advanced Threat Protection, we are also linking information so we can see different threats to the environment that we are mitigating. To retrieve the Commercial ID, follow the steps outlined next.

Note   To retrieve the Commercial ID, you need to have completed the Azure Log Analytics setup described in Chapter 2. If you have not completed those steps, please return to Chapter 2 and configure Log Analytics so can you add data analysis to your environment. Security defenses requires that data is collected form different endpoints and analysis with the data form the cloud services.

Step 1: Select Log Analytics and Update Management

Select Log Analytics and then workspace summary. After you have selected workspace summary, select the Update Compliance blade. Then click Solution Settings (see Figure 3-40).

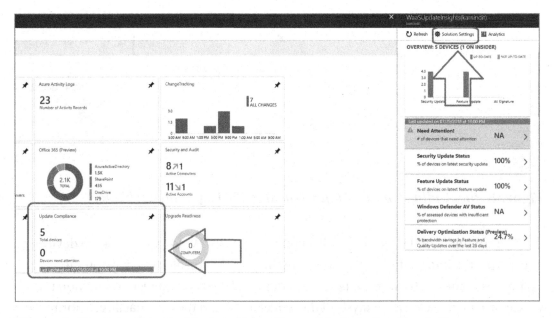

Figure 3-40.   *Selecting the Update Compliance blade in Log Analytics*

Step 2: Copy the Commercial ID from the Update Compliance Blade

The Commercial ID is located in the Update Compliance Settings section of the log analytics (called update Insights). Click Update Compliance Settings, and copy the Commercial ID (Figure 3-41). This is the ID used to organize the data that has been relayed to Microsoft. Our objective here is to make a copy of the key so any information that is uploaded to Microsoft is also uploaded to the security center for analysis.

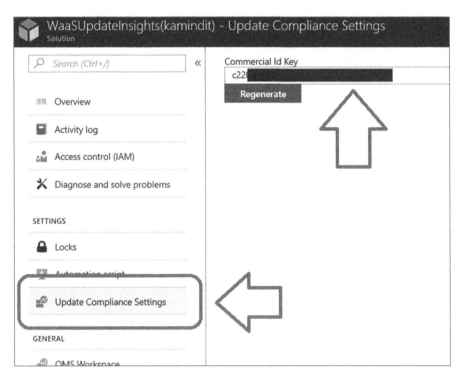

Figure 3-41. *Retrieving the commercial ID from the Update Compliance settings section*

Deploying the Commercial ID on Windows 10 Using Local Policy

There are three ways to deploy the commercial ID. You can deploy this with Group Policy, Local Policy, and EMS deployment (version 1803 or later). In the following steps, we will show how to use Local Policy to configure the commercial ID. In this case, we will use the Group Policy editor to configure the necessary entries for data recording.

Step 1: Edit the Group Policy by Using the MMC Component

On your Windows 10 system, open an administrator prompt and type in MMC (Microsoft Management Console). In the MMC snap-in, select File, select Add/Remove Snap-in, and select Group Policy Object, then Local computer policy. Click Add (see Figure 3-42).

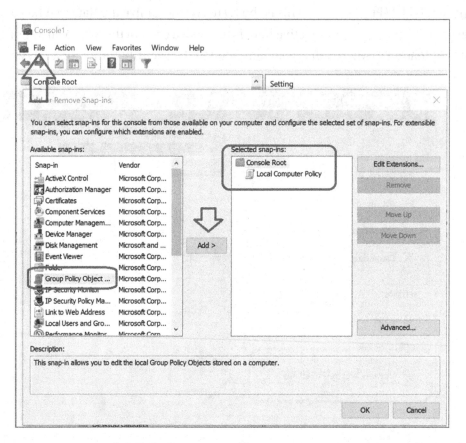

Figure 3-42. *Setting up the MMC to retrieve the group Security Policy Editor*

Step 2: Expand Data Collection and Preview Builds

Once the Group Policy editor is loaded, select Administrative Templates, Windows Components, and then Data Collection and Preview Builds. You want to configure two areas (see Figure 3-43): Allow Telemetry and Configure the Commercial ID.

Setting	State	Comme
🗒 Toggle user control over Insider builds	Not configured	No
🗒 Allow device name to be sent in Windows diagnostic data	Not configured	No
🗒 Allow Telemetry	Enabled	No
🗒 Configure the Commercial ID	Enabled	No
🗒 Configure Microsoft 365 Update Readiness upload endpoint	Not configured	No
🗒 Configure telemetry opt-in change notifications.	Not configured	No
🗒 Configure telemetry opt-in setting user interface.	Not configured	No
🗒 Disable deleting diagnostic data	Not configured	No
🗒 Disable diagnostic data viewer.	Not configured	No
🗒 Configure Authenticated Proxy usage for the Connected User...	Not configured	No
🗒 Limit Enhanced diagnostic data to the minimum required by ...	Not configured	No
🗒 Configure Connected User Experiences and Telemetry	Not configured	No
🗒 Do not show feedback notifications	Not configured	No
🗒 Configure collection of browsing data for Microsoft 365 Anal...	Not configured	No

Figure 3-43. *Options under the Data Collection and Preview Builds*

Step 3: Expand Telemetry

Expand the Allow Telemetry section, select Enabled, and select option 3 - Full (see Figure 3-44).

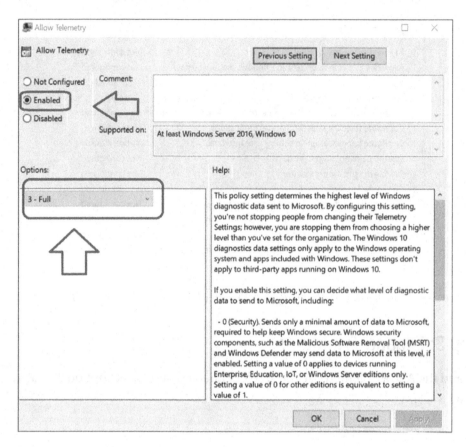

Figure 3-44. *Enabling Telemetry*

Step 4: Enter the Commercial ID and Enable Upload

Expand the Configure Commercial ID section, select Enabled, and enter the commercial ID (see Figure 3-45).

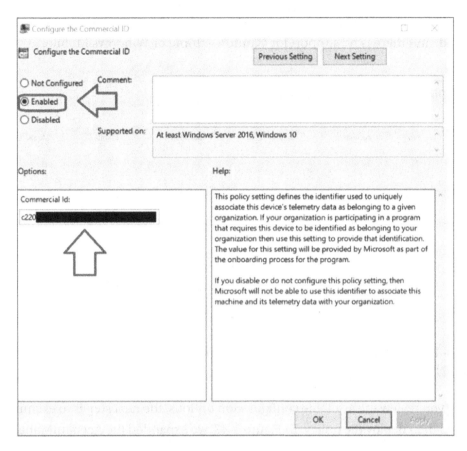

Figure 3-45. *Enabling the commercial ID and entering the commercial ID on Windows 10/Server 2016*

Setting Custom OMA-URI Settings for Microsoft Intune

The Open Mobile Alliance Uniform Resource Identifier (OMA-URI) setting allows you to customize the local security policy settings for Windows 10 and Server 2016 devices. These settings are used to control the features of the device such as the Active Directory group policy. Windows 10 and Service 2016 make many configuration service provider (CSP) settings configurable through Intune MDM policies. Setting up a new policy is easy. (See `https://docs.microsoft.com/en-us/windows/client-management/mdm/configuration-service-provider-reference` for the different CSP policy options.) You need to pay attention to the version of Windows 10. CSP support is variable on the OS build, and you want to deploy CSP only on the latest Windows 10 systems. Figure 3-46 shows a snapshot of the different CSP offerings for MDM/

147

MAM management. The footnote means that only Windows 10 version 1803 or later is supported, and there is no support for Windows Home or Windows Mobile.

CSP support

AccountManagement CSP

Home	Pro	Business	Enterprise	Education	Mobile	Mobile Enterprise
✗	✗	✗	✗	✗	✗	✗

Accounts CSP

Home	Pro	Business	Enterprise	Education	Mobile	Mobile Enterprise
✗	✓[4]	✗	✓[4]	✓[4]	✗	✗

ActiveSync CSP

Home	Pro	Business	Enterprise	Education	Mobile	Mobile Enterprise
✓	✓		✓	✓	✓	✓

Figure 3-46. *Custom OMA-URI configuration settings for Windows 10 (courtesy of Microsoft)*

Once you review the available configuration options, the next step is to examine the policy and then deploy the policy. In Figure 3-47, we expanded the AccountManagement CSP policy to see the policy in a tree format.

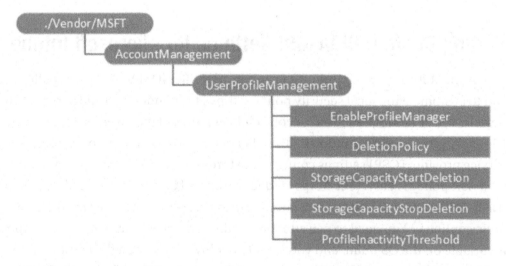

Figure 3-47. *Expansion of the AccountManagement CSP (courtesy of Microsoft)*

Once you have reviewed the CSP policy, you can select the necessary configuration elements. In this case (looking at the AccountManagement CSP for our Windows Holographic Business edition), we want to set up the device so that profiles are deleted when the storage is full or after a period of inactivity. As an example, the data we will need to configure is shown here and in Figure 3-48:

- *Name*: Windows 10 Account Management – Holographic Delete policy

- *Description*: Set Account Delete Policy

- *OMA-URI*: ./Vendor/ MSFT/AccountManagement/ UserProfileManagement

- *Data Type*: Integer

- *Value*: 2

The configuration we are using is Microsoft 365 E5, and we have deployed the Intune MDM/MAM. To configure the policy, log in to `https://portal.azure.com` and select Intune on your Azure dashboard (if this is not present, you will need to add the service through the Azure search or Azure option "Create a resource"). Once you have selected Intune, select Device configuration and then Policies. Click "Create profile" to create a new profile for deployment. Make sure you have selected Windows 10 and Later as well as Custom profile. Once you have set up this information, you can now add the deployment information or Windows 10 Holographic edition.

Figure 3-48. *Deploying a custom configuration to the connected client*

The scope for what you can deploy on Azure-connected clients is extremely broad and is being expended with every release. In Figure 3-49, you see the WiFi CSP. MDM can be set up to fully configure the WiFi configuration for the connected mobile or Windows 10 client.

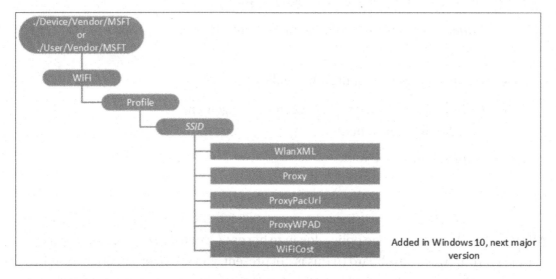

Figure 3-49. *Exploring the WiFi CSP and changes on the connected client (courtesy of Microsoft)*

Deploying DMARC/DKIM

Phishing e-mails and spam are becoming more and more common. One of the ways to combat them is to use Domain Keys Identified Mail (DKIM) in conjunction with the sender policy (SPF) to validate e-mail in Office 365. The combination of these two technologies is called Domain-based Message Authentication, Reporting and Configuration (DMARC), as shown in Figure 3-50. This ensures that the destination servers can trust your company e-mail and you can trust e-mail that has been sent to you from third parties (assuming you are using the Office 365 protection services).

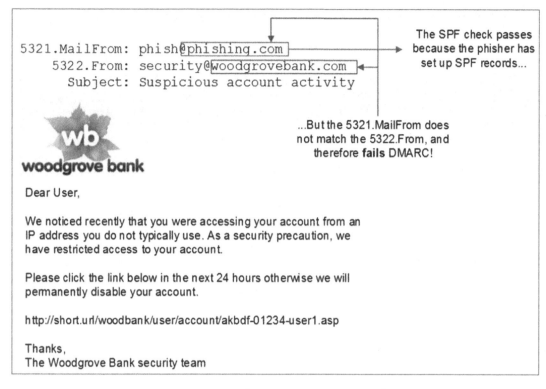

Figure 3-50. *DKIM e-mail analysis (courtesy of Microsoft)*

How does DMARC work? Simply put, it standardizes the send from address (5322 specification) and the mail from address (5321 specification). The deployment of DMARC/DKIM prevents spoofing. As an example, look at the simple mail transcription in Figure 3-50. Normal SPF checks will allow an e-mail to go through the message filters, but a DMARC/DKIM deployment will detect the phishing address and force a failure for DMARC.

DRMARC/DKIM simply forces the domain validation of the e-mail. In the example, DMARC validates that the e-mail addresses comes from a valid domain. This approach validates the sender e-mail; however, you can still be phished, but this minimizes the phishing from fake e-mail domains. The configuration of DMARC involves the following steps.

Step 1: Configure SPF Records

Configure your SPF records for your e-mail domain in Office 365. The typical Office 365 SPF record looks like this:

```
v=spf1 include:spf.protection.outlook.com -all
```

To access your SPF record, log in to the Office 365 admin panel and select Setup and Domains (see Figure 3-51).

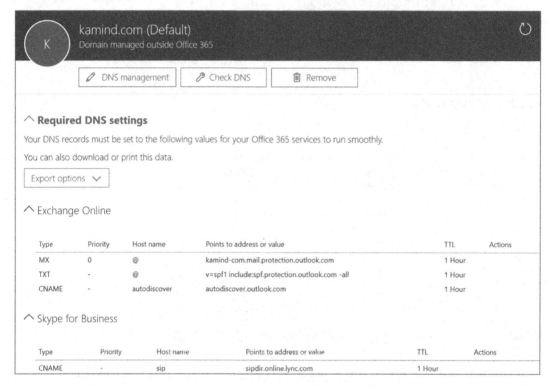

Figure 3-51. *Collecting the SPF record from Office 365*

Office 365 has a default DKIM and uses the `onmicrosoft.com` domain. Once you have verified your domain, you need to create the DKIM record that corresponds to the verified domains.

Step 2: Publish Two CNAMEs for Records in Your Custom Domain

Figure 3-52 shows the mail flow. The first step is to create two CNAME records for your custom domains. Figure 3-53 has the generic DKIM/DMARC records. The changes you make are in domain, domainGUID, initialDomain, and domainkey. Figure 3-54 shows the configured DKIM information for `kamind.com`. Once you have these records defined, upgrade the DNS services with the new records. DKIM works only with records that have been verified. You will need to have a DKIM record for each domain that you use.

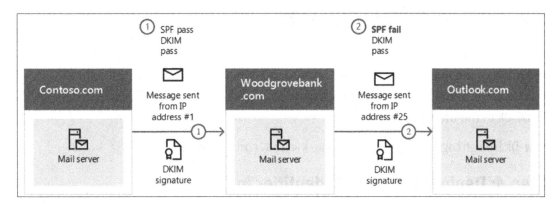

Figure 3-52. *DKIM mail flow (courtesy of Microsoft)*

Host name:	selector1._domainkey.<domain>
Points to address or value:	selector1-<domainGUID>._domainkey.<initialDomain>
TTL:	3600
Host name:	selector2._domainkey.<domain>
Points to address or value:	selector2-<domainGUID>._domainkey.<initialDomain>
TTL:	3600

Figure 3-53. *Microsoft generic Office 365 DKIM records (courtesy of Microsoft)*

Host name:	selector1._domainkey.kamind.com
Points to address or value:	selector1-kamind-com._domainkey.kamindit.onmicrosoft.com
TTL:	3600
Host name:	selector2._domainkey.kamind.com
Points to address or value:	selector2-kamind-com._domainkey. kamindit.onmicrosoft.com
TTL:	3600

Figure 3-54. *Configured KAMIND.com DKIM structure for Office 365*

Step 3: Enable DKIM in Office 365

Once you have created the DKIM records and installed them in your DNS server, you need to run the following PowerShell command. Once you have configured the DKIM, you can look at the internal properties of a sent message and you will see DKIM=pass or DKIM=OK in the Internet header.

```
New-DkimSigningConfig -DomainName kamind.com -Enabled $true
```

Step 4: Deploy the DMARC Identifier in Office 365

The next step is to configure the DMARC name for Office 365. The decision for which record to deploy is based on the policy of the organization. There are multiple policy options that you can deploy. A policy is what happens when you have a DMARC failure. Figure 3-55 shows the different configurations. The recommendation is to use a quarantine (or the junk folder).

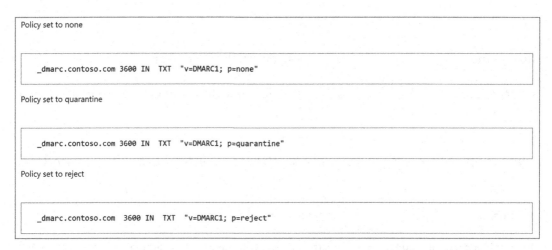

Policy set to none

```
_dmarc.contoso.com 3600 IN  TXT  "v=DMARC1; p=none"
```

Policy set to quarantine

```
_dmarc.contoso.com 3600 IN  TXT  "v=DMARC1; p=quarantine"
```

Policy set to reject

```
_dmarc.contoso.com  3600 IN  TXT  "v=DMARC1; p=reject"
```

Figure 3-55. PowerShell to enable DKIM for Office 365 (courtesy of Microsoft)

Using Azure Advisor

Once you have enabled all the security services, Azure Advisor will begin to analyze your configuration and make suggestions. In Figure 3-56, you see the advisor recommendations for Availability, Security, Performance, and Cost. You can expand the categories to look at the changes that you need to make for your Azure environment to function better. You can load the Azure Advisor from the "All services" option in the dashboard. Don't forget to pin the new favorites to the dashboard for future reference.

Figure 3-56. *Azure Advisor (located in all services)*

Summary

At this point you have expanded the type of data being collected in the Azure security center. You enabled the Commercial Id for windows devices (Server 2019 and Windows 10), and started to collect more data about your enterprise environment. At this point we can now see alerts in our enterprise and drill down on those alerts to remediate issue. One of your other accomplishments, is the integration with Microsoft Secure Score and you started to build a road map on the features you need to implement to secure the environment. We are on the path for success..

Next Steps

Now that our base logging configuration is completed, and the logs are collecting data, we move on to the next step. The next step in this case is the continue build out of the Enterprise Mobility and Security applications. These are not true applications, rather they are Azure extensions targeted to complete specific function, all revolving around Identity protection and information protection. Once we have completed the integration of the EMS services, we can move forward with Mobile application and device management.

Reference Links

There is a lot of information about Office 365 on the Web—the issue is finding the right site. The information contained in this chapter is a combination of my experience doing deployments and of support information that has been published by third parties.

Compliance Manager and Service Trust

- https://servicetrust.microsoft.com/

NIST Guide to Information Technology Security Services

- https://nvlpubs.nist.gov/nistpubs/Legacy/SP/
  nistspecialpublication800-35.pdf

EU Regulation directive 95/46/EC: General Data Protection Regulation

- https://eur-lex.europa.eu/legal-content/EN/TXT/PDF/?uri=CE
  LEX:32016R0679&from=EN

GDPR Compliance and Information Microsoft Collects

- https://docs.microsoft.com/en-us/windows/privacy/gdpr-
  win10-whitepaper

Sharing Diagnostic Data in Your Organization

- https://docs.microsoft.com/en-us/windows/privacy/configure-
  windows-diagnostic-data-in-your-organization

Custom OMA-URI Settings for Windows 10 Devices

- https://docs.microsoft.com/en-us/intune/custom-settings-
  windows-10

CHAPTER 4

Deploying Identity Management with EMS

Office 365 is a suite of technologies delivered as a software-as-a-service (SaaS) offering and reduces IT costs for businesses of any size. Windows Enterprise Mobility & Security (EMS) is a SaaS offering that enhances the security of your Office 365 deployment; The new Microsoft 365 Enterprise E5 suite incorporates Enterprise Mobility and Security E5 suite. My team deploys either the Microsoft 365 E5 suite or the EMS E3/E5 suite for account security. This improves the security of our clients and in doing so reduces our threat landscape. This chapter is about deploying the Azure identity and information protection capabilities included with the EMS E5 (a component in the Microsoft 365 E5) (see Figure 4-1 for an EMS E3/E5 comparison).

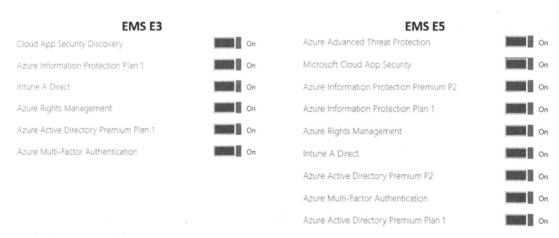

Figure 4-1. *Enterprise Mobility & Security Suite E3/E5 comparison (license feature view)*

© Matthew Katzer 2018
M. Katzer, *Securing Office 365*, https://doi.org/10.1007/978-1-4842-4230-8_4

There are many ways to look at the EMS suites and it is a very large topic. The approach that I used is to break this up into two different chapters, one on Information Protection and Identity Management, and the following chapter on Intune for mobile device management. Figure 4-2 shows the components of the Enterprise Mobility & Security suites.

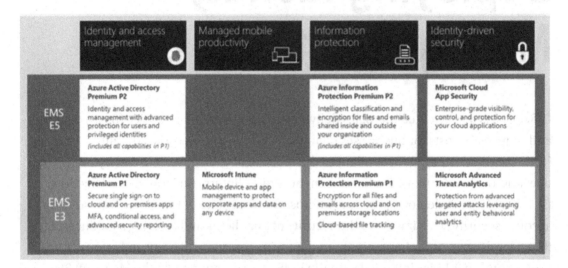

Figure 4-2. *EMS Suite components (courtesy of Microsoft)*

What Is EMS?

EMS (Enterprise Mobility & Security) is a Microsoft security suite for mobile and desktop devices. EMS is designed to work with Windows 10 and to use Azure security to manage the device and user infrastructure. There are two capabilities of EMS that are extremely useful for companies: EMS protects and empowers workers to better perform the duties assigned to them, and EMS allows the CISO to manage the activity of the users and prevent bad actors from accessing the data. One of the latest features to be deployed in Azure AD is *smart lockout*. Smart Lockout locks out bad actors who are trying to guess your users' passwords. The Azure intelligence is developed in such a way that the systems will recognize when a password is being breached and will force password authentication to happen.

There are different password programs and methods. We may think our passwords are unique, but in many cases, they are not and have already been compromised. When you deploy EMS subscriptions (or in this case, when you use one of the Microsoft 365 suites), you are protected by the constantly changing landscape of protecting your users' accounts. This capability is included in the Azure Active Directory Premium P2 component of the EMS suite.

Looking at the business from a CISO point of view, a CISO now can deploy the sets of tools and services that protect the company assets. In Chapter 3, we configured the security score for both Office 365 and the Windows Security Center to manage our environment; now we are taking a deep dive to tightly configure our environment to manage the information that we communicate internally and externally in the organization. To get started, let's look at the components of EMS and understand how we are going to deploy them in our business.

When we created our Office 365 account and validated the domain (see Chapter 7), that action created our Office 365 Azure Active Directory. We have the option to add Azure AD domain services or use our local active directory. You can add this at this step; however, there will be some Azure-configured services that must be set up correctly. These services consist of dedicated Azure subnets and additional configuration (a permanent configuration). Azure AD domain services is not the same as Azure joined devices and is a more involved topic beyond the scope of this book. In our deployment of the EMS security components we can either use the link to the on site active directory, or we can join workstations directory to Azure active directory. Either approach works for our discussion on the deployment of the EMS suite. The services that we are going to add are Azure AD Privileged Identity, Azure AD Identity Protection, and Azure Information Protection (see Figure 4-3). Log in to `https://portal.azure.com` with the global admin account. Select the dashboard and then select *Create a resource*, and select the resource described in the following sections. We will add each of the components of the EMS suite and configure them.

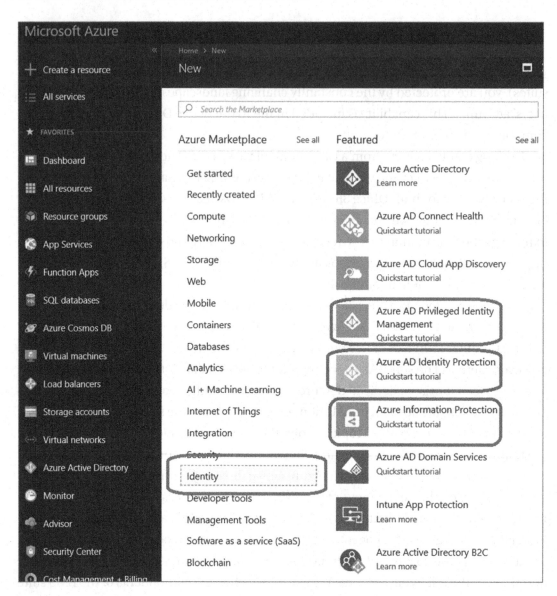

Figure 4-3. *Adding the Azure services*

Adding the Azure AD Privileged Identity Management

There are three Azure Ad services that we will configure in our Azure dashboard. We are going to walk through the steps of the initial configuration of these services. In some cases, the services have additional configuration or customization.

There are three services that we will be configuring for EMS:

- Azure AD Privileged Identity Management

- Azure AD Identity Protection

- Azure Information Protection

EMS includes Intune. Intune is the Mobile Device Management component of EMS and will be focused on in Chapter 5. In Chapter 5, we will set up two types of Mobile Device Management: a Manage Application Management (MAM) and a full Mobile Device Management (MDM) deployment. Before we jump into device management, let's focus on the information protection and identity management.

Let's begin the process of configuring the different information and identity services for our EMS deployment.

Note   Azure Information Protection is briefly covered later in this chapter. My goal is to address the issues associated with identity management and device management and give you an overview of Azure Information Protection. Azure Information Protection is an important topic, but it is an orthogonal topic that is best covered as a stand-alone feature.

Step 1: Adding Azure AD Privileged Identity Management

Privileged Identity Management (PIM) is used to manage user accounts' access to higher-level administrative functions. All of the new compliance audits require that IT administrators operate at the lowest level of permissions possible. Besides, this is just good business practice. Here, we are using PIM to manage administrator access to the global administrator account. The user accounts that require access are set up as password administrators. This is a lower-risk admin account since all users in our environment are running multifactor authentication. So, if we have a bad actor as an administrator, that person can only reset account passwords that have a lower privilege

161

level, and since those users are running MFA, the exposure is minimal (users can reset
their own passwords and requires a mobile number to confirm identity). All of the
administrator accounts have a Microsoft 365 E5 subscription assigned to them. In the
configuration that we are walking through, the administrator account that is used to set
up the PIM service has Microsoft 365 E5. If you are setting up the service with an account
without Microsoft 365 E5, you will generate an error on the configuration. The error is
generated because you need a EMS E5 license component, e.g. the Azure AD Premium P2
license. This license is included with the MS 365 E5 or EMS E5, but not with the EMS E3.

Adding Azure AD Privileged Identity Manager is straightforward. Click the Identity
icon and then click Create (see Figure 4-4).

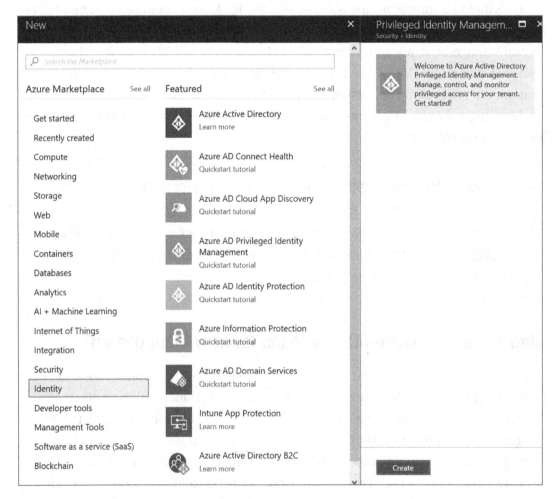

Figure 4-4. *Adding Azure AD Privileged Identity Management*

During the process, the Azure services will create the necessary components in Azure. If the Azure service has been already created or is hidden, watch for the pop-up message (see Figure 4-5) in the left corner. Click the message, which will launch the service to be configured. If you miss this step, just repeat adding the service until you have successfully clicked the message.

Figure 4-5. *Accessing the Azure AD Privileged Identity Management (PIM) service*

PIM creates a new level of security controls for your administrators. Typically, organizations like to maintain control over administrator accounts. So, the user operates at a lower level of administrator. When a user needs to operate at a higher level, such as a global admin, they use PIM to request approval for the higher level of service. The increased credentials permissions are provided for only a limited time, and then the user account is reduced to the previous level. This is a compliance requirement and allows you to control the access of users and verify their access for the type of work they are performing.

Note   In Chapter 3, we touched briefly on Compliance Manager. We did not go into too much detail (Compliance Manager is a book in itself), but we provided some requirements for control. As an example, in NIST 800-35 there is a compliance requirement to use the minimal permissions to manage the environment. To meet this directive, you need to use a tool like PIM where the access to the global admin is activated for a limited period of time. This reduces the risk of a credential breach.

Step 2: Verifying Your Identity

Once you have selected the Azure service, the next step is to verify your identity. The Azure identity service will walk you through the steps to configure your user account and add the necessary information to Azure. The default configuration contains two forms of identification: e-mail address and mobile phone. Click "Verify my identity" and walk through the process of setting up MFA for your test account (see Figure 4-6). You will be prompted on a number of screens to verify your identity.

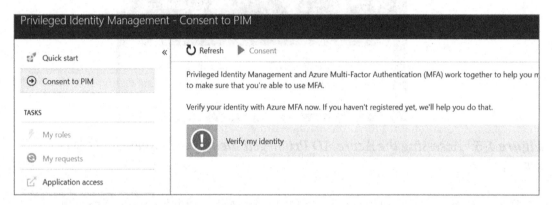

Figure 4-6. *Verifying your identity*

There are different ways you can verify your identity. I use the mobile app when I can. If you have not downloaded the mobile app from the mobile store, you will need to complete this step before you continue. Once you download the app, just select a new account and add the app. The Microsoft service will display a bar code, so scan the bar code to automatically configure the service (see Figure 4-7). Click Next and then enter the code. You will still be prompted to enter your cell number for access in case the mobile app fails (or you lose your phone).

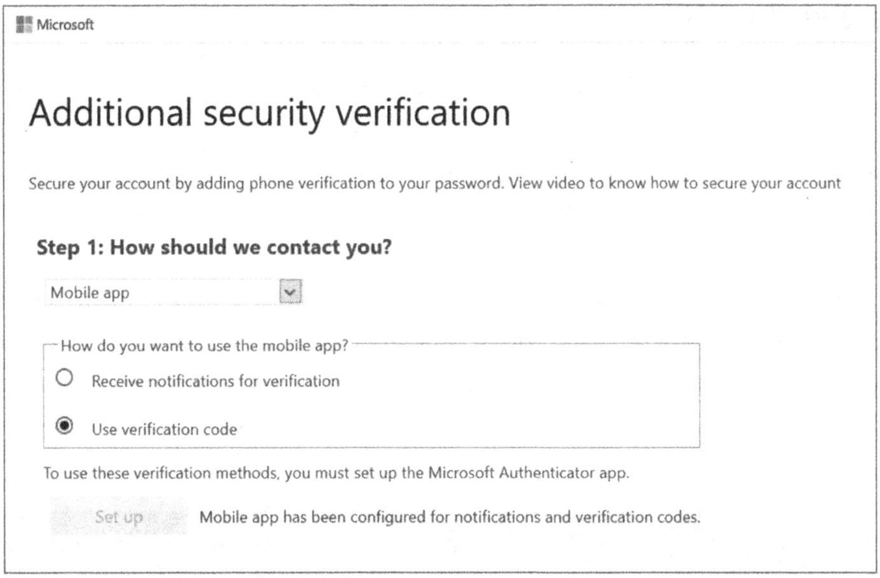

Microsoft

Additional security verification

Secure your account by adding phone verification to your password. View video to know how to secure your account

Step 1: How should we contact you?

Mobile app

How do you want to use the mobile app?

○ Receive notifications for verification

◉ Use verification code

To use these verification methods, you must set up the Microsoft Authenticator app.

Set up   Mobile app has been configured for notifications and verification codes.

Figure 4-7. *Verifying your identity using the mobile app*

Once you have completed the process, you will be redirected to the application to provide your consent. Click Consent to continue the configuration. You will be prompted to verify your actions before the PIM service will be configured. See Figure 4-8.

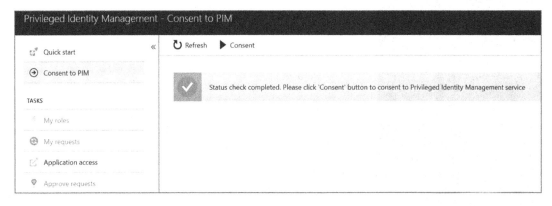

Privileged Identity Management - Consent to PIM

↻ Refresh   ▶ Consent

«   Quick start

⊕ Consent to PIM

TASKS

My roles

My requests

Application access

Approve requests

✓ Status check completed. Please click 'Consent' button to consent to Privileged Identity Management service

Figure 4-8. *The identity is verified; next you need to consent to the use of the PIM tool*

Step 3: Set Up PIM

The next step is to select the Active Directory role and sign up for access. This sets the user account as the security manager for the PIM process. Once you have PIM in place, the users' access is managed. Configuring user access is described later in this chapter. At this point, the goal is to set up PIM so you can manage user access to the global admin account.

Select the Azure AD roles (see Figure 4-9). This will launch an investigation into your tenant and build the Azure AD roles for all users to access the Azure security services. Since you are a global administrator and you are the first user to use the services, the service will be configured around your credentials (see Figure 4-10).

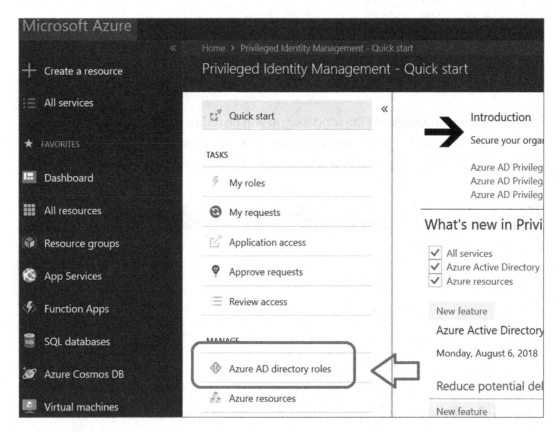

Figure 4-9. *Selecting the Azure AD directory roles for PIM*

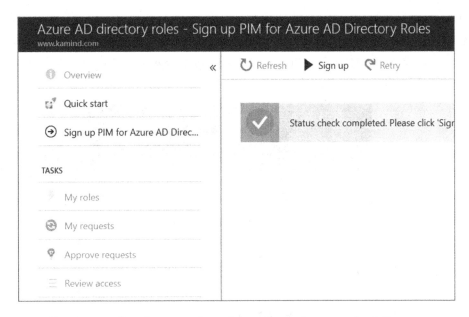

Figure 4-10. *Signing up for the security role as the primary administrator*

Once you have completed the sign-up process, PIM is ready for additional users to access the service. The configured service should look like Figure 4-11.

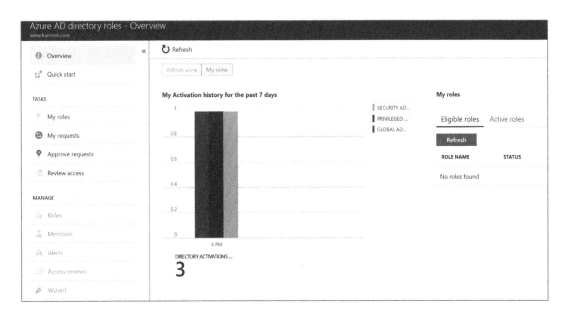

Figure 4-11. *Configured PIM service for future expansion*

There is one last item that you need to complete, and that is pinning the configured PIM service to the Azure dashboard. So before you forget, look in the right corner, and click the pin to pin PIM to the Azure dashboard (see Figure 4-12).

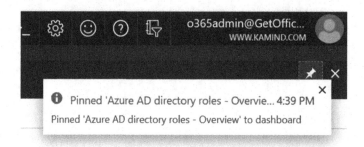

Figure 4-12. *Pinning PIM to the Azure dashboard*

Step 4: Configure the Initial Role

After PIM is installed, the next step is to run the wizard and configure the user roles. The wizard looks for users with different permissions and allows you to assign them temporary administrator rights. The wizard is an important step to run to set up the baseline configuration (see Figure 4-13).

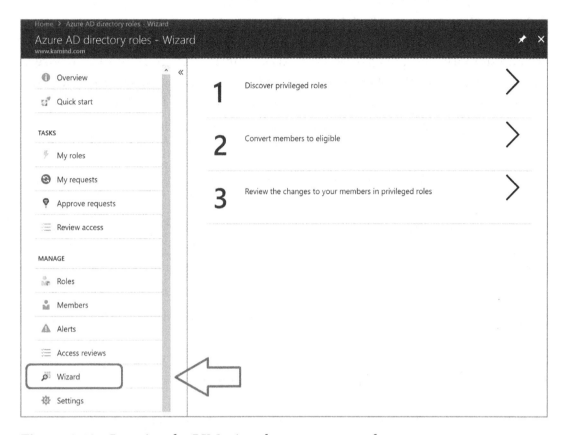

Figure 4-13. *Running the PIM wizard to set up user roles*

As an example, take a user who is a password administrator and wants to run as a global administrator. The user logs into Azure, accesses PIM, and requests the global administrator access. The role is assigned for a limited period of time (30 minutes in this example) to allow the user to perform the necessary actions. Global administrator rights are temporary. At the end of the time period, the user permission is restored to the nonglobal admin permissions.

PIM requires that the user have some administrator privilege level to use the service. We use a password administrator as the default administrator account (all our users have MFA deployed, so this has little impact on the user in the case of an issue with an authorized administrator). At this point, we will move to the next step and set up Identity Access Manager.

Adding the Azure AD Identity Protection

The next service we are adding is the Azure AD Identity Protection. This service manages access and detects whether there is an attack on Office 365 users. This service provides a layer of notification on attempted breaches to Office 365. Figure 4-14 shows the log files on my account and how the account was accessed by third parties.

Application	IP address	Location	Sign-in status	Sign-in error code	Failure reason
Office 365 Exchange Online	13.93.216.68	San Jose, California, US	FALSE	50126	Invalid username
Office 365 Exchange Online	13.91.61.249	San Jose, California, US	FALSE	50126	Invalid username
Office 365 Exchange Online	13.93.216.68	San Jose, California, US	FALSE	50126	Invalid username
Office 365 Exchange Online	40.118.211.172	San Jose, California, US	FALSE	50126	Invalid username
Office 365 Exchange Online	104.209.35.177	San Jose, California, US	FALSE	50126	Invalid username
Office 365 Exchange Online	13.64.196.27	San Jose, California, US	FALSE	50126	Invalid username
Office 365 Exchange Online	13.93.233.42	San Jose, California, US	FALSE	50126	Invalid username
Office 365 Exchange Online	13.91.61.249	San Jose, California, US	FALSE	50126	Invalid username
Office 365 Exchange Online	13.93.216.68	San Jose, California, US	FALSE	50126	Invalid username
Office 365 Exchange Online	13.93.233.42	San Jose, California, US	FALSE	50126	Invalid username
Office 365 Exchange Online	40.118.211.172	San Jose, California, US	FALSE	50126	Invalid username
Office 365 Exchange Online	144.0.94.79	Yaoduzhen, Anhui, CN	FALSE	50053	Account is locked
Office 365 Exchange Online	144.0.94.79	Yaoduzhen, Anhui, CN	FALSE	50053	Account is locked
Office 365 Exchange Online	144.0.94.79	Yaoduzhen, Anhui, CN	FALSE	50053	Account is locked
Office 365 Exchange Online	13.93.216.68	San Jose, California, US	FALSE	50126	Invalid username

Figure 4-14. *Invalid access attempts to Office 365 account*

Follow the next steps to configure Azure AD Identity Protection (see Figure 4-5). After completing these steps, we will install Azure AD Identity Protection.

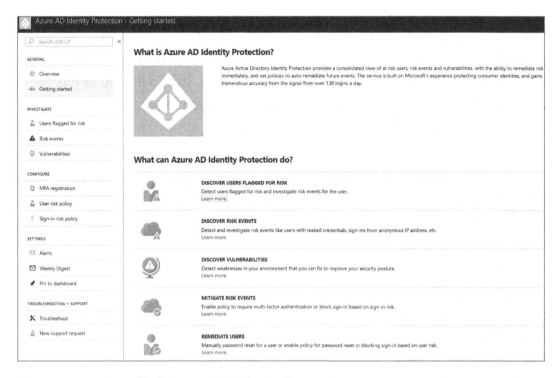

Figure 4-15. *Installed Azure AD Identity Protection*

Step 1: Installing Azure AD Identity Protection

To install Azure AD Identity Protection, open the Azure dashboard at `https://portal.azure.com`, click "Create a resource," click *Identity*, and click *Azure AD Identity Protection* (see Figure 4-16). This will start the installation of the Azure AD Identity Protection service. The Azure AD Identity Protection service is the service that monitors user access to Office 365 and Azure resources. Once you select the resource, then click Create and pin the resource to your Azure dashboard. This will create the Azure subsystems necessary to use the resource you selected.

Note   Azure resources are dependent on the EMS license type. In our case, we are using the Microsoft 365 E5 license for all configuration (which includes the EMS E5 subscription). If you do not have the Microsoft 365 E5 license in your tenant, you may not be able to fully configure the resources we are using.

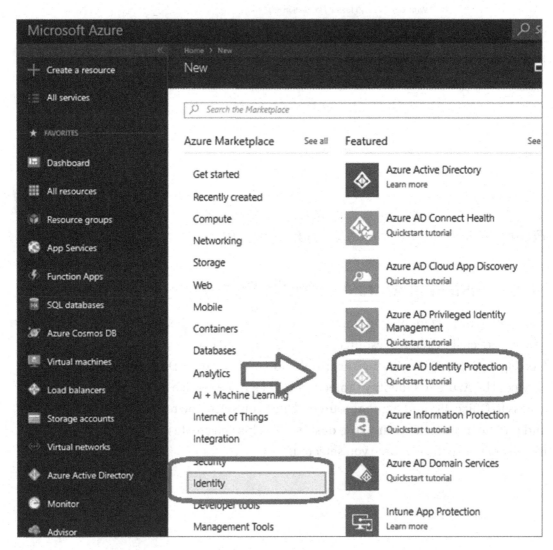

Figure 4-16. *Installed Azure AD Identity Protection*

Step 2: Setting Alerts in Azure Identity Protection

We are focusing on the settings and the configuration. At this point, we want to have alerts in place to let us know when an event happens and to take the appropriate action. After we set up the alerts, we will configure the user policies to manage those alerts. To configure the alert settings, click Alerts (see Figure 4-17) and follow the next steps. In this case, we are sending the alerts to the o365admin test account.

1. Click Alerts.

2. Set the alert to level Low.

3. Click Included and then + Add (to add a user for the alerts).

4. Select the user.

5. Click the Select button.

6. Click Done.

7. Click Save.

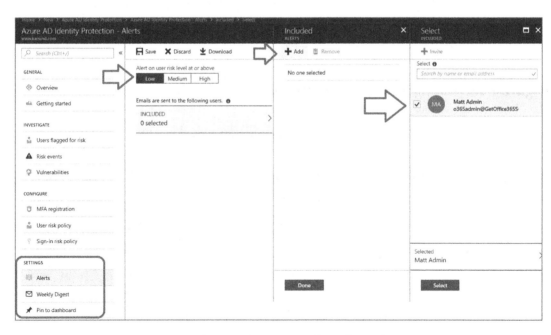

Figure 4-17. *Setting Azure alerts to be sent to the selected user*

Step 3: Setting Up a Weekly Digest in Azure Identity Protection

After you click Save, the next step is to set up the weekly digest. The weekly digest has similar configuration steps that we just completed: you enable the digest and select the user. After you select the user, the screen should look like Figure 4-18 before you click Save.

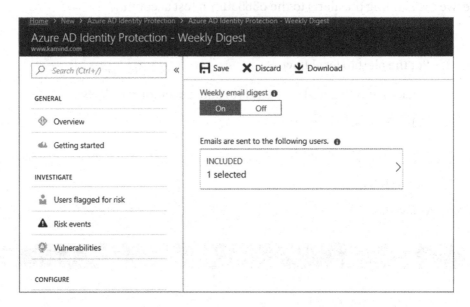

Figure 4-18. *Setting the weekly digest in Azure Identity Protection*

The Azure Identity Protection service will send you a weekly summary of the different activities so you can verify the access (Figure 4-19). What you are looking for are attack trends. The trends of the access by bad actors will give you a better understanding of the threats that you will need to defend yourself.

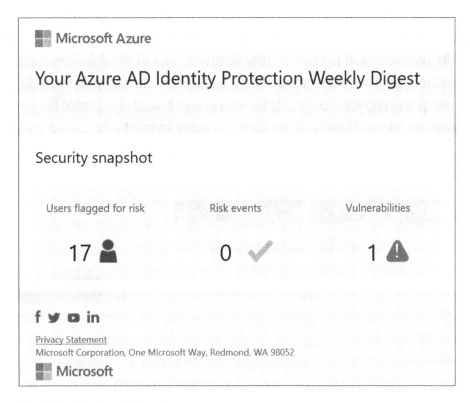

Figure 4-19. Weekly alert digest

Step 4: Configure the Risk Policy

There are three different configurations for a risk policy. Risk policy is actions taken on a user account to protect company information. A risk can be a password attack, or any type of activity that is nonstandard user behavior. Risk level is what the business assigns to different levels of attacks on an account that may become compromised (e.g. the credentials are stolen). To combat risk, you may force users to authenticate with MFA. Keep in mind that any action you take on risk policy is a global action and effects all users. After you have configured Office 365 and see the type of events that are happening, you can tighten the different risk policies to have better control over the Office 365 user access. The critical users that you want to worry about are the administrators. The administrators are the targeted users in Office 365.

Configuring risk policies for the administrators and making them subject to MFA is simple. You add the administrator users that you want subject to the MFA authentication and you enforce the MFA policy. In this example, we selected two users, set the controls to require MFA, and set enforced to on (see Figure 4-20).

Note   Before you start enabling the functionality, take your time and develop a plan for how you want to enforce risky behavior. Look at the data, and then enforce the controls. A lot of companies enable the features. The best practice is to set up a test group and apply the control to the test group, before you enable the control for all users (or administrators). Make sure you leave yourself a back door for testing.

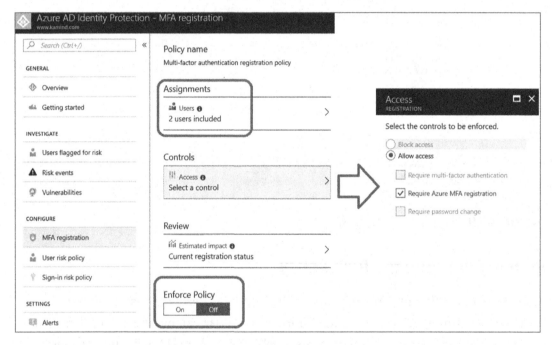

Figure 4-20.   *Forcing MFA on a set of users*

At this point, you have configured the alerting activity for privilege access. You can now turn on additional security features to help manage user accounts. We recommend that you enable only a few test accounts to verify the functionality. Once you are satisfied, then you can roll this out in mass to all users. The next step is to configure Azure Information Protection.

Note   Testing accounts is easy. Just create a test group (set to include) to test out the new feature. Once you are satisfied with the process, you can either include all users or create a new static or dynamic group for the user accounts.

Azure Information Protection

Azure Information Protection allows you to control information, classify documents, and set the information characteristics of those documents that are added. We can also send out documents where the information cannot be shared externally to an organization, the document can be configured to block printing or being forwarded to a third party. We can also add controls in a document template (or the document metadata) to block theses activities. This is known as *data loss prevention* (DLP) rules on documents. This has been enhanced by Microsoft with other third-party services, so those services now understand documents that can be managed. As an example, you can define a set of documents (or rules on documents) that are restricted to internal use. This means when a document is sent externally to another user in a different company, the external user would be forced to login with credentials to access the document. Since the user is unknown to the company, the user would be blocked from accessing the document. As an example, in sales we want to send out proposals and statements of work and have those proposals expire after 30 days. We would use AIP to manage the document type so anyone who received the document would be blocked from reading the document in 30 days.

The following are the configuration steps required to set up Azure Information Protection:

1. Install and configure the Azure dashboard (select Protection Activation).

2. Define the labels for document management.

3. Configure the global document policy.

4. Download the Azure agent for Office applications for document classification.

Once you have taken these steps, you can send protected documents (or block them from distribution).

Document management is a large activity that can easily consume a lot of time. The best way to look at document management is to make it self-service. This model of self-service builds on the labels that the organization puts in place to manage information and train your users on how to classify documents.

To get started with the Azure Information Protection (AIP) service, we need to enable the service and activate the protection. We will complete these steps and set up a basic rule for AIP to process credit cards.. Let's get started with the configuration process so we can protect our organizational documents. So we are on the same page, when I say *documents*, I am referring to any written communications (e-mails, pictures with text, work documents, PDFs, etc.). See Figure 4-21.

Figure 4-21. *Azure Information Protection loaded and set up as a favorite on the dashboard*

Step 1: Install Information Protection

The first step is to enable the AIP service in the Office 365/Azure tenant. To set up the service, go to the Azure dashboard and add the service to the dashboard. You can pin the AIP service, or you can add it to your favorites. See Figure 4-22.

Note   Earlier we used the term *pin*. In this case, we are not pinning the tool to the dashboard, but we are adding this to our favorites (under the star in Figure 4-21). To add to the favorites (the left side of the dashboard), all you need to do is to select "All services" and click the star to add the element to the dashboard. This process is detailed later in the chapter.

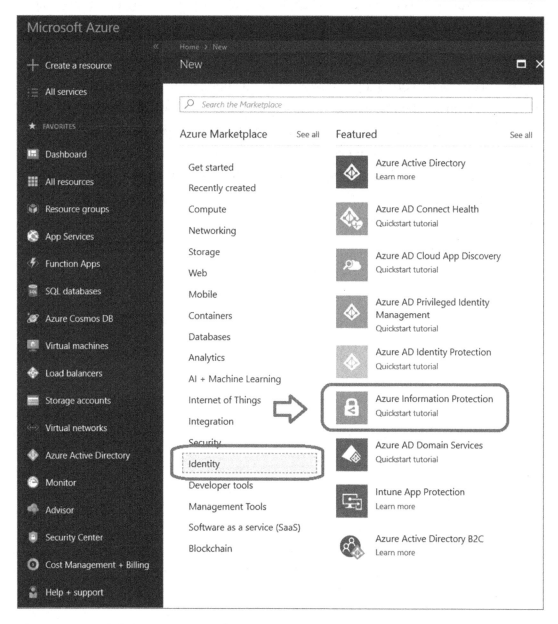

Figure 4-22. *Selecting Azure Information Protection*

Once we have selected the service, we will create the service (see Figure 4-23). This is a simple process; just select the service under Identity and Azure Information Protection and then click *Create to start the service*. This will start the service and set up some of the background configuration that is required for your Office 365 account. Once you have enabled the service, you can add this to your dashboard by selecting *All Services*, finding the services, and then adding them to the favorites (by clicking the star next to the service). Microsoft is working to make this more of an automatic process that is tied to the subscription type.

Note   Classifying information is a large task. To address the classification, the best way to handle this is to configure the base parts of Azure Information Protection and enable data auto classification in the Office 365 Security & Compliance Center. Document classification needs to be created by the end user creating the document. The automated tools (such as the AIP scanner that scans documents located on file servers) need to be used to validate the document classifications that were created.

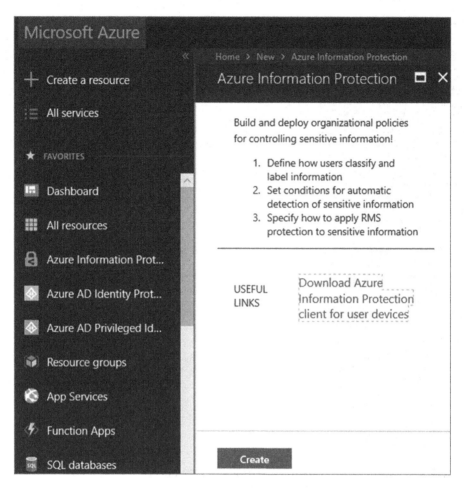

Figure 4-23. *Setting up Azure Information Protection for the first time*

Once you have created the service, the next step is to set up the service (see Figure 4-24). In our service setup, we will be executing two steps. First, we will activate the service, and then we will come back to the service and set up new document classification and organization policies. We highlighted two areas in Figure 4-24: the protection activation and the labels. Click Activation to activate the service. Once you completed this step, the protection status will say "Protection status is activated." After we have activated the service, our next action items will be to create a simple documentation classification (detection for credit card numbers) and then the policy to implement the document protection and classification.

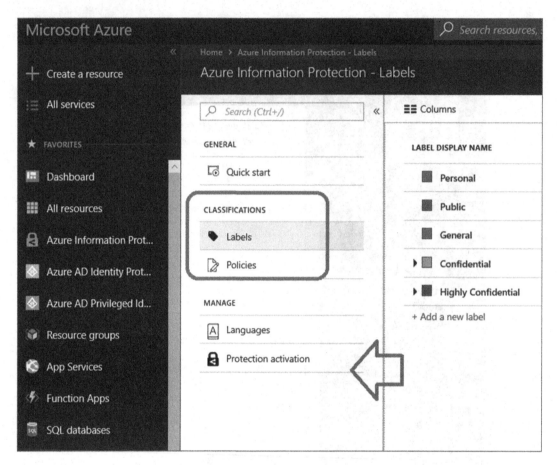

Figure 4-24. *Activating Azure Information Protection*

Setting up a policy on credit cards is simple and has little effect on the organization. Do not get me wrong; protecting the organization from sending out credit card information in the e-mail is critical. We need to protect the organization from violations that will result in fines. Under the new California law (CCPA), this data breach could result in fines of up to $750 per record, on the assumption that the consumer was harmed. The changes that we see in the new laws (like CCPA) are over assumed harm. Under old laws, harm had to be proven by the consumer. Under the new laws, **harm is assumed**. Businesses need to prove that protected personal information was not distributed to unauthorized third parties. This is why the Azure Information Protection is so critical to businesses, and the distribution of information needs to be tracked.

As an example, we can create a credit card protection rule where we allow documents (that contain credit card information) only to be read internally but not e-mailed externally. If a user e-mails the document externally, our labeling will block external user access to the document. The document rules are managed in the Office 365 Security & Compliance Center.

Step 2: Define Additional Label Classification

The first step after you have enabled the service is to define an additional documentation label that can be used to govern your business. Once you have defined the labels, the labels are now part of the documentation classification in the Office 365 Security & Compliance Center administration center.

Our approach is to walk you through the label configuration process on how to set up a credit card for detection and analysis. Once we are completed with this, we will quickly review the automatic label generation process.

The first step in configuration is to review the label structure and create the necessary sublabels and behavior that we want to see on the Office 365 user. In our case, the document that contains credit cards will be marked Confidential. We are going to create a sublabel for this document, as shown in Figure 4-25. Right-click *Confidential* and select *Add a sub-label*.

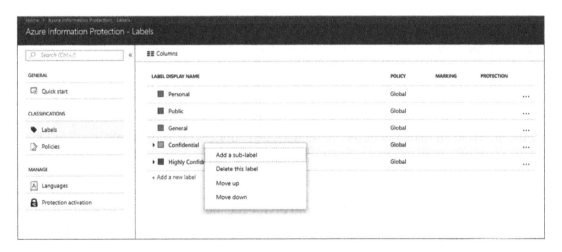

Figure 4-25. *Creating the first sublabel*

This launches the Sub-label windows. Change the default settings as described next (see Figure 4-26).

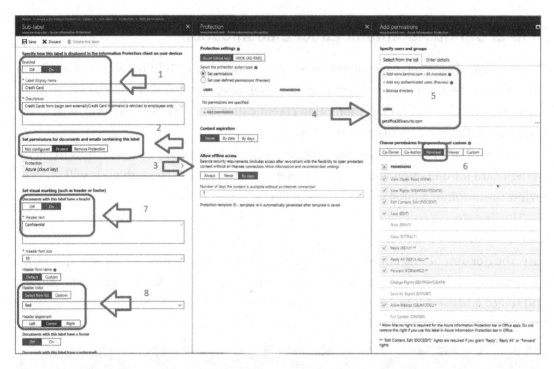

Figure 4-26. *Defining the sublabel functions to classify documents (steps 1–9)*

There are 13 steps we need to follow to enable the credit card protection in our document. The steps are cumbersome because there are many different options that organizations need to follow based on their security polices (so there is no one-size-fits-all solution). The changes that we are making are numbered 1–8 (see Figure 4-26) and described here, and steps 9–13 are shown in Figure 4-27.

1.   Turn on the service (enable it and define the label), in our example we used *Credit Card* as the name of the rule.

2.   Select the label to protect the documents.

3.   Select Azure Protection; this will launch the protection options.

4.   Select Add permissions to the document. (If you want to restrict e-mail distribution, select set user define permissions).

5. Specify the users and groups who will access this document label; in our case, this is only users from our e-mail domain.

6. Define the type of access users will have (make them all reviewers). Click OK and Save to return to the main blade.

7. Set visual marketing's (watermark) on the document.

8. Define a header for the document and a color (in this case red) .

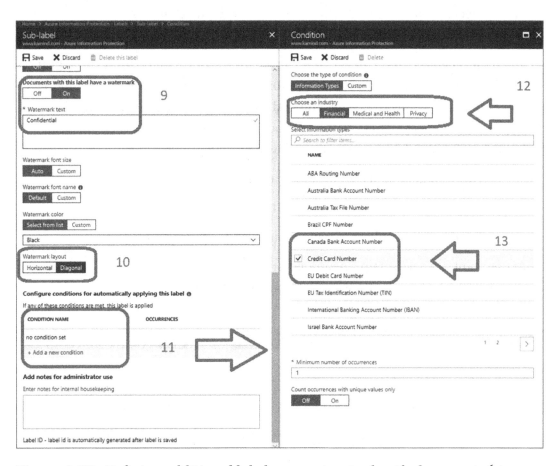

Figure 4-27. *Defining additional label parameters to classify documents (steps 9–13)*

After we have made those changes, let's make some additional changes on the document blade. These are numbered 9–13 in Figure 4-27. Click Save when completed.

9. Select a document to have a watermark and enter the watermark.

10. Display the watermark as a horizontal or diagonal in
    the document.

11. Select the condition for the protection (in this case we are using
    credit cards).

12. Select the industry type (aka financial).

13. Select the credit card condition, in this case we are using card
    number as a condition.

The basic label has been created. Save the changes on each of the blades. The next
step is to apply the new document classification to all documents. There are additional
document selection parameters. I recommend you leave these at the defaults and
change them later after you have tested the document in production.

Looking at Figure 4-27, we notice the following:

-   The new document classification called Credit Card has been added.

-   The document policy requires that the document be marked.

-   The document policy also states that the document is protected.

At this point, we have set up a new document classification label called Credit Card
(see Figure 4-28). Let's apply the changes throughout the Office 365 tenant.

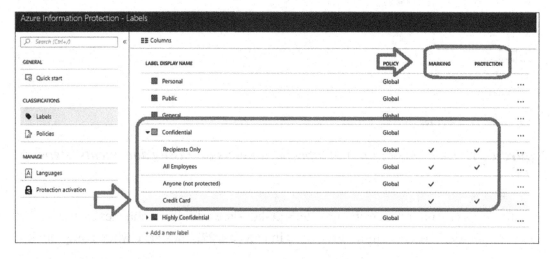

Figure 4-28. *Defining additional label parameters to classify documents (steps 9–13)*

Step 3: Applying the Document Classification Globally

So far, we created a new document classification called Credit Card. This document has a subtype of Confidential, and we have restricted access to the document to users in our company with the e-mail address getoffice365security.com (remember step 5 in Figure 4-26). The restriction that we placed on the document is as a reviewer. Next, let's select Policies (under Classification in Figure 4-29) and then select Global (there should be only one policy in place unless you added a policy).

Figure 4-29. *Adding the Credit Card policy to the global policy*

In Figure 4-29, we need to add the new document classification to our global default policy. This simply requires adding the document classification type. In Figure 4-29, once you are in the global document classification, the next step is to add the document and select Credit Card. This will immediately begin the document classification process. The next step is to download the right management protection tool.

Note   The best way to deploy document classification is by training the end user to classify the documents when they are created. You can also deploy the automated AIP scanner that scans documents located on file servers to collect data and classify documents that have not been uploaded to Office 365.

Step 4: Downloading the Document Classification Tool

Documents are automatically classified based on the process that we defined in step 3. The document classification tool allows users to classify documents according to our company standards. There is so much information that we have created; the only way that we can truly become compliant is that we train the users in document classification. Granted, not all users think the same, which is why we create special rules and procedures to keep our users in check (so to speak). From a compliance management perspective, if you rely only on automated tools, you will not catch everything. You need the users' help.

Once you have downloaded the client, install the client (see Figure 4-30) and start Word (or PowerPoint, etc.). This will display the document classification menu (see Figure 4-31).

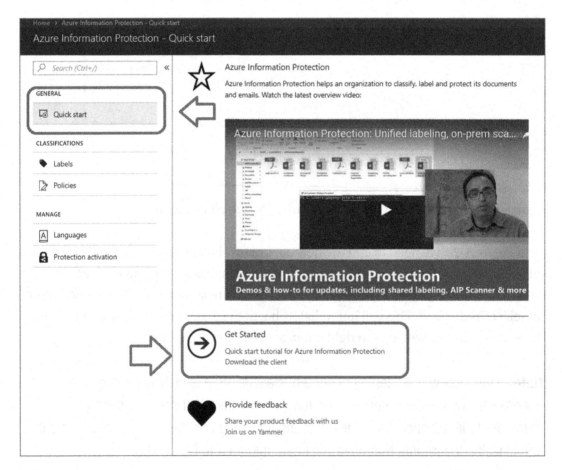

Figure 4-30. *Downloading the client from the Azure Information Protection dashboard*

Figure 4-31. *Installing the Azure Information Protection client management tool*

After you have installed the AIP client, you will need to sign up for the Azure Rights Management Service (RMS) to make sure the document is tracked. Open Word, and select Track and Protect under the AIP icon in the toolbar. Then click *Protect*, then *Track and Revoke* (see Figure 4-32). This is the process you will use to mange access to documents you distribute. This is in addition to any label controls that were created globally on documents.

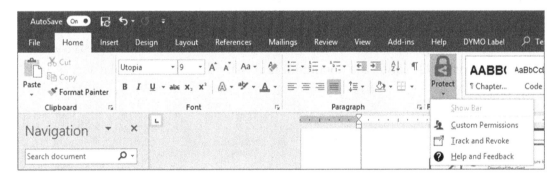

Figure 4-32. *Word 2016 with the Azure Information Protection client installed*

Keep in mind that the user needs to control the flow of information that is sent externally and manage the documentation workflow. As an IT administrator, you can set polices on documents from a global sense, but it will be the individual users who need to manage the document they distribute to their customers. As an example, say we have a sales document that we use and distribute to potential clients. As a salesperson, I will manage my own information based on client needs. You cannot do this action globally; otherwise, you will affect sales in the organization.

Note   The AIP client is the same client as the document scanner for servers. This client tool runs as a background process and can be used to process the document on your server. In this example, we downloaded the document scanner for the end user to use. If this was a server and we wanted to run the AIP scanner, we download the same tool, install it on the server, and run a set of PowerShell commands to process documents. The document scanner requires that the account used to install on the server is the same account with the correct permission (and license) for Azure Information Protection services. See the "References" section for links where you can learn more about the AIP scanner.

Step 5: Enabling the RMS Tracking Service

Clicking Track and Revoke will launch the Azure RMS tracking service. You will need to sign in or sign up for the service (see Figure 4-33). This allows you to track documents worldwide (once the document is classified). You can revoke access and grant access.

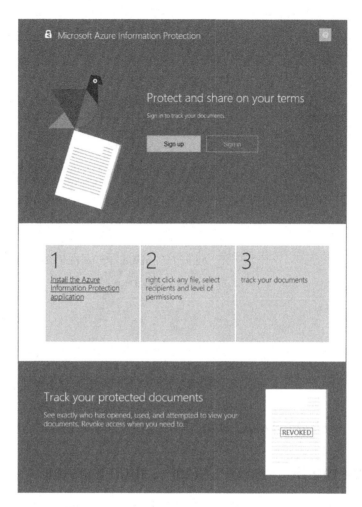

Figure 4-33. *Signing up for document tracking for an external e-mail document*

Once you have completed the sign-up process, download the clients for the different devices that you are using (see Figure 4-34). This way you will have a 360-degree view of all documents and be able to track and revoke rights from users.

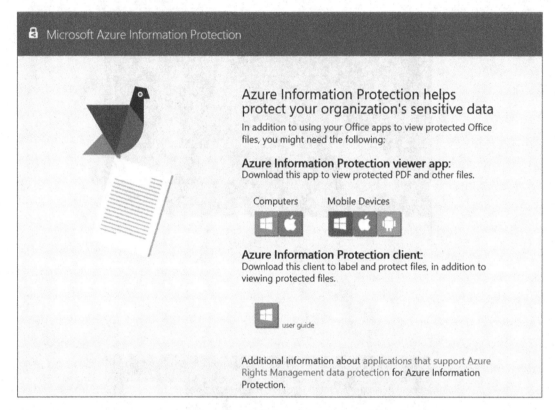

Figure 4-34. Application availability for reading protected documents

Step 6: Test the Document Classification Service

Testing the service is easy. Search the Web for a demo credit card number. The best way to test this is to create a Word document with the information. The AIP systems will prompt you for permission to send the document (see Figure 4-35). If you drop the e-mail into a document, the e-mail will be sent but will be encrypted per company policies.

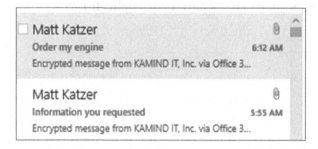

Figure 4-35. Documents are auto-encrypted before being sent

The e-mail encryption is automatically handled, but what about a user trying to send a Word document with protected information (Figure 4-36)? The service works the same way. The e-mail in Figure 4-37 is the document as received by the end user.

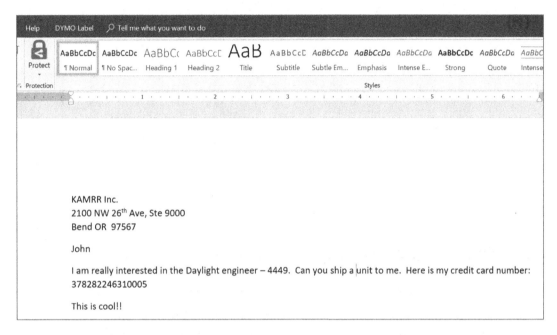

Figure 4-36. *Sample Word document used in our test with protected information*

I sent the Word document using the share function, and when Outlook finished loading, I was prompted to sign in to the Azure information service. If my system was Azure, then there would be no login prompt. If I was an external user and not permitted to read the document, I would be blocked from document access.

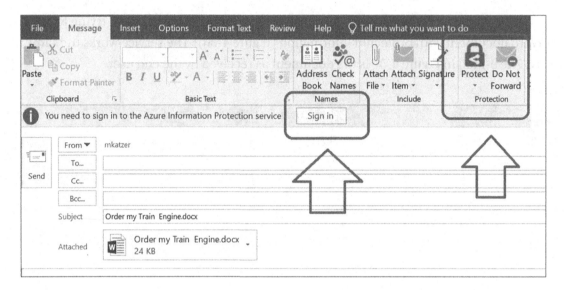

Figure 4-37. Document protection with a credit card number

Step 7: Configure the Data Loss Prevention Rules

The DLP rules allow you to automatically classify e-mail based on content and leverage AIP client for special features (such as Do Not Forward and other actions). In the use of AIP, we customize our e-mail portal and define labels for our document classes. AIP will process the document and recommend a classification based on the document content (see Figure 4-38). Define the document class, and the users will help you with the document classification. Keep the document classification and types to a minimum number for the best results.

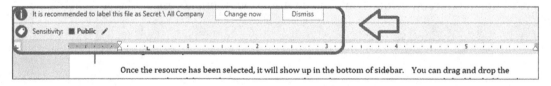

Figure 4-38. AIP automatically classifying documents

Additional Configuration

There are many ways to configure Enterprise Mobility & Security (EMS) for your environment. In this section, I have detailed some of the additional customization that you can do. I wanted to provide you with the information on the service customization but handle that in a different section so you would not be distracted from deploying the service. Once you have the service in place, you can change the service to match your business needs.

Password Smart Lock Protection

A password lock box is an easy configuration to complete. The EMS licenses provide you with access to Azure Active Directory. To configure smart lock passwords, all that is needed is for the systems to be trusted (azure AD joined or hybrid joined) and to have the service enable the features in Azure Active Directory. As an example (see Figure 4-39), we logged into `https://portal.azure.com` and selected Azure Active Directory. Once we selected Azure Active Directory, we clicked "Authentication methods" and enabled the service. In our example, we blocked some common password that users often use.

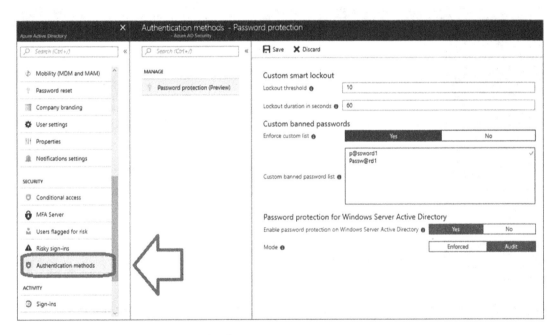

Figure 4-39.   *Enabling smart lock in Azure Active Directory*

Looking at Figure 4-39, you will notice that there are some additional configuration options such as the number of failed attempts (called lockout threshold) and the lockout duration. In our example, we allow up to ten attempts, and then we lock the user access for 60 seconds. Every business is different, and the lockouts will be shorter depending on the organization risk and compliance regulation.

Adding Applications to the Favorites List on the Azure Dashboard

In Figure 4-40, I have highlighted two areas to look at: favorites and all resources. To add an application (or blade) to the favorites, all that is needed is to select the application and add the element. The process is simple; select *All Services* from the sidebar. Find the service you are looking for (in this case, the Azure Information Protection application is located under Identity); then click the star (and turn it yellow).

Once the resource has been selected, it will show up at the bottom of the sidebar. You can drag and drop the resource on the sidebar to the position that makes sense to you. You can easily build a dashboard. Likewise, you can use the same process to remove the dashboard icons.

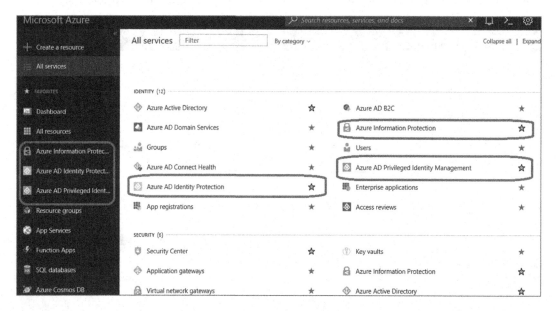

Figure 4-40. *Adding three applications to the Azure favorites in the sidebar*

Adding Office 365 E-mail Encryption

Adding e-mail encryption is easy to do in Office 365. This is a requirement for any type of compliance management. In this section, we will show how to add e-mail encryption and customize the e-mail portal that is presented to clients. Customization is key to ensure that secured e-mail messages that you send to your client are easily recognizable as coming from your organization. In our example, we customized our e-mail encryption with our contact information, logo, and description of who to contact about the e-mail in case there are any questions. This is important because phishing attacks target a large number of different Office 365 users. If you want to reduce your threat level, you need to customize your e-mail encryption portal when you add e-mail encryption.

In Figure 4-41, the e-mail message has two interesting properties. First, we include the organization logo in the e-mail, and since we are requiring that the user click an e-mail, we also include information about the e-mail contents. The objective is to customize the e-mail communications so that third parties can easily see that the e-mail message is from your organization. The areas that you can customize are outlined in the user's Outlook client and later after they click the encrypted e-mail message.

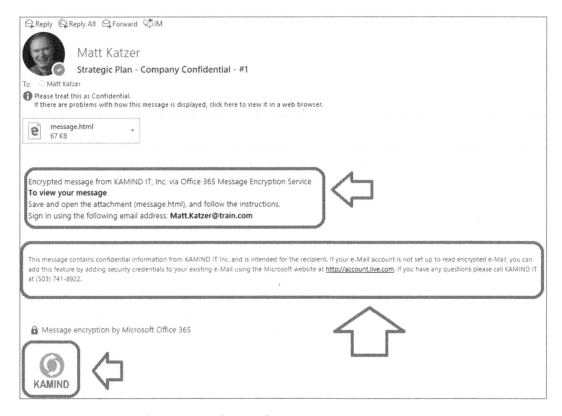

Figure 4-41. *Sample encrypted e-mail*

When a user clicks a secure e-mail that has been configured, they see the configured e-mail portal (see Figure 4-42). The user can enter their ID, or they can request a passcode to be e-mailed to them. Either approach works and is simple to use.

E-mail encryption is a good way to exchange information between users. Once you have sent and encrypted e-mail to the other user, the user can edit the e-mail and return the information to you. The encryption on the e-mail is unique and is maintained in isolation from other encrypted e-mail.

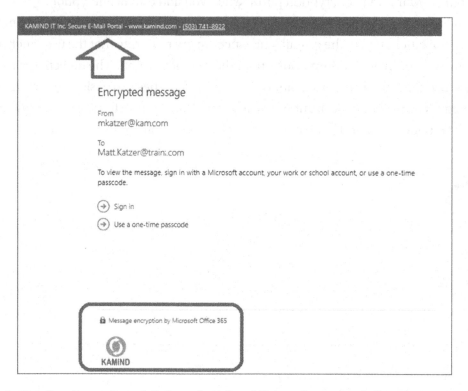

Figure 4-42. *Configured e-mail portal with additional contact information*

To start, you need to purchase an Office 365 plan that includes e-mail encryption. This is included in all Office E3/E5 subscriptions and in the Microsoft 365 E3/E5 suites. We are using the Microsoft E5 suite. To set up e-mail encryption service, follow these steps:

1. Activate the Office 365 Rights Management service (should already be completed).

2. Enable the encryption service in Azure Active Directory (should already be completed).

3. Configure the Automatic Encryption transport rules (optional).

4. Customize the e-mail encryption service for your business.

5. Download the AIP client to allow users to classify and encrypt e-mails.

Let's walk through the steps to configure e-mail encryption.

Step 1: Setting Up the Office 365 Rights Management Service

Office 365 encryption is easy to set up and configure. The first step to use encryption is to enable the Office 365 Rights Management service. Once you have enabled the Rights Management service, you select the various rules that you want the Rights Management service to use in automatic processing communications external to your organization, as well as manual configuration of a confidential service.

Log on to Office 365 and enable the Rights Management service (only global administrators can activate this). Click Settings, click "Services & add-ins," and then click Azure Information Protection (see Figure 4-43).

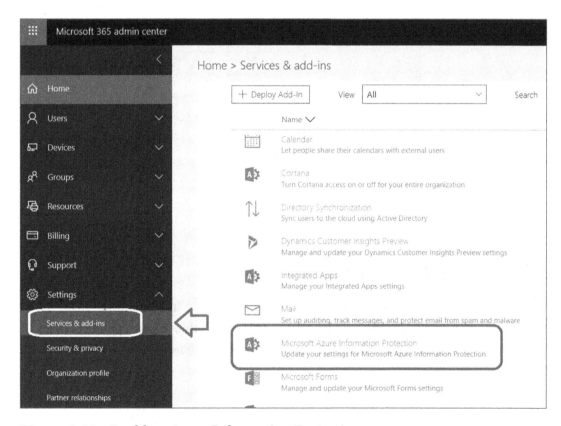

Figure 4-43. *Enabling Azure Information Protection*

After you click Azure Information Protection, select "Manage Microsoft Azure Information Protection settings." This will redirect you to an admin screen that shows the settings of the service. This will show you the status (see Figure 4-44). If the service is not activated, then activate the services. Keep in mind it will take 30 minutes to fully activate the services.

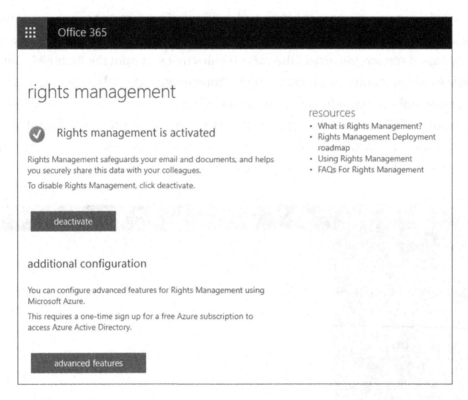

Figure 4-44. *Verifying that the service is activated*

Step 2: Enable Azure Information Protection

Next, click "advanced features." This will take you to the Azure Information Protection application; then select "Protection activation." This will enable the encryption service. This should be already enabled from the earlier steps (see Figure 4-45).

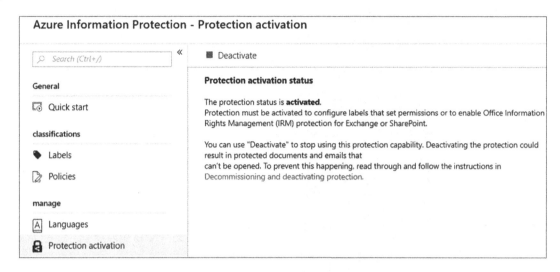

Figure 4-45. *Verifying Azure Protection is activated*

Step 3: (Optional) Configure the Automatic Encryption Rules for HIPAA and PII

You can configure DLP rules in the Office 365 Security & Compliance Center. To configure the rules, go to the Office 365 admin center, and select Security & Compliance Center. Once in the Security &Compliance Center, select Data Loss Prevention and Policy. We are going to create a new policy, so click Create Policy (see Figure 4-46). In our case, we are going to select the "Medical and health" option for our policy and US Health Insurance Act (HIPAA) .

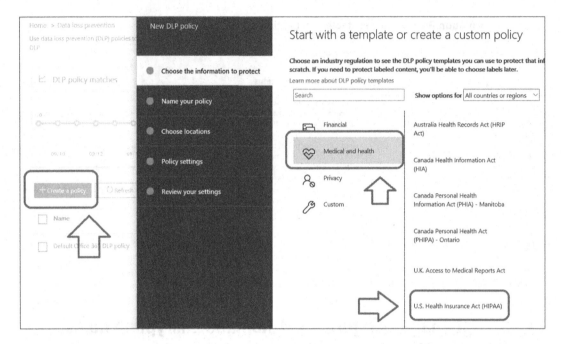

Figure 4-46. *Creating the custom HIPAA policy*

Click Next and name your policy (leave as default); see Figure 4-47.

Figure 4-47. *Naming your policy*

Click Next and choose the locations (leave as default); see Figure 4-48.

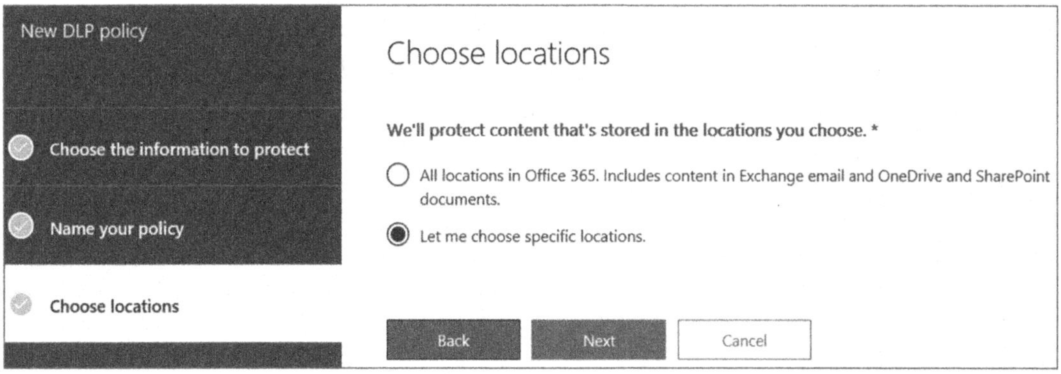

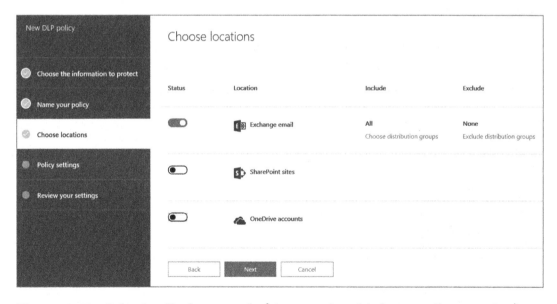

Figure 4-48. *Selecting all locations for content management*

Click Next to restrict the encryption to e-mail only (see Figure 4-49). In this example, we are only setting up HIPAAA rules for Exchange e-mails that are sent externally.

Figure 4-49. *Selecting Exchange only (we are using this for e-mail encryption)*

Click Next to customize the content you want to protect. In this case, we are looking only at HIPAA information. In Figure 4-50, if you click Edit, you can define the accuracy of the content match. As an example, for PII information (such as Social Security numbers), you have a range that starts at 75 percent.

It is important that you check your business rules in your organization on the PII information and what risk factor you want to have. If you set it too high, then all e-mail will be encrypted. If you set too low, then you will have no e-mail encrypted. The recommended setting is the default at 75 percent, but this is really an organization decision on PII/HIPAA information distribution.

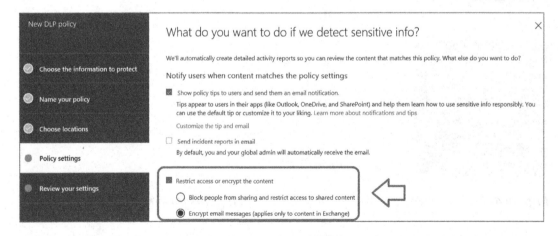

Figure 4-50. *Enabling the default rules*

Click Next to automatically encrypt the content (see Figure 4-51). In one of the previous steps, we excluded OneDrive and SharePoint. This is the reason why. We are encrypting the e-mail that is being sent externally from the organization.

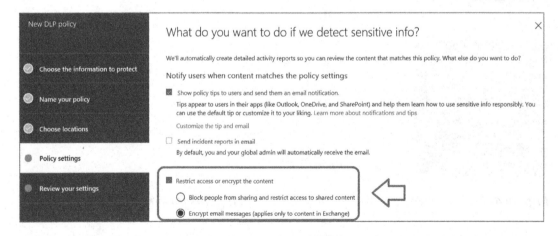

Figure 4-51. *Restricting access and encrypting the e-mail (or blocking if that is your business rule)*

Click Next; then choose your label that is appropriate for this content (see Figure 4-52).

Labels are becoming more important to organizations. Data needs to be typed and configured. In Figure 4-52, we have different labels that we have already configured. We recommend that you look at the documents in your organization and define a tighter granularity for documents. Minimize the creation of new labels as much as possible. A lot of labels, adds complexity and confuses the end users (who will be doing most of the work on classification). Make the label classification process a simple process. This will make your job much easier to manage the document configurations.

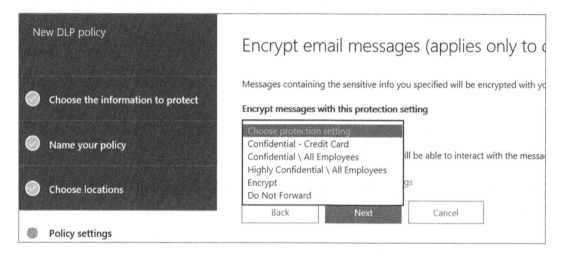

Figure 4-52.   *Selecting the label that reflects the type of content*

Once you have configured the rules, you can test the policy or have it implemented. In this case, we will implement the policy. I recommend that you put the policy in test mode until you have the Outlook Message Encryption (OME) environment configured with your company headers and portal customization. See Figure 4-53.

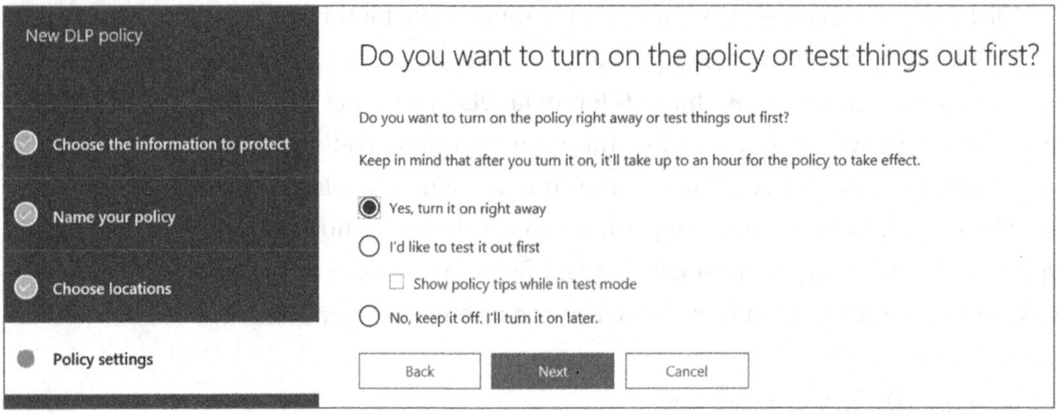

Figure 4-53. *Enabling the policy for execution*

Click Next to review your settings. If everything looks correct, then click Create. This will create the encryption rules for you in your Office 365 tenant. This process of rule creation will take a few minutes. Once the rules are completed, they will show up in the Office 365 Security & Compliance Center's DLP portal.

Step 4: Customize the E-mail Encryption Service for Your Business

There are four customizations you can make to set up an encrypted e-mail: adding your logo, customizing the encryption message, customizing the encryption center, and adding instructions to the encrypted e-mail. These configuration changes are made in PowerShell and are described here.

- Adding your logo

- In Figure 4-54, we branded the encrypted e-mail to use our KAMIND IT logo. To add your logo to Office 365 encryption, run the PowerShell commands shown here. Your customized logo will be displayed to the recipient.

  ```
  #Load the JPG file to the user tenant
  Set-OMEConfiguration -Identity "OME configuration" -Image (Get-
  Content "C:\customers\kamind\kamind_new_2014_v3.jpg" -Encoding byte)
  ```

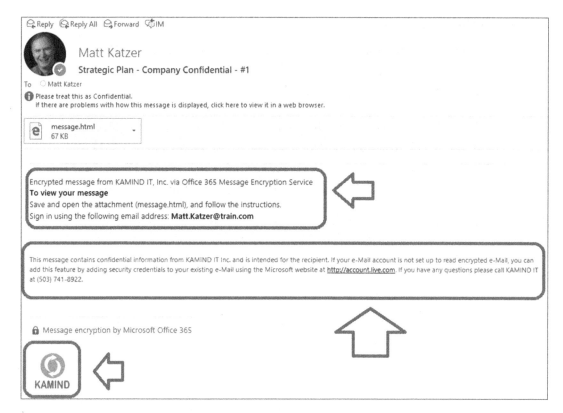

Figure 4-54. *Customization of the encrypted e-mail portal*

- Adding your customized text

- In Figure 4-54 we added customized text to display information for KAMIND IT. To add your customized text, execute the PowerShell command shown here:

```
#Load the JPG file to the user tenant
Set-OMEConfiguration -Identity "OME configuration" -DisclaimerText
"This message contains confidential information and is intended
for the recipient. If your e-Mail account is not set up to read
encrypted e-Mail, you can add this feature by adding security
credentials to your existing e-Mail using the Microsoft website at
http://account.live.com. If you have any questions, please call
KAMIND IT at (503) 726-5933."
```

- Customizing the encrypted e-mail portal

- In Figure 4-55, we added customized text to display the branded portal and our KAMIND message. To add your customize text, execute the PowerShell command shown here:

```
#Set the Customize text and Portal Text
Set-OMEConfiguration -Identity "OME configuration" -EmailText
"Encrypted message from mkatzer@kamind.com" -PortalText "KAMIND IT
Inc. Secure E-Mail Portal - www.kamind.com (503) 741-8922"
```

Figure 4-55. *Portal customization*

The complete PowerShell customization is as follows. The customized portal content from Figure 4-55 is highlighted in bold.

```
Set-ExecutionPolicy RemoteSigned
$LiveCred = Get-Credential
Import-module msonline
Connect-MSOLService –Credential $LiveCred –Verbose
#Createthe PS session
```

```
$Session = New-PSSession -ConfigurationName Microsoft.Exchange-
ConnectionUri https://ps.outlook.com/powershell/ -Credential $LiveCred
-Authentication Basic –AllowRedirection
Import-PSSession $Session -AllowClobber
#Load the JPG file to the user tenant
#Set-OMEConfiguration -Identity "OME configuration" -Image (Get-Content
"C:\customers\kamind\kaminditLogo.gif" -Encoding byte)
#Set encryption text
Set-OMEConfiguration -Identity "OME configuration" -EmailText "Encrypted
message from KAMIND IT Inc. via Office 365 Message Encryption Service"
-PortalText "KAMIND IT Inc. Secure E-Mail Portal - www.kamind.com - (503)
726-5933"
# Sample message
#Set-OMEConfiguration -Identity "OME configuration" -DisclaimerText
"This message contains confidential information and is intended for the
recipient. If you are not recipient you are notified that disclosing,
copying, distributing or taking any action in reliance on the contents of
this information is strictly prohibited."
Set-OMEConfiguration -Identity "OME configuration" -DisclaimerText
"This message contains confidential information and is intended for the
recipient. If your e-Mail account is not set up to read encrypted e-Mail,
you can add this feature by adding security credentials to your existing
e-Mail using the Microsoft website at http://account.live.com. If you have
any questions, please call KAMIND at (503) 726-5933."
#Display the configuration that was just setup
Get-OMEConfiguration
Remove-PSSession $Session
```

Step 5: Download the AIP Client

We have already downloaded the AIP client and installed it in Outlook. There is no additional configuration necessary. For the installation instructions, please review the previous section on Azure rights management. That is all that is required to set up Office 365 e-mail encryption and to customize the portal for our clients to use. Once you have set up the e-mail encryption portal, you can extend the service to other parts of AIP. As an example, you can set up documents with metadata policy strings that the

DLP rules can process to determine the best way to control information that is being sent externally. As an example, strategic plans may have a "Company Confidential" description placed in the metadata. The DLP rules can be configured to find the information and block the distribution of documents externally from the company.

Configuring Manual Encryption for Confidential Documents (Legacy)

You should create all DLP rules in the Compliance & Security Center. However, there are times when you need to go to the Exchange admin center to create DLP rules. In this case, we will create a manual encryption rule for e-mail. The manual encryption feature allows users to manually encrypt documents that are e-mailed with a sensitivity of Confidential. In Figure 4-56, we created a new e-mail, selected the options tag, and changed the message sensitivity to Confidential. The configuration notes in this step enable the manual sending of an e-mail (and all documents attached) as Confidential.

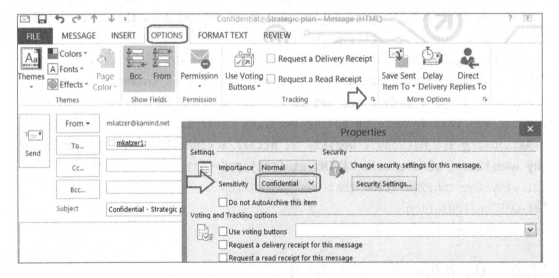

Figure 4-56. *Sending the encrypted e-mail*

To configure these policies, you need to be a global administrator, and the configuration will be made in the Exchange admin center of Office 365. We are going to add a custom Exchange transport mailbox rule. The mailbox rule simply states that if an e-mail has Sensitivity set to Confidential, then encrypt the e-mail. The user has the ability to manually set the document sensitivity. Likewise, you can create transport rules to disable encryption. Let's walk through the creation of a custom transport rule in the Office 365 Exchange administration center.

Step 1: Create a New Rule in the Exchange Admin Center

To create a new rule in Exchange admin center, select the plus sign (See Figure 4-57) to create the rule. The next step is to configure the rules characteristics.

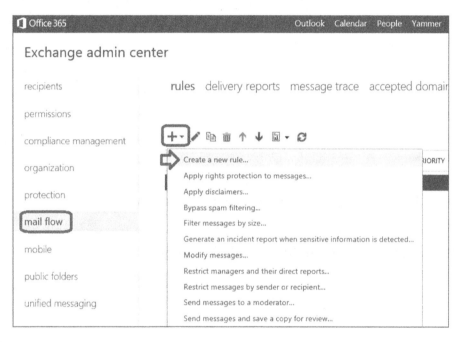

Figure 4-57. *Setting a manual encryption rule to set encryption on an e-mail*

Step 2: Enter the Name for the Rule *ManualEncryptEmail*, and Select the Conditions of the Rule

The exchange steps for the legacy configuration are easy to set up and configure. Follow these steps:

1. Click the blue link "More options" to expand the encryption options (see Figure 4-58).

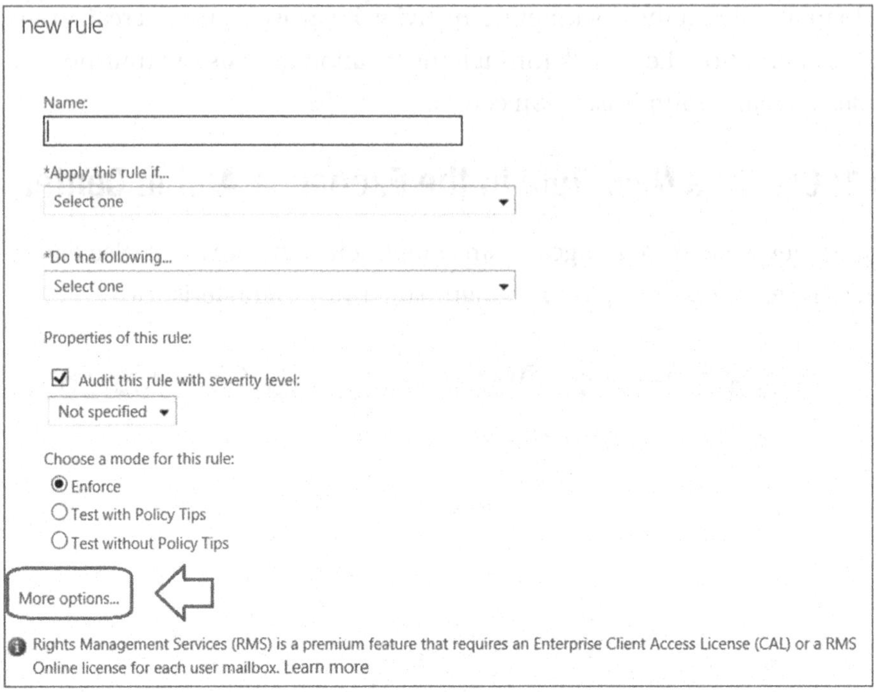

Figure 4-58. Creating the rule in the Exchange admin center

Step 3: Add the Encryption Rule Actions

Define where the recipient is located (outside of the organization) and set the message header sensitivity to include Confidential. In "Do the following," select "Apply Office 365 Message Encryption to message" (see Figure 4-59).

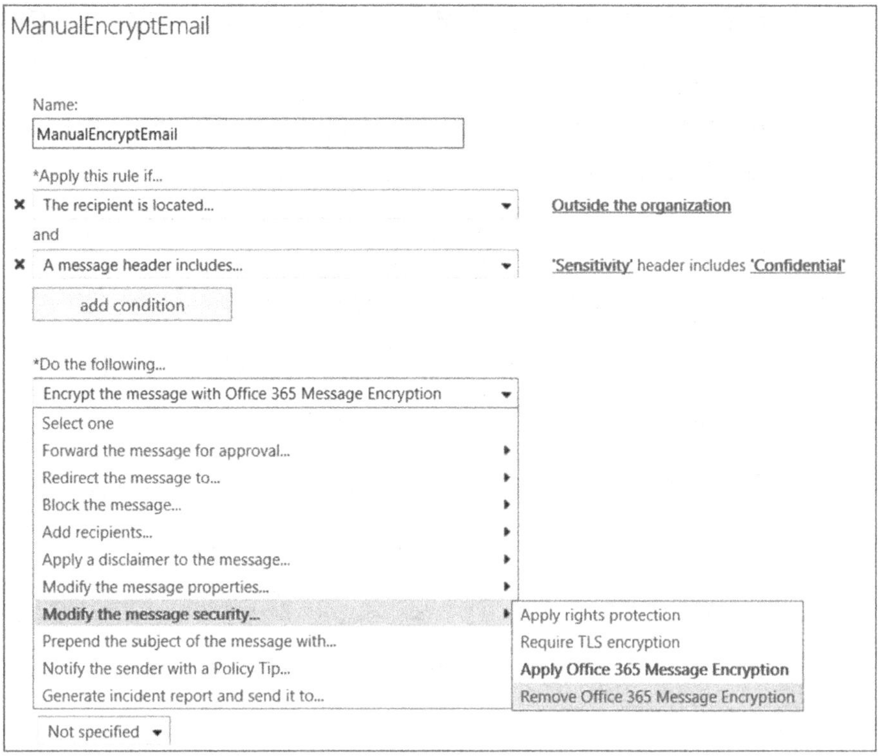

ManualEncryptEmail

Name:

ManualEncryptEmail

*Apply this rule if...

✖   The recipient is located...   ▼   <u>Outside the organization</u>

and

✖   A message header includes...   ▼   '<u>Sensitivity</u>' header includes '<u>Confidential</u>'

add condition

*Do the following...

Encrypt the message with Office 365 Message Encryption   ▼

Select one	
Forward the message for approval...	▶
Redirect the message to...	▶
Block the message...	▶
Add recipients...	▶
Apply a disclaimer to the message...	▶
Modify the message properties...	▶
Modify the message security...	▶
Prepend the subject of the message with...	
Notify the sender with a Policy Tip...	
Generate incident report and send it to...	

Apply rights protection
Require TLS encryption
Apply Office 365 Message Encryption
Remove Office 365 Message Encryption

Not specified ▼

Figure 4-59. *Setting overrides*

The final rule should look like Figure 4-60.

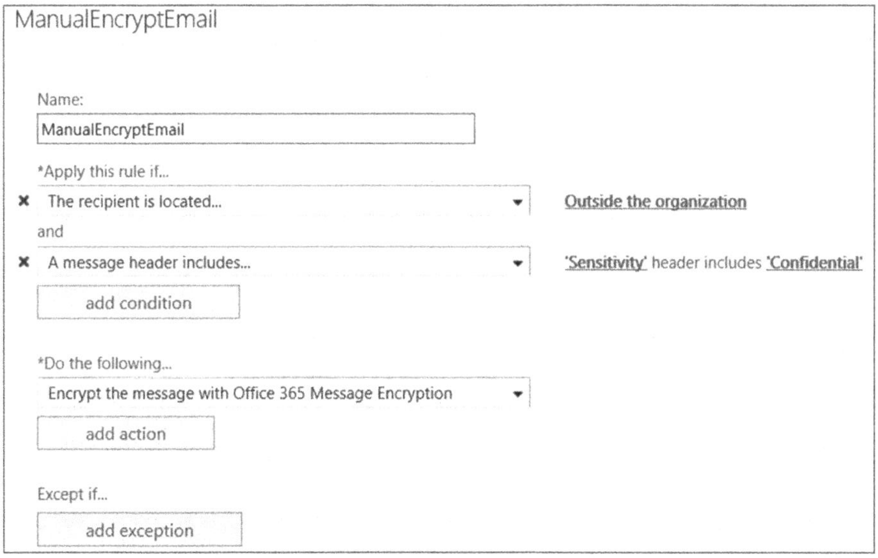

ManualEncryptEmail

Name:

ManualEncryptEmail

*Apply this rule if...

✖   The recipient is located...   ▼   <u>Outside the organization</u>

and

✖   A message header includes...   ▼   '<u>Sensitivity</u>' header includes '<u>Confidential</u>'

add condition

*Do the following...

Encrypt the message with Office 365 Message Encryption   ▼

add action

Except if...

add exception

Figure 4-60. *Fully configured rule to Manually Encrypt email based on message sensitivity*

213

Step 4: Test the E-mail, and Use Outlook to Send an E-mail

Open Outlook and send a test encrypted message. Select the optional options on the message (icon below Low Importance), change Sensitivity to Confidential, and send the message as shown in Figure 4-61.

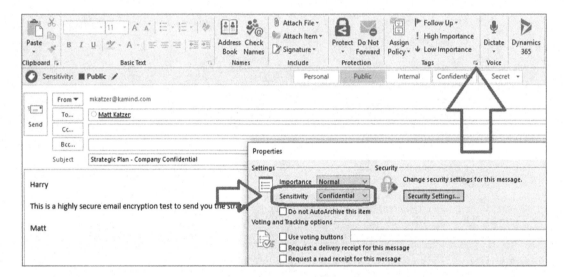

Figure 4-61. *Creating a secure e-mail with a custom transport rule*

The e-mail received by the client will look like Figure 4-62. Click the e-mail to read it and unencode it. In our example, we sent the e-mail with the option "Do Not Forward" (see red "do not enter" icon).

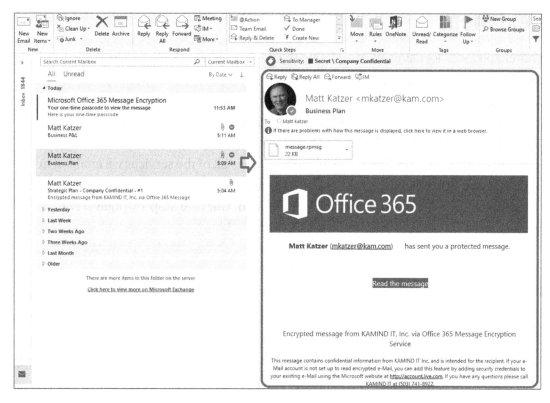

Figure 4-62. *Outlook client receiving encrypted e-mail*

The secret on using encrypted email is to make sure your portal is branded with your business logo. You need to train your customers visually on what is an accepted email from your organization. The customized portal helps your customer recognize messages that come from your organization.

Summary

This chapter focused on Identity Management and Information Protection. These tools are powerful and provide you with the necessary flexibility to configure your Office 365 services. As a bonus, I walked you through the configuration of Exchange encryption. We spent some time setting up e-mail encryptions and customizing the service portal. As Microsoft develops the Security & Compliance Center, these capabilities will be upgraded and enhanced. At this point our baseline is completed and data is being logged for security analysis.

Next Steps

This chapter was focusing on completing the basic configuration for security with Office 365 and Azure. In Chapter 2, we built out the necessary data collection repositories in Azure under Log Analytics. In Chapter 3, we expand the capabilities and added data from Windows device endpoints (Windows 10, Windows servers and Linux devices) to give us the 360 view of activities in our tenant. In this chapter, we built out the remaining identity services for EMS. The next step is to leverage all of the services we enabled in our MAM and MDM deployment. Once this is completed, we have a secure environment where our corporate data and devices are protected. Our next stop - Mobile Device Management!

References

We covered a lot of information in this chapter. My goal was to give you an overview of the various components to give you a head start on the configuration of protection management and security. If you follow the steps, you will be able extend the capabilities of your security deployment. The following are good reference links that will assist you in reaching the next level of securing your Office 365 and Azure environment.

Getting Started with EMS

- https://docs.microsoft.com/en-us/intune/get-started-evaluation

What is Intune and MDM

- https://docs.microsoft.com/en-us/intune/introduction-intune

Deploying Privileged Identity Management

- https://docs.microsoft.com/en-us/azure/active-directory/privileged-identity-management/subscription-requirements

Azure Active Directory Identity Protection

- https://docs.microsoft.com/en-us/azure/active-directory/identity-protection/overview

Quick start on deploying Azure Information Protection

- https://docs.microsoft.com/en-us/azure/information-protection/infoprotect-quick-start-tutorial

About Azure Information Protection

- `https://docs.microsoft.com/en-us/azure/information-protection/requirements-applications`

Using Office 365 Data Loss Protection (DLP)

- `https://docs.microsoft.com/en-us/office365/securitycompliance/data-loss-prevention-policies`

EMS trial subscriptions

- `https://kamindit.azurewebsites.net`

CHAPTER 5

Mobile Device Management with EMS

The chapter is about extending the key security components necessary to operate and manage mobile devices in Office 365 and Azure. This chapter is focused on the deployment of multifactor authentication (MFA), Mobile Application Management (MAM), Windows Information Protection (WIP) and Mobile Device Management (MDM). These four components are compliance components that are included with the Microsoft 365 suites. At the end of this chapter, you will have a good understanding of the MFA, MAM, WIP and MDM components and be able to deploy them with the Microsoft Authenticator application. The Microsoft 365 E5 suite that we are using contains all the features of Office 365, Enterprise Mobile E5, and Windows 10 E5 in one license. Our objective in this chapter is to build out the Azure Intune management portal so it looks like Figure 5-1. Microsoft mobile device management is part of the Intune component of the Enterprise Mobility Suite (EMS).

© Matthew Katzer 2018
M. Katzer, *Securing Office 365*, https://doi.org/10.1007/978-1-4842-4230-8_5

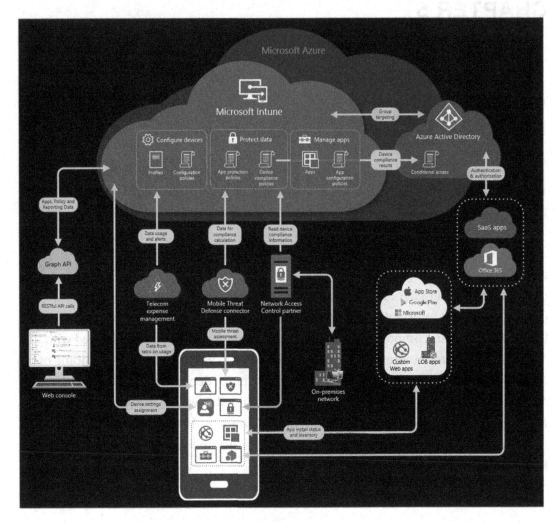

Figure 5-1. *Intune Mobile Device Management*

In Figure 5-2, we have configured the MDM portion of Office 365 and Azure to provide policy management of our Office 365 organization. The configuration includes managing conditional access, managing application deployment, deploying windows information protection, deploying approved applications through the Company Portal (available through the vendors online store), and blocking business data from being deployed to nonbusiness applications through Mobile Application Management (MAM).

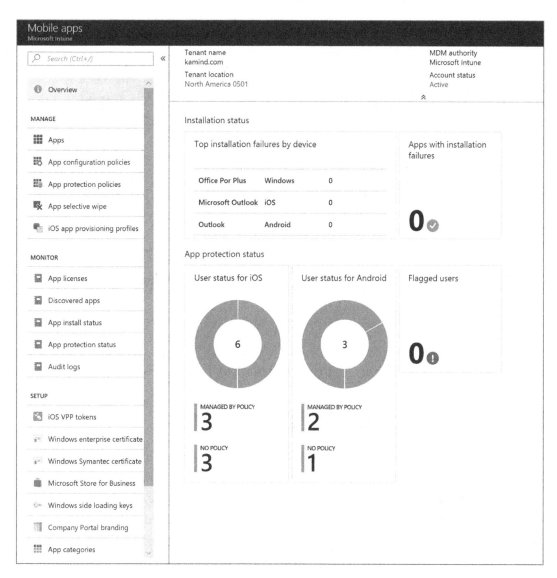

Figure 5-2. *EMS portal build-out for Intune device management*

Before we begin, let's look at the EMS components (see Figure 5-3). We have already covered all of the other components except for Intune and Multi Factor Authentication. (see https://docs.microsoft.com/en-us/enterprise-mobility-security/). Keep in mind that EMS assumes all devices can be managed from Macs, including Windows 10 desktops, laptops, and mobile devices such as iOS and Android devices. The subject is complex, so I broke this down into the logical areas of deployment for device management. We will start with MFA, then progress to simple device management with MAM and WIP. We will close with a compliant device management using MDM.

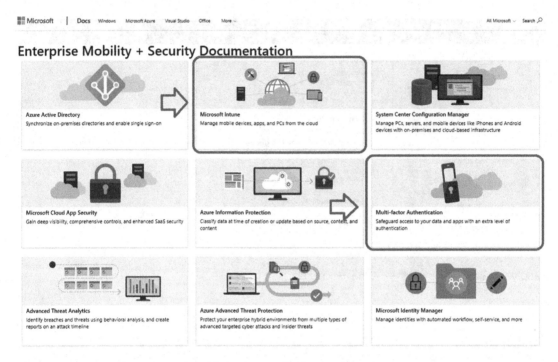

Figure 5-3. *EMS components (courtesy of Microsoft)*

EMS: Managing Mobile Productivity

Access to the Intune portal is controlled with the Office 365 subscription. The subscription that we are using on our account is the Microsoft 365 E5 suite. This suite has the equivalent of EMS E3 and EMS E5 built into the license offering as used to enable EMS is either EMS + E3 or EMS + E5. Since we have already enabled the Azure portal, all we need to do is add the Intune component to our dashboard. To add the Intune, return to the main Azure dashboard (click the dashboard at `https://portal.azure.com`) and type **Intune** in the search component (see Figure 5-4). Once you see the Intune listed in the search window, click **Intune** and pin the component to the dashboard. (Remember the pin icon in the upper-right corner we used previously? This is the way you make the dashboard components appear on the Azure dashboards.)

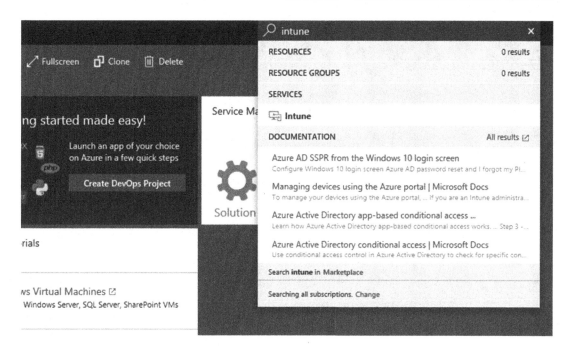

Figure 5-4. *Adding Intune to the Azure dashboard*

At this point we have added the mobility component necessary to manage user and company owned devices. The next step is to configure Mobile Device Management for our business. In this case, we are defining the security aspects of the company-owned devices and employee-owned devices (aka BYOD - bring your own device). In this section, we look at the configuration of Microsoft Intune for mobile devices and desktops. The management of Windows Intune is through the Azure Intune portal (see Figure 5-5).

Figure 5-5. *Microsoft's Intune portal*

Management of mobile devices can be easy or complex to deploy depending on the business needs. We are going to approach the configuration of the management of mobile devices from two perspectives: simple (MAM/WIP) for BYOD devices and compliant (MDM) for company own devices. We will walk through the process of setting up the environment to handle concluded with a fully managed mobile device under MDM. The two approaches are outlined here:

Simple	This is a basic setup for Mobile Device Management to control company information. A limited set of controls are used. This is for a basic level of protection and is our MAM deployment.
Compliant	The organization has a compliance requirement, so stringent controls are used to manage the devices. Compliance oversight may require how the data is used and what data is maintained on the device. The company store is used for device management and compliance checks and is our full MDM deployment.

Before we look at this in detail, let's step back and look at Microsoft Intune and why it is used. I have used Microsoft Intune since it was released for cloud-based device management for the simple reason that it just works. Devices that have Microsoft Intune deployed with Office 365 have fewer support calls and trouble tickets. My own experience is that the Microsoft Intune reduces support calls by 50 percent when deployed with Windows 10 Automatic Updates under ring management and Windows Defender Advanced Threat Protection. Figure 5-6 shows the two different deployment options for Intune, using a stand-alone configuration or with System Center Configuration Management (SSCM). Our focus with Azure is the stand-alone configuration.

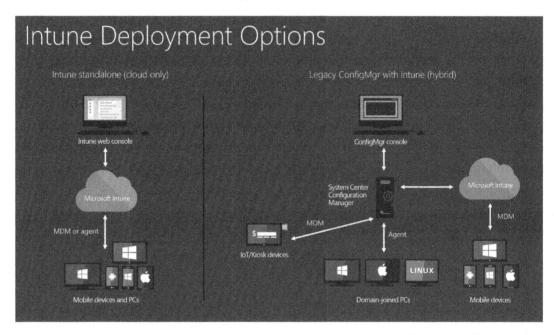

Figure 5-6. *Microsoft Intune management options (courtesy of Microsoft)*

Device management is the process and tools for the management of users, devices, applications, and data. Office 365 and Microsoft EMS/Intune are built with a self-service model providing users with access to Microsoft cloud services worldwide. Microsoft Intune Mobile Application Management and Mobile Device Management provide consistent experiences for all users and the management of the devices. Users (and IT administrators) can add users to the local Active Directory, either through a workplace/ Azure join or the traditional Active Directory Add User/Computer function. Microsoft Intune provides consistency of device management with the following:

– Workplace/Azure join allows you to dynamically add a device with multifactor authentication.

– Windows 10 (version 1809) Domain joined systems can be remotely configured.

- There are consistent opt-in messages across all environments.

- This is a consistent implementation of self-service portals across all environments.

The Office 365 self-service portal (allows users to install Professional Plus software on demand) is extended with Microsoft Intune hosted in Azure. This trend is forcing a change to the management of devices: application distribution via a company-owned application store. As new users enter the workforce, they want to use their own devices and load the software that they need to use to improve their personal productivity. As an IT manager, you need to figure out how to supply these services without adding additional support costs. This is where Microsoft Intune comes into play. Microsoft Intune solves these problems for users and IT managers. IT managers now have a single view to all the devices in the organization (see Figure 5-7), including Apple and Android devices. Device management with integrated Office 365 support is the power of Microsoft Intune.

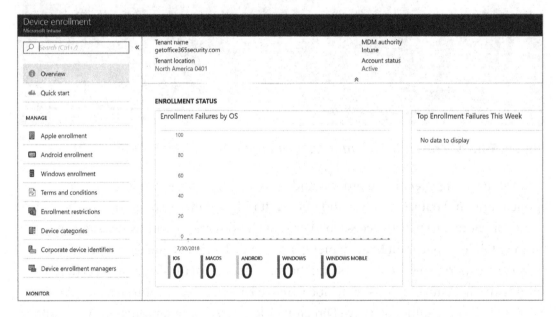

Figure 5-7. *Microsoft Intune Mobile Device Management panel*

Microsoft Intune vs. System Center

Microsoft Intune currently operates with Microsoft System Center or as a stand-alone cloud service. The Microsoft Intune System Center hybrid configuration is a legacy configuration and will slowly be discontinued over the next few years. If you are currently using System Center for the management of Intune manage devices, you can convert the Intune services to the Intune cloud management hosted in Azure.

The selection of the hybrid service versus the dedicated cloud service was because of the limitations of the Intune Cloud services. Those limitations no longer exist. Both the cloud and System Center deployments support the following services:

- Unified EMS admin experience

- Scale of more than 50,000 device restrictions

- Full access to the Graph API

- New advanced reporting

- Role-based access control

It is recommended that you use Microsoft Intune Azure services for your deployment. The scalability of Microsoft's cloud services and the security model deployed with Window's Azure Active Directory federation. The linking of the on site Active Directory is through the Azure join systems and the Intune management portal.

As Microsoft deploys newer operating system (OS) software (aka Windows 10 Pro 1809 or later), these operating systems are shipped with a lightweight management agent integrated into the OS. These management agents simplify the user access in enabling their own devices to be managed by Microsoft Management. These agents are as follows:

- *Mobile Device Management*: Intune management (lightweight management)

- *Configuration Device Management*: Workplace Join (Azure or AD)

The changes that have been made with the Windows 10 solutions have made integrating different products into the management portal easy. Microsoft has expanded the different portals with new configuration options for various market segments. A good example is the integration of the Windows 10 Software Updates rings. See Figure 5-8.

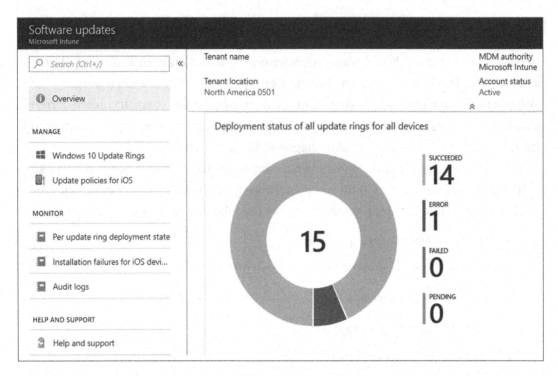

Figure 5-8. *Microsoft Software Updates management portal*

As Microsoft Intune is deployed in Azure, new features are being added that were
available only with dedicated on-premises solutions and massive infrastructure support
using Microsoft's System Center. Microsoft added new features to hybrid Active Directory
Connector (AdConnect), that links the on-premise active directory device metadata
with Azure Intune services. This capability extends the Azure Intune services to provide
greater device control. This capability is extended further with the newer versions of
Windows 10 operating systems (Pro and Enterprise) adding windows telemetry and
security support to operating systems. You can now collect data on the operation and
management of the windows devices with these new features enabled. Better data
collection means less system and security problems and better end user productivity.

Getting Started with Microsoft Mobile Device Management

Intune has significantly changed from the Windows 7 days. No longer do you deploy
Microsoft Windows Intune agents to manage devices. Today you manage devices
and use the Azure Intune center of management. If you are using mobile application
management, there are no agents to deploy. If you are using Mobile Device Management,

you deploy the Company Portal to the company owned device. The company portal is deployed from the store (Windows store, Android Google Play store, or iOS store), and you deploy the Microsoft store to your environment.

The approach that we will be using will divide Intune deployment into two categories: a simple configuration and a compliant configuration. This configuration will give you a better perspective of the work required to deploy a full company managed MDM and the necessary configuration. As an example, Figure 5-9 shows how the desktop will respond to an Office 365 environment where the systems are required to be compliant. Before we start to deploy Mobile Device Management, we need to deploy multifactor authentication and the mobile Microsoft Authenticator application on your iOS or Android mobile devices. This is a key component that needs to be deployed to secure the mobile devices and provide secure access to the Office 365/Azure environment.

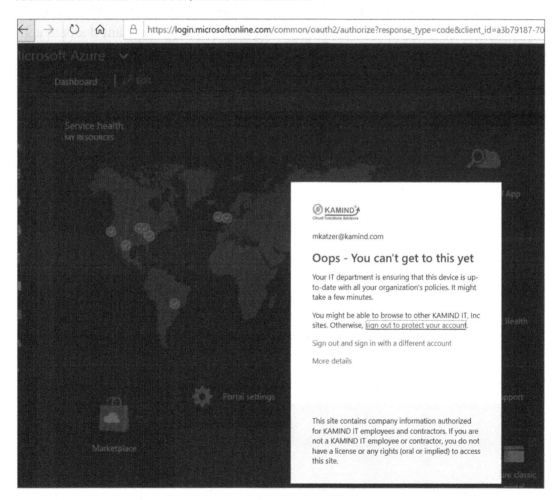

Figure 5-9. *Noncompliant system blocked from accessing controlled resources*

Deploying Multifactor Authentication

Multifactor authentication includes different methods for authentication. Initially you set up MFA to use multiple methods to get users to use the service and train them to use the biometrics of the device (fingerprint visual recognition), and so on. To accomplish this, you will need to use the Microsoft Authenticator on mobile devices and integrated biometrics on Windows 10 systems (1809 or later). As an example, when I use Windows Hello on my Surface, I am providing a biometric login to Office 365 with no password prompt. Biometrics can replace the cell phone text messages for authentication.

There are many people who do not want to deploy MFA and think their passwords are strong enough. For those skeptics, take a look at the sign-ins by location for our Office 365 tenant (see Figure 5-10). This is a 90-day snapshot of the audit logs for our Office 365 tenant. The logins shown below are bad actors from countries that are attempting to access our Office 365 tenant. We only have offices in the US. If you have any doubt that your password is strong and unique, you need to dismiss those thoughts and deploy multifactor authentication and start using the Microsoft Authenticator for single sign-on. Let's walk through the steps and configure your Microsoft 365 E5 subscription with full MFA. What is happening in this case is the bad actors are using a password spray attack to try different passwords against our office 3365 tenant. The bad actors most likely purchased passwords for my email address from the dark web.

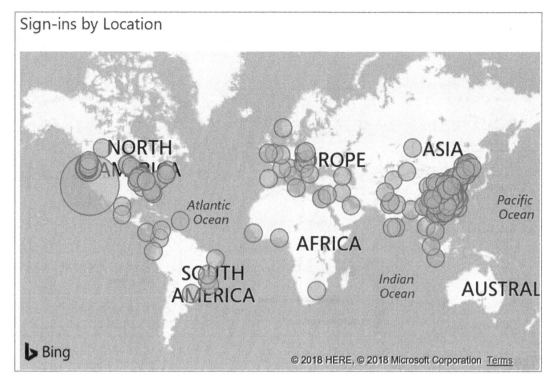

Figure 5-10. *Successful and failed sign-ons in our Office 365 tenant*

Step 1: Enable Azure Password Self-Service Reset

Log into https://portal.azure.com and click Azure Active Directory and "Password reset." Set up the MFA deployment similar to Figure 5-11 by enabling the mobile app notifications, mobile app code, mail, and phone. Click Save when completed.

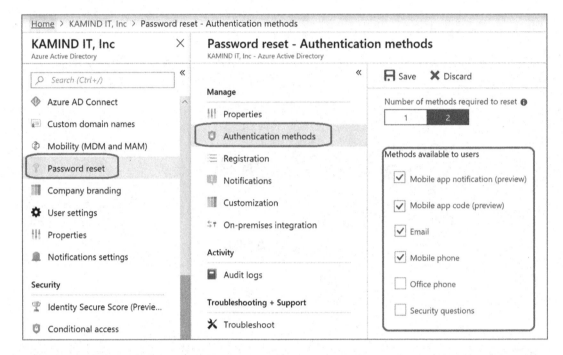

Figure 5-11. *Setting up MFA options*

Step 2: Enable Access to the App

In Azure Active Directory, click "User settings" and then click "Manage settings for access panel preview features" (see Figure 5-12). Set the user to a user group (that is eligible) and then click Save (see Figure 5-13). In this case, we set the MFA test group to all of the KAMIND employees.

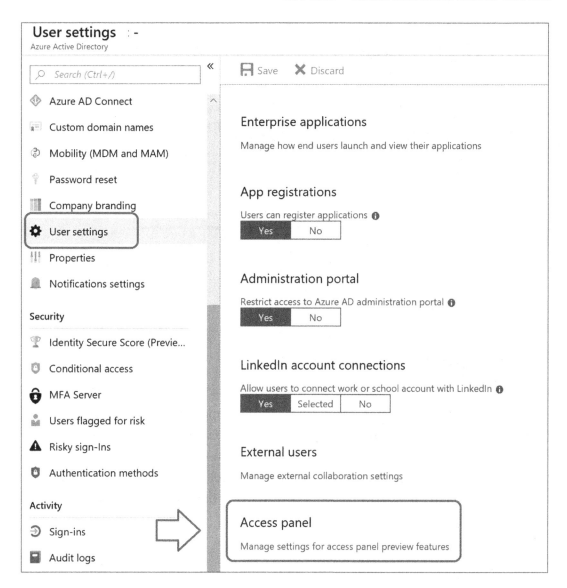

Figure 5-12. Accessing the Access panel for single sign-on

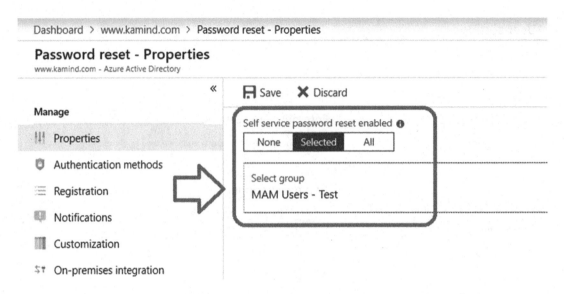

Figure 5-13. Enabling MFA for test users

Step 3: Register the User Accounts

Have all users go to `https://myapps.microsoft.com`, log in with their Office 365 user information. Once logged in, select the user icon (upper right hand corner - see Figure 5-14). Once the user icon is selected, the pop-up menu options will include Profile. Select profile, then set up self-service password reset. Enter your password and follow the wizard to set up the email address and your cell phone. This is used for your account verification for password reset. Proceed to the next step to add additional security information and set up the authenticator app.

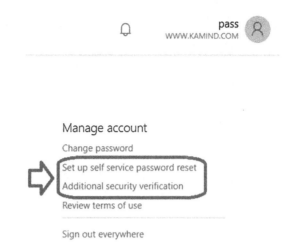

Figure 5-14. *Setting up for password reset*

Step 4: Set an Authenticator App

The Authenticator app will work for modern applications and modern devices. Install the Authenticator app from the mobile device store (iOS or Google Play store). Once the Authenticator app is installed then you are ready to configure the app. To configure the Authenticator App, select "Additional security verification" (see Figure 5-14). Once you have selected the option, you need to select how you want to use the app with your login credentials (see Figure 5-15). The most common configuration is to select "notify me through the app" and select the check box for Authenticator app or Token. You are going to configure the app to link your login credentials. The reason why we do this is to configure your smart phone, so you can later use Mobile Application Management to manage the company data on the device. Once you have configured the application select "save". You will receive an additional verification prompt to verify the codes were set correctly.

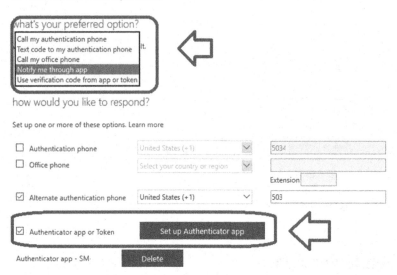

Figure 5-15. *Creating an app password*

Step 5: Test MFA for Deployment

At this point, the infrastructure is set up. Now we need to enable the conditional access so that all users are required to use MFA. In our case, we will set up one user account and test it, before deploying this to all users. To set up the conditional access, click Azure Active Directory and then click "Conditional access" (see Figure 5-16). The next step is to add a location followed by a policy.

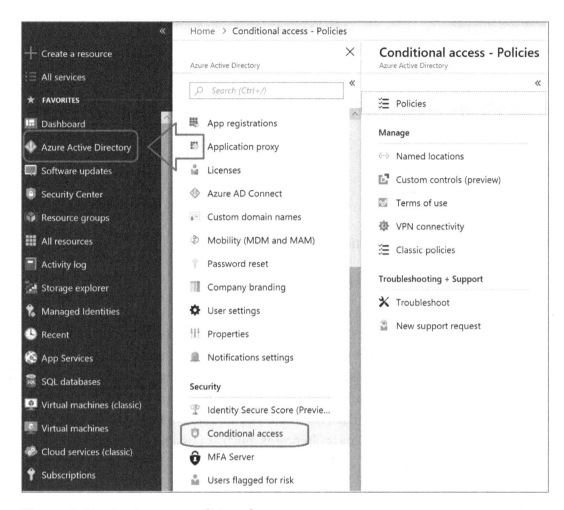

Figure 5-16. *Setting up conditional access*

Name Location 1: Create a Name Location

On the "Conditional access" page, click Name Location. We are going to define a location where users access our business. As an example, if we are in the United States, we should restrict external access to the United States only. Click "Named locations." We will build a name location as the United States and use this later to deny access. See Figure 5-17.

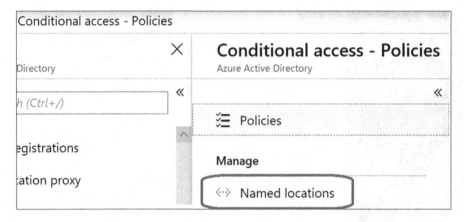

Figure 5-17. *Setting up conditional access*

Name Location 2: Set Up US as a Name Location

Click the name location and then select New location (+ sign). On the new location enter "All US IP Addresses", then select countries and "United States" click "United States" and assign the location name as "Restrict to US". Click the options as shown in Figure 5-18 and then click Save. We are going to use the new policy to reduce the sign-in attempts. You can set up multiple locations. Some organizations have a location for each country they do business in. Keep in mind that bad actors can hop to a system from a U.S. location and still attack you. All we are doing is filtering as much as possible to reduce risk.

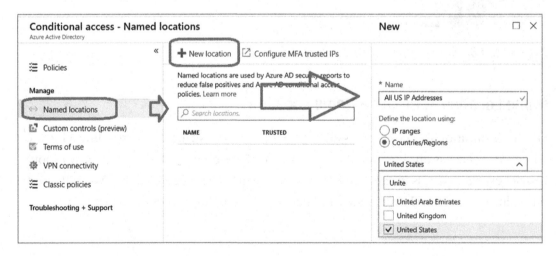

Figure 5-18. *Clicking a U.S. location policy*

Let's create a second location for working at home. In this case, we will set the IP address as a trusted location so we can use this location setting later. When you are completed setting the location, you should have two locations: All U.S. Addresses and a trusted location address (Work-Home). We will use these locations to filter bad actors later. See Figure 5-19.

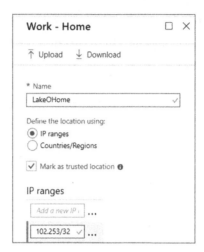

Figure 5-19. *Enabling a specific IP address as trusted to bypass MFA*

After we create the name location, we are going to create the MFA policy for conditional access. Go back to the "Conditional access" options, click Policies, and then add a new policy called US only (see Figure 5-20).

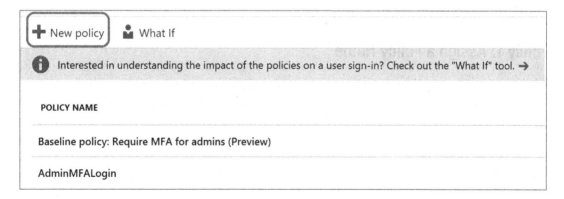

Figure 5-20. *Adding a new conditional access policy*

When you click add a policy, you have to make decisions on five different areas of the policy (see Figure 5-21). I'll outline the five steps with the different options. Our objective here is to create a conditional policy for the enforcement of multifactor authentication on all users. We are going to set this up so that any user who comes in externally from the United States will be denied access when clicking cloud resources. We are also going to require that the user accounts meet some minimal standards. Initially, we will require that the user meets at least one of three requirements. Over time, we will start changing these requirements to be more stringent. The requirements that we are deploying for this conditional access are as follows:

- Must be a U.S. location

- Must be one of following:

  - MFA required

  - Device is compliant

  - Hybrid Azure joined

  - Approved clients

Looking back at the access map shown earlier, we can now see that by deploying these types of restrictions, we will reduce our threat of breach significantly. Let's deploy our conditional access policy. The user in this case will be our test group that has only one user account. When you configure conditional access, make sure that you test out the conditions with a user account before you deploy the polices to the entire organization. In our case we created a test group called MDM test group. In the test group, I added the pass@getoffice365security.

Policy 1: Assign a Policy Name

After you have created a new policy, assign a simple, descriptive name for this conditional access policy. Our policy is called "Require MFA to access all cloud resources".

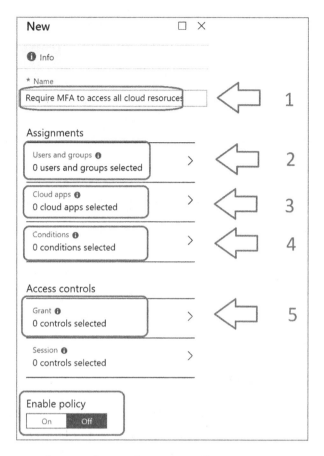

Figure 5-21. *Naming the conditional access policy*

Policy 2: Assign the Users

In the test phase, you include a selected user (Test User in this case), and on the Exclude tab, you click "All users." When you go into production, you reverse this. You include all users, and you exclude selected users (such as certain service accounts), as shown in Figure 5-22.

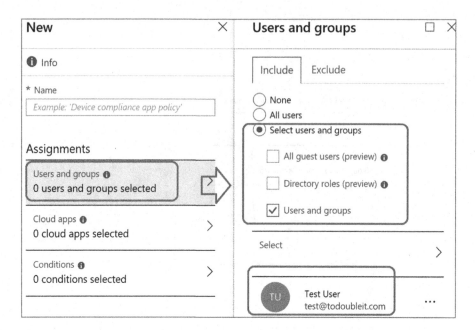

Figure 5-22. *Setting up a test group and exclusion group*

Policy 3: Select the Cloud Apps

The best practice in this case is to select the cloud apps that are being used. Do not select all cloud apps; otherwise, you may find yourself locked out of the Office 365 tenant. In Figure 5-23, we select the cloud apps that we use in our environment. In this case, we are selecting Windows Defender ATP, Office 365 Exchange and Office 365 SharePoint Online. Once you have tested this you can change this later to all cloud apps.

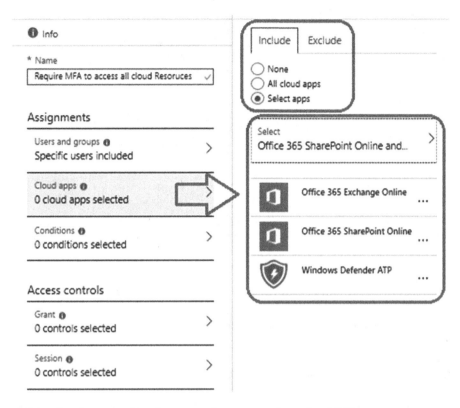

Figure 5-23. *Setting up cloud apps to be covered under MFA*

Policy 4: Select the Conditions: Device Platforms

There are five different conditions that we can use to control the policy: Sign in Risk, Device platform, Locations, Client apps, and Device state. In our example, we will configure device platforms and locations. To start the process, click Device Platform and then select the supported devices in the organization. Since this is a new deployment, click "All platforms (including unsupported)" at this time. Later, after you have a better feel for the hardware in your company, you can deploy additional restrictions. Click Yes and then Save to continue (see Figure 5-24).

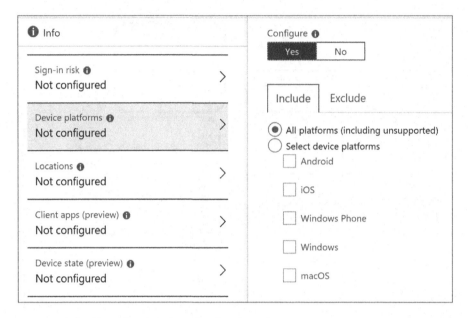

Figure 5-24. *Selecting the Device platforms*

Policy 4: Select the Conditions: Locations

Click Locations and select the new location. We are going to force everyone to use MFA except the trusted locations (see Figure 5-25). You can change this over time, but this will give you a good baseline. Microsoft defines a trusted IP as the corporate network (or configuration). In our current configuration, we have not defined trusted network. Later, we will add a second conditional access policy which we will block any locations, but will exclude all US addresses.

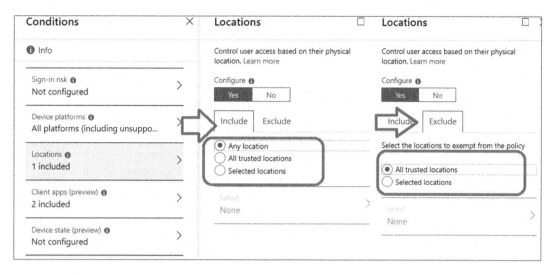

Figure 5-25. *Selecting the device platforms*

Once you have the completed the conditions configuration, save the policy and let's configure access controls.

Policy 5: Select the Conditions: Device Platforms

The policy is controlled by the access controls. Earlier we set the conditions for the policy, and now we need to configure the policy for what we need to accomplish. We are going to set three access controls and enforce the controls. This means that the client will need to meet one of three access controls to access our resources. This is in addition to the conditional access that we have already put in place.

Note   It is easy to build a version of an access control that has everything. Do not do this. Focus the conditional policy on a single task. Do not have a conditional policy that tries to do multiple things, which is difficult to debug.

In our access controls, enable MFA, "Require device to be marked as compliant," and Hybrid Azure AD join. Click "Require one of the selected controls" and then save the controls (see Figure 5-26).

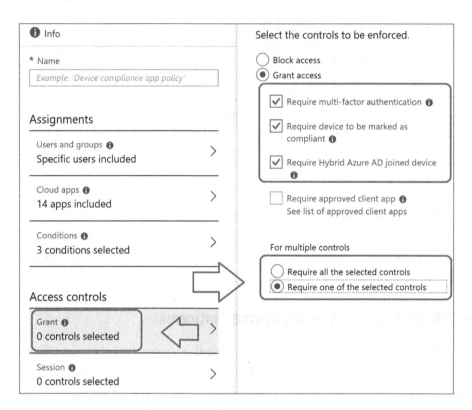

Figure 5-26. *Selecting the Device platforms*

At this time you are ready to apply the controls and test the account. Click "Enforce policy") (See Figure 5-27) to turn the policy on. The best way to select the client is to log into `https://portal.microsoft.com` with the smart phone you used earlier to set up the Authenticator app. You will be prompted to authenticate with the app that was configured earlier.

Figure 5-27. *Enforcing the policy*

Step 6: Deploy MFA to All Users

Deployment is easy. Once you have tested the account, you can add additional users to the test group. Make sure you have tested the policy before you deploy and verify with your users. If your MFA is not working and your systems are not compliant, MDM deployment will fail.

Getting Started with Microsoft Intune

Microsoft Intune is an Azure service for device management. What is different is the way we think about the deployment. When you use the Intune MDM solution, you are thinking about users and devices. We recommend you step back and look at your organization and create dynamic groups for users and systems assignments (this is described in detail later in this chapter). When I deploy MDM, I create test groups for policy deployment, and I use dynamic groups for production deployment.

Setting up Intune requires decisions about the following:

- Which users will have application management?

- Which users will have device management?

- Which groups will have access restrictions?

- Are you going to manage the organization with dynamic groups?

Let's begin the process and set up some of the must-do configuration so we can deploy Mobile Device Management. Once we define a few items and set up some administrative functions, we are going to look at two different types of deployment: a simple deployment and a compliant deployment.

Step 1: Set Up Deployment Groups

We are creating eight groups. These groups are for our organization (based on the department structure) and for our devices. Also, let's create three MDM test groups. If you do not know how to create dynamic groups, see the "Additional Configuration section - Using Dynamics Groups" section later in this chapter. The number of groups you set up is a strategic decision. My philosophy is to automate as much as possible with dynamic groups. When users are added to an organization, I define the department and manager and assign a license. I use dynamic groups to read the metadata of the object and add the user to the appropriate group. Permission and access are assigned to groups. Likewise, in Azure I use the concept of a blueprint and management groups to assign access and permission to Azure subscriptions. When you click groups, you create groups based on the organization strategy. In our case, we are doing a demo configuration and are using the groups listed here:

- Dynamic team groups for the following departments: sales, engineering, marketing

- Dynamic device groups such as Android, iOS, and Windows

- MDM test deployment groups (static)

- MAM test deployment group (static)

When you are done, the groups should look like the list in Figure 5-27. Keep in mind that the production groups are the dynamic groups. The test groups will be deleted once we feel we have the deployment tested and validated.

Note   If you are not ready to build groups, let's keep it simple. You have a test account (as we used in MFA deployment), and you have everyone else. Exclude everyone and assign the test account. Once you have a policy successfully deployed, then apply it to all users or the different management groups.

Figure 5-28 is a snapshot of the engineering team. Note that we have the users, but also, as we build out the security infrastructure, we will have resources assigned to different groups. We can define applications that this group has access to as well as Azure resources. The objective here from a security standpoint is to create processes and standardize the behavior. See Figure 5-29.

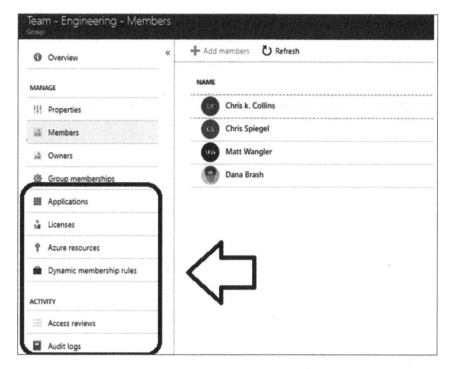

Figure 5-28. *Expansion of the security group with dynamic members*

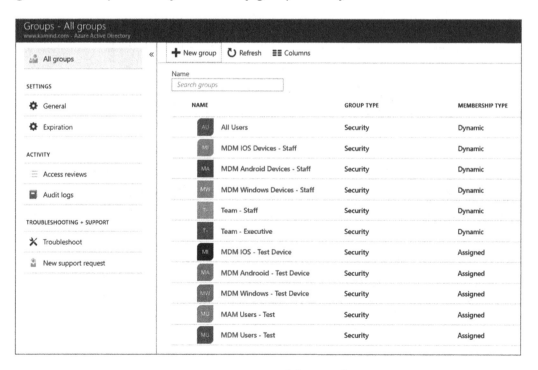

Figure 5-29. *Azure AD test groups: assigned (testing), dynamic production*

Once the group is created, we need to create the membership criteria of the group. We are not going to assign users to the group, but have Azure service assign users based on the membership criteria. When you create the test groups, replace the expression in the "Advanced rule" box with All Users. See Figure 5-30. This will automatically add all users to the group as the user accounts are created in Office35/Azure.

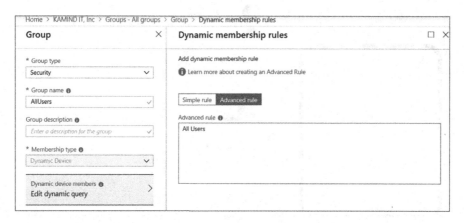

Figure 5-30. *Creating an All Users group*

In a few minutes, the group you created will populate with all of the users in your Office 365 account. If this is a production tenant, please verify that this is the process you will want to follow for MAM deployment in a test group.

Step 3: Set Up the Intune MDM Authority

Intune must be set as the MDM authority, or if you are using Systems Center Configuration Manager (SCCM), then you can set SCCM as the authority. If you are using a third-party product, you will still need to select the none or Intune option. Which MDM do you choose? If you have no plans to use Systems Center Configuration Manager, then choose Intune MDM as the MDM authority (see Figure 5-31). The Intune management plans will be grayed out until you select an option.

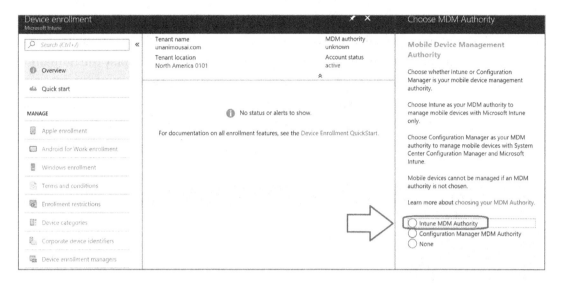

Figure 5-31. *Setting up Intune as the MDM authority*

Step 4: Configure the Mobility (MDM and MAM) Enrollment URLs

After we set the MDM authority, we need to enable the MDM/MAM enrollment URLs. The enrollment URLs should have been set up when you verified your domain in Office 365 and added the necessary cname. If these cnames have not been added to your DNS, then add the cnames listed in Figure 5-32.

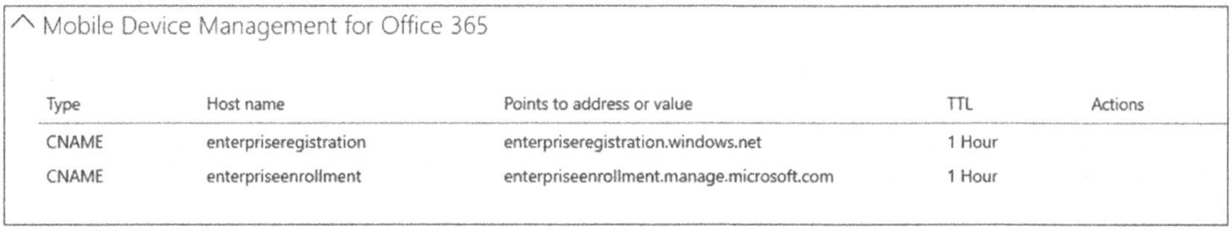

∧ Mobile Device Management for Office 365				
Type	Host name	Points to address or value	TTL	Actions
CNAME	enterpriseregistration	enterpriseregistration.windows.net	1 Hour	
CNAME	enterpriseenrollment	enterpriseenrollment.manage.microsoft.com	1 Hour	

Figure 5-32. *Adding DNS records to your domain for MDM/MAM enrollment*

The cnames are listed in your Office 365 domain setup. To access this record, go to the Office 365 admin center, click Setup, click Domains, and select your domain that you are using for your default domain. The Office 365 admin center will display the domain records that are being used. Verify that all the cnames and other DNS records have been entered correctly. After you have verified that the DNS records are in place, then the next step is to set the MDM/MAM enrollment. To do this, open Azure Active Directory and click Mobility (MDM and MAM) (see Figure 5-33). Then click Microsoft Intune.

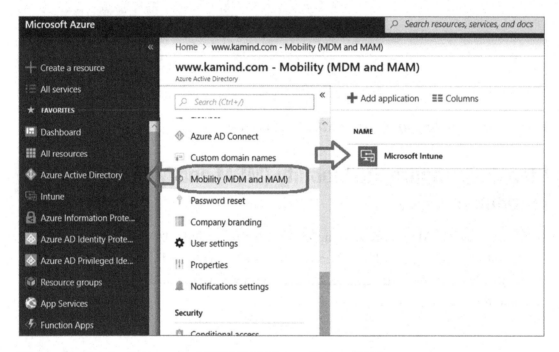

Figure 5-33. *Setting up the MDM/MAM enrollment URLs*

Change the MDM/MAM enrollment for None to All (see Figure 5-34); then click Save.

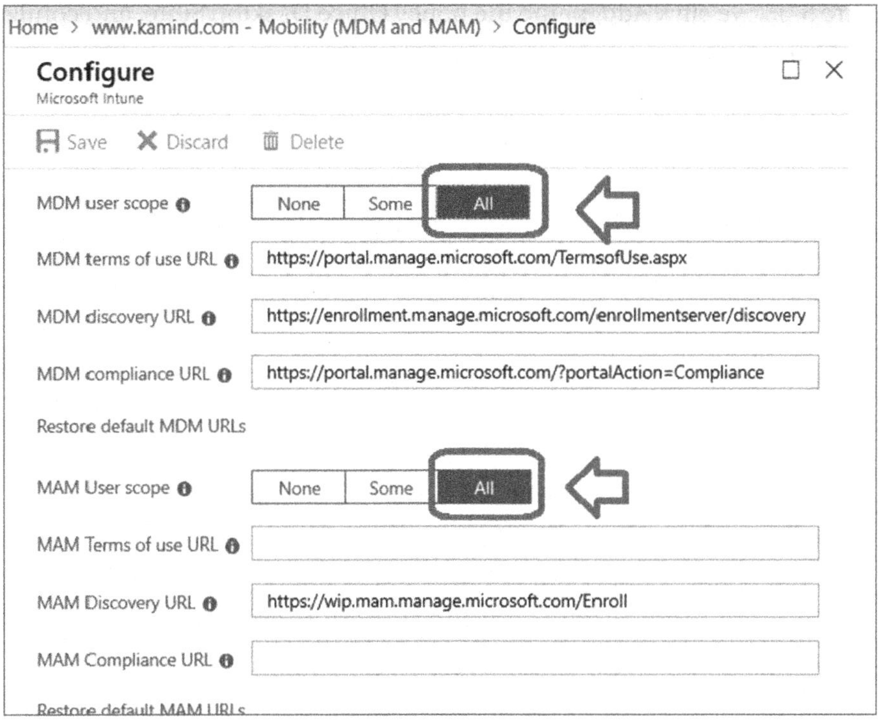

Figure 5-34. *Setting up the MDM/MAM enrollment URLs*

Step 5: Enable the Office Update Policy

The Office update policy is crucial for MAM and MDM deployment. Once we have completed the test group deployment, we need to define the Office Desktop Suite Update policy (see Figure 5-35).

Figure 5-35. *Creating a Mobile Device Update policy for the Office suite*

In Figure 5-35, we click Add, name the policy Office Desktop Suite, and configure the policy (see Figure 5-36).

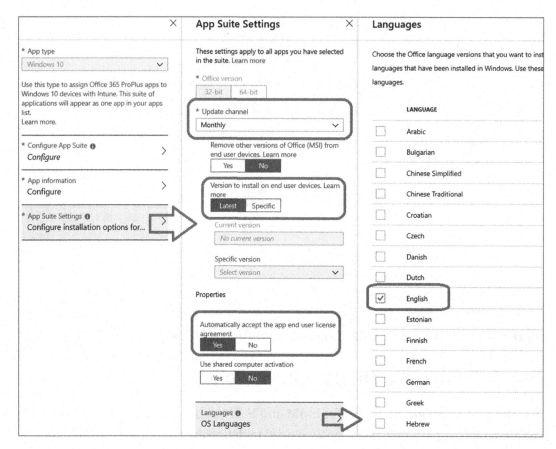

Figure 5-36. *Office Pro Plus Update policy*

There are a lot of different options that we can use; we have detailed this later in the chapter. The typical Office update policy will look like Figure 5-37. The configuration options for Office Pro Plus are described at the end of the chapter. This will ensure that the Office updates are deployed. You can verify the deployment in the Intune management portal (click Intune, Client Apps, Apps, and then Office Desktop Suite).

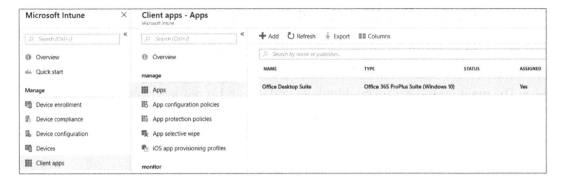

Figure 5-37. *Office Pro Plus Update policy*

If you click Office Desktop Suite, you can see the status of the Office deployment (see Figure 5-38). Our deployment of Office Pro Plus has a required attribute, so users after they log into Office 365 will have the Office Pro Plus software pushed to the client. This is how software is automatically deployed to the client system - worldwide. Let's move on to step 6 and configure the Windows 10 software update ring.

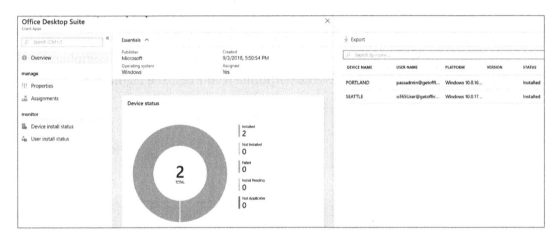

Figure 5-38. *Status of the Office Pro Plus deployment*

Note   There are detailed instructions in the "Additional Configuration" section later in this chapter for the configuration of Windows Updates and Office Updates. I purposely gave an overview in steps 4 and 5 so you would not lose focus on the objective. We are building a framework for Mobile Application Management (MAM), Windows Information Protection (WIP), and Mobile Device Management (MDM). If we go into too much detail (like dynamics groups), we will lose sight of our objective.

Step 6: Enable the Windows Update Ring

We are using a Microsoft 365 E5 suite. As part of the deployment, we need to ensure that Windows Updates are configured and managed. I wanted to focus on the reason for this here. The main reason we are enabling the updates at this point is because we want to have compliant devices (se Figure 5-39).

Figure 5-39. *Compliant devices (select Intune, Devices, All devices)*

When we fully deploy MDM, we are deploying for mobile devices, desktops, and laptops; everything will be managed and must be compliant. If the devices are not compliant, then the user will not be able to access the corporate resources. See Figure 5-40.

Figure 5-40. *Device status for Windows Updates*

The configuration process for software updates is similar to Office updates. You need to define the update target and the dynamic groups and let the system manage the updates (see Figure 5-41).

Figure 5-41. *Update policy for Windows 10*

Step 7: Test for Compliance

The end game is that we must have systems that are compliant. At this point, you need to deploy Windows Updates and Office Updates and test that the systems are compliant. See Figure 5-42.

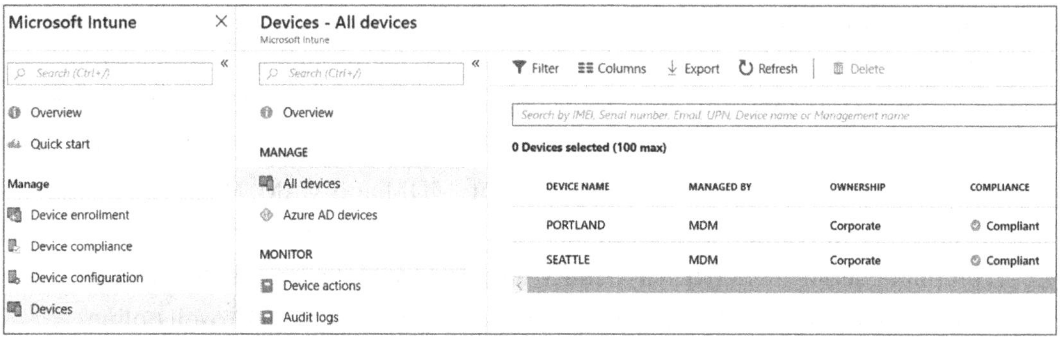

Figure 5-42. *Compliant devices*

If your devices that you want to test with are not compliant, you need to resolve the compliance issues at this point. All compliance is a stake in the ground because your systems are linked to your organization policy on device management. If your devices are not compliant (with all green check marks), find out why and resolve the errors. If you do not do this, your MDM deployment will fail, and your users will be locked out of using your Office 365 resources.

At the end of this chapter, I have detailed information on four important areas for MDM deployment. These are the dynamic groups creation and management of the Windows updates.

Keep in mind that to deploy MDM you will need to complete these four steps:

1.   Set up Intune as the MDM authority (or System Center).

2.   Create the dynamic groups for MDM deployment.

3.   Create dynamic groups to capture the devices for Windows Update.

4.   Assign the dynamic groups to Windows Intune to be updated.

Note   Make sure you have deployed the Windows 10 update ring and that the Office Pro Plus updates are marked updated and are compliant. If this is not the case, fix the problem before you continue.

Mobile Application and Mobile Device Management

We are all ready to go; we have set up the basic components of our Mobile Application Management (MAM, Windows Information Protection (WIP)) and Mobile Device Management (MDM) deployment. We have Intune set up as the Mobile Device Management authority, and we have created our test groups. We are going to walk through two versions of Intune MDM deployment: MDM and MAM. MAM will be the simple deployment. Windows Information Protection (WIP) will be deployed with MAM.

A compliant deployment (such as a full Mobile Device Management deployment) requires that you use the Company Portal from the IOS, Android or Microsoft online store to validate the endpoints (Windows 10, iOS, or Android). Figure 5-43 shows the Company Portal completing an analysis of a device to bring the device up to compliance standard. If the device is not compliant, then the user will not be able to access the Office 365 resources. Our end game will have all compliant devices. If you want to verify your Windows 10 device, download the Company Portal application from the vendor device store and run it. The desktop configuration that we are using is for Windows 10 devices that are either workplace joined or hybrid joined via a local Active Directory instance and AD Connect.

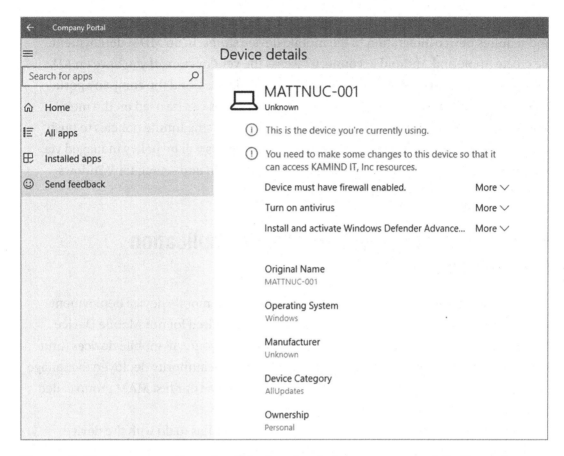

Figure 5-43. *Company Portal validating the desktop system and finding it is not compliant to MDM policies.*

Note   If you are running a local Active Directory and want to deploy MAM/MDM, you will need to install Azure AD Connect for Azure Identity. If you are using a test account and test machines and no Active Directory, the Windows 10 devices must be Azure joined. To Azure join a new Windows 10 device, reset the Windows 10 device (remove all data) and click the Work or School account when you start a first-time Windows 10 installation.

This is a Mobile Application Management style of deployment, with some conditional access. MAM deployment works for Microsoft Intune because Microsoft owns the application that we are deploying on the mobile device. There are enough controls over the device to protect information, but it is not a fully compliant deployment.

MDM is our *compliant* deployment. MDM is a much more robust deployment and requires device integration to the mobile device stores. In an MDM deployment, we create Apple and Android accounts to access the vendor store. If you have an AD, Group Policy is used to push information out to the devices, and the company portal is downloaded to the device and allows what applications can be used on the mobile device. If you have only an Azure joined device, you are using Intune policies to push out information to the mobile device. Windows 10 devices will be policy managed via Windows Information Protection (see docs.microsoft.com and search for Windows Information Protection (WIP)).

Simple Intune Deployment: Mobile Application Management

Let's get started with our simple deployment. Our simple mobile device deployment will be a mobile application deployment and will be required for our Mobile Device Management deployment. The reason for this is a simple one. All mobile devices (and Windows 10 devices as well) have only one mobile device authority deployed to manage the activity of the device. In this section we are going to use our test MAM group called Test Users that we created earlier.

There are some gotchas with running MAM, and this has to do with the device that you are using. If you are using an iOS device, you need to download the Microsoft Authenticator from the Apple store and install it on the device. If you are running an Android device, you need to install the Intune Company Portal. If you do not do this, the device will not work with MAM and cannot be managed.

Note   iOS Users: If you have an iOS (on a mobile phone or an iPad) and you want to run MAM, you must install Microsoft Authenticator and link the Microsoft Authenticator to your Office 365 work account at `https://myapps.microsoft.com`.

Android Users: If you are using an Android device (on a mobile phone, a pad, or a Chromebook) and you want to run MAM, you must install the Microsoft Company Portal from the Google Play store and log in with your Office365 work account.

A MAM deployment does not require us to set up links to the iOS or Android store (this is required for a full MDM deployment). The MAM deployment allows us to directly configure Microsoft applications to the mobile device. The user can download the applications to their device, and the MAM integration will make the device compliant with the policies associated in our business. We are focusing on the MAM deployment in the Windows Intune portal (see Figure 5-44).

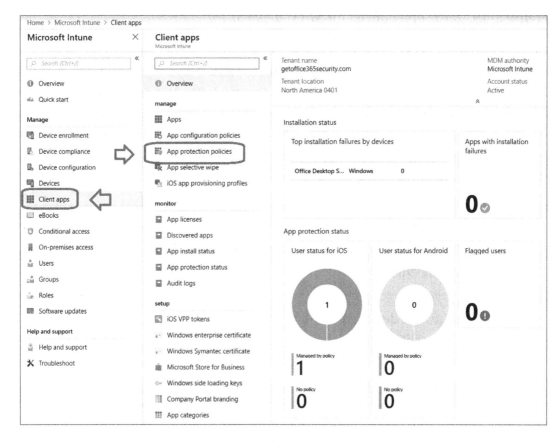

Figure 5-44. *Client apps protection policy: status*

The configuration process is simple; we will define the app protection policy. Once this policy is in place, we will assign users to our test accounts. At the end of our MAM deployment, we will expand the test group for all users. Make sure you have thoroughly tested the deployment before you deploy the test group; otherwise, you will restrict access to the company data by your users. See Figure 5-45.

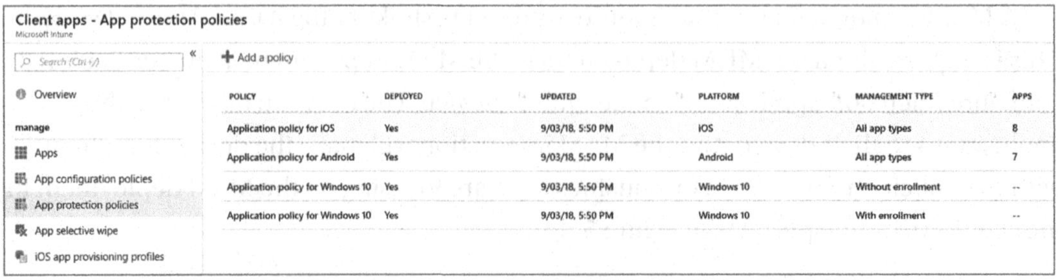

Figure 5-45. Basic app policies for MAM deployment

Let's start the process and get our MAM configuration in place. Before you start this process, you will need to have completed the previous steps. If you have not completed them, you are putting your deployment at risk. The Windows Update, Azure joined/hybrid join devices, and Office updates must all be marked compliant at this stage. If they are not compliant, fix the problem before you continue. Otherwise, your deployment will fail. Let's get started with Mobile Application Management. Our objective for MAM is to build the following policies for Mobile Application Management.

Note   When you deploy policies, you need to develop global policies to all devices and assign all users (Android, Windows 10, and iOS devices). Otherwise, the device will be marked noncompliant.

At this point, we have deployed the Software Updates and Office Pro Plus policy updates. The desktop clients that we have attached are all compliant (Azure join or hybrid join). The next step is to deploy the policy for applications management. If your devices are **not compliant** (with green check marks), stop now and resolve the issues with the devices. Once you have verified the configuration and devices are marked all compliant, you can start the mobile device deployment.

Step 1: Set the MAM Deployment Rules

Before we begin with the deployment policies, let's review the three rules associated with MAM/MDM deployment.

- The iOS device must have deployed the Microsoft Authenticator.

- The Android device must have deployed the Company Portal.

- You must have Intune license for all devices (part of Microsoft 365 E5 suite).

Verify that you have completed all these steps before you continue with the MAM deployment.

Step 2: Set Up the Windows 10 Application Policy for MAM Without Enrollment

What this means is that the device is not enrolled in Intune (aka MDM), but it is enrolled under MAM. We are creating a Windows Information Protection (WIP) app protection policy with Windows Intune. The process is outlined here.

Policy 1: Add the Windows 10 Application Policy

In Figure 5-46, add a new protected app policy by clicking the Intune and then "Client apps: and then "App protection policies." Then click "Add a policy." After you click "Add a policy" enter the following policy blade information for Windows 10:

Name: Enter **Windows 10 Policy No enrollment**.

Description: Enter **Test Windows 10 Policy**.

Platform: Click Windows 10.

Enrollment State: Click Without Enrollment.

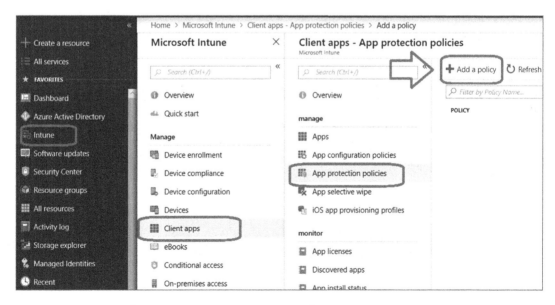

Figure 5-46. *Deploying an app protection policy*

Policy 2: Add Windows 10 Application Policy

After you click "Add a policy," enter the following policy information for policy name, Platform and policy type. After you entered the information, select "add apps" to add the Microsoft applications that will be managed under those policies. See Figure 5-47. We are building two policies. One policy is for devices without enrollment into our deployment, and the other policy is for devices that are formally enrolled. Both are very similar, but only different in the policy type.

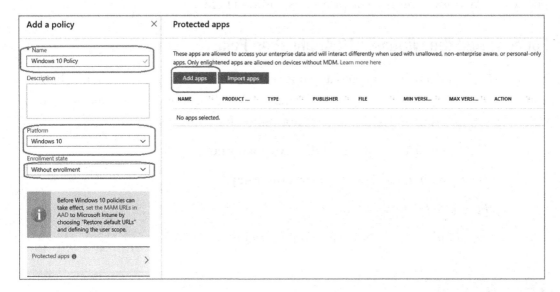

Figure 5-47. *Adding a policy*

Policy 3: Select the Windows 10 Apps You Want to Deploy

Click the apps you want to push down without an enrollment. See Figure 5-48.

	NAME	PRODUCT ...	TYPE	PUBLISHER	FILE	MIN VERSI...	MAX VERSI...	ACTION
✓	Microsoft Edge	Microsoft.Micr...	Store	CN=Microsoft ...				Allow
	Microsoft Peo...	Microsoft.Peo...	Store	CN=Microsoft ...				Allow
✓	Word Mobile	Microsoft.Offic...	Store	CN=Microsoft ...				Allow
✓	Excel Mobile	Microsoft.Offic...	Store	CN=Microsoft ...				Allow
✓	PowerPoint M...	Microsoft.Offic...	Store	CN=Microsoft ...				Allow
✓	OneDrive App	Microsoft.Micr...	Store	CN=Microsoft ...				Allow
✓	OneNote	Microsoft.Offic...	Store	CN=Microsoft ...				Allow
	Mail and Cale...	microsoft.wind...	Store	CN=Microsoft ...				Allow
	Microsoft Phot...	Microsoft.Win...	Store	CN=Microsoft ...				Allow
	Groove Music	Microsoft.Zun...	Store	CN=Microsoft ...				Allow
	Microsoft Mov...	Microsoft.Zun...	Store	CN=Microsoft ...				Allow
	Microsoft Mes...	Microsoft.Mes...	Store	CN=Microsoft ...				Allow
	Company Portal	Microsoft.Com...	Store	CN=Microsoft ...				Allow
	IE11	*	Desktop	O=Microsoft C...	iexplore.exe	*	*	Allow
	Microsoft One...	*	Desktop	O=Microsoft C...	onedrive.exe	*	*	Allow
	Notepad	*	Desktop	O=Microsoft C...	notepad.exe	*	*	Allow
	Microsoft Paint	*	Desktop	O=Microsoft C...	mspaint.exe	*	*	Allow
	Microsoft Rem...	*	Desktop	O=Microsoft C...	mstsc.exe	*	*	Allow
✓	Microsoft Teams	*	Desktop	O=Microsoft C...	teams.exe	*	*	Allow
✓	Office-365-Pro...		AppLocker File					
✓	Denied-Downl...		AppLocker File					

Figure 5-48. Adding apps without enrollment

Click OK and add the apps, as shown in Figure 5-49. Click OK after they have been added.

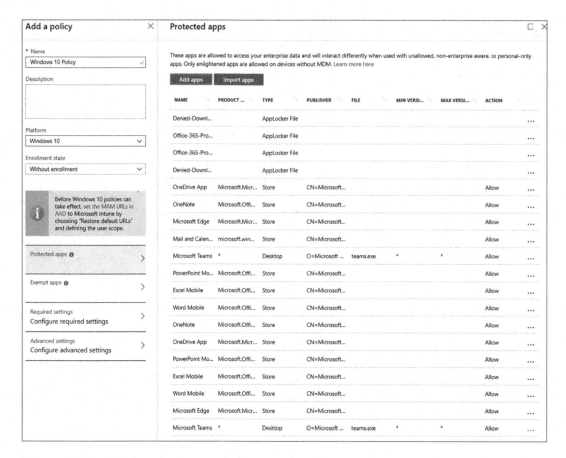

Figure 5-49. *Updated protected apps*

Policy 4: Configure Windows Information Protection

In this case, we will enable Windows Information Protection (WIP) to track inappropriate
sharing modes and block them (see Figure 5-50). This protects corporate data from
data loss. WIP places controls over corporate data and personal data on Windows 10
devices. WIP policies allow corporate data to be managed on personal devices. As an
example, when an employee leaves a company, and the user is removed from Office 365,
the WIP policies will remove the data from the user's personal Windows 10 device. The
configuration below, allows WIP to look for inappropriate data sharing practices and
blocks the user. Typically, you will see this when a user tries to copy data from a one
drive to the desktop that is managed by WIP. The activity will be blocked.

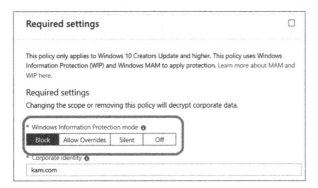

Required settings   ☐

This policy only applies to Windows 10 Creators Update and higher. This policy uses Windows
Information Protection (WIP) and Windows MAM to apply protection. Learn more about MAM and
WIP here.

Required settings
Changing the scope or removing this policy will decrypt corporate data.

* Windows Information Protection mode ❶
| Block | Allow Overrides | Silent | Off |

* Corporate identity ❶
kami.com

Figure 5-50. *Enabling WIP to Block data sharing*

Policy 5: Set the Windows 10 Advanced Settings

The next step is to configure the advance settings. Select configure the advance setting option, and set up the policy and use the defaults. Since this is a device that is not enrolled and managed, we need to define the offline policy. If the device is offline, then our policy is to wipe the persistence data. Once you make the changes, select save and create the policy. See Figure 5-51.

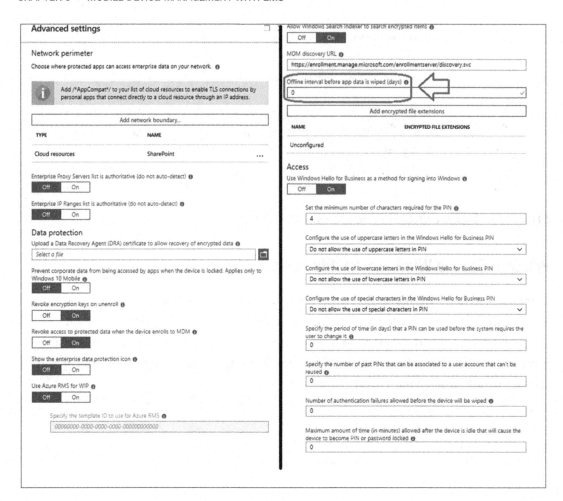

Figure 5-51. *Changing the parameters to wipe persistence data*

Policy 6: Assign the Test User to the New Policy

Once you have completed creating the policy, click the policy and click Assignment. Either assign your test group (recommended) or the All User policy (see Figure 5-52). In this example, I have a test tenant with an all users dynamic group.

Figure 5-52. *Changing the parameters to wipe persistence data*

Step 3: Set Up a Windows 10 Application Policy for MAM with Enrollment

After we created the without enrollment policy, we need to create the corresponding systems with enrollment for our Windows 10 devices. We will create a section with enrollment. With the exception of selecting the enrollment (see Figure 5-53), the steps are the same. Once you have set up the steps, we can move to step 3, policy 2.

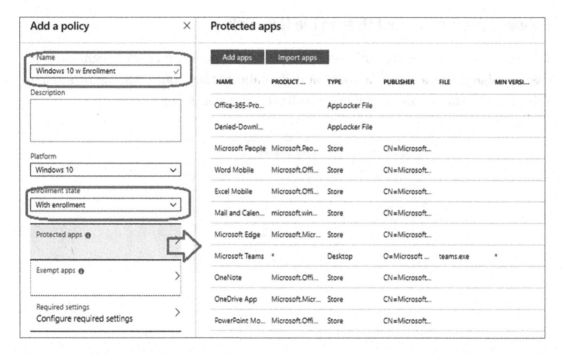

Figure 5-53. *Setting up the MAM policy with enrollment*

Policy 2: Add the Office Pro Plus Exception

The only change that you will make is adding an exempt policy for Office Pro Plus (see Figure 5-54).

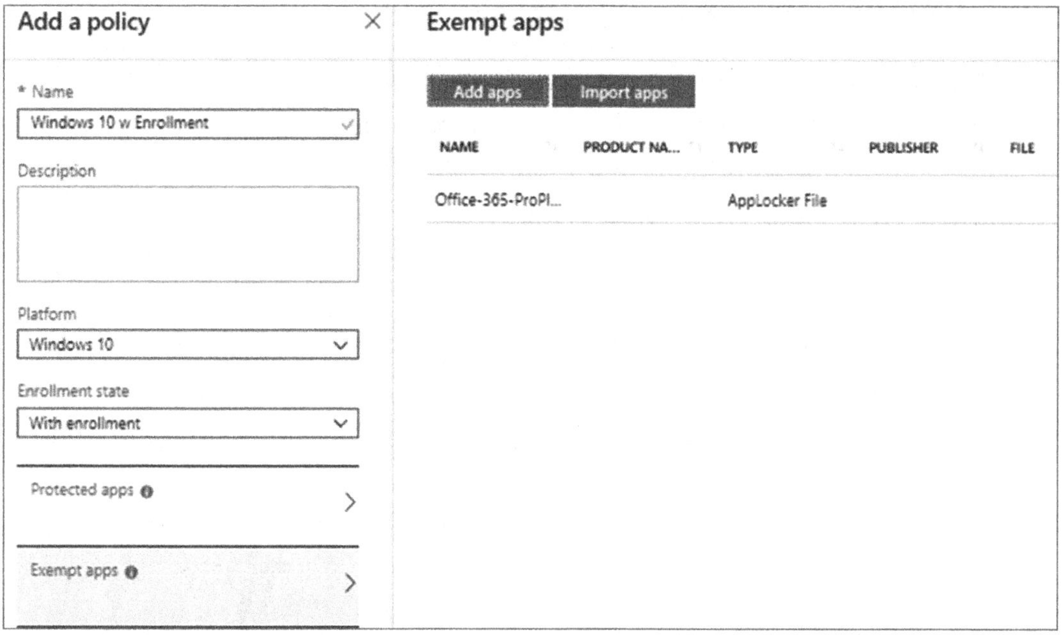

Figure 5-54. *Setting up the exclusion for Office Pro Plus*

Policy 3: Configure Windows Information Protection

In this case, we will enable Windows Information Protection (WIP) to track inappropriate sharing modes and block them. This protects corporate data (Figure 5-55).

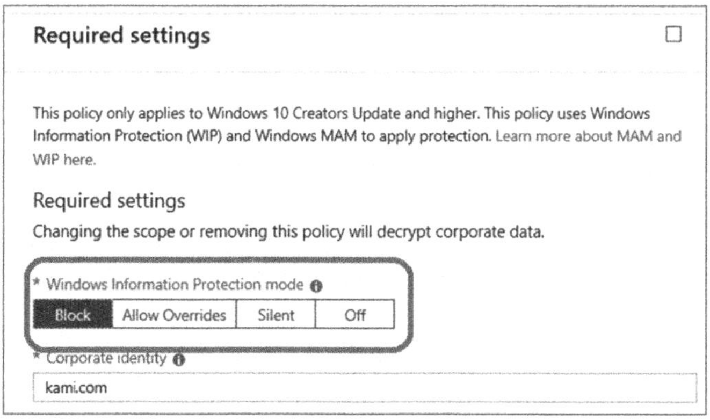

Figure 5-55. *Enabling WIP to block data sharing*

Policy 4: Configure the Advanced Settings

Click "Configure advanced settings" and leave the defaults. When you are done, it should look like Figure 5-56. Click OK and Create. This will create the baseline Windows 10 policy.

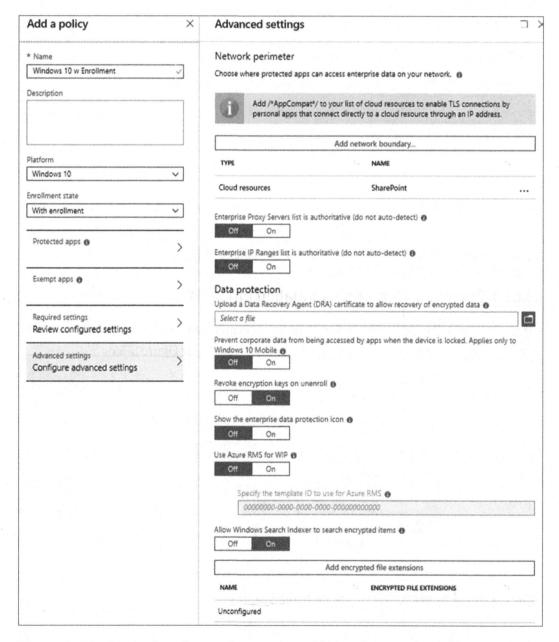

Figure 5-56. *Set up the advanced settings, and leave them at the defaults*

Policy 5: Assign the Test User to the New Policy

Once you have completed creating the policy, click the policy and click Assignment. Either assign your test group (recommended) or assign the All User policy (see Figure 5-57).

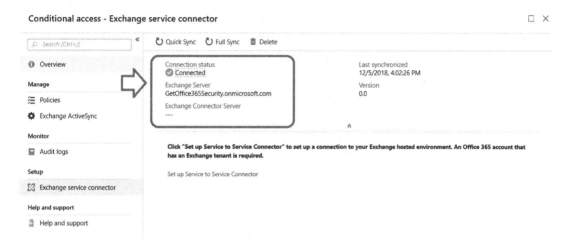

Figure 5-57. *Changing the parameters to wipe persistence data*

Step 4: Set Up an iOS Application Policy for MAM

The process is almost identical to the Windows apps. The difference is in the hardware setup and configuration. In Figure 5-58, we added a policy, and then we clicked the iOS applications to add.

Figure 5-58. *Setting up iOS data*

The next step is to set the device restrictions. The device restrictions are set up to protect the corporate data. In Figure 5-59, we have a section of different options to choose from. The key criteria is to restrict the data from being copied. Set up the data elements and pay attention to the circled areas. This is where the data restrictions are located.

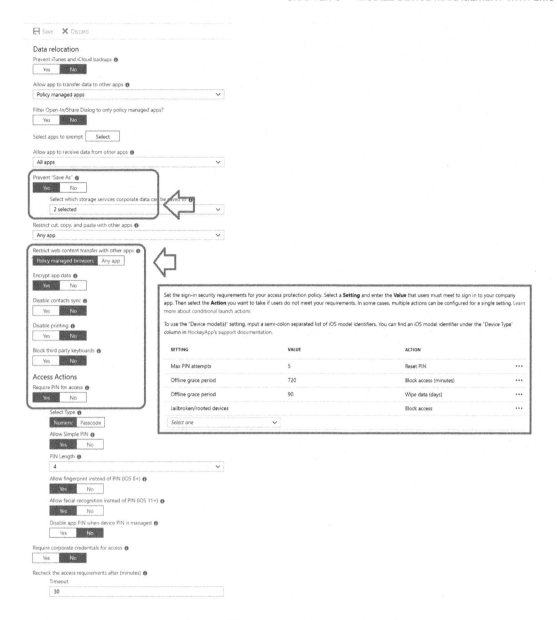

Figure 5-59. *Setting up the iOS device as a managed application*

One you have set up the data, save and create the iOS profile. The next step is like the other policies: edit the properties of the policy and set it to everyone for deployment (Figure 5-60).

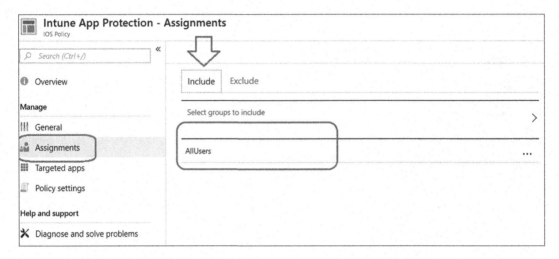

Figure 5-60. Assigning rights to iOS devices

Step 5: Set Up an Android Application Policy for MAM

The Android device is similar to the iOS device. Create a new policy, assign applications, and assign the restrictions in Figure 5-61 for the initial application assignments. Be careful when you select some applications and make sure you test them. As an example, if you select the Android Microsoft launcher, you can effectively lock the user out of using any application on the Android phone.

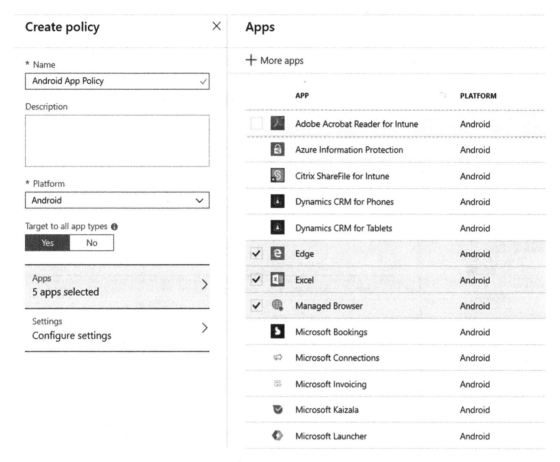

Figure 5-61. *Assigning applications to Android devices*

Once you have completed the applications assignment, click "Configure required settings" to set up a finer level of detail of data management on the device, identical to what we're doing on the iOS devices (see Figure 5-62).

Data relocation

Prevent Android backups ●

| Yes | No |

Allow app to transfer data to other apps ●

| Policy managed apps   ∨ |

Select apps to exempt | Select |

Allow app to receive data from other apps ●

| All apps   ∨ |

Prevent "Save As" ●

| Yes | No |

   Select which storage services corporate data can be saved to ●

   | 2 selected   ∨ |

Restrict cut, copy, and paste with other apps ●

| Policy managed apps with paste in   ∨ |

Restrict web content transfer with other apps ●

| Policy managed browsers | Any app |

Encrypt app data ●

| Yes | No |

   Disable app encryption when device encryption is enabled ●

   | Yes | No |

Disable contacts sync ●

| Yes | No |

Disable printing ●

| Yes | No |

Access Actions

Require PIN for access ●

| Yes | No |

   Select Type ●

   | Numeric | Passcode |

   Allow Simple PIN ●

   | Yes | No |

   PIN Length ●

   | 4   ∨ |

   Allow fingerprint instead of PIN (Android 6.0+) ●

   | Yes | No |

   Disable app PIN when device PIN is managed ●

   | Yes | No |

Require corporate credentials for access ●

| Yes | No |

Set the sign-in security requirements for your access protection policy. Select a **Setting** and enter the **Value** that users must meet to sign in to your company app. Then select the **Action** you want to take if users do not meet your requirements. In some cases, multiple actions can be configured for a single setting. Learn more about conditional launch actions

SETTING	VALUE	ACTION	
Max PIN attempts	5	Reset PIN	...
Offline grace period	720	Block access (minutes)	...
Offline grace period	90	Wipe data (days)	...
Jailbroken/rooted devices		Block access	...
Select one ∨			

Figure 5-62. *Assigning device restrictions for MAM*

The final step is to assign all users to the device (see Figure 5-63).

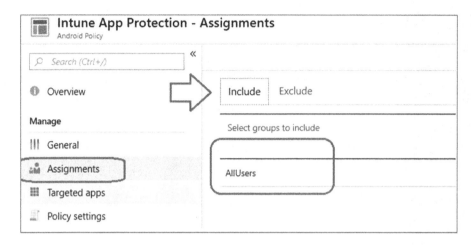

Figure 5-63. *Assigning a policy to the device*

Step 6: Set Up a Default Compliance Policy

One of the other policies we need to put in place is a default compliance policy. If the devices that are connected to our network meet certain criteria, we will make the devices compliant. You can expand on the policies and tighten them down based on your business criteria. Our goal at this point is to put in place a basic policy. To add the policy, go to Azure Active Directory, click "Conditional access," and add a new policy (see Figure 5-64).

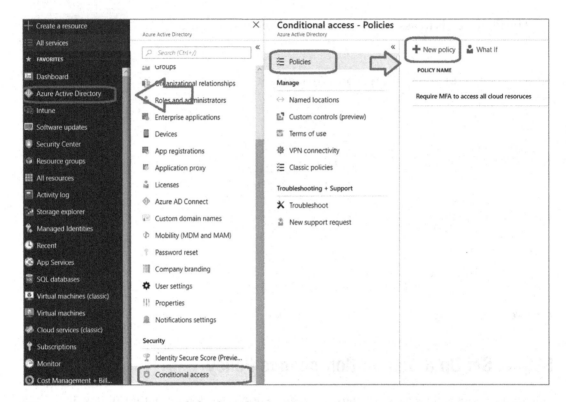

Figure 5-64. *Creating a default policy*

Policy 1: Set Up a Policy for All Users

Name the policy **Default Compliance Policy**, and select "All users." See Figure 5-65.

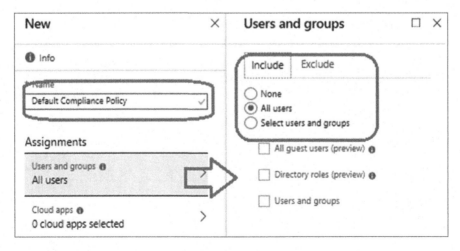

Figure 5-65. *Assigning the Default Client Policy to all users*

Policy 2: Assign the Applications for Access

Select "All cloud apps" and assign them to all cloud apps. Ignore the message shown in Figure 5-66.

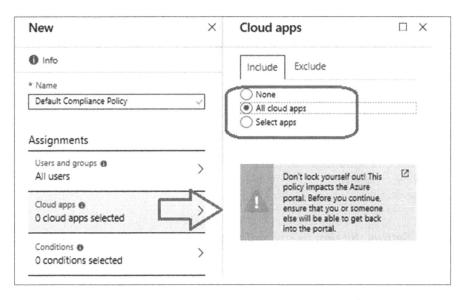

Figure 5-66. *Assigning the Cloud apps policy to all users*

Policy 3: Create the Conditions for the Compliance Status

Compliance is extremely important. If a device is marked non-compliant, then the device will not be able to access corporate resources. In this case, we are adding a compliance factor for risk level. Select Conditions, and we will define three different areas for compliance. These are the sign-in risk, the client apps, and the device state. You can add additional restrictions, but at this point, let's keep this simple and change them later. The goal is to force the clients to authenticate to our network. If they cannot authenticate, we will make them noncompliant. The criteria we are using are as follows:

- Sign-in risk is low (see Figure 5-67)

- Client applications used on network (see Figure 5-68)

- Set up the device state for cloud app security (see Figure 5-69)

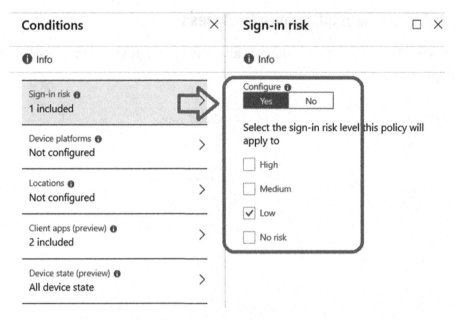

Figure 5-67. *Setting the sign in risk policy that applies to clients with low (and below) risk*

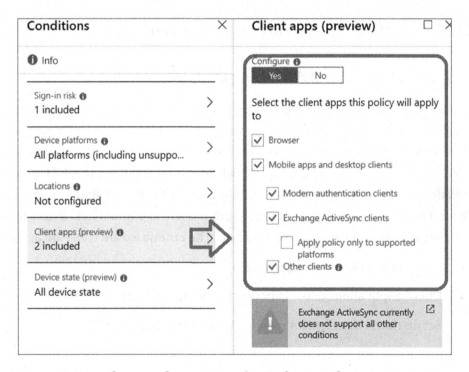

Figure 5-68. *Setting the compliance e-mail interface applications*

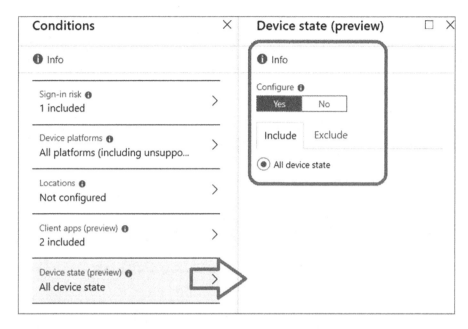

Figure 5-69. *Setting the device to save dates for Cloud App Security*

We will step through the configuration to set up the default compliance policy.

Policy 4: Set the Access Controls

At this stage, we are setting the access controls for the compliance. We are going to grant access based on the Microsoft application being used (see Figure 5-70).

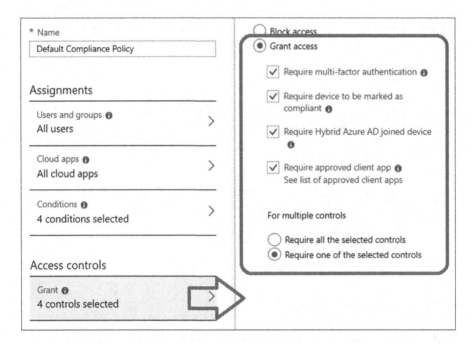

Figure 5-70. *Setting access controls for compliance*

Policy 5: Set the Session Controls

The final policy step is to set the session controls to use CAS. This is important because the data will be monitored in real time in CAS. We configured CAS in an earlier chapter. See Figure 5-71. CAS is used to generate systems alerts for security breaches.

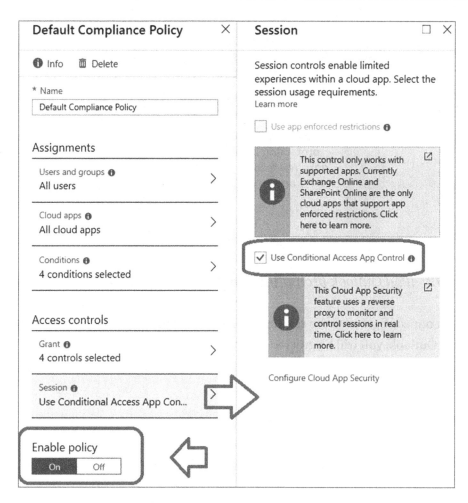

Figure 5-71. *Setting the real-time data recording in CAS*

Policy 5: Enable the Policy

To enable the policy, just click "Enable policy" and create the policy. See the status on the new policy. To see the impact to an organization, open Outlook on your iPad, and you will see the pop-up message requiring you to log out and log back into Outlook (see Figure 5-72).

Figure 5-72. *iPad Outlook prompting to restart application so it can be managed*

Also, in our configuration we set the requirement to use a six-digit PIN code. When you restart Outlook, you will be greeted with the requirement to enter a six-digit PIN (see Figure 5-73).

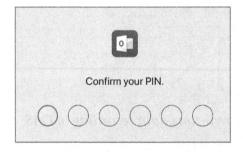

Figure 5-73. *Outlook requiring a six-digit PIN to access the company data (per policy)*

If you do not see this behavior, verify that the Company Portal application and the Microsoft Authenticator application has been installed on the mobile device. Android clients require the Company Portal (from the Google Play store) has been installed. iOS clients require Microsoft Authenticator application to be installed from Apple store.

The basic MAM and WIP management is complete. Now we need to expand our management with conditional access. Conditional access will only allow Microsoft applications to use the service and no longer allow data to be copied between third-party applications. This is how you block the email client on the device. All of the compliance regulations are requiring this feature to be deployed.

Step 7: Lock Down Access to Nonconditional Access

Currently, if you started the Apple e-mail, you would see that local e-mail is permitted to access company e-mail (see Figure 5-74). What we will do next is to block corporate data from being used by the native applications.

Figure 5-74. *Apple Mail client with app permitting access*

There are multiple ways to do block corporate data on mobile devices. The method I use is to set up a global condition that overrides all the other conditions for sharing e-mail information. To do this, we are going into Microsoft Intune; then we will click "Conditional access" and set the Exchange access policies through the Exchange Active Sync connector.

Policy 1: Enable the Exchange Active Sync Connector

In the Microsoft Intune "Conditional access" settings, click the Exchange Service connector and click Set up Service to Service Connector (see Figure 5-75). Once you click the service connector, it will take a few minutes to set up. When you see the setup notification, then click Full Sync (see Figure 5-76).

Figure 5-75. *Setting up Exchange service connector*

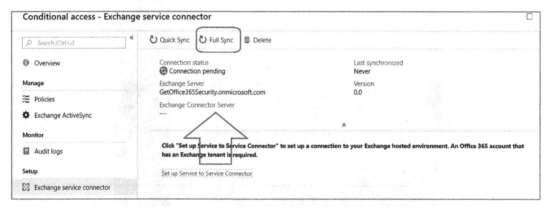

Figure 5-76. *Syncing the Exchange service connectors*

Refresh the browser, and the status will change to a connection status
(see Figure 5-77). At this point you are ready to block e-mail access to nonmanaged
e-mail clients. (When you refresh the browser, it will display on-premise; ignore this.)

On-premises access - Exchange ActiveSync connectors				
⊕ Overview	STATUS	ORGANIZATION NAME	CAS HOSTNAME	LAST SUCCESSFUL SYNC
Manage	⊕ Connection...		GetOffice365Securi...	
▓ Exchange on-premises access				

Figure 5-77. *Sync status with a valid connection to Office 365 Exchange*

Policy 2 : Set the Notification to the End User That E-mail Is Being Blocked

Click Microsoft Intune, click "Conditional access," and click Exchange Active Sync
(see Figure 5-78). We are going to add the notification to the users, followed by the
restrictions on using ActiveSync. Select user notification and the default configuration.

Figure 5-78. *Sync status with a valid connection to Office 365 Exchange*

We are adding a message for users to redirect them to `https://portal.manage.`
`microsoft.com` (also called the *Company Portal*). The is where the device can be
checked for compliance with Mobile Application and Device Management. Compliance
is critical for Mobile Device Management. The Company Portal will help to debug
compliance issues when a device is under management. If the user goes to this screen
at this stage, there will be no applications displayed because we are not deployed
MDM. The sample message is shown in Figure 5-79.

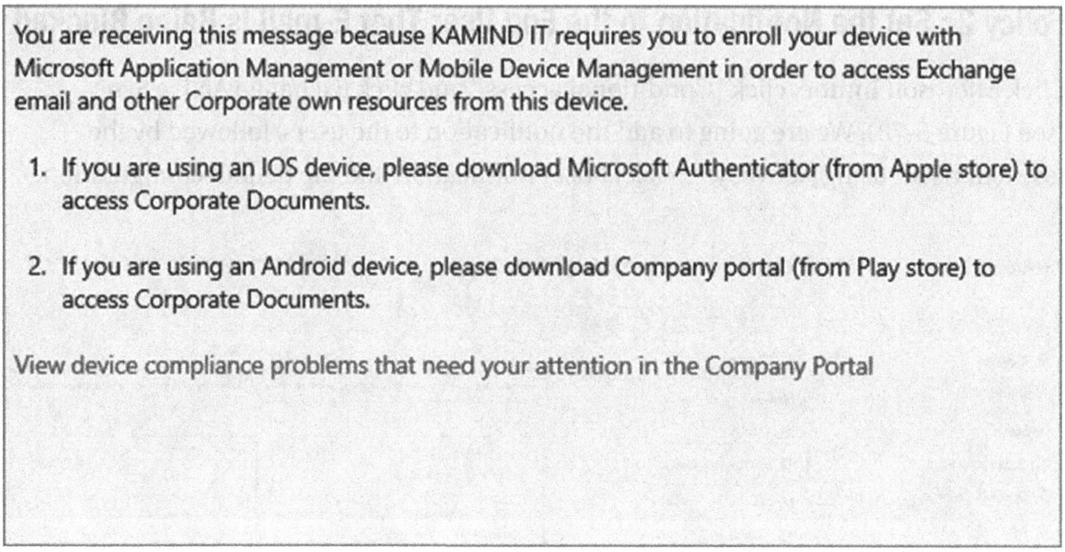

You are receiving this message because KAMIND IT requires you to enroll your device with Microsoft Application Management or Mobile Device Management in order to access Exchange email and other Corporate own resources from this device.

1. If you are using an IOS device, please download Microsoft Authenticator (from Apple store) to access Corporate Documents.

2. If you are using an Android device, please download Company portal (from Play store) to access Corporate Documents.

View device compliance problems that need your attention in the Company Portal

Figure 5-79. *Notification message for the user*

The message gets loaded in the configuration section. Note that we added information for Android devices and iOS devices. iOS requires that Authenticator application is installed (not necessarily running) and that the Company Portal is installed for Android devices (again not configured). These applications must be installed on the device for access to corporate data. See Figure 5-80.

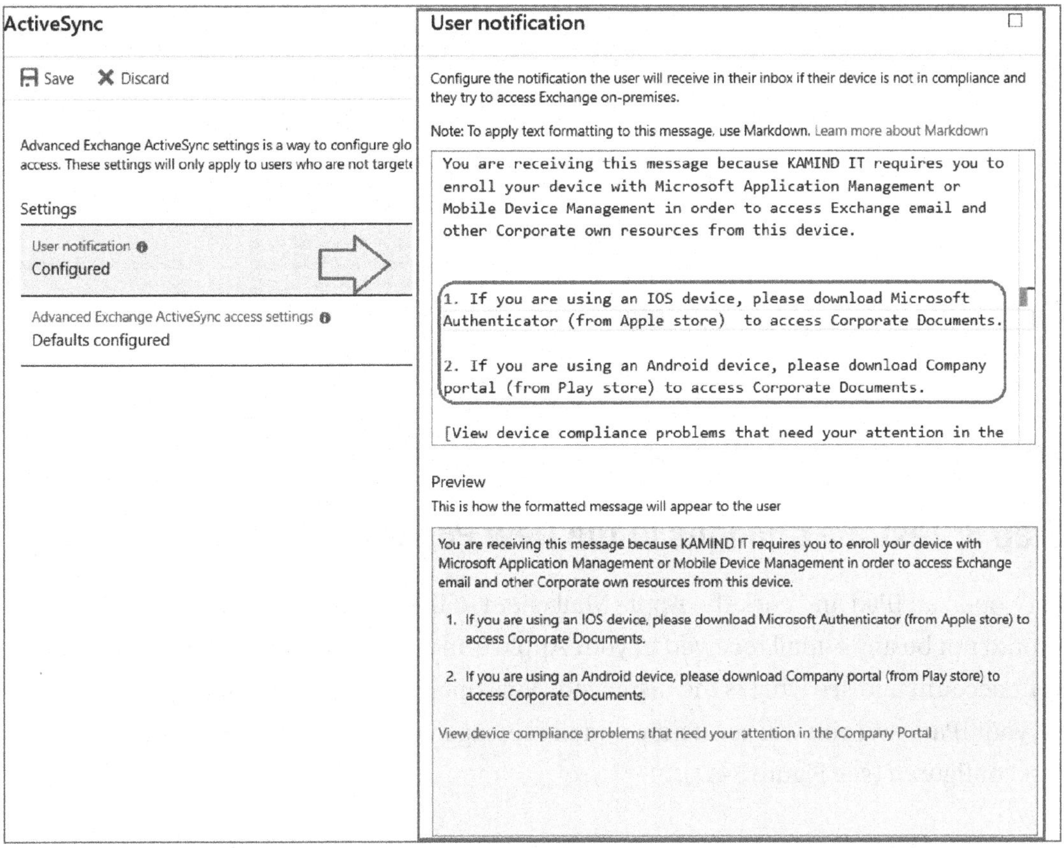

ActiveSync

🖫 Save   ✕ Discard

Advanced Exchange ActiveSync settings is a way to configure glo
access. These settings will only apply to users who are not target∈

Settings

User notification ⓘ
Configured

Advanced Exchange ActiveSync access settings ⓘ
Defaults configured

User notification   ☐

Configure the notification the user will receive in their inbox if their device is not in compliance and
they try to access Exchange on-premises.

Note: To apply text formatting to this message, use Markdown. Learn more about Markdown

You are receiving this message because KAMIND IT requires you to
enroll your device with Microsoft Application Management or
Mobile Device Management in order to access Exchange email and
other Corporate own resources from this device.

1. If you are using an IOS device, please download Microsoft
Authenticator (from Apple store) to access Corporate Documents.

2. If you are using an Android device, please download Company
portal (from Play store) to access Corporate Documents.

[View device compliance problems that need your attention in the

Preview
This is how the formatted message will appear to the user

You are receiving this message because KAMIND IT requires you to enroll your device with
Microsoft Application Management or Mobile Device Management in order to access Exchange
email and other Corporate own resources from this device.

1. If you are using an IOS device, please download Microsoft Authenticator (from Apple store) to
access Corporate Documents.

2. If you are using an Android device, please download Company portal (from Play store) to
access Corporate Documents.

View device compliance problems that need your attention in the Company Portal

Figure 5-80.   *Adding configuration messages for the user*

Policy 3: Block E-mail to Nonmanaged Devices

Once you have the policy in place, the next step is to determine the behavior for
nonmanaged applications when accessing e-mails. In this case, we are restricting e-mail
communications only to devices that have managed applications. This means that the
Apple Mail and Google Gmail clients (and any other third-party clients) will no longer
work on the devices that are subject to this mail policy.

The reason for this is to control data on the personal device. As a corporate
custodian, I need to be responsible for all the business information for any device that is
connected to my network. When an employee leaves, I must be able to remove corporate
data from the user device. All we are doing in this case is blocking the data so it is on
managed applications. See Figure 5-81.

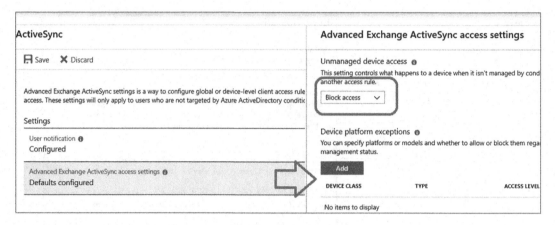

Figure 5-81. *Adding configuration messages for the user*

Step 8: Test the Changes in the New Policy

Let's open an iPad and click the Apple Mail client. If the policy is working correctly, there should not be any e-mail received in your Apple e-mail clients. Send a new test e-mail to your account and see what is the displayed. Now open the Outlook e-mail client that is on your iPad, and you will see a new e-mail message with the block notification that we just configured (see Figure 5-82).

From: Microsoft Outlook
Sent: Sunday, September 30, 2018 11:56:38 AM
To: Test User
Subject: Your mobile device has been denied access to the server because of server policies.

You are receiving this message because KAMIND IT requries you to enroll your device with Microsoft Application Management or Mobile Device Management in order to access Exchange email and other Corporate own resources from this device. [1. View device compliance problems that need your attention in the Company Portal](https://portal.manage.microsoft.com) [2. If you are using an IOS device, please download Microsoft Authenticator (from Apple store) to access Corporarte Documents. [3. If you are using an Android device, please download Company Portal (from play store) to access Corporate Documents.

Your device won't be able to synchronize with the server via Exchange ActiveSync because of an access policy defined on the server.

Information about your device:

Device model:	iPad6C11
Device type:	iPad

Figure 5-82. *Notification e-mail that the old e-mail clients are blocked*

At this point, all that is left to do is to complete the testing and apply the policies from the test user to all of the users. One note of caution: before you apply this company-wide, send out an e-mail notification to users that they are required to download the Outlook clients to the mobile device and that they will need to download the company portal (all Android devices) and Microsoft Authenticator (all iOS devices). Once these applications are in place, the company resources will be protected.

MAM and WIP Setup Is Complete

We have completed the MAM setup and WIP setup for Windows 10 devices and Android and iOS devices. We restricted data to these devices to our Office 365 tenant. This approach allows control over the company data on the user devices but does not give permission for the corporate entity to wipe the company device. If a device is compromised, we can wipe the data from the applications. In our MAM model, we disallowed data from being stored locally.

Once you move outside of applications management to device management, that is when you cross the line to Mobile Device Management. Mobile Device Management is a different configuration altogether and requires additional work to set up and configure the services. If you lay out the services correctly, MDM, WIP and MAM can co-exist with each other. Mobile Device Management will require us to use the Company Portal to manage the device. You can manage mobile phones to laptops (including Mac-based systems). Figure 5-83 shows the company portal with an MDM deployment. Notice that the MDM deployment verifies that the device hardware is compliant with the company policies. This is the topic we will discuss next. It is important that you have tested the MAM/WIP polices and have all the systems marked compliant. If your systems are not marked compliant, those devices will be blocked from accessing corporate resources.

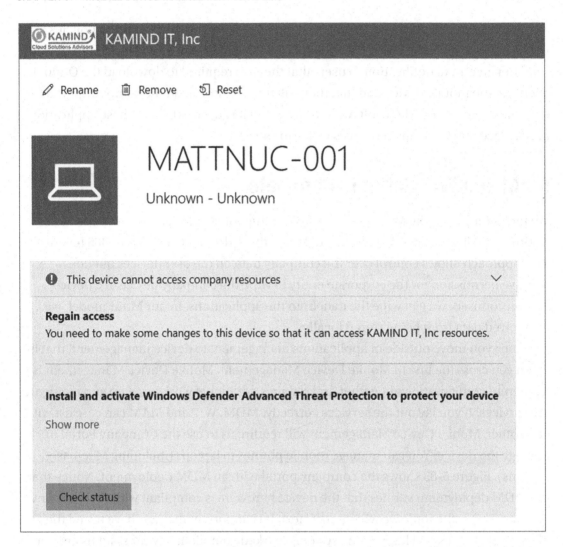

Figure 5-83. Company portal evaluation of a device under MDM

Compliant Intune Deployment: Mobile Device Management

Earlier, we completed the deployment of Mobile Application Management and we have deployed Windows Information Protection (WIP). At this point, you have managed your corporate data and access to personal devices. We have a set of policies around the operation of the devices that connect to our network. In this section, we will deploy a device-managed MDM. There are five different areas associated with MDM deployment in Microsoft Intune (Figure 5-84). These are device enrollment, device compliance, device configuration, mobile apps and conditional access. Earlier in our deployment of Mobile Application Management, we deployed only a basic set of applications on the device. We were restricted what applications we could deploy. As an example, we could not download additional applications for deployment such as the Salesforce applications or a new version of Waze for GPS directions. Another capability that we did not have is the ability to tightly manage the device.

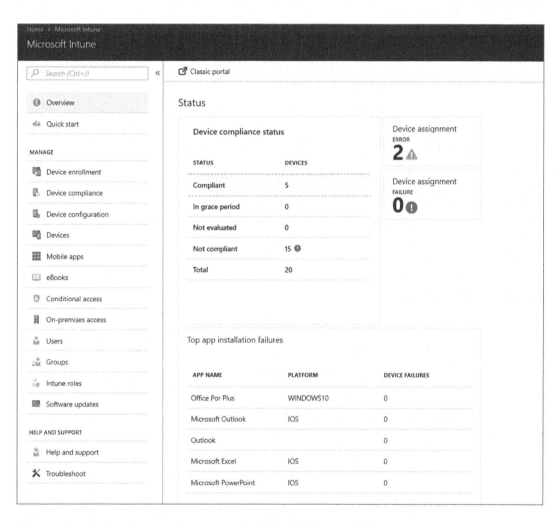

Figure 5-84. *Deploying Intune with full MDM capabilities*

When we integrate a full MDM deployment, we add the application management, conditional access, and full application management on the mobile device. MDM-deployed devices require that we deploy the Company Portal to the device so we can manage and deliver applications securely. The Company Portal is the management agent that is deployed on a managed mobile device (windows, IOS or Android) The Company Portal application can detect if a device is compliant and blocks the device from accessing corporate data. In this section, we will deploy Mobile Device Management in five areas.

- *Device Enrollment*: Setting up accounts in the manufacturer's online store

- *Device compliance*: Setting polices around devices for the management of our corporate data

- *Device configuration*: Setting up policies for device management

- *Mobile Apps*: Managing applications on the device

- *Conditional Access*: Controls on accessing corporate data on devices

A fully managed device means we need to set up and configure each of these areas against the corporate policy. Our objective is to set up an environment where you can have a fully managed device.

Device Enrollment

The first step to building a compliant Mobile Device Management deployment is to set up accounts in the two mobile device stores, Apple and Google. Enrolling in the stores allows you to download a trust certificate that you can use for the deployment of applications to the mobile device. Earlier in our simple deployment, we were deploying Mobile Application Management (MAM) and not Mobile Device Management. See Figure 5-85.

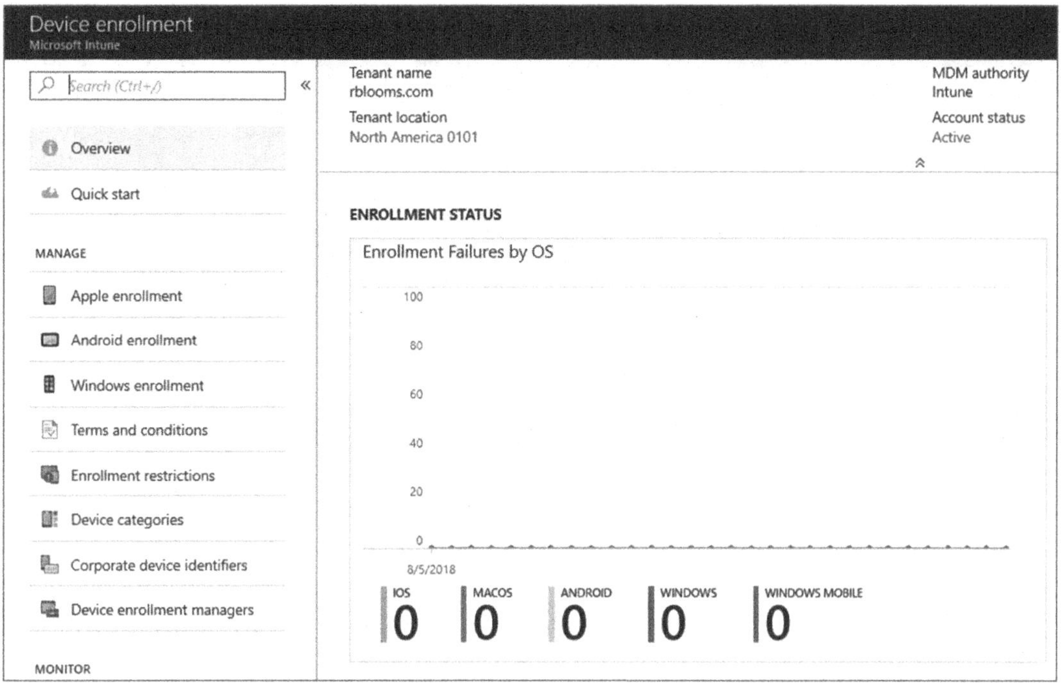

Figure 5-85. Device enrollment, starting at the top configuration

Application support on the mobile devices requires us to download the applications for us to manage them. For this to happen, we need to create accounts and download trust certificates to our Office 365/Azure tenant. The trust certificates allow us to change the mobile applications and push them out to the mobile devices that are controlled. Once we have set up the trust relationship to the iOS and the Android store accounts, we can push out the applications to the device. See Figure 5-86.

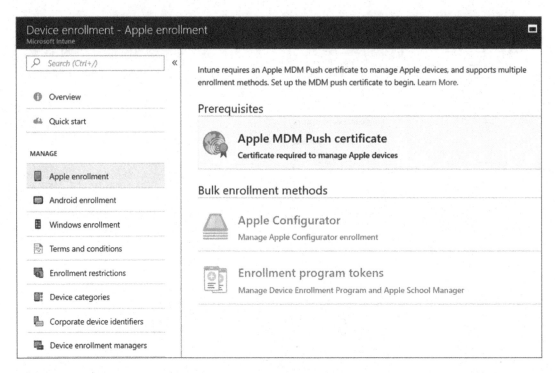

Figure 5-86. *Setting up the device enrollment*

Step 1: Sign Up for an Apple Push Certificate

Click the Apple push certificate and follow the wizard to set up a business ID with Apple. The process is straightforward; you need to create an Apple ID (go to https://appleid. apple.com) that you will use to manage your certificates and portal access. Once you have created the Apple ID, then complete the following steps (see Figure 5-87):

1. Grant Microsoft access to send user and device information to Apple.

2. Download the Apple certificate (you will upload this to Intune in step 4).

3. Enter in your Apple ID so Microsoft can sync data with Apple.

4. Upload the MDM push certificate you received from Apple.

Once you have completed the upload, the status will change from not set up to set up.

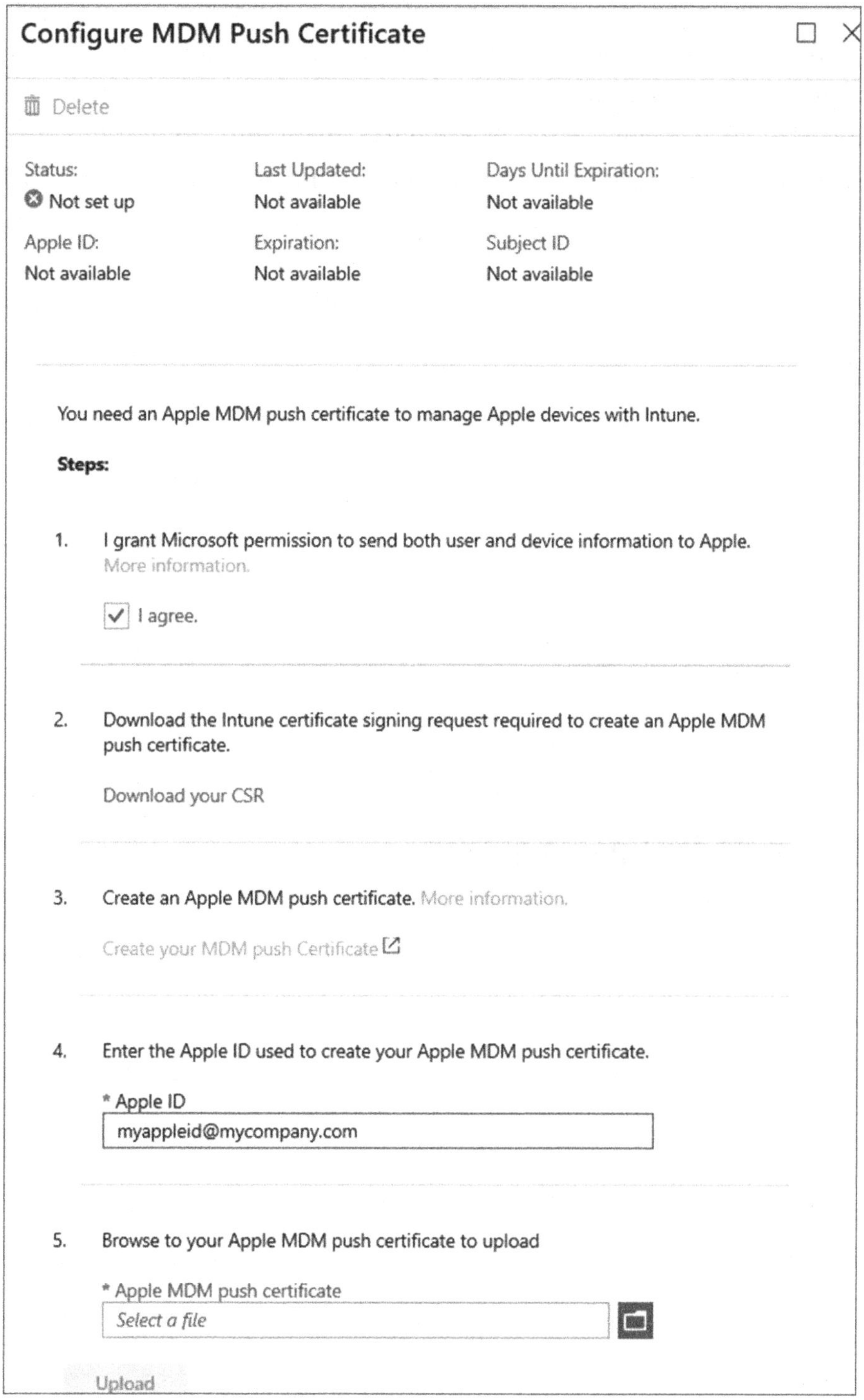

Configure MDM Push Certificate   □   ✕

🗑 Delete

Status: Last Updated: Days Until Expiration:
❌ Not set up   Not available   Not available

Apple ID: Expiration: Subject ID
Not available   Not available   Not available

You need an Apple MDM push certificate to manage Apple devices with Intune.

Steps:

1.   I grant Microsoft permission to send both user and device information to Apple.
     More information.

     ☑ I agree.

2.   Download the Intune certificate signing request required to create an Apple MDM
     push certificate.

     Download your CSR

3.   Create an Apple MDM push certificate. More information.

     Create your MDM push Certificate ↗

4.   Enter the Apple ID used to create your Apple MDM push certificate.

     * Apple ID
     myappleid@mycompany.com

5.   Browse to your Apple MDM push certificate to upload

     * Apple MDM push certificate
     Select a file   🗀

     Upload

Figure 5-87. *Setting up the Apple connection*

Once you have linked Apple and Microsoft Intune, the status will change (see Figure 5-88). At this point, you can access applications from the Apple store and enable applications to be used in your MDM deployment. Once you have a valid certificate installed, you can use the additional configuration options that Apple provides. We are not going to focus on these additional options, rather on the basic MDM deployment.

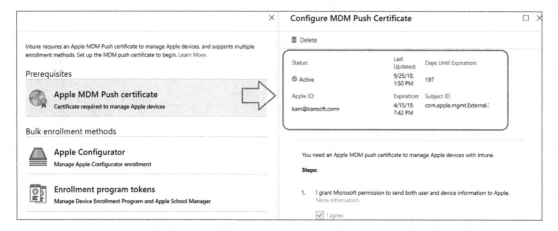

Figure 5-88. Apple ID successfully installed

Step 2: Sign Up for Google at Work

Google has a similar process to Apple. You need to create a Google Gmail account and use that account to manage your Android enrollments. Once the setup is complete, you can configure apps. See Figure 5-89.

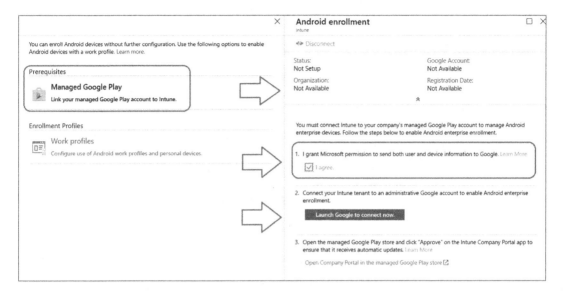

Figure 5-89. *Setting up a Google ID for store access*

When you launch Google to connect, you will connect to the Bring Android to Work site. Like with Apple, you will need to set up a Google ID for accessing data from the Android environment (see Figure 5-90). Be advised that when you sign up for a new Google account, you will be required to enter the GDPR information, such as the data protection officer (DPO) on your Bring Android to Work account. See Figure 5-91.

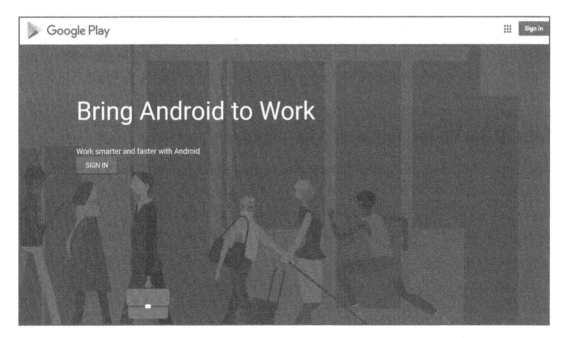

Figure 5-90. *Setting up the Bring Android to Work account*

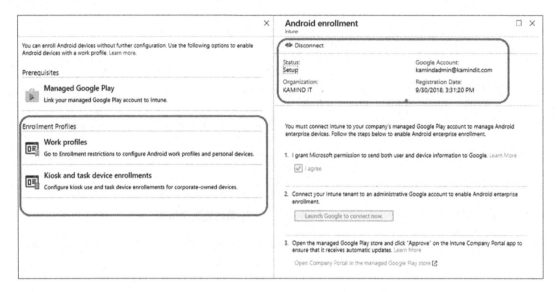

Figure 5-91. *Valid Google account setup*

Once you have completed the Google account setup, you can define the work profile and enrollment restrictions. Likewise, you can restrict user devices. We will not be using these configurations, so leave them at the default settings.

Step 3: Set Up Windows Enrollment

We will use all of the default settings for the Windows enrollment. Earlier in this chapter, we verified the cnames for the Intune portal on device registration. No changes are required at this time because we have already completed all the work in this section for our deployment.

Step 4: Set Up the Terms and Conditions

The terms and conditions should reflect your company policies and what is in your employee handbooks. Typically, these terms and conditions should match your organization's policies. As an example, our terms and conditions are listed in Figure 5-92. After you accept your terms and condition, verify that you assign them to all users.

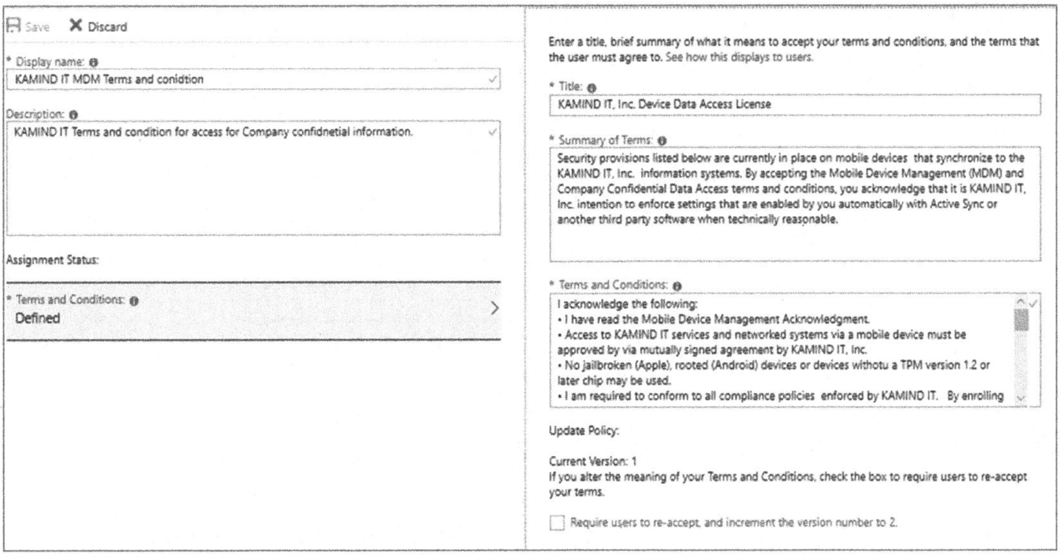

Figure 5-92. *Terms and conditions at KAMIND IT*

After you have completed these steps, you have set up the device enrollment. The next step is to set up the polices for device compliance.

Device Compliance

Device compliance consists of the rules and polices that you want to have deployed in your organization. These rules and policies may be driven internally or through an external organization. The point is that these policies for compliance are driven by the organization for some business need. When we look at Mobile Device Management, we are configuring hardware to meet compliance requirements. When we look at Mobile Application Management (MAM), we have the same goals, but we can configure only the software. MDM allows us to do both. To configure device compliance, you configure policies to manage the hardware deployment. In our case, we are deploying different policies for device management (see Figure 5-93), one policy for each type of device that we are managing.

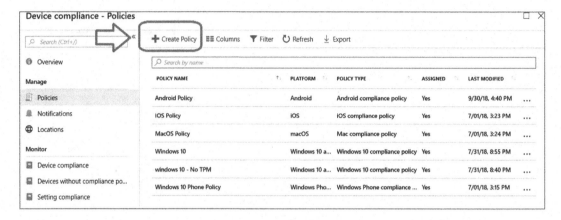

Figure 5-93. *Different device policies*

The device policies can be extremely complex depending on your business needs. Let's start the process.

Step 1: Create a New iOS Policy

Click Create Policy. We will click an iOS device and set up some minimum requirements for the iOS device. In our case, we will require that the password to unlock the device is six characters, and we will block simple passwords (like 123456). Create the policy similar to Figure 5-94.

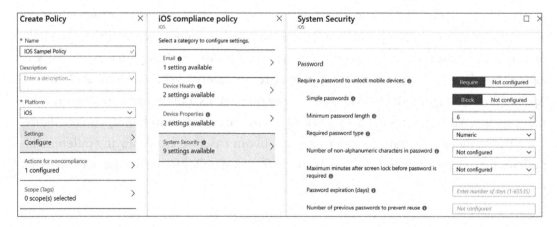

Figure 5-94. *Creating a new iOS policy*

After we have set the base set of parameters, click OK and then Create. This will create a new iOS policy. Our policy is a simple policy and requires a password on the iOS device.

Step 2: Assign the Test User Account to the Policy

After we create the test policy, we need to assign a test user. We need to assign one based on the security groups. If you have not created a test security group, do so at this time and assign the test user to that security group. In our case we created a test group called MDM Test Group and assigned our test user to this group (see Figure 5-95).

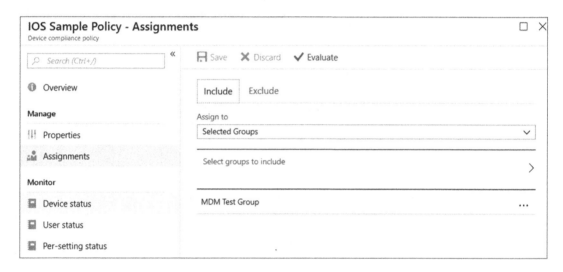

Figure 5-95. *Assigning a test user to a iOS policy*

Step 3: Create the Three Other Policy Groups and Assign the Test User Group

Follow the same process and select four additional policies. If you want to set a policy, then set it. I chose iOS because it is easy to see the deployment. The key to setting policies is that Intune is smart enough to determine what policies apply to which devices. Your objective is to make all devices compliant. To make all devices compliant, you need to cover your bases (as they say) and deploy all policies against the same group. The policies you need to create are as follows:

- Android

- iOS

- Windows 10

- macOS

After you complete the policy deployment and the device is enrolled (we are not at that stage), you should see something like Figure 5-96. In this case, I have six devices in my test group, and only one device (the iPad) is compliant (as I would have expected). For the other five devices, the iOS policy does not apply.

Figure 5-96.   *Policy data overview*

Step 4: Set Up the Compliance Policy

As you deploy your policy, you will have a situation where devices that do not have a compliance policy are set to compliant. See Figure 5-97.

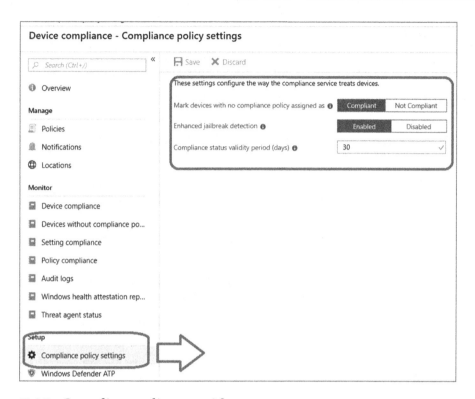

Figure 5-97. Compliant policy override

That is all we need to do at this stage. The next step is the device configuration.

Device Configuration

We have already deployed some policies in the device configuration. One of the policies we deployed is OMA_URI for the Windows 10 commercial ID deployment. We completed this in an earlier chapter. Device configuration is the hardware configuration that you want to have in your MDM policy to be deployed on the devices. In our case, we already deployed the Windows 10 commercial ID. In Figure 5-98, we have a Windows 10 deployment profile. In this case, we can click the different deployment models that we want to follow. As an example, if you click Windows 10 and "Device restrictions," then select that option so you can deploy restrictions on the Windows 10 devices.

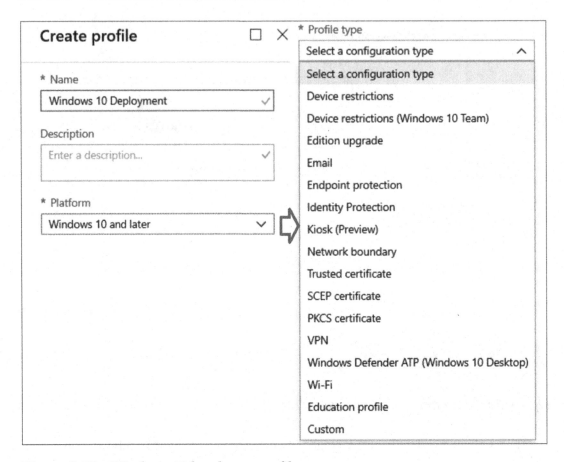

Figure 5-98. *Windows 10 hardware profile*

You will have a complex profile that allows you to set all of the hardware parameters associated with the Windows 10 device (see Figure 5-99). I wanted you to see the options that are available to you. At this time we have only one policy deployed, and that is the commercial ID that we deployed in a previous chapter.

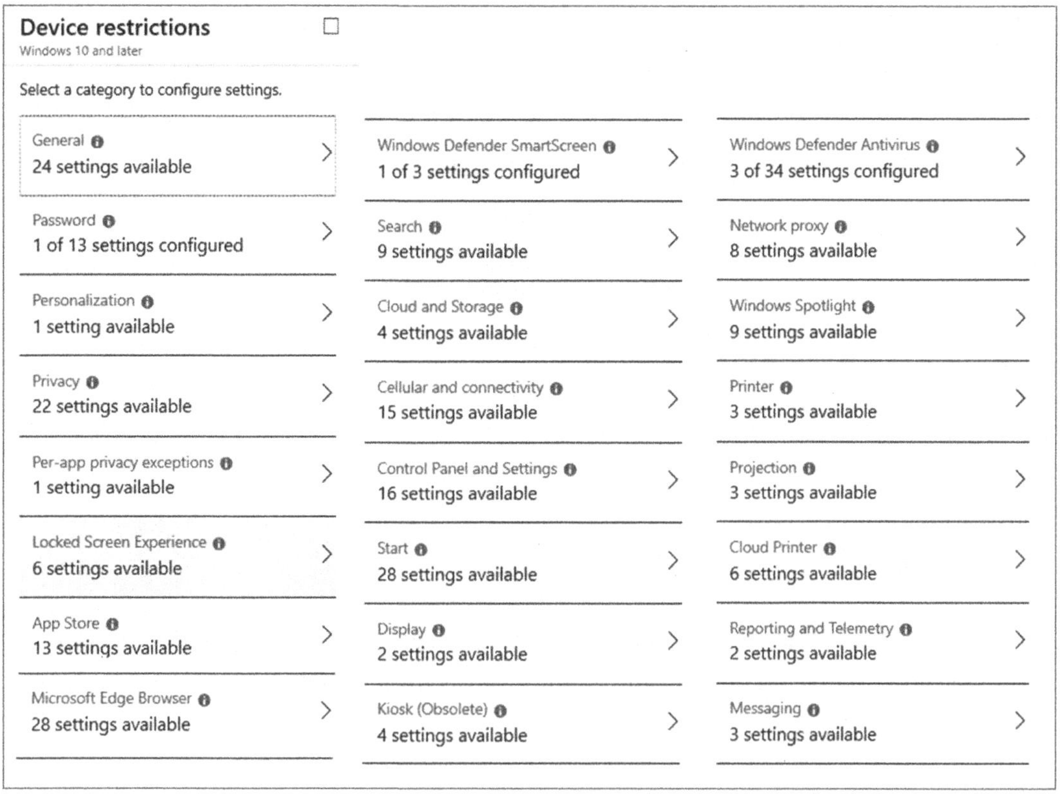

Device restrictions ☐ Windows 10 and later		
Select a category to configure settings.		
General ❶ 24 settings available ⟩	Windows Defender SmartScreen ❶ 1 of 3 settings configured ⟩	Windows Defender Antivirus ❶ 3 of 34 settings configured ⟩
Password ❶ 1 of 13 settings configured ⟩	Search ❶ 9 settings available ⟩	Network proxy ❶ 8 settings available ⟩
Personalization ❶ 1 setting available ⟩	Cloud and Storage ❶ 4 settings available ⟩	Windows Spotlight ❶ 9 settings available ⟩
Privacy ❶ 22 settings available ⟩	Cellular and connectivity ❶ 15 settings available ⟩	Printer ❶ 3 settings available ⟩
Per-app privacy exceptions ❶ 1 setting available ⟩	Control Panel and Settings ❶ 16 settings available ⟩	Projection ❶ 3 settings available ⟩
Locked Screen Experience ❶ 6 settings available ⟩	Start ❶ 28 settings available ⟩	Cloud Printer ❶ 6 settings available ⟩
App Store ❶ 13 settings available ⟩	Display ❶ 2 settings available ⟩	Reporting and Telemetry ❶ 2 settings available ⟩
Microsoft Edge Browser ❶ 28 settings available ⟩	Kiosk (Obsolete) ❶ 4 settings available ⟩	Messaging ❶ 3 settings available ⟩

Figure 5-99. *Windows 10 device restriction options*

Verify that you have deployed the commercial ID. If this not deployed, return to Chapter 2 and review the Log Analytics instructions where we deployed the commercial ID.

Devices

Select Intune then Devices to see the status of the deployment. The only actions we can do on devices is to set up remote support via Team Viewer Connector and the devices cleanup rules. I will not describe Team Viewer here; there are different philosophies on what tools to use for remote support. However, the one device policy that needs to be configured is for cleanup rules on old devices. Be careful with this; this will remove the device from Intune management.

In our case, we will create a policy that remove devices after 180 days from Intune management (see Figure 5-100). This policy is for all devices. When I mark this policy with the deletion option, make sure you copy bitlocker keys for the Windows 10 devices and archive the keys. The BitLocker key for the Azure join system is in Azure Active Directory under the device name.

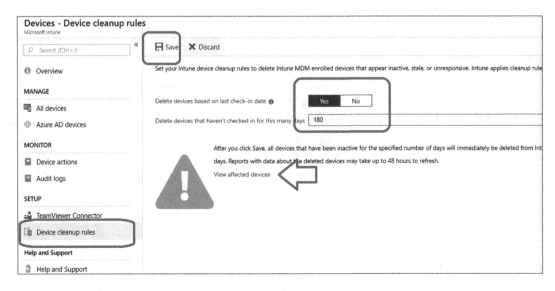

Figure 5-100. *Setting system expiration date*

That is all the configuration that we do with devices. Figure 5-101 shows the status of our enrollment. As you deploy additional systems under MDM, you can see the status displayed under the Device category.

Figure 5-101. *Status of the latest device enrollment*

Client Apps

Earlier we enrolled in the Apple Store and the Google Play store. The enrollment was necessary so we have access to the client apps that we can download and deploy via the Company Portal. What is different with MDM is that we deploy a management policy against the device. The Company Portal is the management agent on the device. The management agent implements the management policy and the agent writes to the device registries if needed. The management agent deploys all the applications to the device. In our MAM world, we are managing applications and not devices. This is the fundamental difference between MAM and MDM.

There are three categories of application deployment: apps, app configuration policies, and app protection policies. When we deployed the MAM deployment, we used the app protection policies. Those policies are in place for the MDM solution that we define. This is why we deploy MAM policies first, and MDM policies second.

App configuration policies are used to customize an application. As an example, if you are deploying a configuration for an app, you need to customize the configuration from the Intune SDK. Configuration policies are available for iOS and Android apps. This setting allows an app to be customized for deployment. The configuration policies are used when a app checks them, usually the first time the app is run. You can configure apps either as a managed device implementation or as a managed app implementation. The best way to look at the capabilities of customizing an app is through the Intune SDK. This is beyond the scope of this chapter.

App protection policies are used to customize the behavior of an application as a managed app with restrictions on what the app can or cannot do. As an example, Microsoft apps can be restricted to handle information to/from the managed applications. This means a user cannot cut data and place the data into nonmanaged applications. This implementation is required for compliance management, and we discuss this in the MAM section. We will not be making any changes for our MDM deployment.

Apps are applications that are downloaded from the various online stores (Apple, Google Play, and Microsoft) and are enabled for deployment to the device under MDM. When we created device enrollment earlier, we created links to download the different applications for deployment. This is the focus of the deployment in this section.

How Are Apps Deployed to Devices?

Before we jump into the app deployment, let's look at the process for MDM deployment. MDM is different than a MAM deployment. MAM deployment is managing applications on the device. The MDM deployment will set up the device as a managed device. The process of enrolling a device in Mobile Device Management follows theses three steps:

1. Deploy the company portal from the device store.

2. Log into the company portal with your Office 365 account and accept the terms and conditions.

3. Install the apps that are permitted by your company to run on your device.

This is how devices are managed under MDM. To get started, we need to install the applications for the device into the Company Portal. The user will start up the Company Portal on the device and install approved applications to the device. This is why it is necessary to make sure the devices that are used are compliant before you deploy MDM. The Company Portal application will check for compliance and block application deployment and users access to corporate data on non compliant devices.

Making Android Apps Available

Before we start to load apps, there is a special Android app configuration that we must complete. We need to select the Android apps from the Google Play store to be able to download them to our MDM devices. In Figure 5-102, click "Client apps" and then Google Play. You log into the Google Play store and select the apps that you want to deploy; once you selected all of the apps, then you click Sync.

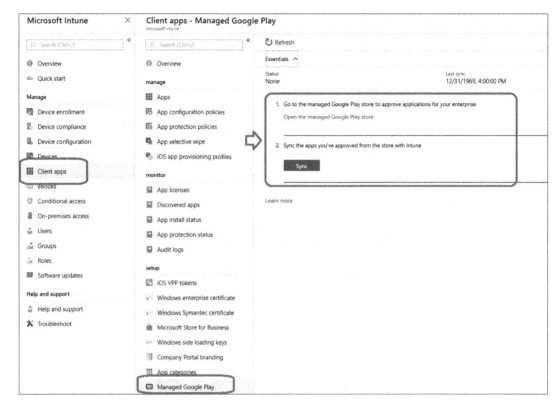

Figure 5-102. *Syncing Android apps for MDM deployment*

The process is a little bit tedious for Android. You need to select each app and approve them for download, one at a time. (see Figure 5-103). After you select the apps, then you sync them.

Figure 5-103. *Approve cycle for Android apps*

The process is straightforward:

1. Log in to the Google Play store with the login you created earlier.

2. Select the apps that you want to enable.

3. Sync the apps to the Intune MDM platform.

Once you complete this, the only step left is to configure the apps for the Company Portal. At this time, complete these steps for Android and sync the apps so we can configure them for the company portal and MDM deployment. After you click Sync, the dashboard will update the status.

Load Apps for the Company Portal Management

To load apps, click App. You will notice that the apps that are available are already displayed. There may be Android apps present but no iOS apps. To add the iOS or Windows apps, follow the steps outlined next.

Click Add (see Figure 5-104).

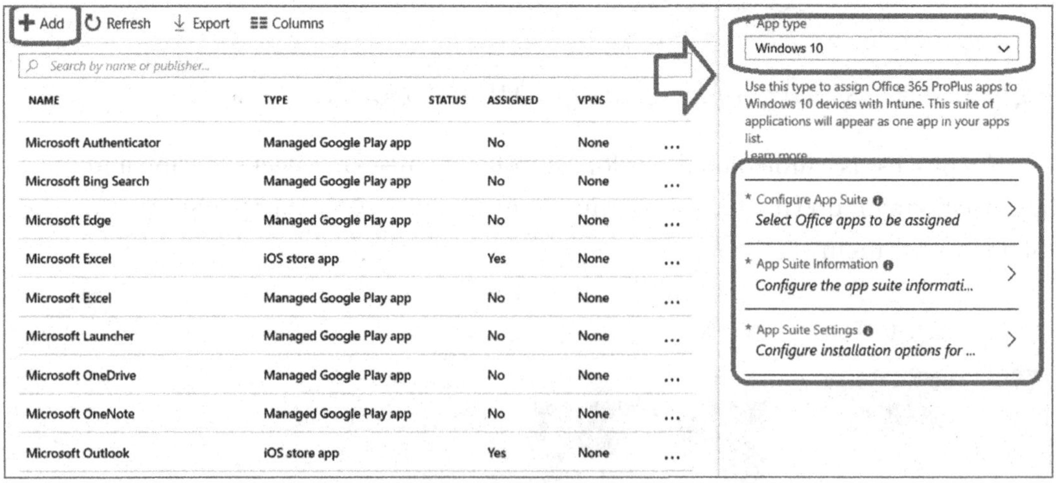

Figure 5-104. *Adding apps to the company portal*

You repeat the process to add all of the apps to the company portal. When you add an app, pay attention to the app characteristics. Make sure you set the updates (if available) and you select to display the application in the company portal. This will allow the end user to see the availability of the apps in the company portal and how the apps interact with each other.

In our MAM deployment, we define the apps as a managed app. This means that the apps cannot share data with third-party apps; they can only share data with managed apps approved by the company. The MDM deployment uses the MAM app condition access configuration as part of the deployment.

The final step in the app configuration is to make sure the apps are assigned. In Figure 5-105, we show how to assign an app. If an app is not assigned, it cannot be downloaded to the company portal and used.

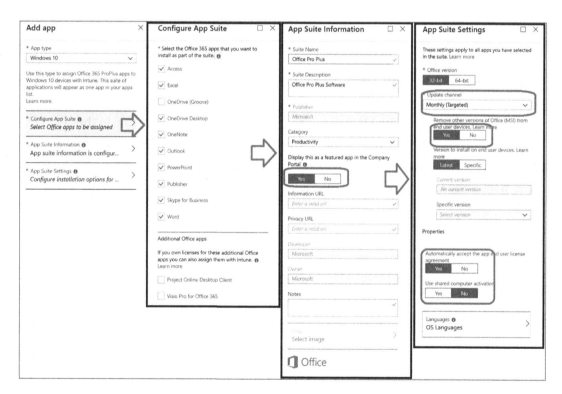

Figure 5-105. *Adding an app to the portal*

When you click an app (see Figure 5-106), you must do the following to make the app available for distributions:

1. Click Assignment; then click "Add group."

2. Click the drop-down to make the group available for all devices.

3. Select the included groups and click Yes for all enrolled devices.

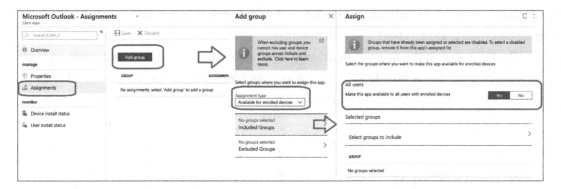

Figure 5-106. *Outlook configuration data for adding to the portal*

Perform these steps with all the apps that you want to make available in the Company Portal. After you are completed, the client apps should display Yes for an assignment. Review the apps that display No, and go back and assign the app or remove the app from the Company Portal (see Figure 5-107).

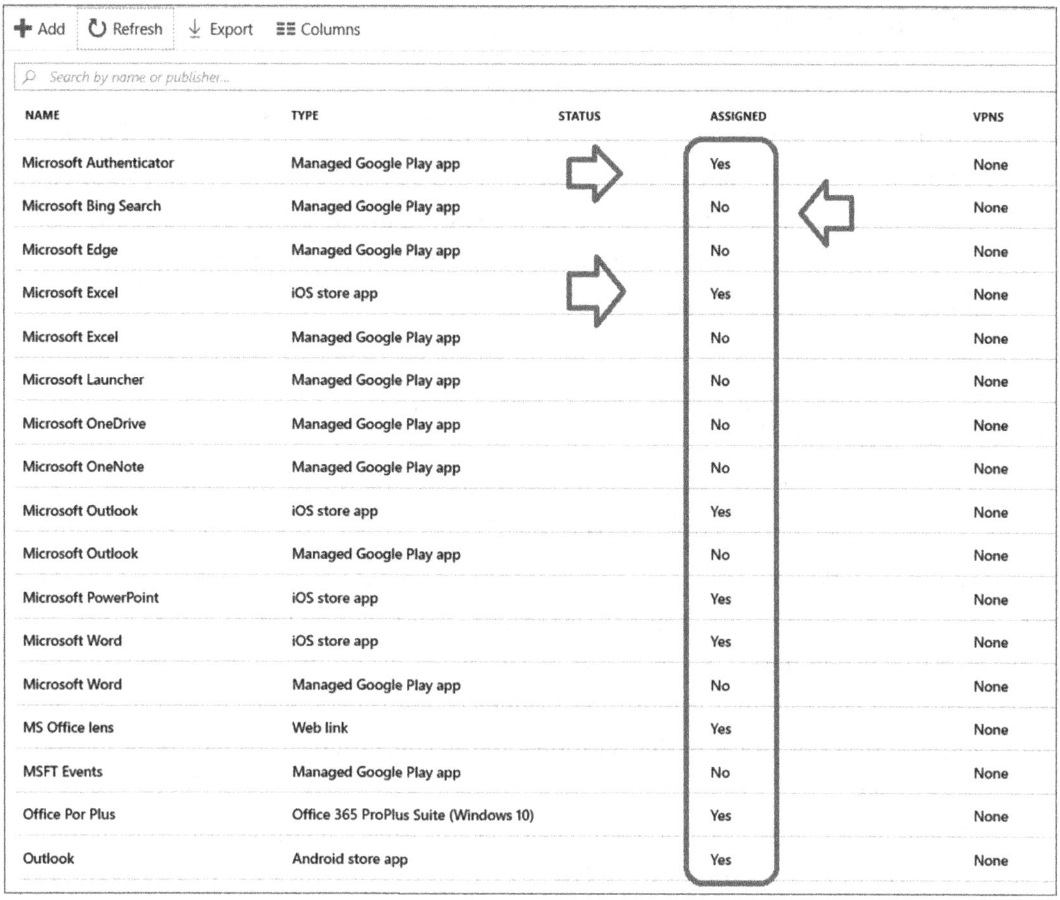

NAME	TYPE	STATUS	ASSIGNED	VPNS
Microsoft Authenticator	Managed Google Play app		Yes	None
Microsoft Bing Search	Managed Google Play app		No	None
Microsoft Edge	Managed Google Play app		No	None
Microsoft Excel	iOS store app		Yes	None
Microsoft Excel	Managed Google Play app		No	None
Microsoft Launcher	Managed Google Play app		No	None
Microsoft OneDrive	Managed Google Play app		No	None
Microsoft OneNote	Managed Google Play app		No	None
Microsoft Outlook	iOS store app		Yes	None
Microsoft Outlook	Managed Google Play app		No	None
Microsoft PowerPoint	iOS store app		Yes	None
Microsoft Word	iOS store app		Yes	None
Microsoft Word	Managed Google Play app		No	None
MS Office lens	Web link		Yes	None
MSFT Events	Managed Google Play app		No	None
Office Por Plus	Office 365 ProPlus Suite (Windows 10)		Yes	None
Outlook	Android store app		Yes	None

Figure 5-107. *Assigning the app to the company portal for accessing the client*

Conditional Access

Conditional access is used to restrict applications that are not approved to access corporate data from accessing corporate data. A good example is using your third-party mail applications to access corporate data versus the approved managed applications. This access enables data loss on the device. You should not need to make any changes here. The settings that we deployed for MAM and MFA are all that are needed for our MDM deployment.

MDM Setup Is Complete

We are now ready to test. What is the best way to test? Grab a new laptop or iPad, load the Company Portal, and log in with your work e-mail address. The Company Portal will tell you what needs to be fixed on the device and will attempt to fix it. What is happening is that the Company Portal is making the device compliant based on the standard that you have deployed. Continue testing your deployment. It is important that you get this right before you deploy to all of the clients at large.

Deploying MDM

In our MAM deployment, the final step was to make sure that we had a fully compliant system before we started to deploy MDM. We have taken a slower approach on the deployment of MDM with test groups to ensure that we didn't create a situation where the users are locked out of accessing the corporate resources on Office 365 and Azure. To make sure that we deploy MDM successfully, we used test groups. At this point, we are making one last check with our Windows 10 devices before going live in a production environment. After you are sure the Windows 10 devices deploy correctly, then deploy iOS and Android.

Once you have configured and tested the iOS and Android configuration, you need to test in the production environment. The MDM/MAM configuration discussed in this section makes the following assumptions:

1. You have fully deployed a MAM configuration.

2. You have deployed MDM in a test group model.

3. The Windows 10 and Mac desktops/laptops are compliant devices.

4. Windows 10 devices need to be running version 1809 or later.

See Figure 5-108.

Figure 5-108. *Device compliance policies in place prior to deployment*

The common mistake that is made is that the desktop systems have not been verified with the Company Portal application and are not compliant before the MDM services are deployed to the users. What causes this is the conditional access policies. For the conditional access policies to work correctly, the Windows and Mac desktop clients must be compliant. If you do not have desktop systems that are compliant, then the mobile policy may work on the mobile devices, but the desktop will not work. When a noncompliant policy is deployed, the user will be unable to access corporate resources on Office 365 and Azure services from the desktop and web applications on their workstations. Deployment of the Company Portal is mandatory. If you are not using Group Policy to push changes, you can use the Company Portal (the downloaded application from the Microsoft store) to identify problems and make changes and to bring the desktop/laptop systems into compliance.

Microsoft has supplied an end-user Company Portal for the deployment of the Intune MDM/MAM solutions to user desktops, available from the Apple store and Google Play store. Accessing the Company Portal is easy; go to the Microsoft store (or Apple or Google Play) and search for *Company Portal.* You download the application to the system and install the software. If you are using a Windows 10 system or Mac, make sure you pin this to your Start menu or Finder (see Figure 5-109).

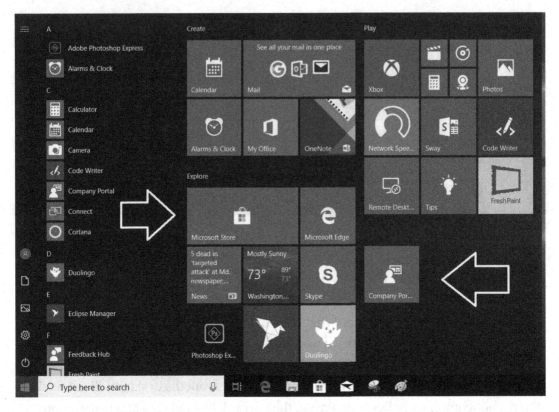

Figure 5-109. *Accessing the company portal*

The steps are easy for the end user.

1. Add the user to the Windows 10 (or MAC) MDM group (discussed earlier).

2. Download the company portal from the Microsoft store, and run the application.

3. Log in with the company credentials and accept the corporation's terms and conditions.

4. Follow the steps outlined in the application to make the system compliant.

The steps walk the end user through the configuration. Once the end user has deployed the Company Portal, the managed applications will work as expected. In Figure 5-110, the Company Portal was deployed, and the system that it was deployed on is not compliant. To make a system compliant, expand the item in question and click "Check status" (see Figure 5-111).

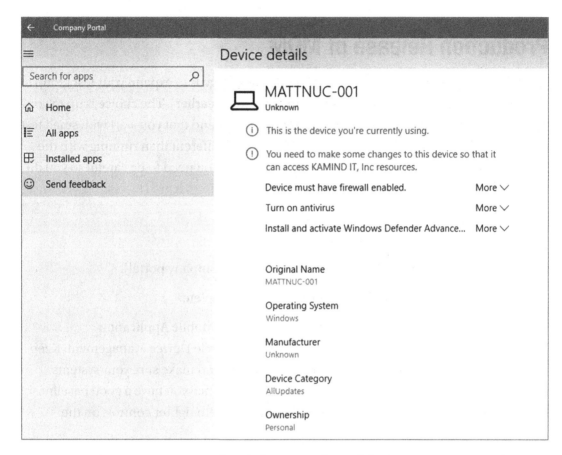

Figure 5-110. *Company portal, validating node and finding it is not compliant*

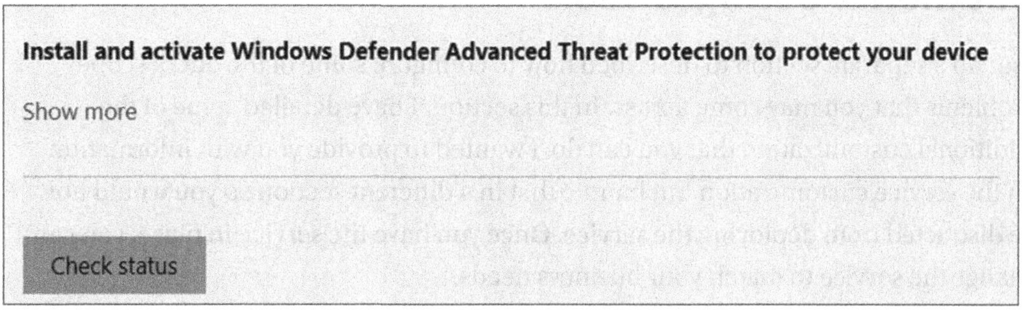

Figure 5-111. *Company portal, expanding the area in question to determine current status*

That is all there is to do with the company portal. This is useful when you are troubleshooting an MDM solution that is deployed on a client, either remotely or on-site.

Production Release of MDM

All of the hard work is done. All that is needed at this stage is to expand your test group to all users (or to use the different dynamic groups created earlier). The choice is up to you on what is the best type of rollout. On MDM we recommend that you start with small test groups and slowly expand the test group. MDM is a lot different than running with the MAM solution. MDM requires control of the hardware. You need to be careful so you do not block users from accessing corporate resources.

These are the next steps:

1. Add additional users to test groups.

2. Verify connectivity and compliance (use the company portal).

3. Deploy to the organization once testing is complete.

At this point you have completed the deployment of Mobile Application Management, Windows Information Protection and Mobile Device Management. Keep in mind that it is best to deploy the basic infrastructure and make sure your systems are marked compliant before you start a MDM rollout. Once you have a good baseline deployed, then you can expand the MDM deployment with tighter controls on the devices.

Additional Configuration

I set up a separate section to described how to configure some of the out of scope problems that you may come across. In this section, I have detailed some of the additional customization that you can do. I wanted to provide you with information on the service customization but handle that in a different section so you would not be distracted from deploying the service. Once you have the service in place, you can change the service to match your business needs.

Using Dynamics Groups

You have new users who constantly bring devices to your network, and you are trying to manage those devices. Do you individually create groups for management and manually move users to those groups, or do you use dynamic groups for managing devices? The correct answer is that you use dynamic groups for the management of the devices and users. The reason for this is simple; you have better control of the mobile device policies as devices are added in your network. See Figure 5-112.

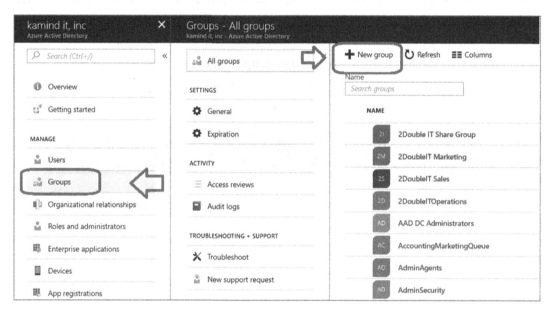

Figure 5-112. *Azure Active Directory*

Most organizations have some type of functional structure in place; in our case we have the engineering, sales, marketing, security, and service departments. Looking at the device types in the organization, we have Android devices, iOS devices (phones and iPads), Windows 10 devices, and unknown devices. Instead of manually adding the groups, we are going to set up the groups for dynamic enrollment. The initial policy we are using will be simple, but you will be able to use this model and expand the group model based on your business needs. In our case, we are setting up the dynamic enrollment for the management of our environment. We will walk through the process of creating dynamic enrollment groups for devices and users for our iOS group and for our service group. You can repeat this process for the organization as needed for other devices and users.

Step 1: Set Up a Dynamic Device Group: iOS

Go to https://portal.azure.com, select the group, and add a new group called MDM iOS Devices Staff. In our organization we have two classes of iOS users - Staff and Management. The capabilities are different, and the controls are different. That is why we set up two different groups, in addition to our test group (non-dynamic group). This allows us to manage our compliance requirements.

The groups are set up as dynamic groups. Looking at Figure 5-113, we have made a decision on the characteristics of the device that we want to use for device auto selection. In this case, we are looking for all devices that are iPhone devices. The expression that is used to find the devices is device.deviceOSType -contains "iPhone" or device.deviceOSType -contains "iOS". You can look up the device parameters, but typically they are iOS, iPhone, Windows, Android, or Other. See Figure 5-114.

Figure 5-113. *Setting up dynamic groups for iOS*

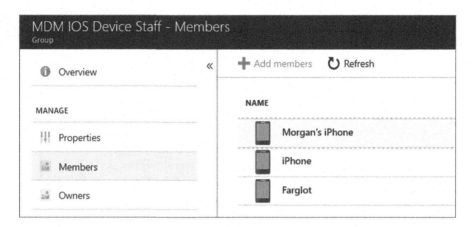

Figure 5-114. *Devices detected in our iPhone search in Azure AD*

Step 2: Set Up a Dynamic User Group: Service

When we add a new user in our organization, we add attribute information about the user. In this case, we assigned the user to a department (service, security, engineering, sales, marketing, or executive). The user in our Azure AD is assigned to a functional department. When we hire, transfer, or fire folks, we will make adjustments in the records, and this in turn adjusts the rights in the organization. If we remove a user from the functional organization, we have to remove their privileges from the resources that they were accessing. I use *department* as a filter (like iPhone earlier), and the user was assigned to the correct functional group (see Figure 5-115 and Figure 5-116).

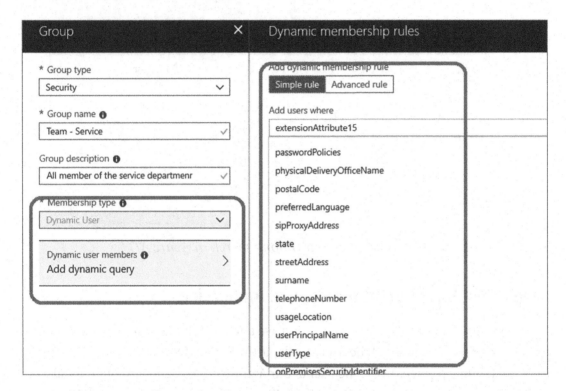

Figure 5-115. *User detected in the service department*

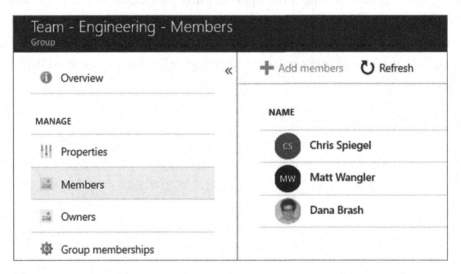

Figure 5-116. *User added to the correct functional group*

Software Updates: Office Pro Plus

Office Pro Plus updates can be managed through Azure deployment. The management process is simple; you can use an Office deployment group, or you can allow Intune to manage the deployment for all enrolled devices. The model that we are using here is to allow Intune to manage the deployment for all enrolled devices. This means when you use your Office 365 account to enroll your device (either through a hybrid join or an Azure join), the device becomes an enrolled device, and the management of the device is subject to the MDM deployment. See Figure 5-117.

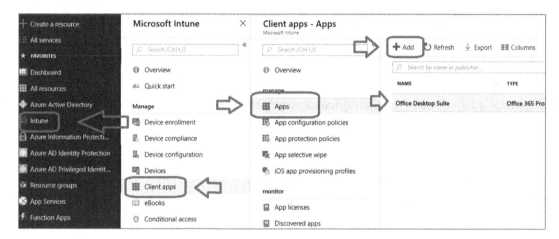

Figure 5-117. *Setting up the Office deployment group*

In our case, what this means is that we will deploy the necessary updates and configuration changes to the device when the device is enrolled in our company's Office 365 account. When a user leaves and we remove the user, then the access to the company's software and resources will also be removed. Let's walk through the configuration process of adding a controlled software update process for Office updates.

Step1: Add a New Office Deployment Group

Click + Add to add a new deployment group. Click Office 365 Suite – Windows 10 (see Figure 5-118). Select the suite as indicated. This will set up additional configuration options for Office Pro Plus deployment. In our case, we want to enable updates but not force deployment of the software.

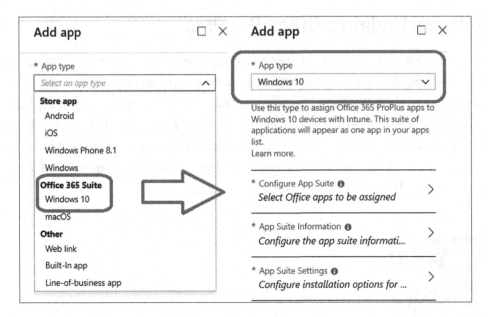

Figure 5-118. *Setting up the Office deployment group*

We are going to select the Office apps that are used in our deployment. This should look like Figure 5-119. The reason for this is that we are going to manage the updates for all connected devices). Click OK once the selection is completed.

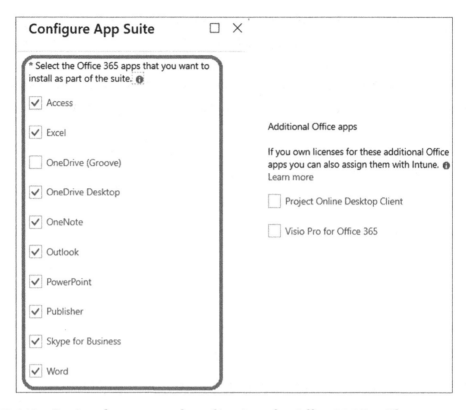

Figure 5-119. *Setting the managed applications for Office 365 Pro Plus*

We need to define information associated with the update for the desktop suite. Click OK once the selection is completed (see Figure 5-120).

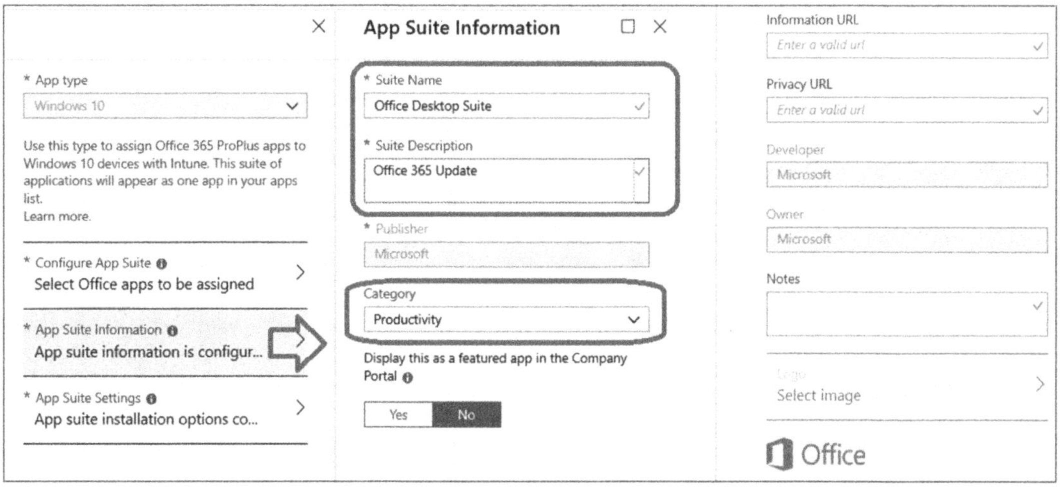

Figure 5-120. *Office Pro Plus update configuration*

Our goal is to put in place an update policy for all Microsoft Office applications that have been deployed. This way we can ensure that all users have the latest software on their managed device, independent of our MDM or MAM/WIP deployment. The update channels are listed in Figure 5-121. Take a quick look at the chart so you understand the update process. We are going to use a Monthly Channel update for our Office updates.

Update channel	Primary purpose	How often updated with new features	Default update channel for the following products
Monthly Channel	Provide users with the newest features of Office as soon as they're available.	Monthly	Visio Pro for Office 365 Project Online Desktop Client Office 365 Business, which is the version of Office that comes with some Office 365 plans, such as Business Premium.
Semi-Annual Channel	Provide users with new features of Office only a few times a year.	Every six months, in January and July	Office 365 ProPlus
Semi-Annual Channel (Targeted)	Provide pilot users and application compatibility testers the opportunity to test the next Semi-Annual Channel.	Every six months, in March and September	None

Figure 5-121. *Office Pro Plus update options (courtesy of Microsoft)*

The next step is to click the channel for the update. As part of the process, you also want to set up device management to remove the previous version of the Office software and automatically accept the license agreement. Configure the updates like in Figure 5-122. Click OK when completed and then Save.

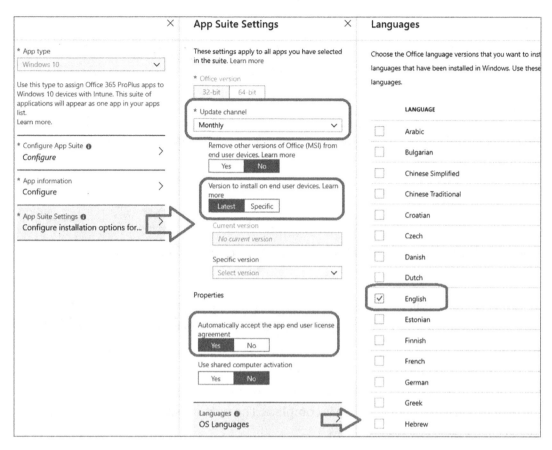

Figure 5-122. *Clicking the update channel and deploying Office*

After you have clicked the updates, the next step is to click who the updates are supposed to apply to. In this case, all updates will be applied to all users or to one of our Office test groups. If you have a mixed environment with kiosk users (no desktop software), you will need to create a separate group. In their case, you will use a dynamic group and pick the users based on the license type that they are using. If the user is provisioned with Pro Plus, then set the dynamic group to only deploy Pro Plus to those licensed users.

In this case, we will select the required option and the "All users" group (see Figure 5-123) to set up the deployment groups, click Assignment, and then click "Add group." The assignment type is required. Click "Make this app required for all users." This will deploy the Office software to all connected devices that meet our criteria.

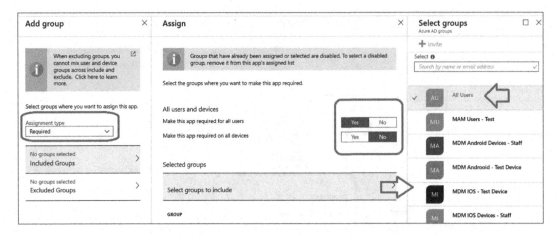

Figure 5-123. *The update will be required for all users who use the Office 365 tenant*

You can make this have a smaller granularity than all users. Keep in mind that if a user opens Office and is not licensed, the software will exist after loading. Each organization is different on the types of software to deploy and the business, so be careful on how you push the software out to the clients. Our objective here is to make sure the client systems are using the latest version of software to reduce the support cost.

At this point, the configuration is complete. The next step is to verify the deployment and see if we have any system errors.

Step 2: Verify That the New Office Software Has Been Installed

The Office deployment software installation will need to be checked for errors. In Figure 5-124, the Office software tried to push an update out to the client, but the updates failed because the Office software was open on the desktop.

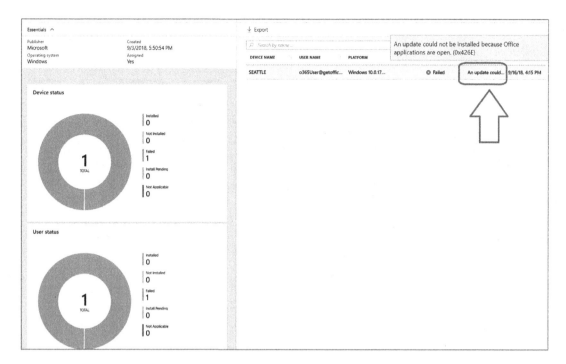

Figure 5-124. *The update will be required for all users who use your Office 365 tenant*

In Figure 5-125, we have two systems installed. The one system that had an error now has a valid installation, and the second system's installation is pending. To see the error, move your mouse over the error.

Figure 5-125. *Update showing installed status and pending update*

Software Updates: Windows 10 Update Rings

Once you have set up your dynamic teams and dynamic device groups, the next step
is to set up the Windows Update rings. What we do is assign the update rights to all
detected members in our company. If you are running Windows Insider, you need to set
up the condition in the dynamic group to separate the Windows Insider users from the
dynamic users. In our update case, here we are using all user groups to manage updates
corporate-wide.

Step 1: Set Up the Software Update Rings

The software update ring group was added to the Azure dashboard. Click Intune, click "Software updates," and then click "Windows 10 Update Rings." In Figure 5-126, we have our Windows 10 update group. In our case, our Windows 10 update group is set to all users (similar to the Office Pro Plus update group). You can set up multiple groups, and how you set up groups is dependent on the license type. You cannot mix devices and users in the same group.

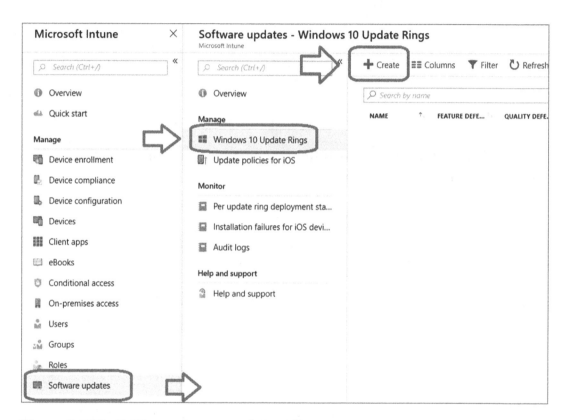

Figure 5-126.   *Setting up a new update policy*

Office 365 Windows 10 licenses come in two flavors: device licenses and user licenses. The test subscription we are using is Microsoft 365 E5, and this is a user license. To set up a group, click Intune, click "Software updates," and then click Windows 10. Then click Create.

The key to picking an update strategy is to understand the update channels. The standard update channel that you want to use is the semiannual targeted. This will give you the standard updates on a released schedule. The update options are listed in Figure 5-127. If you have users in different update programs, you will need to configure a service channel for them and adjust the dynamic group.

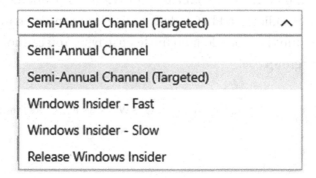

Figure 5-127. *Windows 10 update channel options*

The update configuration that we are using in our deployment is shown in Figure 5-128. Click these options and then click OK; then save and create the policy.

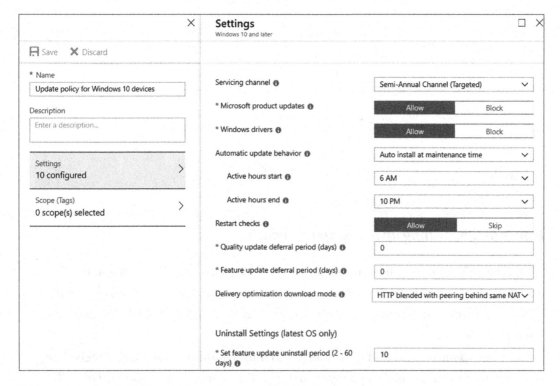

Figure 5-128. *Windows 10 update configuration*

In our case, we are not using a Windows 10 Insider group, so we assign the update policy to all users (see Figure 5-129).

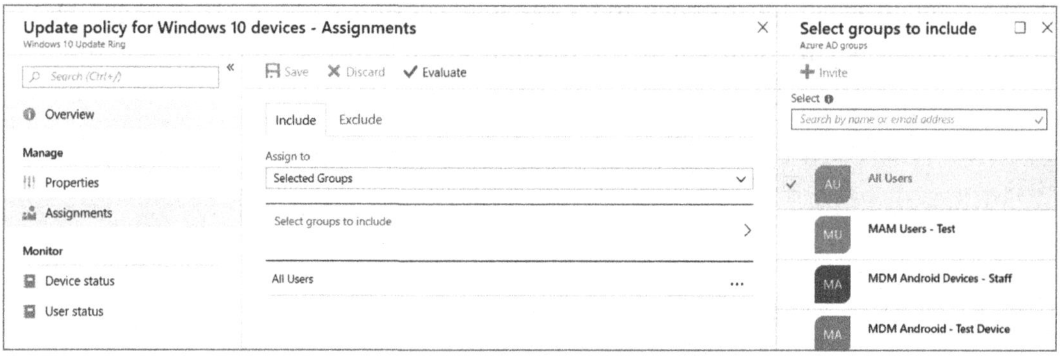

Figure 5-129. *Selecting Users for Windows 10 device configuration*

As users join the organization, our dynamic group is automatically updated. You can easily make changes in the update policy. In our case, we created another group for all users that we managed the Windows Update and a Windows 10 insiders group. Our Windows Insider group is a static group, since the users need to be manually added and managed. See Figure 5-130.

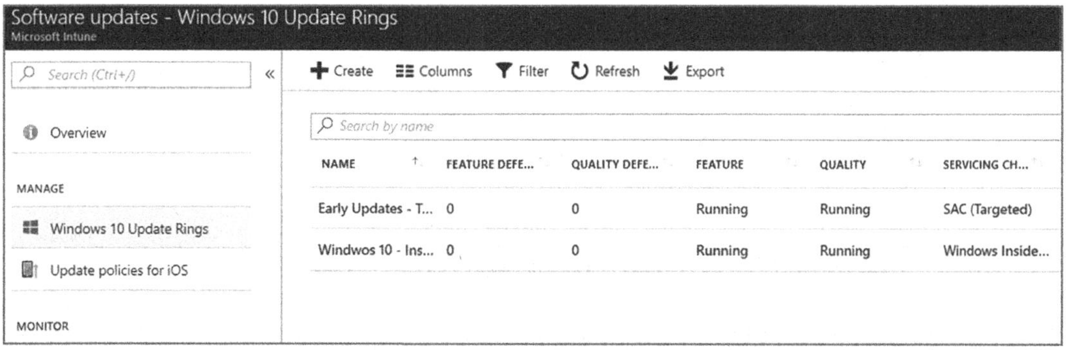

Figure 5-130. *User Windows 10 update rings*

Step 2: Check the Update Status

Once you have deployed the updates to the device, you can easily check the status of the deployment. Just click the overview to see the status of your Windows 10 deployment update. You will see the status of your deployment (see Figure 5-131).

Figure 5-131. *Checking the status of all Windows 10 update deployments*

Legacy: Password Multifactor Authentication

Microsoft has not removed the legacy multifactor authentication. I included this here as a reference, but it is recommended that you use the Azure multifactor authentication. The Azure process based on Office 365 has integrated multifactor authentication with Azure. All administrators are enabled by default. When you enable a user for multifactor authentication, the user needs to have two forms of identity.

We recommend that you check the user status before you enable MFA at `https://aka.ms/setupsecurityinfo` (see Figure 5-132) or use `https://myapps.microsoft.com` (MS moves the url around, so you may find one URL works and the other does not).

Our desktop systems in this example are Windows 10 Pro (or Enterprise) systems are linked to Office 365 via Azure Join. What this means is that the "password reset of MFA" action will affect the user desktop device. The user desktop is using Office 365/Azure identity to manage the security.

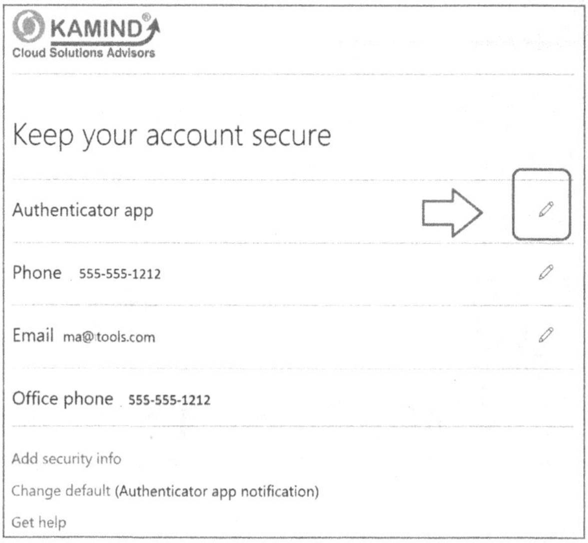

Figure 5-132. *Reviewing the account configuration for multifactor authentication*

There are two different types of multifactor authentication: Office 365 and Azure. Office 365 MFA is enabled on certain subscriptions and is in place for all administrators. Azure MFA is set up for all accounts with Azure Identity Plan 2. In a previous chapter, we discussed the Microsoft Enterprise Mobile + Security suite MFA configuration. In this section, we will look at the Office 365 MFA deployment. We will deploy the Azure EMS Identity solutions versus the Office 365 MFA.

Multifactor authentication uses a secondary device (such as your smartphone) to supply you with additional login information for a Microsoft service. To use multifactor authentication, log in to Office 365 with your username and password. The Microsoft Office 365 service prompts you to enter a PIN (usually six or eight digits). The PIN comes from three different sources.

- Microsoft calls your cell phone and supplies you with a number.

- Microsoft texts your cell phone with a number.

- You supply a PIN from your smartphone via the authentication app.

The PIN is unique and has a short lifetime. You use this PIN to log in to the Office 365 service (see Figure 5-133).

Figure 5-133. *Logging in to Office 365 with multifactor authentication enabled*

There are two ways that you can set up multifactor authentication: log in to `https://portal.azure.com` (described in Chapter 2) or log in to Office 365 (if not using EMS/Intune) and click Azure Multifactor (click Grid and then Admin ➤ Admin Center ➤ Service & Add-ins ➤ Azure Multifactor, as shown in Figure 5-134). The services are similar in some respects but different. Office 365 is a basic service (like what Apple deployed for iCloud), or there is an advanced service that is part of the Enterprise Mobility + Security (EMS) suite. The main difference is that it is an enabling/disabling function, where the Azure EMS identity allows you much more customization of the MFA features.

Note   If you are planning to use MFA across the organization, the best approach is to use an EMS E3 or EMS E5 subscription. This service is more robust than the base service supplied in Office 365.

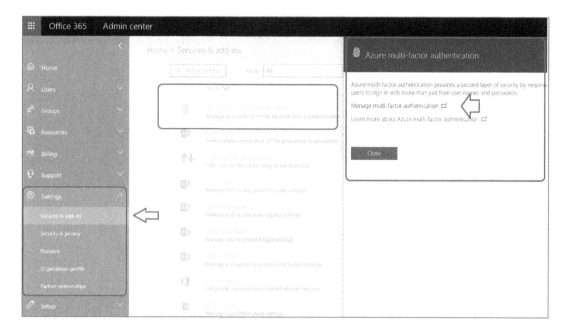

Figure 5-134. *Setting up multifactor authentication (not using EMS)*

Setting up multifactor authentication is straightforward. Click the link Manage Multi-Factor Authentication. Office 365 will direct you to Azure to authenticate your credentials. All user identities are managed in Azure. To set up multifactor authentication on a user account, follow the next steps.

Step 1: Enable the Users

Select the user to enable multifactor authentication for, and set the policy (see Figure 5-135). Then click Enable to set up the multifactor authentication properties.

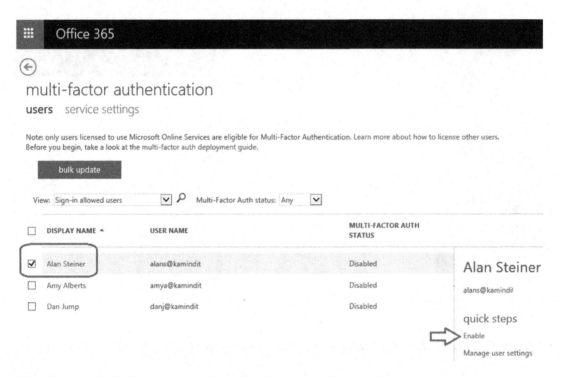

Figure 5-135. *Selecting users for multifactor authentication*

Step 2: Set Up User Credentials

After you have enabled the user (click "enable multi-factor auth"), have the user log in to Office 365 to set up the credentials (see Figure 5-136). If you want to set up the credentials for the user, you need their smartphone and login credentials for Office 365.

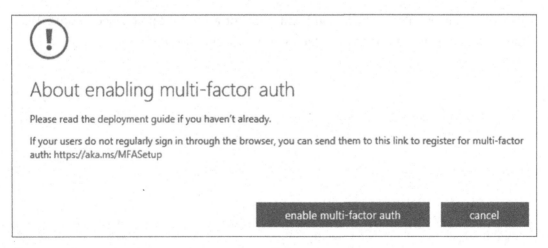

Figure 5-136. *Enabling multifactor authentication*

The next time the user logs in to Office 365, they are informed of the setup to the new services (see Figure 5-137).

Figure 5-137.   *User setting up multifactor authentication*

Step 3: Authenticate Smartphones

Azure is used to authenticate the service for Office 365. The authentication service is an international service and requires that you own a phone that can receive a text message for login or can install an Office authentication app on your smartphone. You need to pick the service that makes business sense (see Figure 5-138). If your phone does not receive text messages, you can elect to have Microsoft call you in your native language.

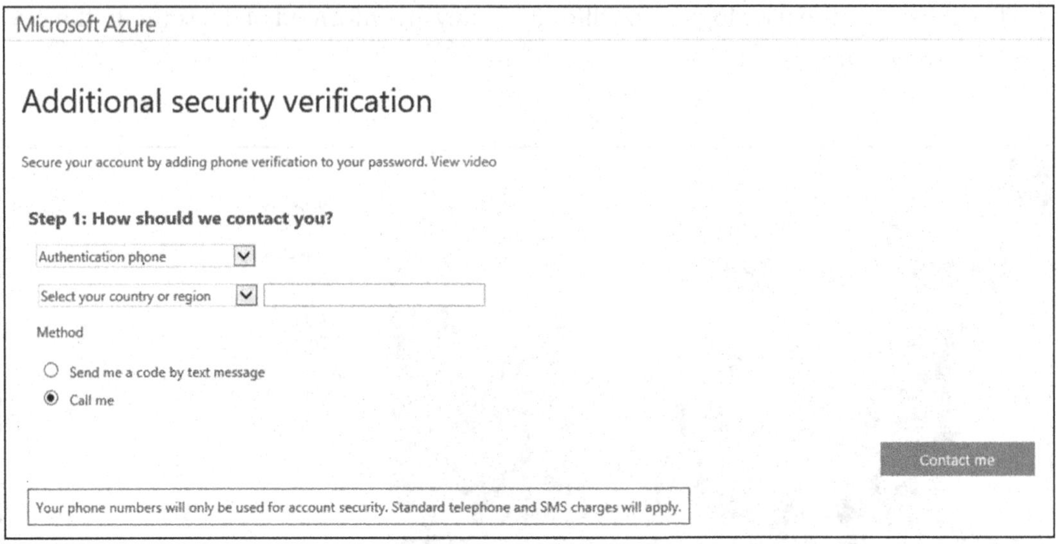

Figure 5-138. *Setting up the service for login*

Once you have verified your smartphone with Microsoft, you are supplied with a security token to allow your mobile device to access the Office 365 account. This passcode is unique and is used to configure mobile applications that do not use two-factor authentication (see Figure 5-140). Use this passcode as the new password for your mobile applications that access Office 365 services. Click Done when completed.

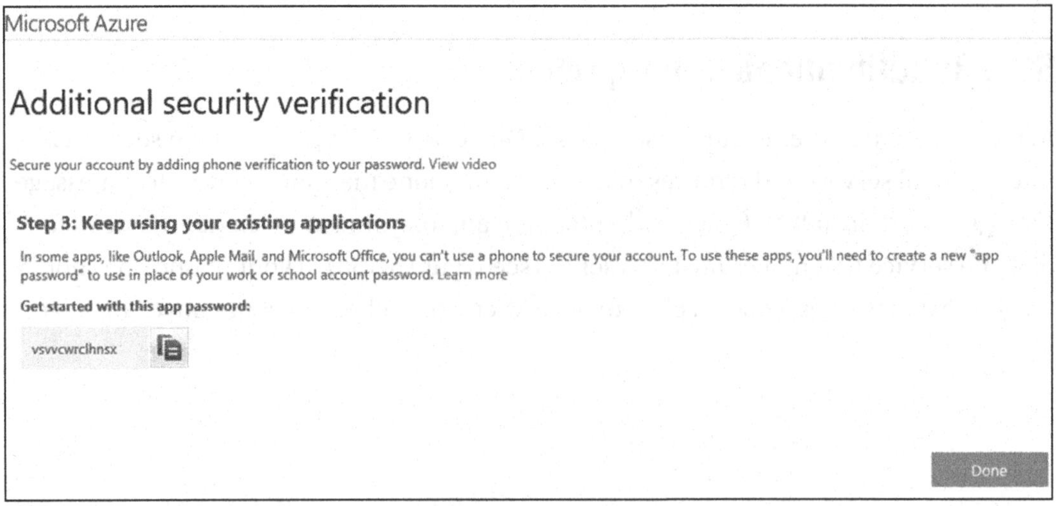

Figure 5-139. *Setting a new password for your mobile application*

Step 4: Test the Service

Log in to the Office 365 service at `https://portal.microsoftonline.com`. Office 365 will text or call your cell phone with the authentication password (see Figure 5-140).

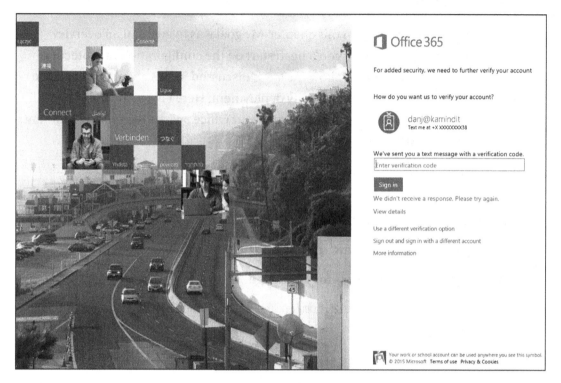

Figure 5-140. *Testing multifactor authentication*

Summary

This chapter focused on setting up Mobile Application Management and Mobile Device Management. We looked at the different configurations and how you set up software upgrades for Windows 10 and the Office 365 software. MDM deployment is a process. Make sure your deployment focus on MAM (and WIP) deployment with continued compliance check process before you deploy MDM. I introduced you to dynamic groups as a management tool for Mobile Device Management and Mobile Application Management. At this point, you have the security configuration in place for Office 365 and Azure. The next step is to look at the different tools for compliance and eDiscovery. We wrap up the book with a chapter on migrating to Office 365 (for those who are still contemplating moving to Office 365).

References

We covered a lot of information in this chapter. My goal was to give you an overview of the various components to give you a head start on the configuration of protection management and security. If you follow the steps discussed in this chapter, you will be able extend the capabilities of your security deployment. Here I list some links that will assist you in getting to the next level of securing your Office 365 and Azure environment.

Getting Started with EMS

- https://docs.Microsoft.com/en-us/intune/get-started-evaluation

What is Intune and MDM

- https://docs.Microsoft.com/en-us/intune/introduction-intune

Deploying Conditional Access for Exchange

- https://docs.microsoft.com/en-us/intune/conditional-access-exchange-create

EMS Trial Subscriptions

- https://kamindit.azurewebsites.net

Deploying Azure Multifactor Authentication

- https://docs.microsoft.com/en-us/Azure/active-directory/authentication/howto-mfa-getstarted

CHAPTER 6

Using Office 365 Compliance Center

Office 365 is a suite of software products that Microsoft offers via a software-as-a-service subscription. The goal of the service is to reduce the IT costs for business implementations. The Security & Compliance Center is an admin center that provides security dashboards for the subscription you purchased. A good way to view the Security & Compliance Center is as a data aggregation site of the different security services in Office 365. The driving factor for Office 365 security features are regulatory standards and user feedback. As an example, services are set up to meet the requirements of the National Institute of Standards and Technology Cybersecurity Framework (NIST-CSF) or the NIST-800-53 compliance standard for government contractors (see the Microsoft Compliance Manager). If you explore the NIST-CSF standard, which is based on the pillars of identify, protect, detect, and response, you will see a detailed relationship with Office 365 security features. As an example, in Figure 6-1, the four pillars are built into Windows Defender ATP (part of the Microsoft 365 E5 subscription) to remediate attacks.

© Matthew Katzer 2018
M. Katzer, *Securing Office 365*, https://doi.org/10.1007/978-1-4842-4230-8_6

Agentless, cloud-powered
No additional deployment or infrastructure. No delays or update compatibility issues. Always up to date.

Unparalleled optics
Built into Windows 10 for deeper insights. Exchanges signals with the Microsoft Intelligent Security Graph.

Automated security
Take your security to a new level, by going from alert to remediation in minutes – at scale.

Synchronized defense
Microsoft 365[1] shares detection and exploration – across devices, identities and information - to speed up response and recovery.

Windows Defender ATP helps stop breaches

The security platform for intelligent protection, detection, investigation and response. Windows Defender ATP protects endpoints from cyber threats; detects advanced attacks and data breaches, automates security incidents and improves security posture.

Unified endpoint security

Windows Defender ATP is a unified endpoint security platform using built-in security technologies working together and powered by the cloud.

Figure 6-1. *The Windows Defender Advanced Threat Protection services (courtesy of Microsoft)*

In previous chapters, we looked at some of the components of the Security & Compliance Center. In this chapter, we will expand our discussion into additional areas, such as alerts, data governance, and threat management. The configuration of the admin center (see Figure 6-2) is based on our subscription, which here is the Microsoft 365 E5 suite. The Security & Compliance Center is your one-stop location where you can review the security logs and configure the services to support your business.

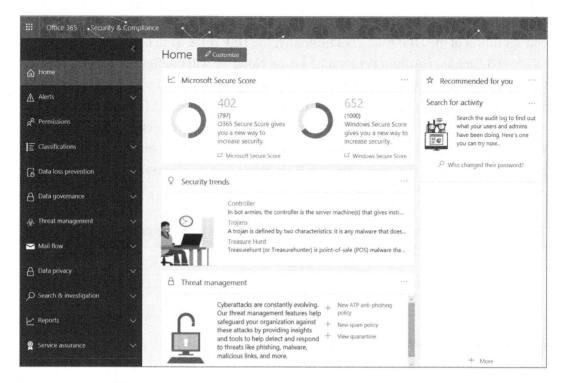

***Figure 6-2.** Office 365 Security & Compliance Center*

In previous chapters, we walked through the different configuration options available in the Security & Compliance Center. These previous configurations supported a unique feature, such as labels or data loss prevention (DLP). We added DLP rules for encrypting e-mail communications and documents. In Chapter 3, we completed a detailed review of Microsoft Secure Score to give administrators guidance on the configuration of the security-related capabilities of Office 365 (see Figure 6-3).

***Figure 6-3.** Microsoft Secure Score from the Compliance Center*

The document classification that we set up in Chapter 4 (see Figure 6-4) led to the configuration of the DLP rules. Traditionally, the DLP rules were configured in the Office 365 Exchange Admin center and Azure. Now, we will configure the rules in the Office 365 Security & Compliance Center. In Figure 6-5, we have a number of DLP rules configured to address HIPAA, the Gramm–Leach–Bliley Act (a 1999 federal act to enhance competition in the financial market), and PII data protection. The Security & Compliance Center also gives an overview of how the rules are being used, both from a policy rule execution viewpoint and a false match analysis viewpoint (this is where the end user overrides the DLP rule).

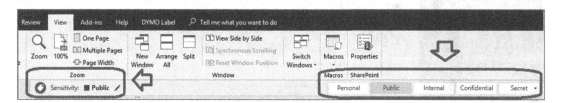

Figure 6-4. *Document classification*

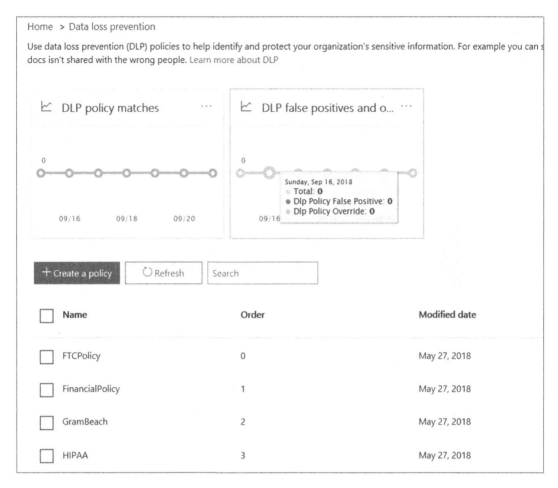

Home > Data loss prevention

Use data loss prevention (DLP) policies to help identify and protect your organization's sensitive information. For example you can s
docs isn't shared with the wrong people. Learn more about DLP

DLP policy matches   ...   DLP false positives and o...   ...

0   0

09/16   09/18   09/20   09/16

Sunday, Sep 16, 2018
Total: **0**
Dlp Policy False Positive: **0**
Dlp Policy Override: **0**

+ Create a policy   Refresh   Search

Name	Order	Modified date
FTCPolicy	0	May 27, 2018
FinancialPolicy	1	May 27, 2018
GramBeach	2	May 27, 2018
HIPAA	3	May 27, 2018

Figure 6-5. *DLP rules in place for different data loss policies*

Compliance is a way of life for any organization that has a digital footprint. I know it seems like a lot of information, but IT administrators need to fulfill our roles as custodians of information and help organizations manage information to ensure it is in compliance with the new data breach and privacy laws, such as the CCPA. Where a data breach is assumed to have happened, it is now up the IT professional to prove that the breach did *not* happen.

Note that the CCPA is about *presumed* breaches. In previous years, any claim for a data breach had to be proven by the person who was damaged. Under the new CCPA regulation (passed June 2018), the cyberbreach damage is assumed, and it is up to the organization to prove the breach did *not* happen and the information was not compromised. A task of this magnitude requires the ability to review historical data and the activities of the organization. As an example, Figure 6-6 shows the type of data in an organization that needs to be managed. In addition to this data, historic logs need to be reviewed. This is the purpose of the Security & Compliance Center.

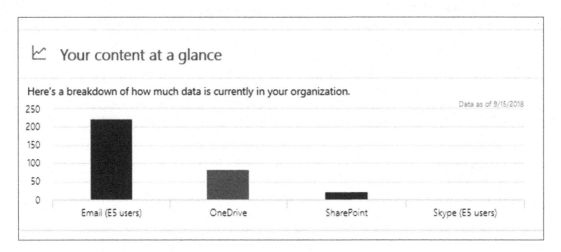

Figure 6-6. *Types of content in the organization*

In this chapter, we will review the areas that we have not already reviewed in this book. Specifically, we will be looking into the data governance, defining what it is and how to use it. Our review will look at the threat management systems and how to use the threat dashboard and the different activities with mail flow analysis and Exchange Advanced Threat Protection. We will look into data privacy, and finally we will walk through requests for production with eDiscovery in the Search & Investigation Center. The eDiscovery capability allows you to search and compile information to satisfy requests for production (in response to document requests from court-ordered subpoenas). This is where we will investigate user messages and document content for compliance. Let's begin our investigation into the capabilities of the Security & Compliance Center.

Overview of Office 365 Security & Compliance Center

Security is built from the ground up. When you look at the Microsoft Cloud (in other words, the core Microsoft infrastructure that hosts Office 365, Azure, and other services), you'll see it meets all current and future compliance and security regulations. When you build a cloud infrastructure that has a security mind-set, the applications and services that run on it have the same mind-set. Likewise, if you are building a set of services designed to sell information, then any application that is built on those services has inherent security flaws built into it for the simple reason that the core service is to sell information, not to protect it.

Microsoft cloud services are transparent. The service offerings (see Figure 6-7) are based on a model of security and transparency. The data your company places in Office 365 and Azure is *your* data. Microsoft has as strict policy not to mine or process your data for business purposes. Microsoft's policy is that the customer owns the data, and if you choose to leave Office 365 for some other service, the data you leave behind will be destroyed within 90–120 days of your subscription termination.

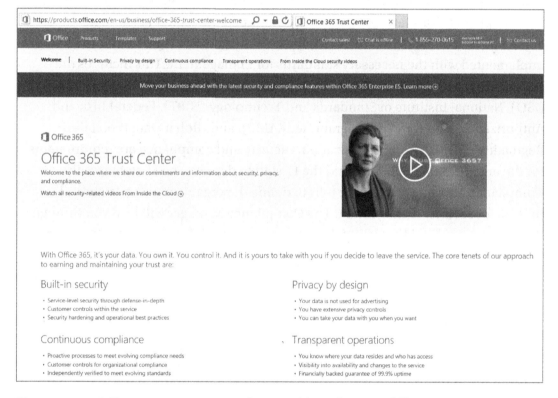

Figure 6-7. *Office 365 Trust Center,* `https://products.office.com/en-us/business/office-365-trust-center-welcome`

There are two parts to compliance in the cloud with Office 365: your business processes in the management of your Office 365 data and Microsoft's management of Office 365 and Azure services. Earlier, we talked about the service trust with Office 365. Microsoft has published the standards that are used to meet its side of the compliance issue on the Microsoft Trust Center (see Figure 6-7). If you are looking for a Health Insurance Portability and Accountability Act (HIPAA) of 1996 business associate agreement certification or want to request a copy of the service audit logs, you can request them directly from Microsoft. Microsoft is transparent in its process on Office 365 and built the service around protecting your company information. This is in contrast to other cloud services that require an intellectual property rights assignment, which allows them to use your information to sell advertising, among other things. The business process starts with your organization and specifically with your business processes that you use to manage Office 365. The best guide for all business to use to meet your portion of the compliance requirement is for you to deploy the Compliance Manager from the Service Trust Portal (`https://servicetrust.microsoft.com/`).

Compliance is a shared responsibility between Microsoft and you. The Service Trust Portal deploys the Compliance Manager (see Figure 6-8), which has implemented with the necessary standards for management. This includes the Service Organization Controls (SOC), International Organization for Standardization (ISO), National Institute of Standards and Technology (NIST), Federal Risk and Authorization Management Program (fedRAMP), and Global Data Protection Regulation (GDPR). As an organization, security and compliance are requirements for the organization to manage and the IT staff to deploy. The IT staff uses the Compliance Manager (see Figure 6-9) to define the organization's business process for security management. The Compliance Manager will lead you through the audit process and help you define the ownership of the management processes for your organization.

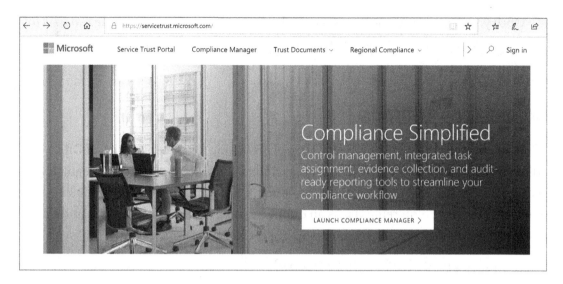

Figure 6-8. *Office 365 and Azure Service Trust Portal (`https://servicetrust.microsoft.com`)*

Most organization do not have a compliance requirement. However, what all organizations can do is deploy the Compliance Manager and set up a necessary process for either NIST 800-35 or NITS-CSF and see the areas that are lacking controls for a cyber security defense. The Compliance Manager helps you to define the necessary processes and controls that your organization needs to follow. The issue many of us have is where to begin on a large task like this. How do we make our organization compliant, and what are the things we need to do to make our business more secure? The steps are easy now: launch the Compliance Manager and start an assessment. Usually NITS 800-53 will get you started. This has many of the requirements that you need to run your organization on a daily basis.

Figure 6-9. *Office 365 and Azure Service Compliance Manager*

Once you have started the process with the Compliance Manager, the next step is to deploy the various alerts of organization changes that you need to follow to ensure that your organization has the necessary processes in place.

Compliance Settings

When we refer to Office 365 compliance, we are referring to the capabilities of Office 365 data governance to preserve and manage information. Compliance and regulatory settings are the services you enable on the Office 365 site and that meet your business needs or regulatory requirements. As an example, you can group information into three categories: compliance, information review, or business data retention.

- Compliance (HIPAA as an example)

  - Rights management and the protection of personal information

  - Encryption of personal information external to your organization

  - Document classification and encryption

- Information review (regulatory like the Financial Industry Regulatory Authority [FINRA]) or judicial order

  - Litigation hold and eDiscovery

  - E-mail review to meet FINRA requirements

- Business data retention

  - Business processes on age of data

  - Data management: how to archive, how to delete

In the discussion in this chapter, we will group information into these categories. For example, HIPAA requires you to manage certain types of data in a way to protect information. To meet HIPAA requirements, you must protect personal information by encrypting the information before it is sent externally to the organization. One of the HIPAA requirements is that the service you are using provides a Business Associates Agreement (BAA) for the services you are using. If you are subject to HIPAA, you need to ensure that you have completed a yearly a HIPAA assessment audit to make sure you comply with the regulations. The fines are significant, and the federal government is looking into business of all sizes to make sure the business complies with the regulation.

Information review typically means that the information is subject to an audit and is immutable—meaning it cannot be changed or deleted by the users or the organization—prior to review. Any type of regulator review requires that the data is immutable. The most common is litigation. When an organization enters into litigation, all information is frozen at that period in time. We refer to that as a *litigation hold*. Regulator reviews such as FINRA and SEC are nothing more than an extension of a litigation hold in conjunction with business process reviews.

Business data retention is nothing more than the business processes used to maintain information, subject to the regulatory requirements. As an example, if the business policy (or user policy) deletes information subject to the retention policy, the information is deleted from the user perspective but may be kept for a very long time subject to the compliance needs of the organization. The user may delete information, but the compliance setting keeps the information in an area where it is immutable and fully searchable and hidden from the user.

The Office 365 administrator has complete control over the configuration of the compliance and retention polices. The administrator can enable these settings, and all actions are auditable. The settings can be changed by using the Security & Compliance Center or by using PowerShell commands. As Microsoft enhances the Office 365 service, these settings will be simplified in an easy-to-use graphical interface. The rest of this chapter discusses these concepts for data governance and provides a step-by-step implementation with examples of data loss protection (compliance), regulatory review (discovery), and business data retention policies.

Best Way to Proceed

The best way to understand the Security & Compliance Center is to look at the Trust Center. After looking at the Trust Center, the next step is to review NIST-CSF, the cybersecurity framework, and to review the NIST-800-35 compliance framework. There is a lot of work to be completed.

Note   There are three sets of logs that you need to collect monthly: the Azure login logs, the Azure sign-in logs (located in Azure Active Directory), and the audit logs located in the Security & Compliance Center. These logs need to be stored in a SharePoint site for future analysis.

The Security & Compliance Center gives you a focal point for the security process in the organization. However, security starts with your IT team. If your IT team lacks the capability to do the necessary work, you need to address this quickly and either fix the internal problem or contract the security services externally. This book was designed to help you determine what you need to do and how you should do it. If you consciously choose not to secure your Office 365 environment, you are the breach. The ownership is with you and your IT team and not your license provider. Let's continue our journey through the Compliance & Security Center.

Data Governance

Governance has taken on a new meeting in the cloud. The best way to look at governance in the cloud is in the role of cloud custodian. In today's model, the polices are put in place to manage the business operation and roles and controls. Once governance is put in place, then developers and the operation teams can implement the necessary changes and help drive the business to be more innovative. This is cloud governance in Office 365 and Azure. This is to make sure the right people have access to the right resources and the behavior is governed by a set of rules and polices that is baked into the platform.

The best way to view Microsoft governance is to think of a road with guard rails. As you drive down the road, you are kept from going off-track because the guard rails are there to keep you aligned on the role. The Security & Compliance Center and the governance activity are guiderails for organization policies. This applies to older resources and new resources. The difference with governance today is that the polices that are deployed are consistent with the policy that is deployed for the organization. The enforcement of governance in Office 365 begins with the Security & Compliance Center and through the Compliance Manager and the new Azure Blueprint platform. The goal is to build compliance into the Azure and Office 365 subscriptions that are the base of all activities. The new strategy is to use management groups, which are container groups on top of a subscription (or a resource group). This allows a policy to be deployed as a management group with full access and control. This is the only way an organization can scale and empower the individuals in the organization to innovate. Governance in the Microsoft Cloud was built into the core of the platform, not as an afterthought like with the other major cloud providers.

We explored some data governance issues in the previous chapters. Specifically, we deployed labels and DLP. These services were deployed in different administration centers, including the Exchange admin center, Azure Information Protection, and finally with the Security & Compliance Center. All of these services could be deployed from the Security admin center in the Data Governance section, and they apply to all subscriptions in the organization. In Figure 6-10, we have a summary dashboard of the different governance sections that we have deployed. In this example, we have deployed 11 different labels for data, and we have long-term compliance for data retention. The top label that was used is Attorney-Client Privilege.

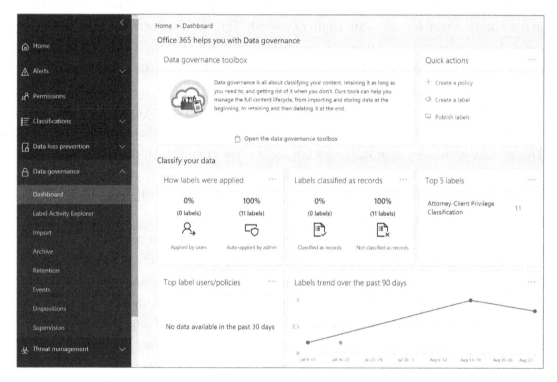

Figure 6-10. *Overview of data governance in the Security & Compliance Center*

Data Governance Concepts

Data governance provides a policy-based management service on Office 365 that meets or exceeds the regulatory compliance. The policy-based service is applied across subscriptions and aligns with the Azure policy manage process. The data in Office 365 (and the subscription types) is managed and owned by the company. The Office 365 business owners need to look at the business and decide what makes business sense based on the needs of the business. To put this in perspective, when an external entity looks at e-mail storage, it is considered modifiable by the user and is noncompliant to certain regulations. A compliant system requires that the email and document storage systems must be incapable of being modified, or *immutable*. The owner of a mailbox must not be able to go in and delete information or documents. These capabilities are options in the Office 365 enterprise plan and are included at no charge in some of the subscription suites (such as the Enterprise E3/E5 subscription).

You are probably familiar with the various *CSI* and *NCIS* shows on TV. A key message that these shows highlight lies in the evidentiary collection of information and that there must be a "chain of custody" regarding information collected. Think of data governance in the same context. It is all about chain of custody. Data governance on Office 365 is the same. Access to information that is under discovery or access cannot be tampered with. Further, access is recorded and auditable for all those who access the information. This is the data governance model of Office 365.

Traditional approaches, such as journaling, record information external to the organization structure and mostly just contain copies of the e-mail communications. This archaic journaling approach does not address the changing landscape of data governance and data management. Journaling does not link data from storage sites and draft documents in an integrated form. An archive is nothing more than another mailbox that is used to store information.

Immutability, audit policy, archive/retention, and data loss prevention are all part of the Office 365 data governance structure. It is designed around chain of custody and the preservation of information. If information is tampered with, then a full audit trail of access, as well as the original information that was modified, is created.

Before we discuss the practical aspects of the configuration of retention policy and eDiscovery, we need to frame the discussion with a definition of each of the four key areas of data governance to put them in perspective. There has been much written about information immutability, and there are many misconceptions as to what this is and how it is managed in Office 365. The definition is simple: the preservation of data in its *original form cannot be changed and is kept in a form that is discoverable.*

Recall the discussion of chain of custody. The information that you are accessing and providing for data governance needs cannot be changed, and you must not have the ability to change it. In addition, any access to the information must be fully traceable. If you access information, the information that you extract will not change the underlining information.

The best example is to look at an e-mail that flows in or is created by a user in the cloud (see Figure 6-11). In this case, information that arrives or is in a user mailbox can be changed and modified by the user. This is the normal process that we use in writing an e-mail. An e-mail that is immutable, on the other hand, keeps all parts of the message in a form that can be fully discoverable through searches. When an e-mail message is drafted, all changes and drafts are kept and not deleted. Nothing is purged—all information is fully discoverable.

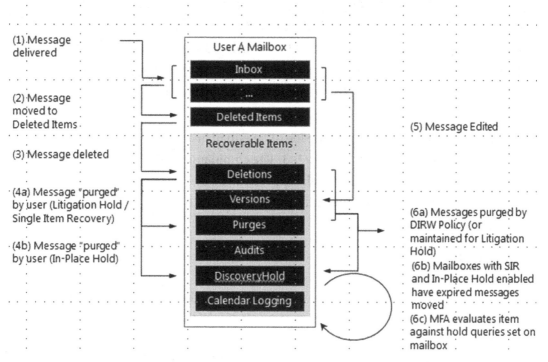

Figure 6-11. *Life of an e-mail message (courtesy of Microsoft)*

When we refer to *compliance*, we are referring to our ability to access communications and documents that are immutable. Retention rules are based on business policies in the management of e-mail communications, specifically what e-mail is visible to the user in the mailbox and what is kept in the archive. For example, you may have a business policy that dictates the movement of e-mail from a user mailbox to an archive if the e-mail is too old or if the user deletes an e-mail. One company has a retention policy of 90 days; after 90 days, a user's incoming e-mail is moved into the compliance archive. These retention rules move the mail from the user mailbox (or delete folder) into the archive. These rules can be systems level (the user has no control), they can be local level (the user has complete control), or they can be any combination thereof.

A *litigation hold* is an action that is placed on a mailbox to meet compliance requirements for future discovery and searching. What a litigation hold does is to ensure that the data in a user mailbox is immutable. As an example, if the user tries to delete an e-mail, the e-mail is deleted (or purged) from the user's view, but the litigation hold function blocks the e-mail from being deleted in the system and is fully discoverable by the administrator (or compliance officer).

Note   When data is placed under litigation hold, the data is locked from deletion. Once the litigation hold is lifted, the data will automatically be deleted subject to the retention tags. If your policy is to stop data from deletion, then set up the retention policy to move data to the online archive after deletion.

Referring to Figure 6-11, we see the life of an e-mail in a user's mailbox. In Figure 6-11, the user only sees the message in steps 1–3. The compliance officer has access to all transactions in steps 1–6. When a discovery action—a search—is executed, all information is displayed in the search request, including the information in the deleted items, purges, and draft folders.

Audit Policy

Companies in the cloud need to know who has access to their company data. The ability to monitor and produce the necessary reports are part of the Office 365 audit capability. Companies need to do the following:

- Verify that their mailbox data isn't being accessed by Microsoft

- Enforce compliance and privacy regulations and access by nonowners

- Have the ability to determine who has access to data at a given time in a specific mailbox

- Have the ability to identify unauthorized access to mailbox data by users inside and outside your organization

The ability to monitor the mailbox data is a fundamental part of the Office 365 organization (see Figure 6-12). Once the audit capabilities are enabled (via PowerShell), the audit reports can be generated by the administrator or an individual who has been given this capability.

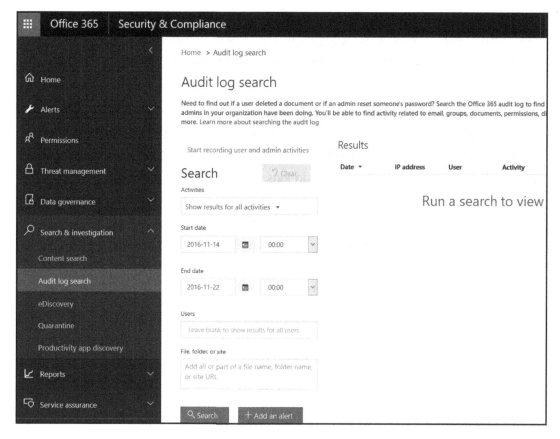

Figure 6-12. *Audit and retention capabilities*

The audit reports are displayed in the search results shown in Figure 6-12. However, the audit report must be enabled. To enable the audit reports, select the "Start recording user and admin activities" option. The audit reports are only for 90 days and can be extended via PowerShell. Typically, I set audit reports for a 12-month period. Each audit report contains the following information:

- Date of access

- IP address of the access

- User who performed the activity

- Activity performed

- Detailed description of the item

- Detailed description of the activity (usually the object's name such as a file name)

The first step in setting up a compliant organization is to enable the audit capabilities to ensure that you have a complete record of all accesses to user mailbox data by nonowner users. This information is used to supplement future reports.

Note   Earlier we mentioned that the organization needs to have a policy of collecting the primary three logs and archiving them in a SharePoint site for future forensic analysis. This is extremely important. Every month you need to download a copy of the audit logs, the Azure sign-in logs, and the Azure audit logs.

The audit reports that are generated contain detailed information about who has accessed the information and how they have changed it. As you'll see in Figure 6-8, once audit logs are enabled, all information is tracked. The discovery center adds another level of detail in tracking information accessed under legal hold.

Figure 6-13. *Tracing access of users through the administrative center audit log search*

Information Immutability

Information immutability takes this one step further and integrates Skype for Business and SharePoint documents (as well as OneDrive for Business document synchronization) into the equation. The Office 365 approach is designed to reduce the amount of information by removing duplicate information. This reduces the complexity of the searches and allows the compliance officer to clearly see the thread of the information and the root cause (if any) of the discovery request. The searched data can be exported in the industry-standard Electronic Discover Reference Model (EDRM) standard in an XML format to provide content to a third party. The Office 365 approach is designed to remove duplicate data from searches and does not remove any data from the user's SharePoint or e-mail mailbox. The data stays where it is and is immutable.

Figure 6-14. *Setting up an eDiscovery search*

The configuration of the eDiscovery search is robust and allows you to specify the areas and mailboxes that you need to search. The scope of the discovery is reduced to the specific set of key words and mailboxes (see Figure 6-14) and can be easily restricted to a few users in question. It is not uncommon that an eDiscovery request on Office 365 would cost 90 percent less than an eDiscovery request using an older journaling system for e-mail communication management.

As you read the rest of this chapter, the discussion on archive and retention polices is built around data immutability to manage an organization's compliance needs. In Office 365, this is referred to as *compliance management*. Administrators are enabled to set up controls based on the business polices of the organization.

Office 365 Archiving and Retention

The term a*rchive* is overused. It often implies more than what it really is. An archive is nothing more than a second mailbox designed for long-term storage. The relevancy of an archive is based on the business process rules that are used to manage it. This is where immutability and retention policies come into play. Immutability refers to how information is retained (in a form that can't be changed) in the mailbox and the archive. Retention policies describe the length of time you need to keep the data that is not subject to any legal action (legal hold to guarantee immutability).

It is important to describe the length of time you need to keep the data that is not subject to any legal action (legal hold to guarantee immutability). These policies are located under Retention (see Figure 6-15).

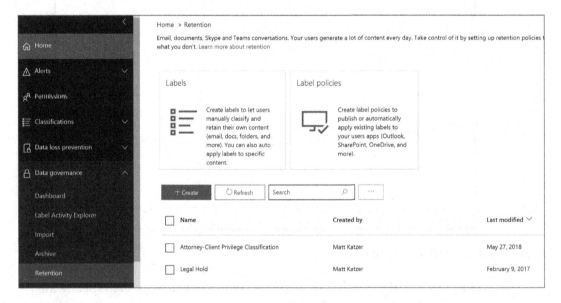

Figure 6-15. *Retention policies*

It is easy to create a new retention policy. In Figure 6-15, just click + Create and set up the policy. The wizard will walk you through the process. The retention policy created is almost the same way the retention policy was created in the Exchange admin center. So, depending on how you want to approach the problem, you can create a legacy retention policy or a new policy. The legacy retention policy is composed of retention tags. A group of retention tags constitutes a retention policy, as shown in Figure 6-16. The new retention policy is a wizard that allows you to fill in the same information.

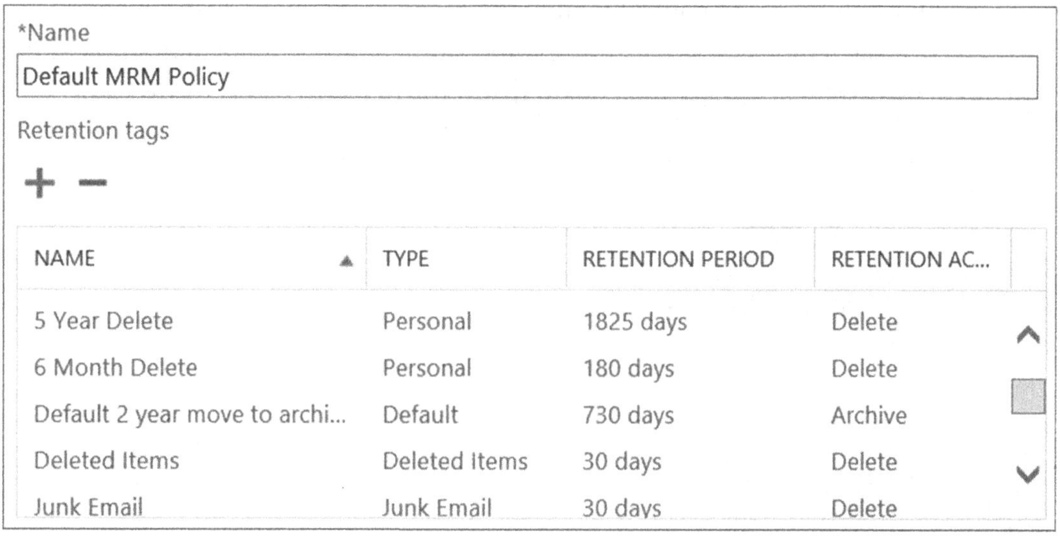

*Name

Default MRM Policy

Retention tags

+ —

NAME ▲	TYPE	RETENTION PERIOD	RETENTION AC...
5 Year Delete	Personal	1825 days	Delete
6 Month Delete	Personal	180 days	Delete
Default 2 year move to archi...	Default	730 days	Archive
Deleted Items	Deleted Items	30 days	Delete
Junk Email	Junk Email	30 days	Delete

Figure 6-16. *Retention policies (legacy view located in the Exchange admin console)*

There are two types of archives in Office 365: personal archives and Office365 Exchange server mailbox archives. The Office 365 Exchange server archives can be immutable (meaning they can be configured to ignore any change via a litigation hold or in-place hold). Personal archives are stored locally on the user desktop and are not immutable (users can change the contents). The retention policies refer only to the moving of data from the user mailbox to the archive. To make an archive and retention policy work, you need to enable the archive in the Exchange admin console (edit the mailbox in the Exchange admin console and select Enable for archive; this is discussed in Chapter 8). This feature will be moving to the Security & Compliance Center at a later date. Litigation hold (or in place hold) locks the Office 365 Mailbox from having contents deleted - regardless if it is in the main mailbox or the archive mailbox. Users will see data being deleted, but administrators can access data in the Security & Compliance center under Search and Discovery.

Retention Policy

A *retention policy* consists of the business processes that define the movement of data to the archive or delete folders. Retention policies are a set of rules that are executed concerning a message (see Figure 6-17). A retention policy is a combination of different *retention tags*, which are actions placed on a message. You can have only one retention policy applied to a mailbox. In an organization where you have compliance requirements, retention tags are used to manage the user mailbox information and to control mailbox sizes. As an example, you can have a retention tag that deletes messages in a mailbox after 30 days. If the mailbox is under legal hold, the user will see the data deleted, but the deleted data is recoverable.

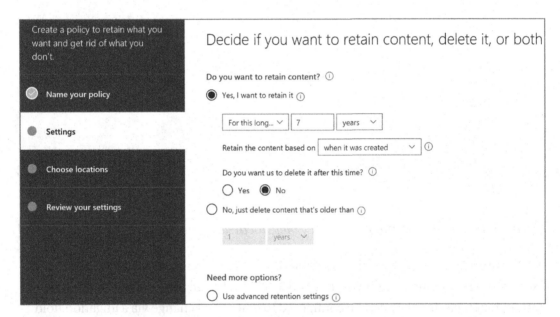

Figure 6-17. *Retention policy created in the Security & Compliance Center*

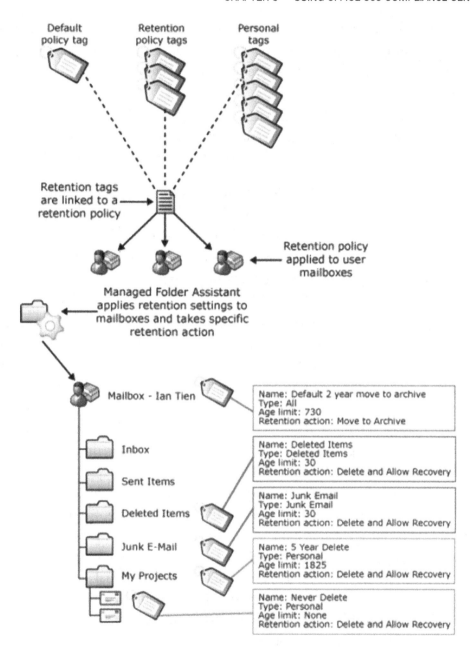

Figure 6-18. *Legacy Office 365 retention tags (courtesy of Microsoft)*

Retention tags define and apply the retention settings to messages and folders in the user mailbox. These tags specify how long a message is kept and what action is taken when a message reaches the retention age. Retention tags are used to control the amount of information that is on the user's desktop. Typically, this means that a message is moved to the archive folder or it is deleted. Looking at Figure 6-17, you can see three types of retention tags: default retention tags, policy retention tags, and personal retention tags.

Default	The default policy applies to all items in a mailbox that do not have a retention tag applied.
Policy	Policy tags are applied to folders (inbox, deleted items, and so on) and override the default policy tags. The only retention action for a policy is to delete items.
Personal	Personal tags are used only for Outlook clients to move data to customer folders in the user's mailboxes.

Keep in mind that a retention policy directly affects the amount of information kept in a user mailbox. A retention policy requires that an archive mailbox is enabled. The default configuration of Office 365 is to have the archive mailboxes disabled. Retention tags (which make up the retention policy) are just another tool used for information management. Depending on your business needs, you may have different retention polices to manage information of different groups in your organization. In one organization we managed, the data retention policy was 90 days, unless the mailbox was placed on an in-place hold for litigation or discovery.

Compliance archives may or may not have a retention policy applied to them. Typically, a compliance rule requires that all documents (emails, files etc) are placed on legal hold for the regulation hold period. The legal hold also includes documents in OneDrive and SharePoint site through the Compliance & Administration site. User mailboxes that are placed under a litigation hold with the external audit enabled meet all compliance requirements because the data is immutable. Later in this chapter, I will walk you through an eDiscovery search to collect information in response to a court-ordered subpoena. For now let's continue with our review of the other features of the Security & Compliance Center.

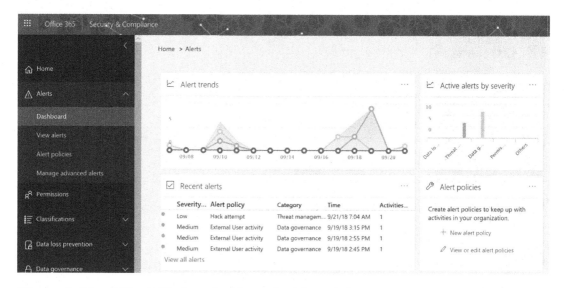

Figure 6-19. *Office 365 alert dashboard with trends*

Alert Structure

Looking back over any of the NIST compliance reviews, there is one requirement that will need to be deployed, and that is alerts to provide an early warning of potential problems. The type of alerts depends on the business and what processes you need to examine. The place to start is with the alert dashboard. To add a new threat, just add a new threat policy, and the wizard will walk you through the threats and what to add. Looking back to our NIST-CSF discussion, one of the pillars is to *detect* the security incident. In Figure 6-20, we have a couple of different threat detection ranging from accessing data to forwarding e-mail.

After you have deployed the alerts, the next step is to review the threat dashboard and establish a policy of review and analysis on the threats. In the Compliance Manager, we need to put in place business processes where we review the alerts in the logs and look for trends to decide. Because of the Compliance Manager activity, we put in place the necessary alerts and processes that we use to analyze the alerts.

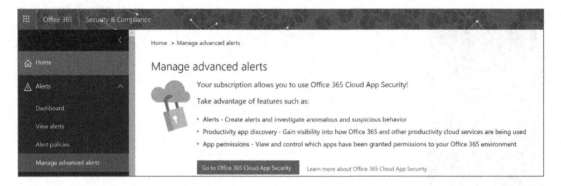

Figure 6-20. *Alert dashboard with CAS integration*

Alert Types

There are different alert types that you can create or add. Some of the alerts are system-wide and are enabled based on other dashboards. The alert dashboard is a data aggregation dashboard in Office 365 (see Figure 6-20) with integration to other services. "Manage advanced alerts" is a link to Cloud App Security (CAS). Depending on how you configure CAS, you can have a number of alerts that show up in the alert dashboard. Figure 6-19 shows the alert dashboard with two types of alerts, those that are from other services (not highlighted) and those that were created in the alert dashboard (highlighted with an on/off slider). As the compliance officer in Office 365/Azure, you want to enable alerts to help you manage the environment for the necessary processes.

Adding new alerts from the dashboard is a simple process. Just click "New alert policy" and create an alert. The following are the key items to set in an alert:

- Name and description
- Severity
- Class of alert

The issue that we all face is the quantity of information that we need to manage. It is important that you define a model for data collection and classification. If you have not set up a classification model, then step back and define the model that you want. In our case we organized information based on class of alerts, such as threat management and severity. Follow the wizard and add additional customization to the alert (see Figure 6-20). Once you are satisfied with the alert, click Save to create the alert (see Figure 6-21).

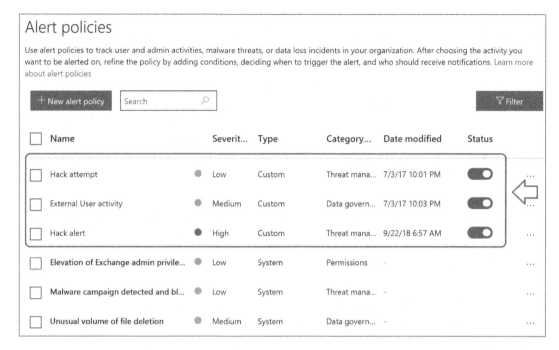

Figure 6-21. *Alert dashboard with alerts highlighted created locally*

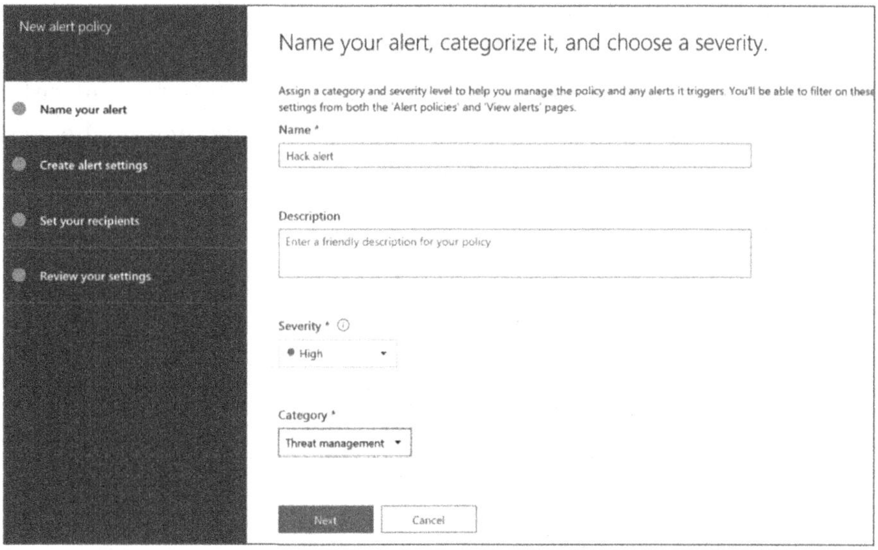

Figure 6-22. *Adding an alert to the Azure notification*

The processes that you use to create and review the alerts are the same. As you expand your security polices, you will establish different capabilities on access and how you want to enable the tracking in the environment. Alerts give you an early warning. You leverage information that is in the Security & Compliance Center along with the security information located in the Azure Security Center.

Threat management

Once you have defined the alerts, the next step is the configuration of Threat management for the threat dashboard. The threat dashboard is a summary of the different threats that are active in your Office 365 tenant. The threat dashboard is another data aggregation function that allows you to see data differently. Threats are about having multiple eyes on a group of systems.

Figure 6-24 shows the threats as they are attacking users, and what we have configured in Office 365 to block is an AI-driven engine; over time you will see trends on the attack and what you did as part of the threat attack. The threat dashboard is expanding and will include other services such as Advanced Threat Protection (ATP), Cloud App Security (CAS), and other solutions that track threats. The Threat management dashboard present a summary of the information to the various services. As an example, the threat management dashboard allows the simulation of phishing attacks and keeps track of the threats and activities to address them. The dashboard information used in the analysis is based on the raw information from the security and audit logs.

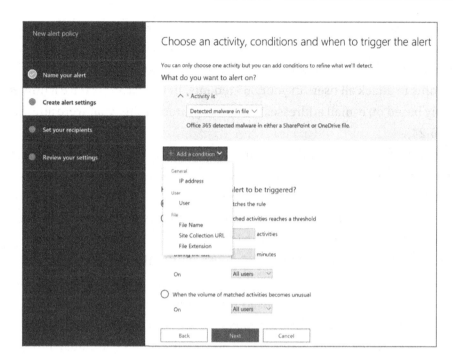

Figure 6-23. Adding additional customization to the alert

Figure 6-24. Finalizing the alert that was created in the Security & Compliance Center

Threat management provides an overview of the threats that are affecting the Office 365 organization. The trend analysis can let you know which users are being targeted and what approach is being used. If this is a coordinated attack, you will see a number of attempts to attack all users in your 365 tenants. In this case, we have a limited attack, probably based on e-mail addresses that we captured in sites that were attacked (see Figure 6-24).

The threat management dashboard also includes simulated attack phishing e-mails. This is a new feature that has been added to the Security & Compliance Center. All of the new regulations such as GDPR, CCPA, HIPAA, and NIST standards require security training (or penetration testing) for the end users. Traditionally this has been contracted to third-party service providers, such as HIPAA Secure, Breach Secure, Knowb4, and others. Office 365 now includes the ability to send out simulated penetration attacks to test users. The attacks are measured and reported. The Office 365 penetration testing includes the ability to modify the security e-mail to test to design it so it is appropriate for the industry. The simulated campaigns are no different than any modern marketing campaign. You pick the target campaign and set up a number of e-mails to trick the end users into clicking the campaign and executing it (see Figure 6-26). To launch a campaign, click Attack Simulator and then the phishing campaign to execute.

Figure 6-25. *Threat dashboard in the Security & Compliance Center*

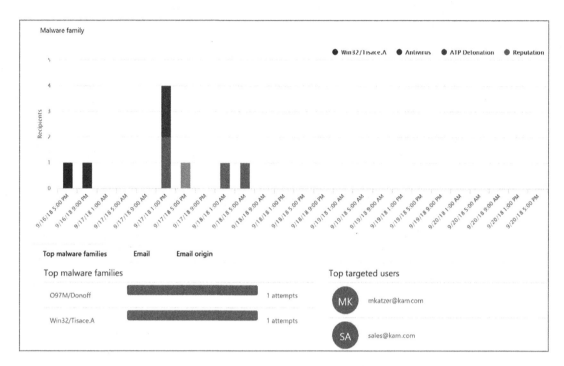

Figure 6-26. *Attack summary with details on targeted users and methods*

As an example, let's select the prize campaign. This campaign is about harvesting user credentials. To make the campaign effective, you have the option to modify the text in the campaign. If you wanted, you could build this as an Amazon campaign or even mirror a gift campaign that one of your businesses sends out in your local community. Executing the campaign is easy; just follow the steps outlined next.

Step 1: Select the Campaign

The campaign we are using is the credential harvesting campaign. Click Launch to start the campaign. Name the campaign and click Use Template. Make sure you do not send more than a one campaign a week (see Figure 6-27).

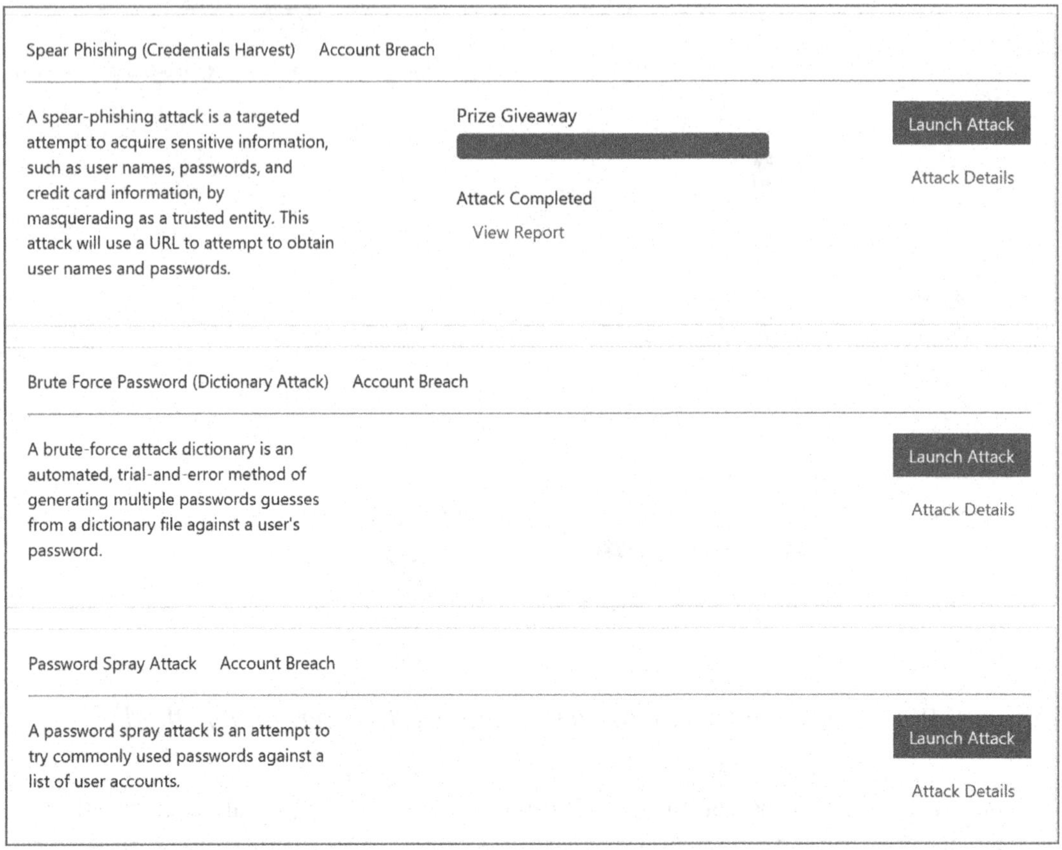

Figure 6-27. *Attack Simulator options*

Step 2: Customize the Offer

It is important to customize the offer so it mirrors an offer in your local market. A modification may be a free Amazon gift card, for example. Pick something that is unique and you can clone from your existing e-mail offers (see Figure 6-28). In this case of a "prize offer" I would use an Amazon gift notification or a survey, such as "Take the Survey, Get a $25 Amazon Card." The goal is to make this as real as possible.

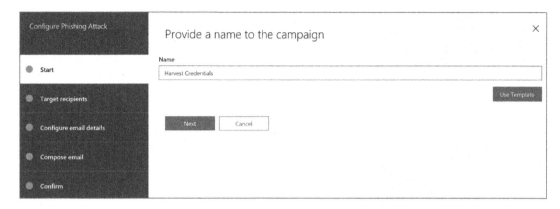

Figure 6-28. *Selecting a campaign and naming the campaign*

Step 3: Select the Distribution List for the Campaign

Select the distribution list to send to. If you do not have one, then create one for your organization. I recommend you create a dynamic list that is targeted to all users who have a license (see Figure 6-29).

Figure 6-29. *Customizing the offer*

Step 4: Select the Distribution List for the Campaign

Build out a web portal with a message to the end user. Let them know you been phished. Your web portal could contain a description of the attack and what to look for. Train your users, and be creative (see Figure 6-30)!

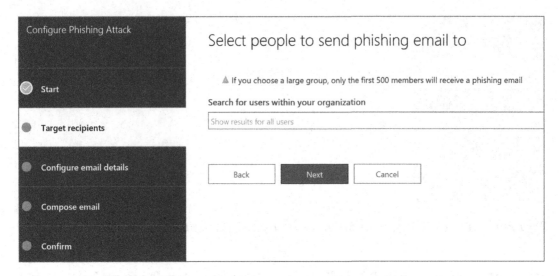

Figure 6-30. *Target the campaign to the users in your tenant*

Step 5: Customize the E-mail

The best e-mail to use is one that you have received. Figure 6-32 shows one that I received from a vendor on a survey for IT services.

Step 6: Execute the Campaign

Send the e-mail (see Figure 6-32) and look for the responses from the simulated phishing.

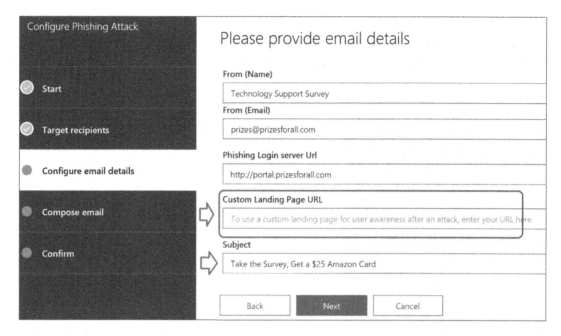

Figure 6-31. *Fill out the campaign and create the destination portal*

Figure 6-32. *Be creative with the campaign*

Once you have executed the campaign, the next step is to review the results (see Figure 6-33). Like any other marketing campaign, you want to make the campaign as realistic as possible. Invest the time to train the user.

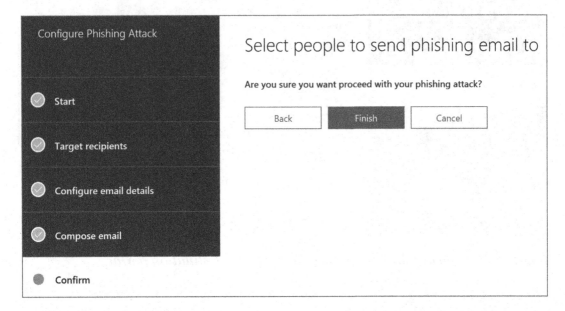

Figure 6-33. *Execute the campaign*

Make sure you review the threat dashboard for the status and trends. You have a responsibility to set up the necessary business process and training to keep your users informed. It is a battle between the good guys and bad guys. Figure 6-34 shows a status dashboard of the attacks against some users.

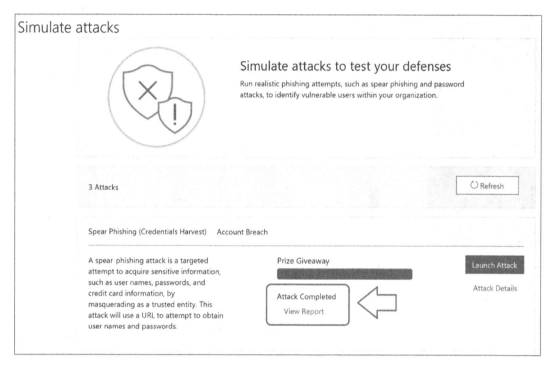

Figure 6-34. *Review the results*

Search and Investigate

Organizations that perform electronic document discovery (attorneys, compliance officers, etc.) are empowered based on the rules in the organization. Typically, there are three levels of management with eDiscovery cases. These management roles are the compliance officer, compliance manager, and reviewer. In small organizations, you have one person completing tasks in all three roles. In a larger organization, this is either completed with a large staff, and some functions are contracted to a third party such as management specialist. Figure 6-35 shows the permission structure in the Security & Compliance Center used to manage these roles. In our small company example, the compliance officer could be the compliance administrator/compliance manager and eDiscovery manager. Usually the IT pro will partner with the compliance officer to set up the environment. The first step in the eDiscovery process is to add the roles that are needed to access information as part of the document review process. The IT pro may not have a role in the discovery process.

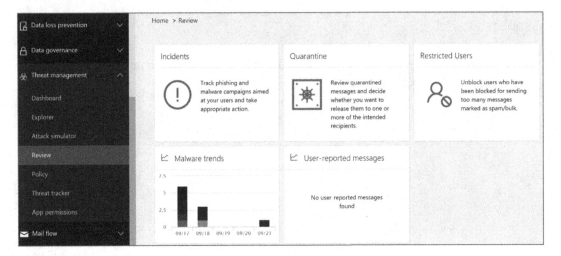

Figure 6-35. *Summary dashboard of the attacks in an Office 365 organization*

My philosophy on eDiscovery issues when using the Security & Compliance Center is to upgrade the subscriptions to an E5. This will give you access to all of the advanced eDiscovery tools available in Office 365. There is an additional cost, but it is significantly less than the sanctions, fees, and penalties associated with losing a case because of poor discovery in the document production phase. As an IT professional, your job is to provide all the information requested as soon as possible.

There are many questions that IT professionals have when setting up the Security & Compliance Center. This chapter is a compilation of the best-known methods in use to implement a compliant cloud storage system that meets the needs of various regulation entities. Our implementation for Office 365 is using the Microsoft 365 E5 subscription, which contains the Office E5 component (see Figure 6-36). I will now show how you can set up service to provide documents in response to a request for production (if you have a been served a court order for document production). Our discussion will review two aspects of Office 365 data collection: the compliance capabilities of Office 365 and later suppling documents to a request.

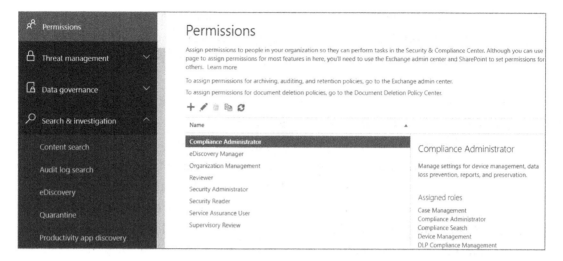

Figure 6-36. *Office 365 eDiscovery roles*

Note   Figure 6-5 shows two different types of eDiscovery search tools: Search Content and eDiscovery. These tools are similar but different. Search Content is a scalable eDiscovery tool that can handles large amounts of data, searching SharePoint, OneDrive for Business, and multiple mailboxes (no limit). The eDiscovery tool does similar functions but is limited in scope. What I do is create a blanket search in eDiscovery to lock the mailboxes under legal hold and perform searches in Content Search.

The Security & Compliance Center roots are in the eDiscovery process. Organizations have discovery requests from presiding authorities, and as part of different request, they need to product documents. Sometimes these documents are covered under a protective order, and sometimes they are not.

Setting Up an Office 365 Discovery and a Retention Policy

Office 365 is flexible in how the different policies for the management of information can be set up. The problem is where to start. Earlier, we reviewed the different capabilities that you have in Office 365. There are three different areas that need to be configured before you can begin to use the services. The following section outlines the steps required to set up the 365 organization for a compliance, discovery, and retention policy. Follow the steps to set up the different features. Note that you will find additional details about compliance steps in the section "Configuring Compliance."

What you are trying to avoid is the generation of paper documents. Figure 6-37 is a sample of the old way of producing documents for eDiscovery. This is a sample of what you want to avoid. Litigation is expensive, and discovery is an expensive process (from $1–$2 a page). In this example, there were 200,000 pages of documents generated to satisfy a request. Cost-wise, this was $250,000 to $400,000 worth of work. Office 365 allows you to create a "discovery center," where you can process the queries and generate a SharePoint library that has the information requested in the response. In this case, information was generated for the other side's attorneys that was in response to a judicial order. Access to the discovery search results can be shared with the other side's attorneys. This discovery center approach is a lot lower in cost than the traditional document production shown in Figure 6-37.

	Office 365 ProPlus	Office 365 Enterprise E1	Office 365 Enterprise E3	Office 365 Enterprise E5
Compliance solutions to support Archiving, Auditing and eDiscovery, mailbox and internal site search and legal hold capabilities depending upon subscription type		✓	✓	✓
Information Protection including Rights Management and Data Loss Prevention for emails	✓		✓	✓
Advanced eDiscovery with Predictive Coding and Text Analytics				✓

Figure 6-37. Subscription types supporting the Security & Compliance Center

Figure 6-38. *Production in response to a judicial discovery order (approximately 200,000 documents produced)*

Discovery Walk-Through

The discovery process seems daunting at the start. The simplest way to understand the eDiscovery process is to walk through an eDiscovery search; then we can look at the process to set up the search. I have found that if you understand the end game, then it is easier to understand how to create an advanced search. To frame the situation, you are a compliance officer and your IT pro has set up your Office 365 site with the correct permissions and access. The IT pro has sent you an e-mail with a notification that your site is set up. Your response (like many of us) is simply, "Great, what do I do now?" Let's walk through the process on what do you do next to put our mind at ease. Discovery is not that difficult; it just takes time.

Step 1: Log In to Office 365 and Click the Security Icon

To access the Security & Compliance Center, log in to Office 365, and click the Security & Compliance Center icon. Users need to be an Office 365 global administrator or a member of one or more Security & Compliance Center role groups. The Security & Compliance role groups are different than the Exchange Online Organization Management role group. These permissions are not shared.

If you do not see the Security & Compliance Center, this is because you do not have access. To access the Security & Compliance Center, a global admin will need to grant you permissions by adding you to the Organization Management role group.

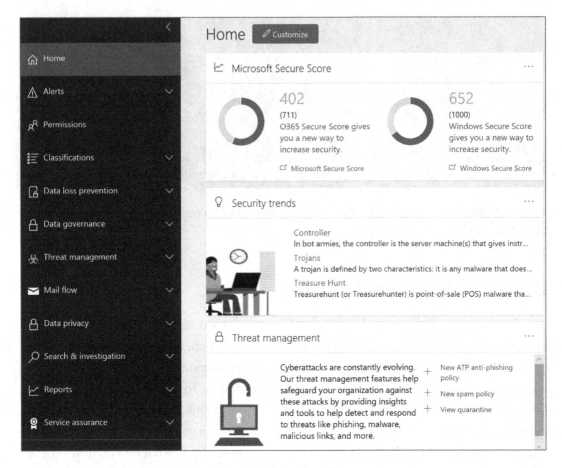

Figure 6-39. *Security & Compliance Center landing page*

Step 2: Select Search & Investigation, and Review Logs

Earlier, the IT support staff added us into the group where we have the correct permission to access the features in the Security & Compliance Center. Our job is simple; it is to perform a search on the data that we were requested to provide. In Figure 6-40, we expand Search & Investigation to begin our query on the eDiscovery process. There are three areas that we focus on: Content search, Audit log search, and eDiscovery.

In Figure 6-40, we are looking at the audit logs to verify who has access to the data and who has recently accessed the data in Office 365. The audit log search will provide that information to you. In our example, the admin has recently logged into the Security & Compliance Center and retrieved the compliance configuration.

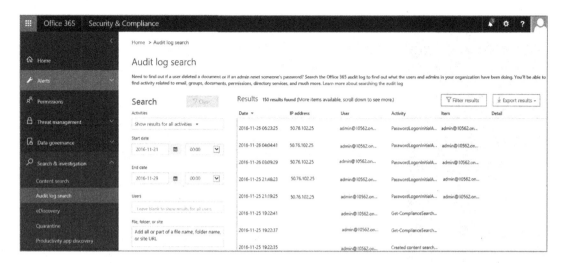

Figure 6-40. *Audit log search*

Once you are satisfied, the next step is to review that a hold has been placed on the data for the content search.

Step 3: Verify That a Case Has Been Created to Place Data on Hold

There are different philosophies on this, but what works the best is to make sure that you have at least one case where all data that you are looking for has been placed on hold. The Office 365 Security & Compliance Center allows you to place multiple data sources on hold for specific searches. However, it is easy to lose yourself in the searches and accidently remove a legal hold and delete data. To prevent this from happening, go to the eDiscovery tool and verify that we have a case and the subject matter of our inquiry is placed on hold (see Figure 6-41).

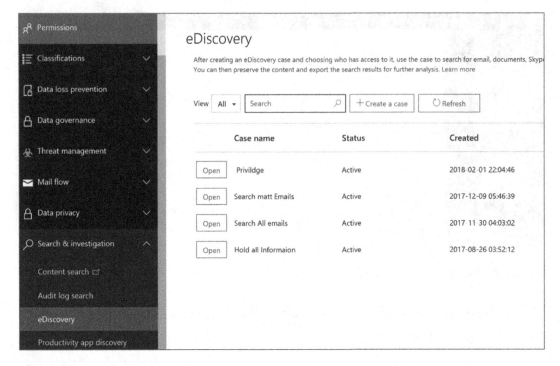

Figure 6-41. *Placed on hold*

If the data has not been placed on hold, a case needs to be created to lock the appropriate mailboxes and SharePoint sites and put the user's OneDrive for Business sites on hold. Once this case is in place, our focus will be on using the Content Search tool.

Note If you do not see a case, create a case and place the accounts you want to search on hold to protect data from accidently being deleted. If you make a mistake and delete the hold, the data will be deleted according to the retention policy. The case in this example has two mailboxes selected, and all data has been placed on hold. The hold is visible only to users who have permission to view the case (more about this later).

Step 4: Start the Content Search

The next step is to start the search for data and export the data for review. So far we have the data on hold (step 3), and we are searching for specific information. We select the content search and look for an existing case. If we do not see one, we create a new case and begin our search for information.

In Figure 6-42, we are creating a new search called Smart Phone Search, and we are looking at three different users' mailboxes: Dan Jump (CEO), Karen Berg (VP of sales/marketing), and Amy (product manager). The process is similar to the actions in the eDiscovery Center; the difference in this case is that we are looking at specific information in user mailboxes, and we do not need to worry about the data being deleted since we have verified that we have all of the user mailboxes and SharePoint sites on hold.

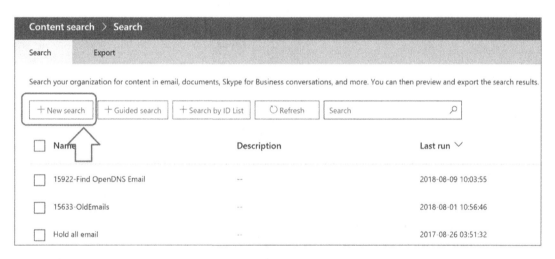

Figure 6-42. *Setting up the content search*

As part of the search configuration, you specify the area of search. In this case, we are looking for all phones and what to exclude the term *cell phone*. If you have an existing case, you can edit the query or create a new query as part of the search setup (see Figure 6-43). Click Add and then Run. Correct any errors that you have (usually the location is not specified correctly); then click Save and name the search.

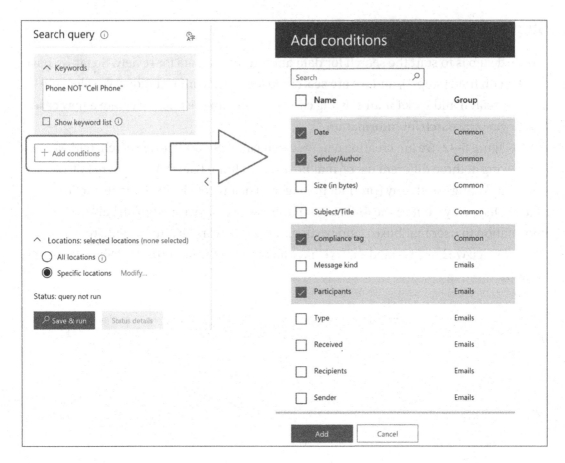

Figure 6-43. *Doing a content search*

Step 5: Preview the Data

As the content search engine crawls the mailboxes, the information is displayed on the number of items and size of the items. The compliance officer can add additional searches as needed.

To preview the search data, select "preview search results" in Figure 6-44 to see the initial set of documents (*documents* in this case are any forms of communications: e-mails, Skype conversation, marketing materials, etc.)

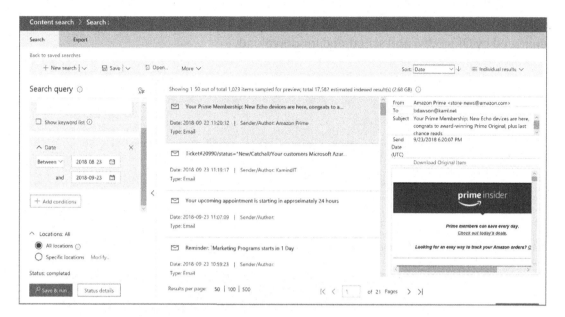

Figure 6-44. *Initial search statistics*

Note   The compliance officer can add and delete searches as needed. Therefore, it is important to have a case created with all of the content under hold for eDiscovery. In the case of a content search, when the content search is deleted, the hold is also removed, unless you have another hold in a content search or under a case in the eDiscovery Center.

If your access is blocked at the preview stage, you need to request permission from the admin on the Security & Compliance Center to give you access to the search results. Otherwise, your results on the search preview will be displayed as shown in Figure 6-44. Keep in mind that search preview is limited. Complete review will require you to export the documents.

Step 6: Export the Documents

Once you are satisfied that you have all of the documents you are looking for, the next step is to export the documents for a full review. To export the document, click More and then "Export results" (see Figure 6-45). Follow the wizard to generate the document export. The documents are exported in PST format to be loaded in a local version of

Outlook. At this stage you are creating an export job. The export data will need to be collected by Office 365 and scheduled for download.

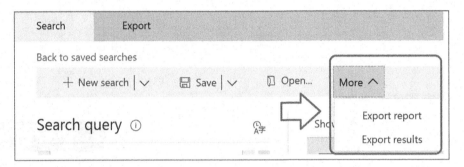

Figure 6-45. *Content search on documents for query "phone Not 'Cell Phone'"*

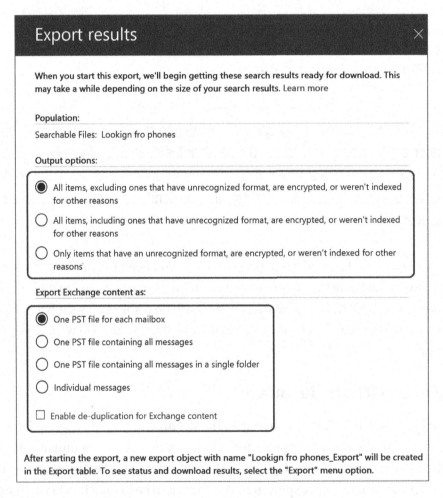

Figure 6-46. *Exporting the documents to a PC*

Click Export, which will start the document export wizard. The first step is to confirm the export and destination. Because of the privacy concerns, documents exported are encrypted, and you will need to keep a copy of the key to decode the documents.

Select the Export tab and then select the job that was created (see Figure 6-47). This will start the data export process. The data will be downloaded to your PC in the format you specified earlier.

Note   If you are responding to a request for production (RFP) on a court order discovery order, you want to export all documents from the eDiscovery Center after you place the documents on hold. I have found it better to give all documents requested and not duplicate information. Most likely you will be using a third-party tool to process the documents and stamp them. We will look at document production later in this chapter.

Figure 6-47. *Start the export process by clicking the case*

The export process runs smoothly in the background. The export process starts and displays the status of the job (see Figure 6-48).

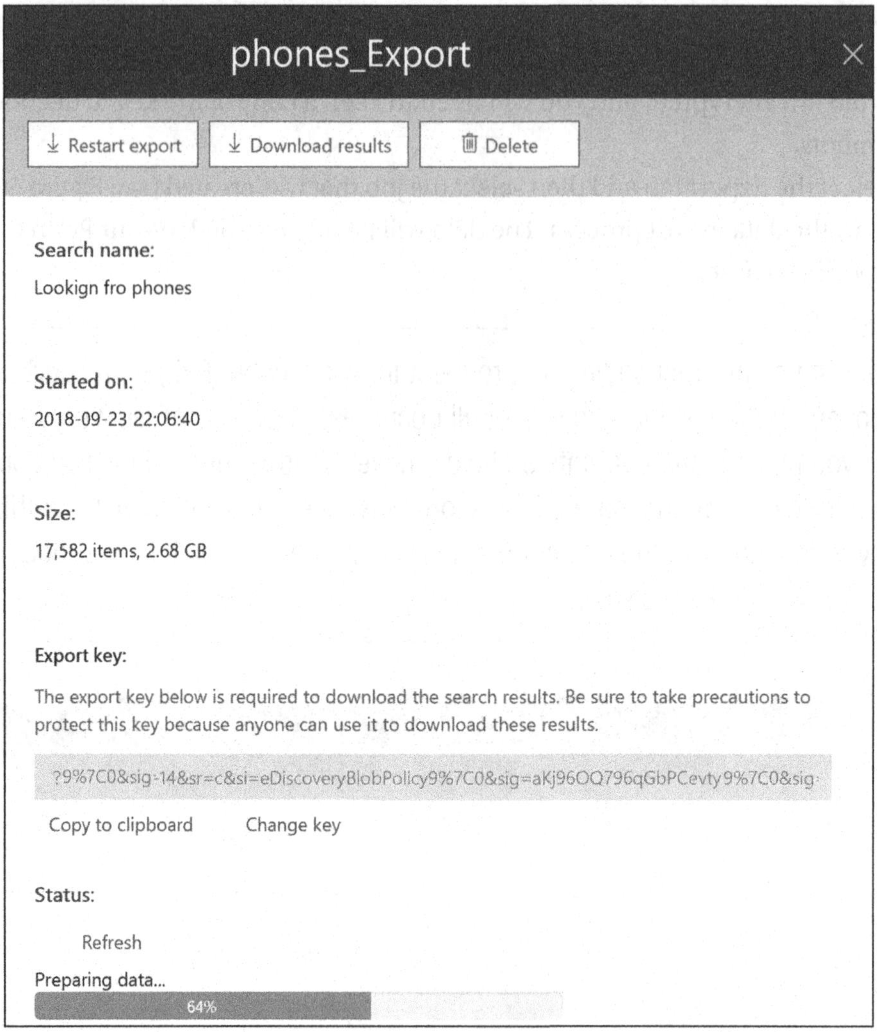

Figure 6-48. *The export process begins to assemble the data for export*

The export wizard handles large downloads. I completed a recent eDiscovery project where the export PSTs were over 30GB in size (about 407,000 e-mails and attachments.). To export the documents, select "download export results" to download the documents to your local system. When you download the documents, the documents are encrypted in transit (se Figure 6-48). Make sure you keep a copy of the key. You will need this key on the client to remove the encryption to access the PST files.

Note   If you are searching for information, the best way to search for information is to use the Content Search Center. In a discovery request, what I have found works is that you define a new user account for the response to an RFP, and you upload the data into the OneDrive for Business. This way you can use the Content Search tool to look for data. Also, if you are building bates-stamped documents, upload them to your OneDrive for Business account. This way you can search for the original document and find the bates-stamped document that matches your search. This saves a lot of time in preparing for litigation.

Once the data is ready, you can download the results. You will need the encryption key to unencrypt the data. All search data in the Compliance Center is encrypted. Once you have copied the key, click Download Results to start the download process. The files will be downloaded to your PC in an Exchange folder structure (see Figure 6-49). We will go through this process later in the chapter; I wanted you to understand the end results and what the discovery process looks like in a response to an RFP.

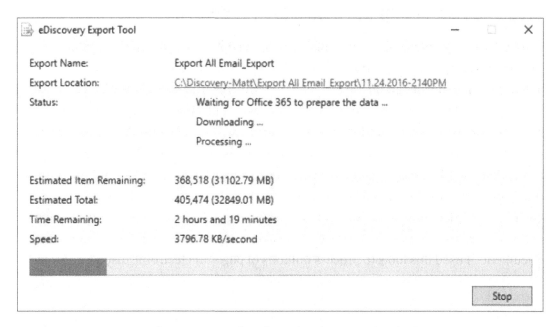

Figure 6-49. Export data process, loading the data on the desktop

After the data is downloaded, it will be in a directory similar to Figure 6-26. Once the data is exported, you can now bates-stamp the material and filter it out as needed.

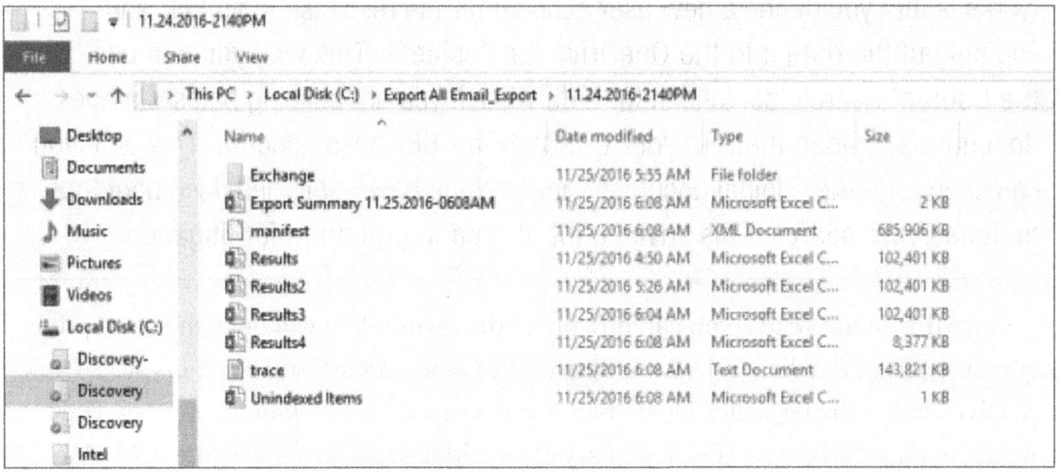

Figure 6-50. *Export data structure*

Step 7: Bates-Stamp the Discovery Production

Once we have completed the export of the data, the only step left is to bates-stamp the material in a response for production. Depending on your business size, you may have a department that will handle the production of the material. Most IT professionals stop at this step and turn over the production to the legal staff. However, if you are a small business, you will need to produce the material yourself to keep costs under control and add bates stamps. There are different tools that you use to process the production. I use a tool called Bates Express. What this tool from Bates Express provides is a unique number that is used to track documents in the legal system. This is called a bate-stamp. When you complete electronic discovery, you are producing millions documents, each page of the document needs to be numbered. This is one of the tools available to bate-stamp documents. I used this tools to process millions of pages in electronic discovery project.

Figure 6-51. *Bates Express website (*`www.batestexpress.com`*)*

What I like about this tool is that it is really easy to use. In the e-discovery production that I am creating in response to the subpoena, I have filtered Exchange information with 120,000 messages in each PST. With Bates Express, I configure the bates stamp (the header and footer on the document), and I point the tool to the downloaded PST. A few hours later, I have 120,000 PDF files, all searchable and all bates-stamped for production (see Figure 6-52).

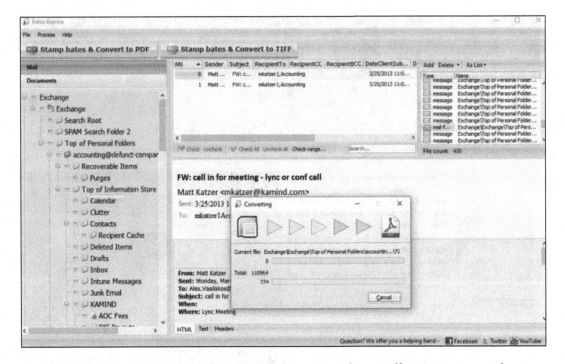

Figure 6-52. *Bates Express processing a document from Office 365 exported archive*

The documents are produced with the necessary header and footers for your discovery project. Bates Express produced documents similar to those in Figure 6-53. The bates stamp I use in this production request is the string "Confidential - <case number> - < document ID>."

Note   Every document that will be produced will need to be bates-stamped, and the document header "Confidential" may be optional but is subject to the production order. In some cases, there will be material designated as "Attorney Eyes Only." In this case, "Confidential" is replaced with "Attorney Eyes Only."

Production of material is not that difficult; it is just time-consuming. Traditional discovery firms charge around $1 a page for each document produced. You can see with automated tools you can sharply reduce the amount of time that it takes to produce material. At this point, you understand the discovery process enough that you can do your own search and produce the documents required. In the final sections of this chapter, we will review some additional configuration process configuration that you can use in your discovery project.

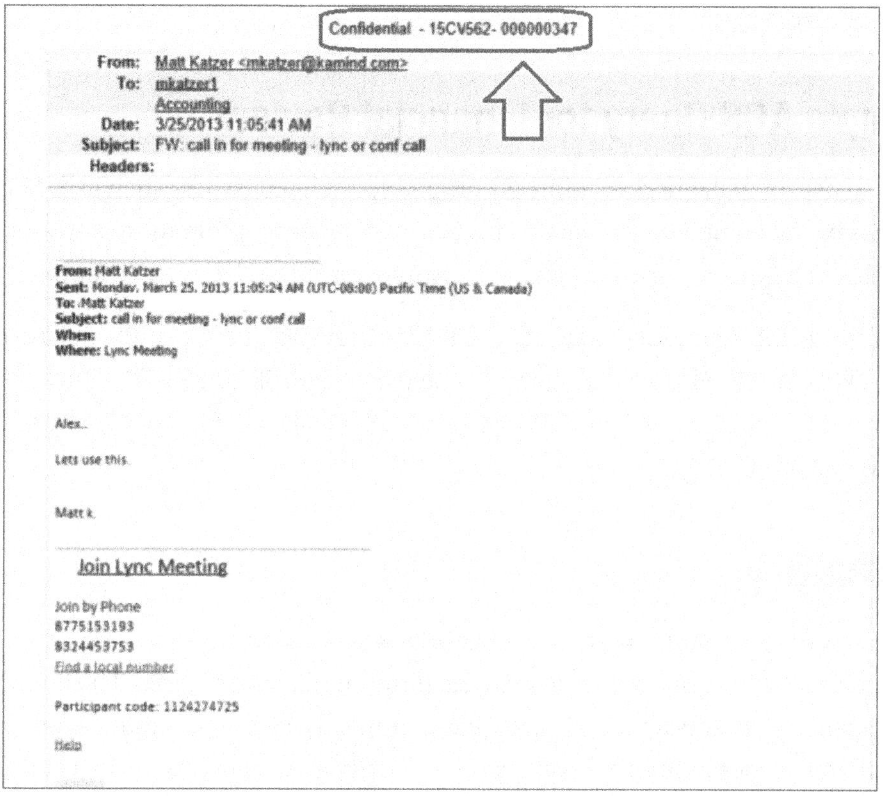

Figure 6-53. *Bates-stamped document with case header*

Building Discovery Searches

In some cases you may want to delete e-mails; in others you may want to preserve them in the long term. When you are experimenting with retention policies, use a mailbox with a trial set of sample data. If you are afraid of deleting information, then enable a litigation hold (or in-place hold) on the account that you are setting up the retention tags for. If the retention tags are not set up correctly, information will be deleted.

Before we address any of the examples, we need to step back for a brief review of advanced query strings (AQS). The syntax can become complex. AQS is provided by the Windows operating system using Windows Desktop Search (WDS). All AQS searches must be fully qualified. A fully qualified search requires that you add parentheses every time you add a Boolean operator (AND OR NOT) to a search query. (The queries are processed based on the location of the parentheses.) There is a good description of AQS queries at `https://docs.microsoft.com/en-us/windows/desktop/lwef/-search-2x-wds-aqsreference`.

Sample AQS Query for Financial Review

You can use an AQS query to address compliance-related issues (such as FINRA audit reviews by the compliance officer). The AQS can be any combination of words. The more complex, the longer it takes to generate the query request. Here's an example:

```
(Guarantee OR Money OR Compliant OR Attorney OR Transfer OR Security OR
Loss OR Loan OR Misrepresented OR Unauthorized OR Yield OR Stock OR Bond OR
Security OR Percent OR Pay* OR Promise OR Funds OR Risk OR Secure OR Take*
OR Pissed OR Churn)
```

Summary

The focus of this chapter was on the Security & Compliance Center as well as on data collection and analysis of the data via the different discovery tools. The Security & Compliance Center is a hub or data aggregation service that contains a repository of the different types of information used in security analysis tools. As an example, the eDiscovery Center has become a key compliance tool used to show that a company has complied with federal and state regulations. This is the audit logs that we enabled in chapter 2 in our initial configuration of the Security & Compliance. The stored logs can be exported and analyzed via tools like Power BI.

It is extremely important that your IT team actively manages the data and records information. The days of not reviewing logs or storing logs on a long-term basis are over. At a minimum, you need to have a process that does the following:

1. Download and archive the Office 365 Compliance & Security Center audit log on a monthly basis.

2. Download the archive of the Azure Active Directory log on a monthly basis.

3. Download and archive the Azure audit log on a monthly basis.

Where do you store the logs? Create a SharePoint collaboration site and upload the logs to that site. At KAMIND IT, this is what we do for all of our customers who are on one of our security plans. The logs are available for forensic analysis. If you are looking at an automatic way to store logs, you can configured this features in the Azure log analytics site. In this case the logs are uploaded to an azure data storage area. This is no longer just nice to have; it is a requirement to be compliant - you need long term archive of the logs.

References

There is a lot of information about Office 365 on the Web—the issue is finding the right site. The information contained in this chapter is a combination of my experience doing deployments and of support information that has been published by third parties.

Microsoft Office 365 Blog: Latest News about Office 365

- http://blogs.office.com/b/microsoft_office_365_blog/

Searching Mailboxes on Legal Hold

- http://help.outlook.com/en-us/140/hh125820.aspx

Understanding Legal Hold in Office 365

- http://www.networkworld.com/community/blog/doing-e-discovery-message-retention-legal-rec

Understanding Retention Policy PowerShell Commands

- http://help.outlook.com/en-us/beta/gg271153.aspx

Understanding Permissions on Discovery Mailboxes

- http://help.outlook.com/en-us/140/ee424425.aspx

Search for Deleted Messages

- http://help.outlook.com/en-us/beta/gg315525.aspx

Benoit's Corner – Useful Tips and Tricks on Exchange and SharePoint

- http://blog.hametbenoit.info/default.aspx

AQS Query Syntax: Discovery

- https://docs.microsoft.com/en-us/windows/desktop/lwef/-search-2x-wds-aqsreference

CHAPTER 7

Step-by-Step Migration

The focus of this book has been mostly on compliance, configuration, and security. My editors suggested that I place this chapter at the beginning, but I wanted the migration information near the end. The reason is a simple one, I wanted to explain the why, and discuss how the security landscape is changing. You need this information to understand what you need to do to make sure you are configuring your office 365 correctly. However, some of you may not have decided to move to Office 365 and I wanted to give you a roadmap on how to move you company to Office 365. It may seem challenging, but the steps are easy. This chapter is your roadmap to Office 365.

There are a variety of ways to get started with Office 365. The key is to remember that you can mix different subscription types based on the job function. For example, in this book, we use the Microsoft 365 E5 suite as the license type. If you are looking at e-mail and OneDrive migration to Office 365, you can get started with different subscription types such as a Business Essentials plan (limited to company sizes with fewer than 300 users) or an Enterprise E1 subscription. Any subscription choice you make is your decision. Microsoft is slowly transitioning the subscription service to be purchased only from an authorized cloud solution provider (CSP). A Microsoft CSP can offer you different subscription types and allow you to change the subscription at any time. If you do not have a relationship with a Microsoft CSP, go to `https://www.microsoft.com/en-US/solution-providers/search` (see Figure 7-1).

© Matthew Katzer 2018
M. Katzer, *Securing Office 365*, https://doi.org/10.1007/978-1-4842-4230-8_7

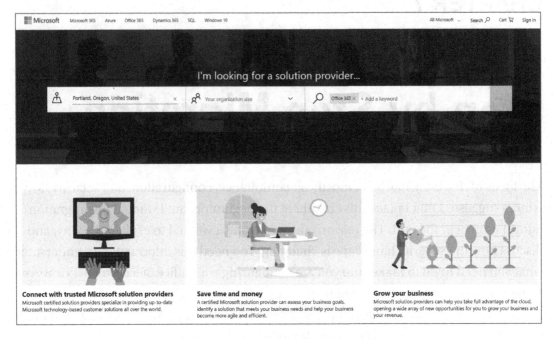

Figure 7-1. *Office 365 solution partner selection*

The focus of this chapter is to provide you with guidance on how to migrate to Office 365. At the end of this chapter, you will have a fully functional Office 365 solution, and you can configure the security services using the techniques discussed in earlier chapters.

Purchasing Office 365

Office 365 plans are designed for different target markets and are organized into suites. Microsoft has set up suites for different styles of companies, based on business needs. In the early days, these suites had fixed configurations that were difficult to change. This has changed considerably. You can now mix different suites and Office 365 plans to reflect your business needs. For example, if you want to purchase a direct-dial number for Microsoft Teams (aka Skype for Business), you add the phone system (included in Office 365 E5) option to your subscription (or upgrade to a different suite that has a domestic calling option). Subscription upgrades and downgrades are common. It is recommended that you work with a CSP to handle these requests. Most cloud partners make the change for you as a courtesy if the cloud partner is added as a subscription advisor (or partner of record) on the account. When you decide to move your IT services—mail, phone, or local file storage—from your current supplier to Office 365, this is referred to as *migration* or *onboarding*.

There are two methods used to move to Office 365: cutover migration and federation migration. Each of these approaches has its pros and cons. In cutover migrations (you move mail to office 365 immediately, then bring over historic mail after email is on Office 365), the end user typically loses the Outlook cache of e-mail addresses (users typically call these *contacts*, but they are not contacts) and local tasks/categories on older versions of Office. Cutover migrations create a new Outlook profile, and the local address cache is not migrated. Federation migrations maintain the same user profile, and moving the mailbox to Office 365 requires an Exchange Server mailbox move (called a *federated move*). The method you use depends on your business requirements and how fast you want to move to Office 365. Cutover migration is fast: you "cut over" your mail services to Office 365 from the old service at a specific point in time. Federation is a stage migration, or a slower, nonintrusive migration. If you are on a POP or IMAP server (such as Google or One on One), you will be using a cutover migration. Typically, we see federation migrations when there is an on-premise Exchange Server (Exchange Server version 2010 or later) and the number of users is greater than 50. The reason for the 50-user limit is cost. The cost of moving 50 users is close to the cost of setting up a federation move, in other words, the cost break-even point. Fewer than 50 users, and it's less expensive for the cutover. More than 50 users, a federation move is less expensive than a cutover migration.

Note   Cutover migrations are typically used when environments have fewer than 50 users and there is not an Exchange Server deployed. There are different ways to complete a federation move. The federation approach depends on the Exchange Server deployment. Keep in mind that if you have users on Exchange 2003 or earlier, you can only use a cutover migration. Exchange 2007 requires an Exchange Server 2013 deployment for federation moves. Exchange DAG deployments are exceptions to these recommendations.

Once you have made your selection to either federation or cutover, the next decision is how to integrate the user accounts into Office 365. If you have chosen a federation approach, you need to use the Azure Active Directory Connector

(AD Connect) to link your on-site Windows Active Directory instance to Office 365. If you do not have an Active Directory instance, then you manually input the user accounts in Office 365 or use a third-party migration tool. There are multiple tools on the market for cutover migration. Two common tools are BitTitan's MigrationWiz (`www.bittitan.com`) and the SkyKick migration tool (`www.skykick.com`). Each tool has different capabilities and features, so it is best that you look at the tools and decide which one makes sense for your migration.

The focus of this chapter is to provide a "how to" approach in moving your business to the cloud, using our 14-step migration process. We will highlight when you must make the decision for migration, and we have a special section for federation moves.

Note   Cutover migration is a manual process, and there is an impact on users during the migration process. Federation migration will move the users' mailboxes with no impact to the users.

It no longer matters what type of Office 365 plan you have; all the Office 365 suites have Exchange mail services that can support migrations. The Office 365 Business version allows you to mix and match the subscription based on the roles in the organization. Individuals who have a requirement for more mail storage and document storage have enterprise plans. Those with fewer storage requirements have different plans with more limited storage requirements. If you have fewer than 300 users, you can use the small business plans intermixed with the enterprise plans. If you have more than 300 users, you can only use the enterprise subscription plans.

Note   Office 365 also has not-for-profit and education plans. These two special plans allow you to deploy enterprise subscriptions in large numbers at $0. Check with your cloud solution provider on the options. The $0 plans are equivalent to the $8 E1/E2 subscription.

The Office 365 subscriptions support iOS and Android devices, Macs, and PCs, and they provide both cloud and desktop software. These productivity tools are needed for businesses of all sizes to control operating costs and to improve productivity. One of the great features of the Business version of Office 365 is the access to all the software components for Microsoft Office desktop client suites.

An Office 365 user can install up to five copies of software for desktop and mobile devices. As you can see in Figure 7-2, we have three copies of software installed and seven more to use (two for desktop devices and five for mobile devices, whether iOS and/or Android).

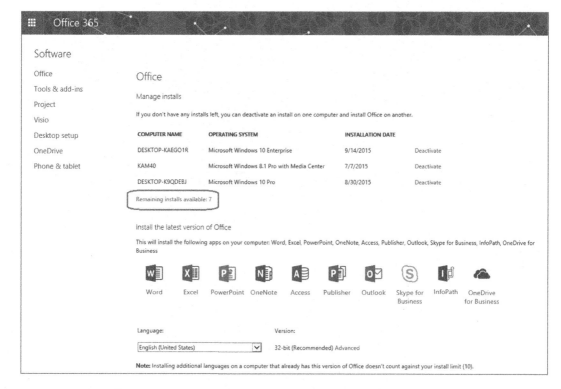

Figure 7-2. *Office 365 service administration software download*

All IT changes—no matter how big or small—require planning. Figure 7-3 shows the planning and deployment steps for moving to Office 365. There are various paths to move your users to Office 365, manually or by using Active Directory. If you are using Active Directory, you can use Azure AD Connect to synchronize (copy) your user accounts (e-mail addresses) to Office 365. This is useful because the other approach requires you to manually enter user e-mail addresses into Office 365 (which is tedious and time-consuming). Once your accounts are in Office 365, you can move your e-mail services to Office 365 and start using the services. Our planning process walks you through the configuration steps to successfully move to Office 365.

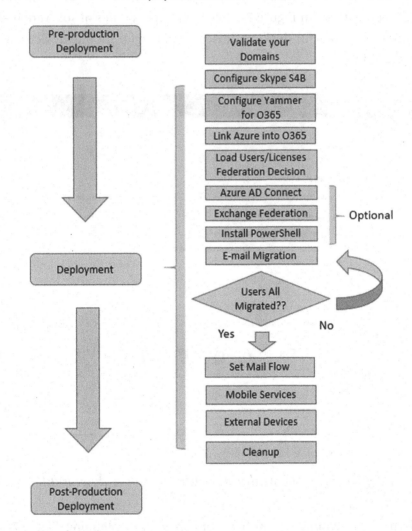

Figure 7-3. *Deployment process overview*

Note   You must have control over your DNS server. If you do not have control over your DNS server, you cannot move to the cloud or the process will be very time-consuming.

Office 365 is composed of different tools to assist you in running your business better. Once you have moved to Office 365, you can extend your capabilities by using Microsoft Enterprise Mobility Suite (EMS) with Microsoft Intune and Teams

(Skype for Business) and Office 365 subscriptions with phone system (Cloud PBX). The combination of these services allows you to manage your desktop and mobile devices with a set of cost-effective and powerful tools designed to improve productivity. Office 365 includes many different services (see Figure 7-4) that can be customized for your business and that are configurable, including the following:

- Exchange

- Teams (Skype for Business and Phone Systems Option)

- SharePoint (Team Site)

- OneDrive for Business

- Compliance Management

- Azure AD

- Bing Places for Business

There are also numerous option services that you can add to your subscription based on your needs. Typically, these include Project, Business Intelligence (Power BI), and Dynamics 365 (CRM).

Figure 7-4. *User portal to Office 365*

Configuring Office 365

Office 365 is simple to configure if you have a plan in place that answers these two questions:

- How do you plan to deploy the clients?

- How do you plan to move historical e-mail to Microsoft Online services?

The simplest migration is a cutover migration. The most complex is hybrid coexistence. Our migration approach uses a 14-step plan that you can complete in an evening or over many days. If your migration requires the Active Directory Connector (AD Connect) or Exchange Federation, see the "Configuring Azure AD Connect" section later in this chapter. There are different ways to complete the data migration (using third-party tools, doing an Exchange mailbox move, or shipping the data files to Microsoft for import to Office 365). The direction to take is up to you. The approach that we have taken is to highlight where these migration options are used in our 14-step process. I have outlined the process here, and the areas where you have choices are emphasized.

1. Purchase your Office 365 services.

2. Validate your domains to Microsoft and add DNS records.

3. Configure Teams (Skype for Business).

4. Configure Yammer for Office 365 (optional).

5. Link Office 365 into Azure Active Directory and EMS.

6. Load users, install the Azure Active Directory Connector (AD Connect), and assign a license.

7. Deploy the Hybrid Configuration Wizard for Exchange Federation (optional).

8. Adjust the mail flow (coexistence).

9. Manually install PowerShell (optional).

10. Migrate e-mail.

11. Finalize all DNS records.

12. Configure mobile services (using EMS/Intune).

13. Configure automated devices (copiers, scanners, fax servers).

14. Clean up.

The first step in any process is one of commitment. With Office 365, you need to sign up for a trial subscription. If you are migrating to Office 365, any subscription will work that contains Exchange e-mail services, however any azure services will require a paid subscription. This chapter is about migrating or moving your e-mail services from one provider to Office 365.

Step 1: Purchase Your Office 365 Services

There are different ways to purchase your subscription, either from the Web or through a URL supplied to you from your Microsoft Partner. As shown in Figure 7-5, you can set up a 25-user trial at `https://www.kamind.com/contact-us/` and request a trial subscription. You can also purchase a 1 user subscription form our website select the Office 365 floating web page (lower-right corner). Once the web page loads, select Try Office 365 to launch the 25-user trial subscription.

Figure 7-5. *Purchasing Office 365 subscription (`www.kamind.com`)*

Once you have requested the business premium trial subscription, you will receive a link in your email account. Click on the Business Premium Trial subscription link (see Figure 7-6), you need to enter your company information (see Figure 7-7). After you have done this, enter an administrator name and domain (see Figure 7-8). You can request any trial subscription form our website. In this example, we used a small business subscription called *Business Premium*.

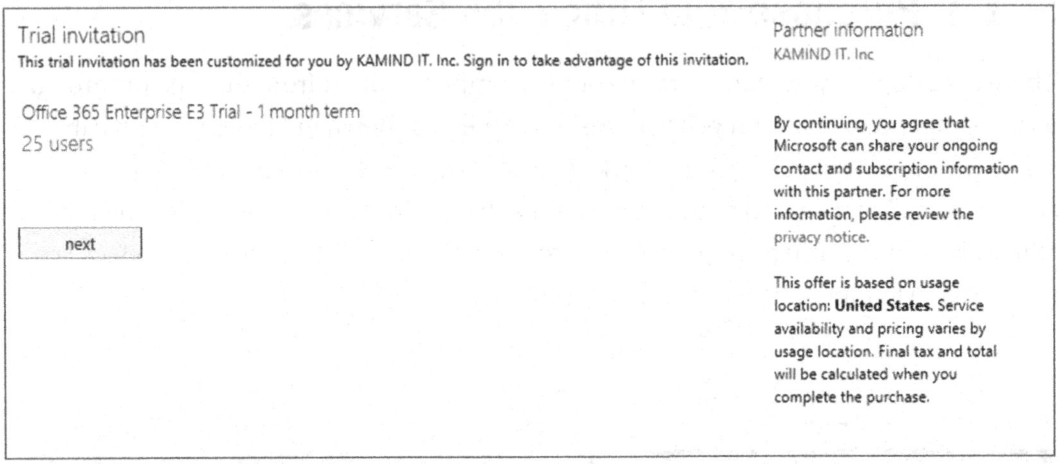

Figure 7-6. *Accepting the 25-user trial offer*

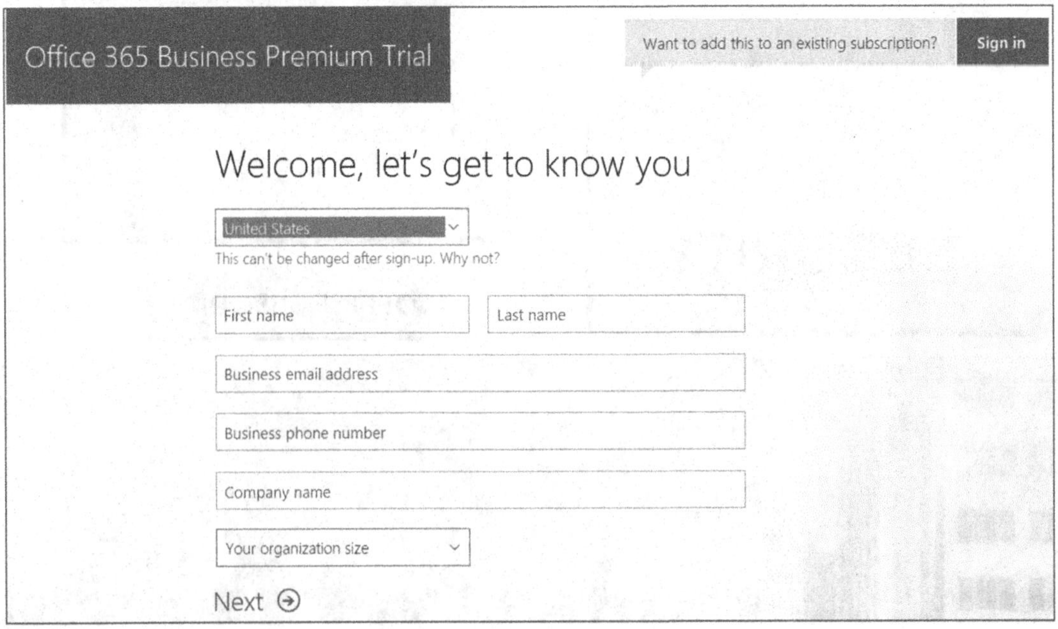

Figure 7-7. *Setting up the 25-user subscription*

414

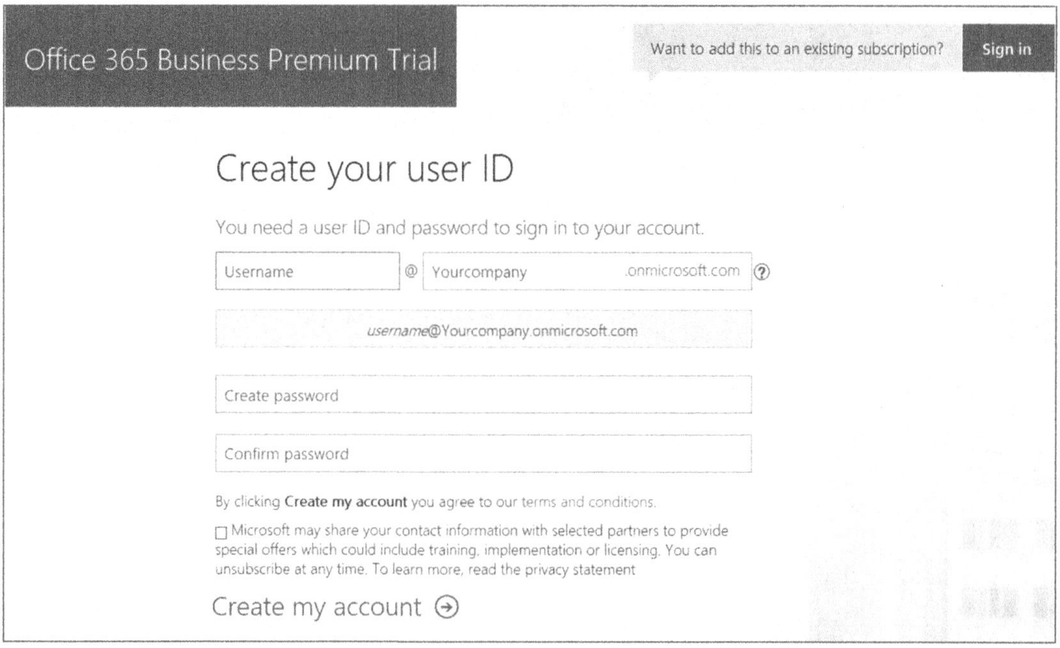

Figure 7-8. *Creating the login ID*

Once you have selected "Text me" or "Call me," enter the verification code and create your account (see Figure 7-9). When your account is created, the screen should look like what's shown in Figure 7-10.

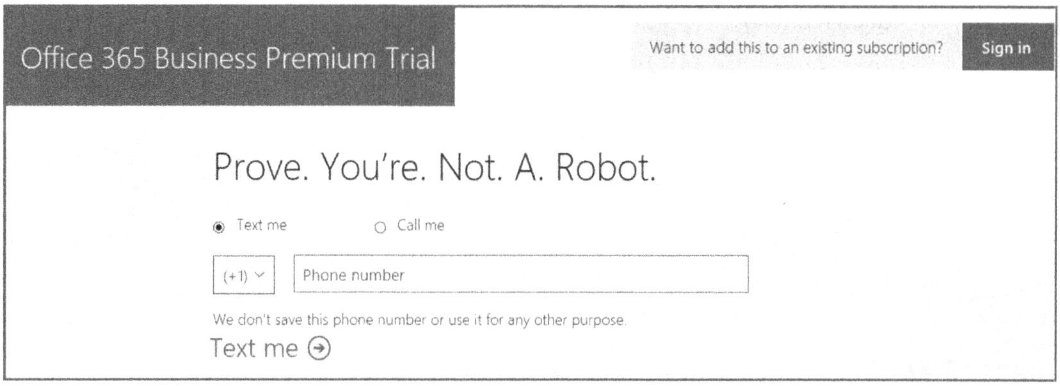

Figure 7-9. *Validating the subscription*

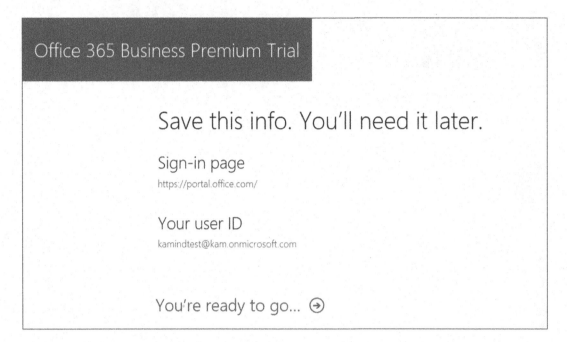

Figure 7-10. *Subscription confirmation*

Figure 7-11 shows that the account has been created.

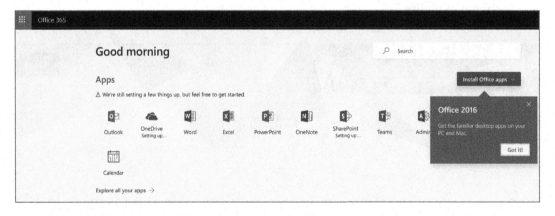

Figure 7-11. *Business Premium Trial account created*

Step 2: Validate Your Domains to Microsoft and Add DNS Records

After you have created the subscription, the next step is to validate the domain. Validating the domain proves to Microsoft that you own the domain in Office 365. Sign in at http://portal.office.com using the account that you created in step 1. Click the Admin icon (or select the nine-block grid in the upper-left corner to select Admin). You will be at the Office 365 dashboard. On the left side, click "Show more," then Setup, then Domains, and then "+ Add domain" to start the process of adding your domain to the Microsoft Online environment (see Figure 7-12).

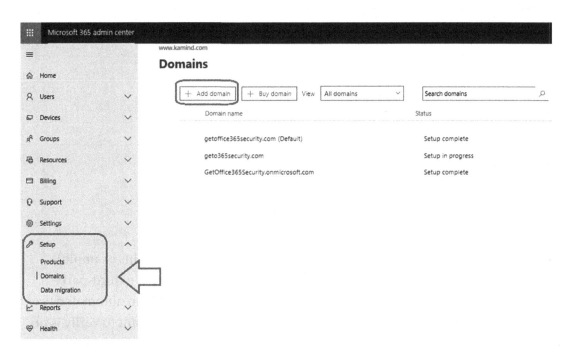

Figure 7-12. *Adding a domain in Office 365*

Office 365 requires you to prove that you own the domain you are using. Figure 7-13 explains DNS and outlines the process of Office 365 configuration. Click Next.

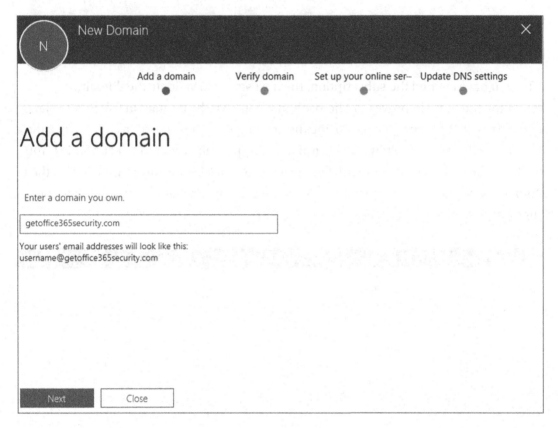

Figure 7-13. *Starting the DNS configuration for Office 365*

Enter the domain you want to use (GetOffice365security in this example) and click Next. If you do not have a domain, you can buy one from a third-party reseller. Office 365 examines your domain and provides you with an automated way to set up your domain. If Office 365 detects that the domain you want to verify is on GoDaddy, it prompts you to use an automatic configuration of the domain and DNS records.

The Office 365 domain wizard prompts you to select the service for verification. If you are going to cut over to Office 365 (move all mail services immediately to Office 365), then use the wizard. If you are not planning to use Office 365 this instant, then click "Step-by-step instructions" and manually configure your DNS service (see Figure 7-14); then click Verify.

Figure 7-14. *Enter the TXT record to validate the domain name*

Office 365 looks up your DNS information and recommends a record to enter for domain validation. In some cases, you may be prompted to enter a wizard. We recommend that you *do not use the wizard,* unless you are setting up a new Office 365 account and have no plans to migrate any e-mail into the Office 365 service.

Note   Use the wizards only if you plan to immediately use Office 365. The wizards configure your domain and move/point your mail records to Office 365. If your mail records are changed to Office 365, your existing mail on the third-party hosting service may be deleted. We use the wizards only if this is a new e-mail domain that has never been used.

To manually add the domain verification record, follow the directions on the screen. Sign in to your domain registrar and add the TXT record as specified on this screen. Figure 7-15 shows a GoDaddy TXT record, and Figure 7-16 shows a TXT record at Network Solutions for the domain getoffice365security.com. The process is the same for all domain verification.

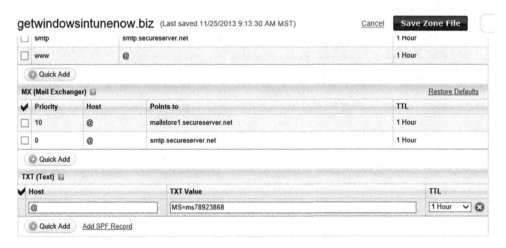

Figure 7-15. *GoDaddy TXT record configuration*

Each domain supplier has different tools and processes to add a domain record. You can only add domain records if the domain is managed by the domain supplier. In the GoDaddy case, the name servers are at GoDaddy, so we are adding records to the GoDaddy servers. This is also the case for Network Solutions.

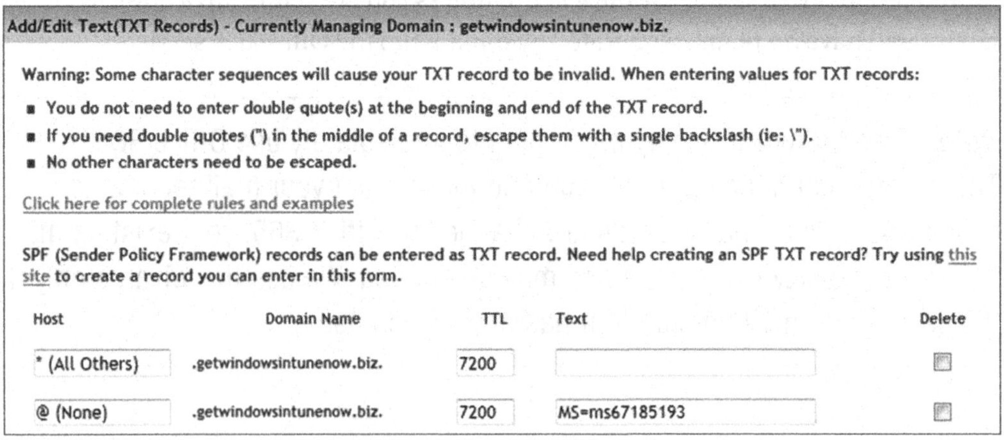

Figure 7-16. *Network Solutions TXT record domain verification*

After you have configured the domain for validation, if the domain does not verify, use MxToolbox (`www.mxtoolbox.com`) to verify that the TXT records have propagated. Once the TXT records show up in MxToolbox, you can validate the domain in Office 365. In Figure 7-17, we verified the record on MxToolbox. The purpose was to check whether the changed record in the DNS had replicated to the other World Wide Web DNS servers. These records also replicate to Office 365.

In this example, we are looking for the TXT record that we inserted into our DNS earlier. On MxToolbox, we enter the command `txt:getwindowsintunenow.biz`. When the record shows up (see Figure 7-17) in MX toolbox, we can verify the DNS record in Office 365 and validate the domain. The domain should validate within an hour. If it does not validate, you need to submit a ticket to Microsoft Online Services or contact a Microsoft Partner to help resolve the issue.

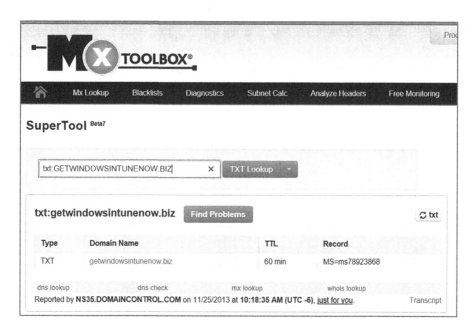

Figure 7-17. *MxToolbox TXT record validation*

Once you have the record in the MxToolbox, then select "I'll manage my own DNS" in Office 365. If the domain verifies correctly, you are provided with an acknowledgment that your domain is valid (see Figure 7-18). If the record does not verify, you will not be able to add the domain to Office 365.

Note   Usually adding the TXT records takes 5 to 10 minutes before the domain is verified. If the domain has not validated, check the values to make sure you have entered the information correctly. If the domain is validated in another Office 365 account, you cannot validate a second domain until the original domain name is removed.

The Office 365 wizards are useful if you are creating an Office 365 account and a new domain for the first time; if this is the case, then select "Set up my online services for me (Recommend)." Any business that has an existing e-mail service will use the option "I'll manage my own DNS records." We will walk you through the next steps of adding and validating the DNS records.

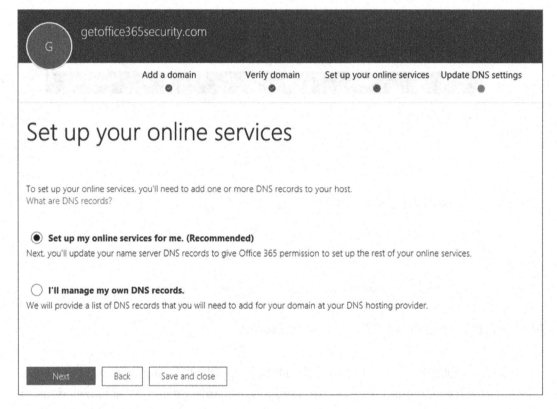

Figure 7-18. *Domain validated, proof of ownership*

After you select "I'll manage my own DNS records," you are prompted to update your DNS settings. When you manually change your DNS records, keep in mind the following:

- Unless you are cutting over e-mail (at this instant), do not change your MX, TXT (SPF), or Autodiscover DNS records. These records are changed when you are ready to receive e-mail services on Office 365.

- Configure all other DNS records, such as Teams (Skype for Business) and other CNAME records (only add theses records if the records are not being used).

In this example (see Figure 7-19), we do not have an existing service, so we will configure all the records for Office 365.

Note   If you cut over to Office 365 and change all the records, mail will flow through Office 365. If you have an existing Exchange server, you want to leave the Autodiscover, TXT (SPF), and the MX records pointing to the old mail service.

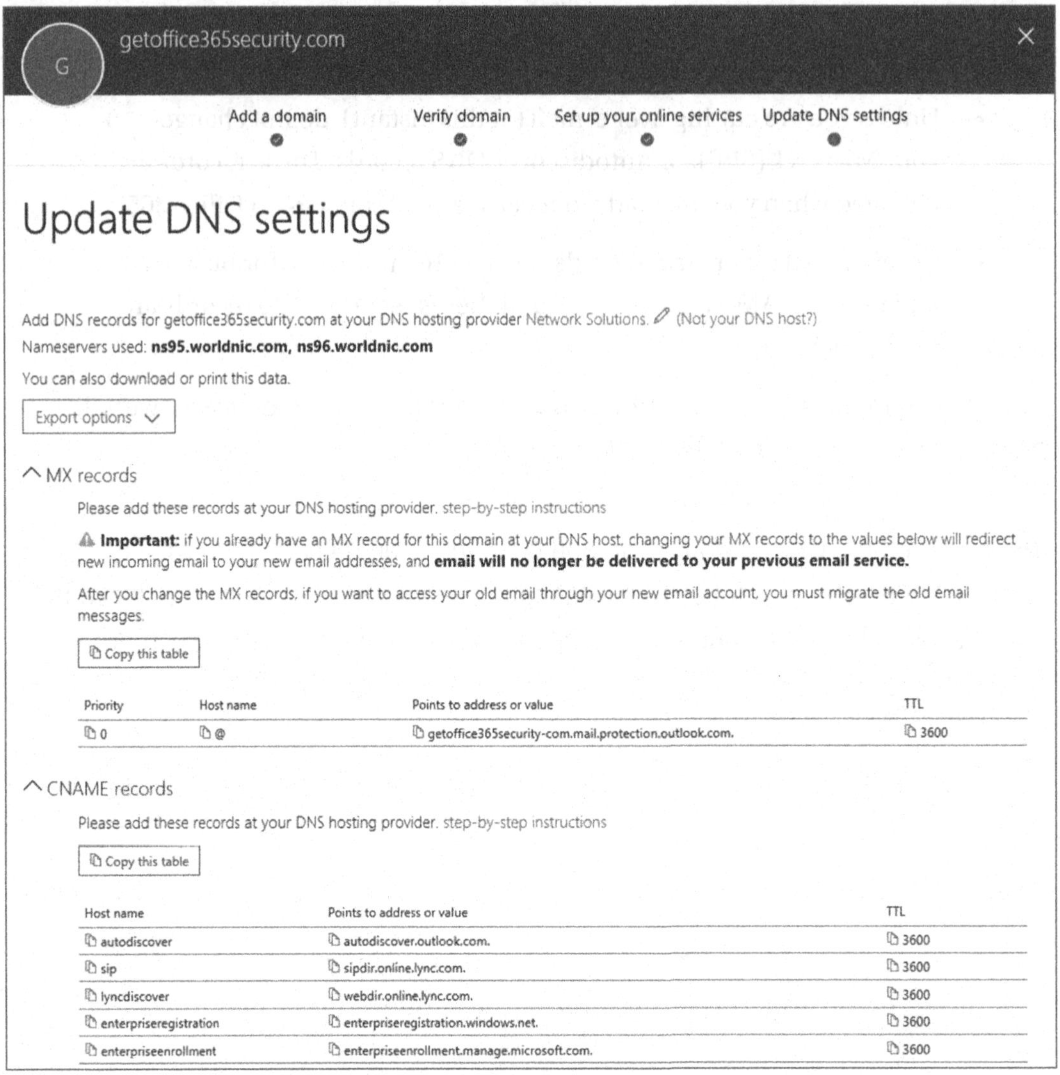

Figure 7-19. Getting the DNS records ready for Office 365

When we validated the domain earlier, we are letting Office 365 know how you are planning to use the domain that you just validated. Once you have added the DNS records, select verify to check the records for errors (see Figure 7-20). After you click Verify (on the bottom of the "Update DNS records" page), the changes you have made in the DNS registrar are validated. If there are errors, then correct the errors and click Verify again. Repeat the process until all checkmarks are green.

Note   You never want to transfer your DNS to a third party for hosting services. Always maintain the ownership separate from the hosting service. In this case, our domain DNS is at the Network Solutions registrar.

Figure 7-20. *Verifying the records : errors are identified for changes*

After you complete the configuration of the domain services on Office 365 and correct the errors, you are ready to use Office 365. Keep in mind that unless you are moving mail service over to Office 365, *do not change the MX, Autodiscovery, or TXT (SPF) records.* You only change these records if you are using a cutover migration. In this step, you are adding some of the DNS records (mail records are not being added).

- CNAME (alias or canonical name) records. These records are used to provide standard names to other Microsoft web services for Office 365. We will be adding the following:

  - `lyncdiscover`

  - `sip`

  - `msoid`

  - `enterpriseregistration`

  - `enterpriseenrollment`

- SRV (service record) records. These records specify information about available services. SRV records are used by Teams to coordinate the flow of information between Office 365 services.

After the records are added, you verify the records. If the records are entered correctly, they validate with a green check mark. If the records are incorrect, there is a red X. The mail records show up with a red X. After you have made the changes in the DNS (only change the records that were highlighted), then click Verify and complete the wizard. The wizard indicates errors in the records that you have not changed. If all the records are correct (making a cutover migration), then you will see a screen like Figure 7-21.

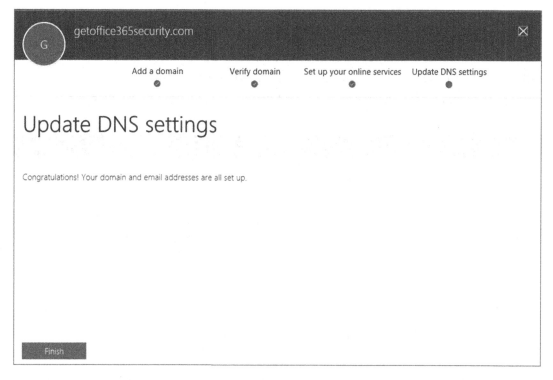

Figure 7-21. *Office 365 wizard showing all records validated*

At this point, you are completed with the setup as far as you can proceed, or you have completed adding all the records required for a cutover migration to Office 365. To return to the Office 365 admin center, click the nine-square grid (in the upper-left corner next to the Office 365 logo). The other DNS records that have an X next to them will be entered when you start the cutover migration for Office 365.

Note   Do *not* change your DNS MX, Autodiscover, or SPF-TXT records. When you change your MX records, you stop the mail flow to your existing e-mail server. If you change Autodiscover, the Outlook clients cease to work with your current e-mail server.

At any time you can add additional DNS records. If Office 365 finds a mismatch of the DNS records (with the records that it expects), Office 365 will display the "Complete setup" message (see Figure 7-22). Click "Complete setup" to fix the DNS issues. Office 365 will display the records that need to be added. If Office 365 determines that some of your DNS entries are valid, these valid entries will have green check marks. If there are errors, there are red Xs. Fix the errors until you have green check marks. You may run into a situation where the DNS server cannot be fixed because your provider will not support the advanced DNS records. In that case, you will need to move your DNS to a different provider. Once the records have been validated, you can change the primary domain to the user account domain and add the necessary users to the account.

Figure 7-22. *Domain configuration status for setup*

You should only have three red Xs on the MX, Autodiscover, and SPF-TXT records. All other records should have green check marks. If you have red Xs on records other than the three described, then correct those problems.

Note   The Office 365 automatic DNS wizard configures the DNS server and assumes that you are completing a cutover migration and you have loaded the user accounts into Office 365. If you are not planning to move to Office 365 at this instant, do not use the automatic configuration tool. Once you move the mail records to Office 365, mail will be received on Office 365, not your existing mail server.

The next step is to add users and assign licenses. We have found that it is better to complete the domain configuration (with the exception of changing the MX records) and add users after you have validated the domain.

Note   Unless you are setting up a new Office 365 account, it is best to set up users after you complete the configuration. If you choose to add users, follow the bulk user instructions. The wizard is designed for new users to 365, not for the migration of existing accounts.

Step 3: Configure Skype for Business (S4B) for Teams

When your Office 365 site is created, Teams is ready to operate within your intranet. As an administrator, you need to decide whether you want to open Teams communications to external users and allow instant messaging. Microsoft calls this *federating the domain*. To enable these services, log in to the Office 365 admin center and select Skype for Business below the Admin menu (see Figure 7-23). If you have purchased or enabled the trial for Skype for Business calling, there are additional licenses that are assigned to your subscription. Configuration of the phone service is completed after you have migrated your users to Office 365.

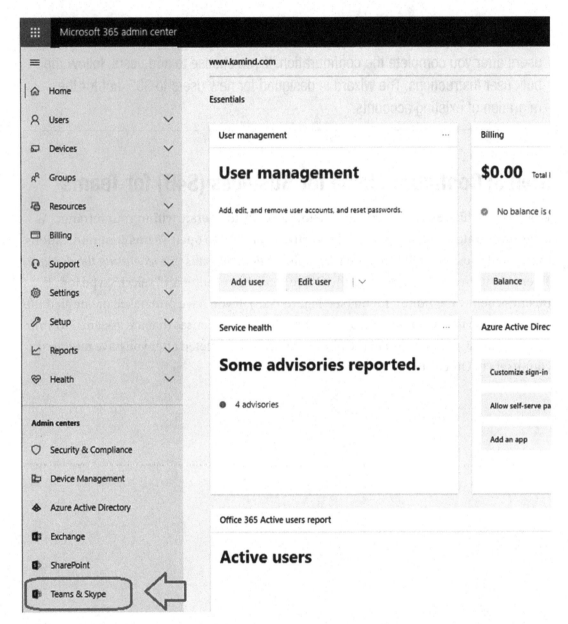

Figure 7-23. *Accessing the new admin center for Teams and Skype for Business*

The Teams "domain federation" allows your intranet to interact with other Office 365 customers and non–Office 365 e-mail addresses that support Microsoft Federation services. For example, domain federation allows your users to see the presence of external vendors (see Figure 7-24). At this point, we are not going to configure Teams/

Skype voice or dial-in conferencing. These services require that the user accounts be loaded into Office 365.

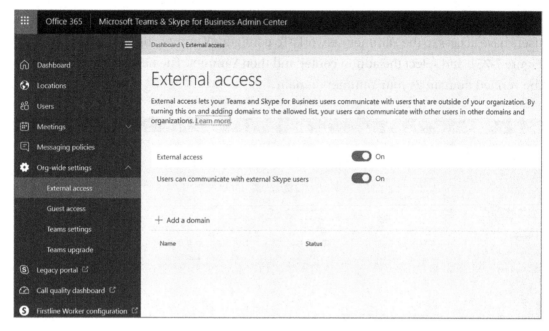

Figure 7-24. *Admin screen: Teams & Skype setup*

The public instant messaging interface allows you to communicate within your intranet with other Office 365 organizations that have federated with Office 365 and Live Messenger. Public IM connectivity is supported with Skype.

In the Teams & Skype control panel, click "Org-wide settings" and then "External access." Enable "External Access," and select "User can communicate with external Skype users." This action enables these services. On is the recommended setting for both services. The default is off (disabled). After you have made the two selections, click Save.

Note   Office 365 users can talk to Skype users via a Skype handle (or Microsoft Live ID). To communicate with Skype users, Skype for Business must add Skype users as a "contact" in their Skype for Business client. If the Skype user is not listed as a contact, you cannot connect with them.

Step 4: (Optional) Configure Yammer Enterprise for Office 365

After the Office 365 domain is verified, the next step is to configure Yammer so that all users have access to the Yammer network. To configure Yammer, log in to Office 365 (see Figure 7-25), and select the admin center and then Yammer. The next step is to enable the verified domain as your Yammer domain.

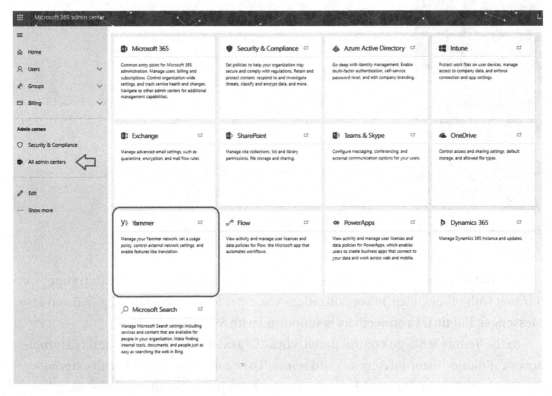

Figure 7-25. *Selecting Yammer for Office 365*

Once you have selected Yammer, Yammer prompts you for your domain for integration to Office 365. Select the verified domain that you entered earlier and then activate. In Figure 7-26, we use the verified domain `kamindit.net`.

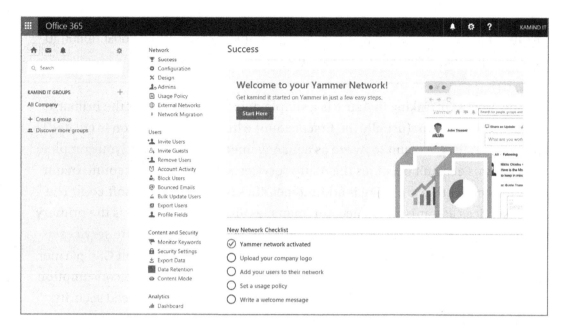

Figure 7-26. *Enabling Yammer for verified domain*

Step 5: Link Office 365 into Azure Active Directory and EMS

The underlining Microsoft cloud that holds all of this together is called Azure. Office 365 user management takes place in Azure. As the owner of the Office 365 organization, you need to manually link Azure to Office 365. This is not automatic, but it is key to managing the security in your business.

Why is this linking of EMS and Azure important? The answer is a simple one. We need to add Microsoft security services to our tenant (to prevent data breaches), and we need to have access to the Azure AD Connect (so we can link our on-premises Active Directory to Office 365). If you are not using the Azure AD Connect in your migration to Office 365, then you do not need to worry about this step. However, the Azure security services are extremely important to the health and well-being of your Office 365 tenant.

Before you set up the Azure link to Office 365, contact your Microsoft Partner and request a trial subscription for the Enterprise Mobility + Security suite (request one from `https://www.kamind.com/support-center/`) and request an Azure $100 consumption subscription account (consumption accounts are discussed later in this chapter).

433

> **Note**   You need to contact a Microsoft Partner for a 25-user trial subscription to the Enterprise Mobility suite (see Figure 7-27).

The process of linking to Azure is a simple one; you need to pick the primary global admin account (usually the first account when the subscription is created) and link that user account to Azure as a management account. Once you complete this task, this account becomes the Azure services administration account. In our case, the account we are using is admin@getoffice365core.onmicrosoft.com. The Azure services administration account manages all Azure activity. It is the primary billing account for all Azure services and is used to assign other Azure services to user accounts. Once you selected this account, inform your Microsoft CSP partner to assign the Azure consumption services to this account. The Azure consumption account is not needed for the migration but is needed for the advanced security services discussed in previous chapters.

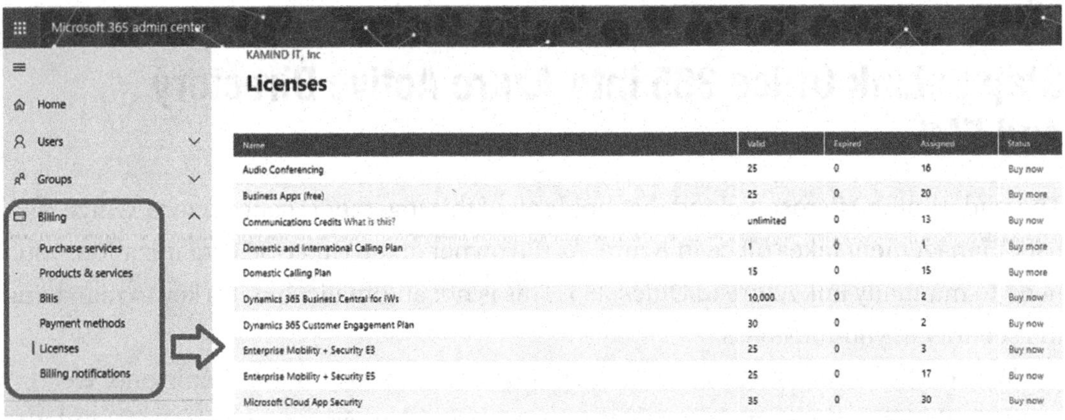

Figure 7-27. EMS trial subscription from a Microsoft Partner

Once you have received the trial subscription for the Enterprise Mobility suite, verify that you have the subscriptions assigned to your account. To verify the subscriptions, go to the admin center, click Billing, and then click Licenses (see Figure 7-27). Assign a license of EMS/E5 + Office 365/E3 to the admin account you are using to manage the subscription.

The process of assigning the licenses is straightforward. To get started, make sure you are logged in to Office 365 with the global admin account you are using to manage your Office 365 Azure services. In the admin center, select Active Users, double-click the selected user account (in our case this is admin@getoffice365core.onmicrosoft.com), and edit licenses. Once you complete this step, assign the licenses Office 365 E5 and EMS E5 to the account (see Figure 7-28). Then you can move forward and link the Office 365 tenant to the Azure management services. Once you have assigned the licenses, you now must link the services into Azure. Click Azure AD under the "Admin centers" menu (see Figure 7-29).

Figure 7-28. *Assigning the licenses to the admin account*

Figure 7-29. Linking Azure Active Directory to Office 365

The Azure interface will launch into the Azure Active Directory interface. This is the interface where you will manage the user's security and identity (discussed earlier). The Azure Active Directory admin center is used to manage the user account properties and capabilities. In our case, we need access to the Azure Active Directory center to download and configure the Azure Active Directory Connector to link our Office 365 services to on-premises Active Directory.

In Figure 7-30, I highlighted the option Sync with Windows Server AD. This is the link you will use to install the Azure AD connector on your domain controller (if you are linking accounts from Office 365 to Azure). Do not select this option now until we complete step 6. If you have an on-premise Active Directory and you have an Exchange Server instance, you must decide the type of migration you will be using, either a federated move or a cutover migration.

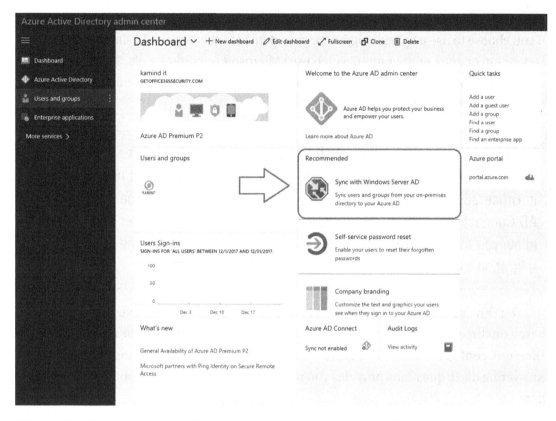

Figure 7-30. *Azure Active Directory account setup with Office 365*

Note   If you are not using the on-premise Active Directory Connector, you will manually load the user accounts into Office 365. Loading users will be discussed in more detail in step 6.

Step 6: Load Users, Install Azure Active Directory Connector, and Assign Licenses

At this point, you are ready to load users, but before you start, you have a decision to make on the migration approach for loading users into Office 365. There are two ways to load users in Office 365. You can use Active Directory (via the Azure AD Connect tool) and Exchange Federation (hybrid) or manually bulk-load the user accounts from a spreadsheet. The direction you choose is based on your business needs. Azure Active

437

Directory sync is required in hybrid migrations but is optional in cutover migrations. If you choose to use a hybrid migration, your data must be migrated using Exchange Federation or cutover migration, which uses Microsoft migration tools. Third-party tools such as MigrationWiz, User Activation, or DeploymentPro are used for cutover migration.

Note   Be careful which migration approach you choose. If there is an Exchange Server on-site and you use Azure AD Connect to load user accounts in Office 365, a user mailbox will not be created. This is because the Azure AD Connect tool detects that there is an on-site Exchange server and will not allow you to create two mailboxes, and it requires you to use the Microsoft migration tool.

You can use the Azure AD Connect in all migration approaches. The decision is based on three factors: whether you using Exchange Server, whether you have an Active Directory configuration, and whether the e-mail services are on Exchange Server. Answering these questions provides you with the different migration options described here:

- On Exchange Server 2010 or later, you can use a federated move and will need to use the Azure AD Connect and using the Hybrid Configuration Wizard.

- For Active Directory and no Exchange server federation, you must manually load the accounts, then connect Azure AD Connect to sync Office 365 user accounts.

- For e-mail services not on Exchange Server, then you will use cutover migration and AD Connect to load accounts if you have an Active Directory.

After you have identified where your e-mail services are coming from, and if you have an on-premise Active Directory, you are left with two different types of migrations. The methods for loading and migrating e-mails are simple, but different approaches are used to move mail to Office 365. My goal at this point is to provide you with enough background material to allow you to make a choice and refer to the section that is appropriate for your move to Office 365. Many partners will provide you with all sorts of different migration paths. All the paths come down to two choices:

- Cutover migration

- Federation migration (or hybrid)

Cutover Migration

Cutover migration is when the accounts have already been created on Office 365. The mail records (MX records) are "cut over" from the old mail servers and pointed to the new Office 365 mail servers. The end user loses their profile unless third-party migration tools are used. These third-party tools (such as BitTitan DeploymentPro) mitigate the issues associated with a new Outlook profile. Old e-mail either can be migrated before the cutover event (users have two mailboxes) or can be migrated after the cutover. If you are coming from an older Exchange 2003 server (or any POP/IMAP or other hosted Exchange service), you will use cutover migration.

The Office 365 configuration has already been completed, so all that is left are the changes to support a cutover move. To complete a cutover move, you need to follow these three steps:

1. Load user accounts into Office 365.

2. Deploy the Azure Active Directory Connector, sync passwords/users accounts, and perform a soft match (if you have an Active Directory).

3. Use BitTitan's migration tool to copy user e-mails to Office 365.

Federation Migration

If you have deployed Exchange Server in your organization (2010 or later), you want to seriously look at using a federation move. Federation moves are simple to do and require work to clean up your Active Directory, but they benefit your users. When a federation move takes place, the end user will receive a notification to close Outlook with the message the "Administrator has made a change." Once the end user closes Outlook and reopens it, they have been moved to Office 365. This is a good user experience with little impact to the user.

The Office 365 configuration has already been completed, so all that is left are the changes to support an Exchange Federation move. To complete a federation move, you need to follow these four steps:

1. Deploy the Azure Active Directory Connector and sync passwords/users accounts.

2. Deploy the federation Hybrid Configuration Wizard.

3. Validate the Office 365 mail flow connector.

4. Use the remote move mail migration wizard.

The process is straightforward, with minor issues in deployment. Typical deployment issues revolve around public folders and Exchange Server configuration and external spam filters. As an example, if you are running an Exchange 2007 data availability group (DAG), then the migration becomes complex. Another case is with a large number of public folders. Public folders can be migrated but are in a proxy model for Outlook only (and not OWA), until the public folders have been cut over to Office 365. Finally are the third-party spam filters. These always cause migration problems.

A *hybrid* migration is a combination of Active Directory synchronization and Exchange federation. A hybrid migration does not require Active Directory Federation Services (ADFS) and is composed of deploying Active Directory synchronization and Exchange Federation (linking the on-site Exchange Server to the cloud). The reason you would use a hybrid migration is to move users to Office 365 to maintain a user's Outlook profile and make the migration 100 percent transparent to the user. This approach allows you to use a staged migration. The hybrid model leverages the Exchange server mailbox move function. When an Exchange administrator implements a mailbox move, all the user sees is a message that the user needs to log out and log back in to Outlook when the mailbox move is completed.

Cutover or Hybrid: Which One?

At this point, you need to decide. If you choose to use cutover as a migration option and want to use your Active Directory, there is a process that you need to follow in moving users to Office 365 (described shortly). If you want to use hybrid migration (and are running Exchange 2007), you need to deploy Exchange 2013/2016 and use Exchange 2013/2016 servers to move mailboxes to Office 365.

You want to be careful with using Active Directory synchronization. AD synchronization will disallow the creation of mailboxes in Office 365 if there is an on-site Exchange Server. To get around this, you need to manually load users into Office 365 and then enable Active Directory synchronization. This approach bypasses the AD synchronization checks and forces Active Directory synchronization to "soft match" the Office 365 accounts with the on-premises Active Directory. The result is that you have an Office 365 mailbox ready for migration and password synchronization with the on-site Active Directory—and a destination mailbox created in Office 365. Figure 7-31 shows a flow chart summarizing the two migration options.

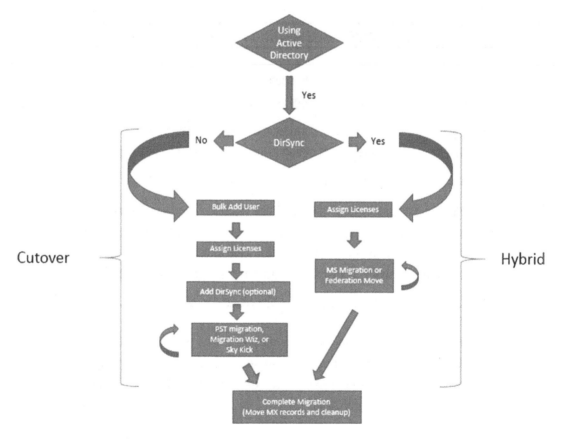

Figure 7-31. *Onboarding flow chart*

Once you have decided on the migration direction (cutover or hybrid), the work follows the process outlined earlier. There are no technical limits on the number of users you can deploy. If you are using cutover, there is no partial deployment groups (or test groups). If you want a test group, use a federation move.

If you are using a federation move, you can deploy in groups based on departments or other criteria. The deployment group size is a function of the capabilities of the support organization. Technically, you should not have any additional support calls because you had a good business process for deployment. However, users will call you anyway because they do not like change, so your support team will need to manage the change.

THERE ARE THREE METHODS TO LOAD USERS

- Add each user (see the "Onboarding Users" section later in this chapter). This method is appropriate for a few users or a test group.

- Bulk-add users using a specially formatted CSV spreadsheet with the user information. Use the Bulk Import option to load the information into Office 365.

- Enable Azure Active Directory synchronized users for access to Office 365.

Pick your method to load users into Office 365. Once you have selected your method (manual or using directory synchronization), you are ready to begin moving user data to Office 365. If you choose directory synchronization, you are restricted to using Microsoft migration tools (if you have an Exchange server in your Active Directory). After you have selected your user-loading approach, then you can begin the mail migration process.

Cutover migration may need to have the user accounts reloaded before the Azure Active Directory Connector is installed. On cutover migrations, the on-premise Active Directory instance may not be cleaned from the old Exchange Server instance. If this is the case, you will need to manually load the user account to Office 365 and then perform a soft match with AD Connect.

Onboarding Users (Cutover Migration Only)

There are three ways to load users: Azure Active Directory synchronization, the Office 365 graphical user interface, or the bulk-load process. The GUI is great for maintenance and small numbers of user accounts (see Figure 7-32), but it is not an effective tool for loading many user accounts. If you choose to use directory sync and you have an on-premises Exchange server, you need to use the Office 365 migration tools.

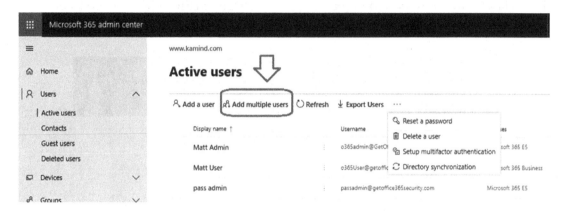

Figure 7-32. *Office 365 administration screen*

Bulk-Load Users Through Azure AD Connect

AD Connect links your on-premises Active Directory to Office 365. This allows you to import existing e-mail addresses, contacts, and distribution lists into Office 365 through a process called *directory synchronization*. When you install AD Connect, you select the directory from Active Directory to sync with Office 365. This is a simple process. If the user AD object is in the sync directory, it is replicated to Office 365. You need to be careful when you use AD Connect. If you have an on-premises Exchange Server instance and you are planning not to use a federation move and want to link AD, load the users into Office 365 (bulk import) and then set up AD Connect and soft match the Office 365 user accounts to the Active Directory. This will allow you to use a tool like the migration wizard and move users to Office 365 as a cutover migration.

Manually Bulk-Load Users

There are two ways to manually load users: using the Office 365 graphical user interface or using the bulk-load process. The GUI is great for maintenance and a small number of user accounts, but it is not an effective tool for loading many user accounts. The process that we use is to bulk-add users.

Log in as an administrator at `http://portal.office.com` and then click Active Users. Then click More and Import multiple users. This will launch the import wizard (see Figure 7-33). Follow the import process to load the users from the CSV file to Office 365.

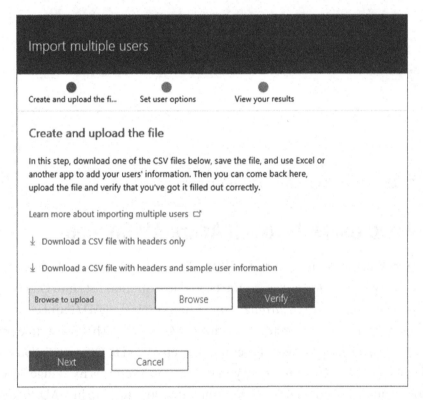

Figure 7-33. *Adding users with the bulk-add method*

The first step is to build and then select the CSV file with the appropriate users to be added. Download a blank CSV file to get the format. You can open this file in Excel (be sure to save it as a CSV file, without extra lines or columns) or edit it with the text editor.

We recommend you use the optional fields and enter all the data possible. If you are accurate at this step, it significantly reduces the amount of work necessary to manually fix user profiles. After you have built the CSV file, click Browse and load the file.

Installing the Azure AD Connect

If you are running an Azure Active Directory and you want to link the user account into Office 365 (regardless if you are running a hybrid or cutover migration), you will need to follow the steps to install the AD Connect software.

If you have an Active Directory environment (log in to a Windows server) and you are not running a small business server, using Azure AD Connect to load users into Office 365 is simple. It gives you a single-password login to Office 365. The caveat on this is the Exchange configuration. If you cannot use Exchange Federation as a method to move mailboxes to Office 365, you need to manually load user accounts into Office 365 before you install the Azure Active Directory Connect tool.

To integrate your local AD and Microsoft cloud, you need to have the following:

- An Office 365 global admin account (like `SyncOnlineAdmin@domain.onmicrosoft.com`)

- A local AD enterprise admin account (like `SyncAdmin@domain.com`)

- A Windows Server 2012R2 or a later server that is domain joined

Before you begin the configuration of the Active Directory integration, please verify that you have created these user accounts and have a server available to deploy the Active Directory integration tool.

Note   The Office 365 Active Directory synchronization tool (DirSync) has been replaced with Azure Active Directory Connect (AD Connect). Microsoft merged the different versions of the directory synchronization tool into one. The Azure AD Connect tool is downloaded from Azure. If you plan to use Azure Active Directory Connect, you need to complete step 3 and integrate Office 365 into Azure. This integration requires that you have purchased a license.

To download the Active Directory tool (refer to step 5, shown in Figure 7-30) and click Sync with Windows Server AD (see Figure 7-34). Select the Federation option, the domain (in our case `Getoffice365security.com`) and to download the Azure AD connector (see Figure 7-35). Install the software using the Sync Admin account on your domain controller.

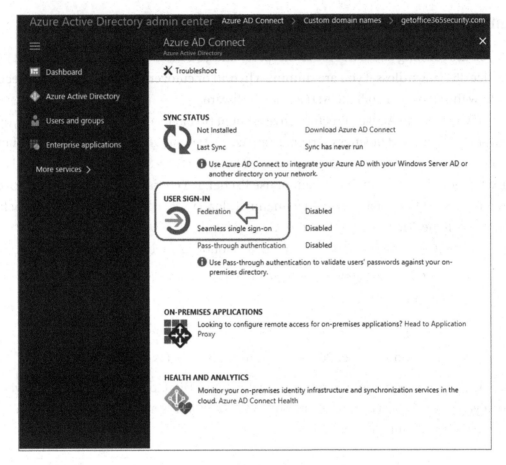

Figure 7-34. *Selecting the Azure AD Connect from portal.azure.com*

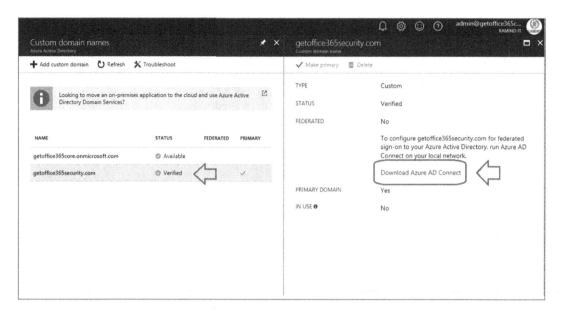

Figure 7-35. *Downloading the Azure AD Connect software*

After you have installed the Azure Active Directory Connector, you will need to make some changes in your local AD. Office 365 and Azure require that the domain account be Internet routable. Traditionally, AD accounts were installed with a local extension (and were not Internet routable). You will need to change the UPN and make additional changes in Active Directory to make sure the user accounts show up in Office 365. The steps to accomplish this are outlined here:

1. Set the UPN to the routable Internet name in the on-premises Active Directory. (In your domain controller, start Active Directory Domains and Trust, select Properties, and enter an alternate UPN).

2. Run the IdFix tool to correct any issues with the on-site Active Directory. (Download IdFix DirSync Error Remediation Tool from `www.microsoft.com`.)

After you have installed the Azure AD Connect software, select Azure AD Connect Health (see Figure 7-36), and validate the Azure Active Directory Connect health. You should see the services fully deployed. If you see any errors, you need to remediate them.

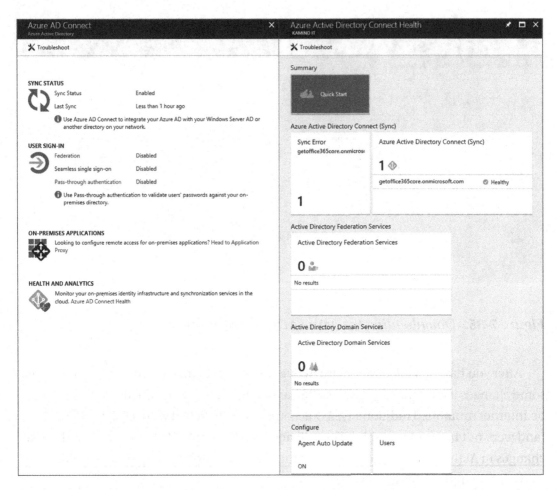

Figure 7-36. Downloading the Azure AD Connect software

Once you have completed the installation of the Azure AD Connect service, your on-site user accounts will appear in Office 365 (as synced users) and in the Azure Active Directory on the Users and Groups tab.

Note   Once you've installed AD Connect, those accounts can be managed from the on-premise Active Directory or Azure Active Directory. A password reset requires the Azure AD Write Back feature. This feature is available if you have deployed either Azure Premium or Enterprise Mobility + Security (EMS).

License Assignment

If you selected Active Directory Sync, you do not need to assign licenses until you begin the migration. Directory-synchronized objects from the on-site Active Directory appear as disabled users in Office 365, and no mailbox is created. Once the user object is created in Office 365, you can manually assign licenses or bulk-assign them with PowerShell. If you selected manual loading, you need to purchase licenses to create the mailbox for the user. It is not possible to load a disabled user in Office 365.

If you do not see a mailbox created from an Active Directory Synced user (after you assigned a license), this is because Active Directory thinks that there is an Exchange Server instance installed in your AD. If this happens and there is no Exchange Server instance, you need stop syncing and delete the user accounts from Office 365 (and the delete all users in the deleted users folder) using PowerShell. Once this is completed, create the user in Office 365, assign a license, and then resync the user account for the on-premises AD. The AD Connect tool should soft match the user and set the user as a synced user.

Note   If you're planning to allow passwords again (which you should do), you must assign an Enterprise Mobility + Security license to the user account.

Step 7: (Optional) Deploy the Hybrid Configuration Wizard for Exchange Federation for staged migrations

The simplest way to migrate to Office 365 is to use the Exchange Server federation wizard. This wizard can be installed on any server. What this wizard does is to create the necessary connections to migrate to Office 365 using your existing Exchange Server instance. The federation wizard works only with Exchange Server 2010 or later. If you have a federation migration, make sure you look at the Microsoft Exchange Assistant planning guide. This guide will walk you through the process of setting up an exchange server for migration (see `https://docs.microsoft.com/en-us/exchange/exchange-deployment-assistant`). The federation Hybrid Configuration Wizard completes the following steps for deployment:

1. Detects the Exchange Server installation

2. Links the Office 365 credentials and the AD credentials

3. Validates the credentials and DNS (using federation token)

4. Configures the federation organization and enables the MRS service

5. Builds the send and receive connectors for Exchange and Office 365

6. Validates the on-premises and Office 365 configurations

The federation wizard is easy to install. Once you have set up the Azure Active Directory Connector with Office 365, all you need to do is log in to Office 365 and click "Admin center," then "Exchange admin," and then "hybrid" (see Figure 7-37). The latest version of the wizard will be downloaded and installed on the server. We recommend that you log in with the credentials that you are using for the AD Connect.

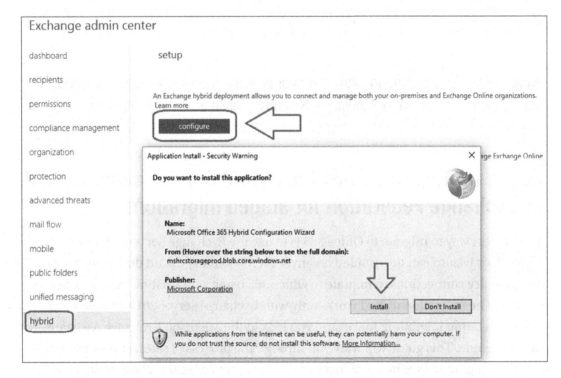

Figure 7-37. *Downloading and installing the Hybrid Configuration Wizard*

Once you have completed the download, start the wizard and begin the installation process (see Figure 7-38). The wizard will find out where the Exchange Server instance is located and will automatically configure all footed services. That is why it is important that you are logging into the systems with the correct credentials. We recommend you use the credentials for the Active Directory Connector installation. The dynamic account will be modified with the correct security extensions to make this work.

The Hybrid Configuration Wizard will need the Office 365 global admin account (use the same account that was used for the Azure Active Directory Connector, as well as the account for access to the Exchange Server instance (such as the adminsycn account). During the process you will be required to provide a TXT record for the federation token to validate the hybrid configuration for Office 365. The federation token is a GUID that needs to be inserted as the primary domain DNS as a TXT attribute. This TXT attribute is read by Office 365 and used to encrypt the data in transit.

Once the wizard is completed, you will need to complete the following:

1. Validate the Office 365 send connector to the on-site Exchange Server instance.

2. Add the IP address for the on-site Exchange Server instance to bypass the Office 365 spam filter.

3. Adjust the Office 365 Exchange retention tags.

4. Adjust the mail flow (set Office 365 as the internal relay).

After these four steps are completed, you are ready to perform a mailbox move to Office 365.

Figure 7-38. *Federation Hybrid Configuration Wizard login screen*

Connector Validation

Once you complete the wizard, go to Office 365 and the Exchange admin center, select "mail flow" and then "connectors." Select the outbound connector to Office 366. On the right side (see Figure 7-39), select "Validate this connector." If the connector fails for any reason, you need to troubleshoot the failure. Typical failures happen when you have a third-party spam filters that do not permit the Office 365 address to send messages to the on-site Exchange Server instance. If the validation fails, debug the issue. Usually the validation fails because the firewall will strip off the TLS on the email form Office 365. In this case, set up an IP address (not in DNS), that goes directly to the exchange server and bypass the firewall scanning. Once this is in lace and validated, then enter the external IP addresses of Office 365 servers to restrict access only to email coming from Office 365. You must validate the connector before you can move any mail.

Figure 7-39. *Exchange connector validation*

Bypass the Spam Filter

The final configuration (besides the adjustment for mail flow) of the connectors to set up the spam filter to bypass all e-mails that come from a specific IP address. The on-premise Exchange Server instance has an IP address that it uses to send mail out to the public net. You will need to retrieve this address and add a bypass for the spam filter in Office 365 in the transport rules (see Figure 7-40). To add the rule, do the following:

1. Select "mail flow" and then "rules" and then select "Bypass spam filtering" from the drop-down.

2. Enter the IP address for the new rule (do not use domain names).

3. Save the rule.

4. Set the rule's priority to 0.

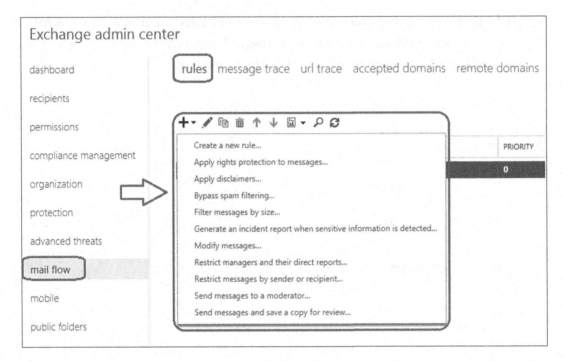

Figure 7-40. *Bypass the spam filter*

At this point you are almost ready to move the mail. The final step is the adjustment of the mail flow to allow an internal relay to the other e-mail accounts that have not migrated to Office 365.

Step 8: Adjust the Mail Flow (Coexistence)

There have been many different strategies on mail flow. Looking at the Internet rules, you can have only one authoritative domain and many different relays. If you are completing a hybrid migration (or a test group migration with forwarders), you will need to adjust the Office 365 domain connector to allow mail to flow from Office 365 to the authoritative domain until you cut over to Office 65.

To set the mail flow, you need to access the Exchange control panel. To access the Exchange control panel, do the following:

1.   Select Office 365 as an admin.

2.   Select "admin centers."

3. Select Exchange.

4. Select "mail flow" and then select "accepted domains."

Select the domain and change the record to "Internal relay domain." The domain type is set to "Internal relay" until all the users have been migrated. When the user migration has been completed, the domain changes to Hosted, and the MX records change to point to Office 365.

The changes that you make for internal relay (see Figure 7-41) are also the changes that you would need if you were running a coexistence strategy with Office 365 and a third-party mail service. Test groups and coexistence are rarely used unless you have a massive migration from Google services to Office 365. I have used this strategy on many occasions when migrating user accounts to Office 365. The strategy is to allow e-mail to flow to Office 365 and Google so users can move their services over to Office 365. In this case, Google is the primary tool for MX records; it is set to be Authoritative, and Office 365 is set to internal relay. Once the e-mail accounts have been moved, then the mail records are pointed to Office 365, and the Google service is shut down.

Note   If you have an on-site Exchange server and you want to create a test group, you will need to manually configure the desktop clients to bypass the on-site Exchange server. It is not clean and requires you to edit the registry. Test groups will not work in Office 2016.

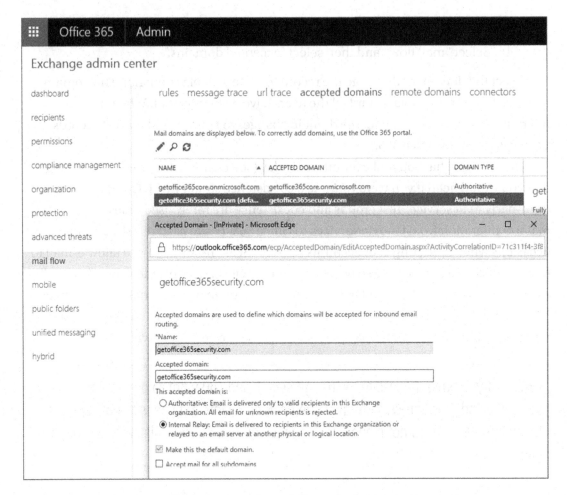

Figure 7-41. *Setting a domain as a shared domain (some users are on an external server)*

Internal Relay Mail Flow (and Test Groups)

An internal relay mail flow uses a combination of forwarders from the on-site server to Office 365. The on-site server uses `onmicrosoft.com` as the forwarding address (see Figure 7-42). This approach works and is useful for testing, but it is not a recommended practice. Test groups are not integrated into the on-premise Exchange server.

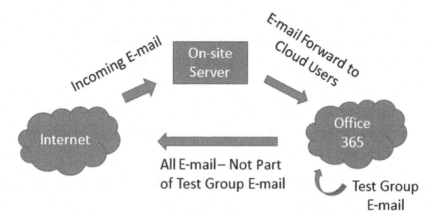

Figure 7-42.   *Test group mail flow*

When you add users to Office 365, these users have an active e-mail address. This means the following:

- E-mail that is sent to one of these new Office 365 e-mail accounts from outside Office 365 or from other Office 365 tenants will *not* be received until your MX records are configured and verified by Office 365.

- Any e-mail sent from one of these new accounts will be routed to your other new accounts. (E-mail to outside addresses will route as expected.)

We recommend you configure mail routing as follows:

- Only load users who are using Office 365 (during test or evaluation).

- If you are using both the Office 365 service and an on-site Exchange server, you need to set your e-mail domain type to Internal. You should have e-mail for these Office 365 users forwarded from the on-site Exchange Server to the Office 365 e-mail accounts using the "long" address of user@<domain>.onmicrosoft.com.

Coexistence E-mail Flow

When you initially purchase Office 365, one of the items created is the subdomain yourdomain.onmicrosoft.com. This is a valid e-mail domain and is the "long" e-mail address. You can send e-mail to <user>@<yourdomain.onmicrosoft.com>, and your e-mail will be delivered into your e-mail box. When you validate a domain and add a user account, the user account is created with two e-mail addresses: `<user>@<yourdomain.onmicrosoft.com>` and `<user>@<yourdomain.com>`.

Coexistence works as follows:

- E-mail is forwarded from the on-premise domain or other hosted e-mail address to your Office 365 "long" address (i.e., `@yourdomain.onmicrosoft.com`).

- When e-mail is sent from inside Office 365, it looks to see whether the e-mail needs to be delivered to a migrated user (i.e., `@yourdomain.com`). If not, the e-mail is forwarded to the real e-mail domain (via the DNS MX records).

Note   After you have moved all users to Office 365 and changed the DNS to the MX records, point to Office 365 and change the domain from Internal Relay to Authoritative. At this point, your e-mail is 100 percent on Office 365.

Once you have moved all the e-mail addresses to Office 365, the MX records are changed to point to Office 365. When the MX records are changed, coexistence mode is completed, and you have implemented your cutover migration, or you have completed the hybrid or a cutover migration. That is all that is really needed to move users to Office 365 for mail flow.

Note   Exchange Server instances may be problematic. You cannot ignore these instances or turn the power off. At the bare minimum, you will need to add a mail forwarder for each user to send mail to the long address of `<user>@<domain>.onmicrosoft.com`. The preferred way is to convert the users to a mail-enabled user or delete the user mailboxes from the Exchange server and uninstall the Exchange server. If you are running Small Business Server (SBSS, then your only option is a forwarder).

Test Groups (or Simple Coexistence)

This is an iterative coexistence migration. Cutover migration will happen at the point that all users are moved to the cloud. Simple coexistence is used to train IT staff and to build experience using Office 365. In simple coexistence, a "test group" of users is migrated to Office 365, and those users who migrate do not have access to the Global Address list and shared calendars of the other users who have not migrated. E-mail for converted users is forwarded from the on-premises or hosted e-mail server to their "long" e-mail address (discussed shortly) in the cloud. The iterative approach requires that only a portion of the users are loaded in step 6 and that the domain type is set to Internal Relay.

Note   Do not use simple coexistence unless you have no other option. There is no sharing of calendars, contacts, or other information with users who are not on Office 365. The users who are migrated are an island. It is much better to use a cutover migration. Everything just works better.

Step 9: (Optional) Manually Install PowerShell

PowerShell allows you to configure Office 365 features via a command line. This step is an optional step, and it depends on whether you need the capability for your management of Office 365. The simplest way to install the latest version of PowerShell is to go to `https://docs.microsoft.com/en-us/office365/ enterprise/powershell/connect-to-office-365-powershell`. This installation will provide you with the basic features necessary to use PowerShell for Office 365 (Figure 7-43).

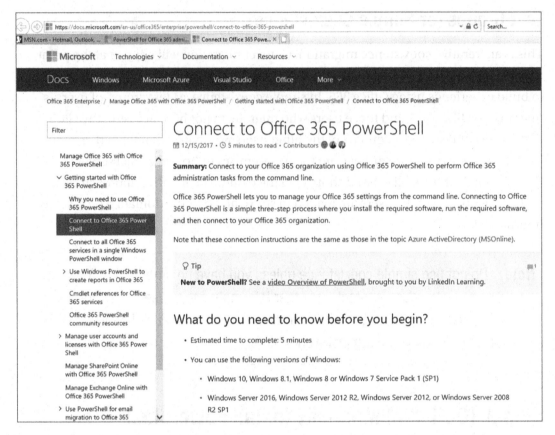

Figure 7-43. *PowerShell installation process*

Typically, we recommend that if your organization has more than 20 accounts, you may find it more convenient to use PowerShell. This is a command interface in Office 365. In Chapter 8, we offer additional troubleshooting steps and configuration options (such as shared mailboxes) using PowerShell. The account that you will use for PowerShell management is the global administrator user account. Users without global administrative privileges will not be able to use this feature.

Once you have Office 365 PowerShell libraries installed, you can access the PowerShell admin center on `https://docs.microsoft.com` and download different PowerShell modules for Office 365 located at `https://docs.microsoft.com/en-us/powershell`.

Once you have installed Office 365 PowerShell, launch the PowerShell module and enter the following commands:

```
Set-ExecutionPolicy RemoteSigned
$LiveCred = Get-Credential
Import-module msonline
Connect-MSOLService –Credential $LiveCred –Verbose
Get-MsolGroup
```

The result of running these commands should be like what's shown in Figure 7-44.

Figure 7-44. *Validating PowerShell commands*

You have completed the base PowerShell setup; now use the preceding command to validate the installation. If the command does not work, you have installed the PowerShell GUI incorrectly, there is a lack of permissions, or you have not installed the desktop connector for Office 365. Using PowerShell requires administrative privileges.

Step 10: Migrate E-mail

We have completed a lot of work to lay the groundwork for migrating e-mail to Office 365. At this point, we are using either a cutover migration or a hybrid migration. Earlier, in step 6, our method of loading users defines the toolset you should use for copying e-mail to Office 365 (this moving of e-mail is called *migration*). Depending on the method you selected, you can use Microsoft tools or external tools. The key decision factor in the toolset you use is based on Azure Active Directory Connect (AAD Sync Connect) integration. If you use AAD Sync Connect and there is an on-premises Exchange Server, you are required to use Microsoft migration tools or Exchange Federation. There are cases where you can use AAD Sync Connect (with an on-site Exchange server) and external tools, but we recommend you consult a Microsoft Partner if you use this approach.

E-mail Migration

E-mail migration is nothing more than copying the e-mail from the old mail server to the new mail server. The mail is not destroyed in the process. You are just copying the e-mail messages (and other mailbox information) to Office 365. There are different approaches to moving the e-mail to Office 365 (see Figure 7-45). Depending upon the approach you are using for migration, you may choose to cut over the mail records before you move e-mail or you may move e-mail and then cut over records. The decision is based more on the source of the mail server and the size of the organization. There is no hard-and-fast rule on the migration of e-mail, with one exception: if you are running some type of coexistence (such as a stage migration), then place a mail forwarder (to the "long" name) in the older mail system before you start the migration. Once the MX records are moved, there is no need to add a forwarder.

Note   Our policy on e-mail migration is to move at least the first 200 e-mail messages for each user (one to two weeks' worth), along with the contacts, calendars, and folder structure, into the new mailbox. The older e-mails can come later. We use MigrationWiz to move historical e-mail as our first choice.

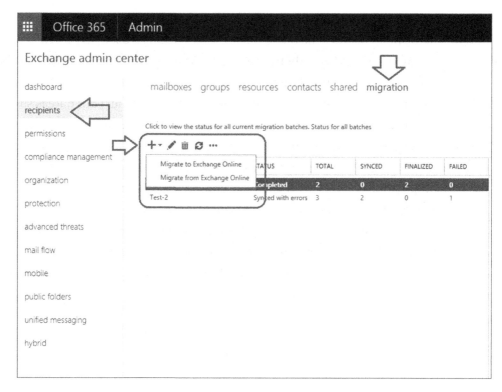

Figure 7-45. *Selecting the Office 365 migration tool*

There are four tools that you can use for e-mail migration: PST export/import, third-party external tools (such as MigrationWiz), the Microsoft Office 365 migration tool, and moving mailboxes with Exchange Federation. Each tool has its fans and critics (see Table 7-1).

Table 7-1. *Different Migration Methods*

Description	Pros	Cons
PST migration	Simple	E-mail addresses are not complete. Requires upload to hosted service or execution at a workstation. Network bandwidth (copy up, and copy down).
MigrationWiz	Simple	Costs $12 per mailbox to migrate.
Exchange 2007/2010/2013	License	Requires Azure Active Directory Connect and Exchange Federation. Exchange 2007 requires adding Exchange Server 2013 for a remote mailbox move.

If you are using a federation mail move (see more later in this chapter), you can use the wizard to pull the mailbox from the on-premises server to Office 365. This also allows you an easy way to preload users (sync them) to Office 365 so you can have a gradual cut over.

There are different deployment methods that you can use depending on how your data is kept. As an example, if you have been using POP mail and all your data is stored in PSTs, then you can only use a PST migration. There are no other options. If your mail is stored on a web server (such as on an Exchange server), you can use the other tools for mailbox migration. We use MigrationWiz (`www.bittitan.com`) tools and use the Microsoft internal migration tool as a backup. If you have chosen to use Exchange Federation, you can only use the Exchange mailbox move for synced accounts. Public folders can be moved with MigrationWiz tools. We discuss the process for each of these approaches later in this chapter in the "Onboarding E-mail" section. The onboarding process is like what's shown in Figure 7-46. If you are using AD Connect (see Figure 7-47), user accounts in Office 365 are synced from AD and are not entered manually.

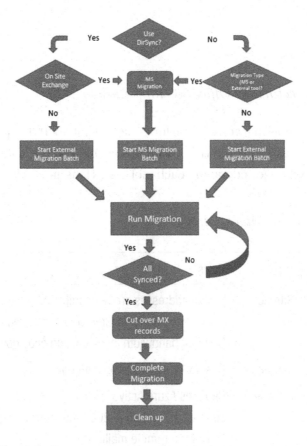

Figure 7-46. *E-mail migration*

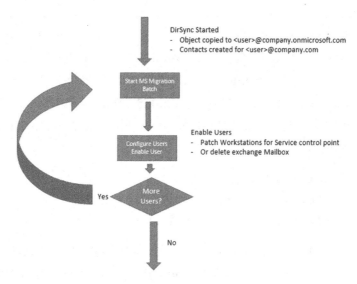

Figure 7-47. *AD Connect synchronization migration approach*

Note   If you want to use MigrationWiz (`www.bittitan.com`) in your migration, please see the MigrationWiz section later in this chapter. Typically, we use MigrationWiz and DeploymentPro for our cutover migrations.

Exchange Server: Mailbox Changes

When you use the Microsoft migration tools, what the Microsoft tools do at the end of the data sync step is to convert the mailbox from an Exchange mailbox to mail-enabled users. What is really happening is that the Exchange mailbox is converted to a contact, and the existing mailbox is placed in a disabled state. When e-mail is received by the on-premise Exchange Server, the server looks up the contact and sends the e-mail to the destination. The contact for the user of the on-site Exchange Server contains the Office 365 long address (*user*`@company.onmicrosoft.com`).

If you are using a third-party migration tool such as MigrationWiz, you need to manually convert the Exchange mailboxes to mail-enabled users. Microsoft Support has published a set of conversion scripts for Exchange Server 2007 and 2010. These scripts convert a migrated Exchange server mailbox to mail-enabled users. If you are running SBS server and decide to keep the SBS server around, you will need to add a mail forwarder to the Exchange server.

Note   If you have used a cutover migration before you install clients and you have an on-premise Exchange server, you need to remove the Exchange service control point (e.g., the CAS Autodiscover record from Exchange Server 2007, 2010, and 2013 by running the following commands. They do the following: (1) retrieve the CAS server identity <name> and (2) set the CAS server Autodiscover record to $NULL.

```
(1) Get-ClientAccessServer
(2) Set-ClientAccessServer -Identity "<name>" -
    AutoDiscoverServiceInternalUri $NULL
```

In some cases, you may also need to remove the Autodiscover record from the Exchange server service control point. Run the command Get-OutlookProvider (to retrieve the Autodiscovery records and set certprincipalName to $null) using the command set-OutlookProvider.

After you have run these commands, the Outlook clients use the DNS Autodiscover records to look up the Office 365 Exchange Server. If you do not remove the Exchange Server CAS role, the Outlook client will bypass the Autodiscover record lookup and connect to the old Exchange Server instance.

Step 11: Finalize All DNS records

At this point, we are done with the mail migrations and are ready to set the mail flow to Office 365. If you chose to cut over all users at one time (cutover migration), the Office 365 Global Address List (GAL) contains all the new user accounts. This limited GAL also applies to sharing calendars and free-busy status. If you choose to move users in groups (simple coexistence), the GAL will only contain those users who have been moved.

Earlier, we discussed three possible migration plans.

- *Cutover migration*: All users are loaded, MX and Autodiscover records are changed, and Office 365 receives all e-mail.

- *Test group (nonhybrid)*: Some users are loaded. E-mail is forwarded from on-premises servers to Office 365 (temporary). This is not recommended.

- *Hybrid coexistence*: Exchange Server and Office 365 operate in tandem.

The hybrid coexistence migration is a complex migration and is beyond the scope of the chapter. Earlier In step 7, I showed you were you would add the hybrid connector for a federation migration. This is detailed in the Microsoft Exchange Assistant planning guide (see `https://docs.microsoft.com/en-us/exchange/exchange-deployment-assistant`). Once you have moved the mail to Office 365, the process of moving MX record (and TXT and autodiscover) to Office 365 in a federation move is the same, you move the records at the end of the migration. If you are using Public folders, you move the public folders at the end of the migration after all users have been moved. (public folder migration is beyond the scope of this chapter).

Cutover Migration and Hybrid

At this point all users mailboxes have been moved to Office 365. If you have public folders, you have move them as well, and no other records are left. This is also a 100 percent conversion, and you are ready to change the final MX records and cutover to Office 365. Cutover means that you have loaded up the users and you point the e-mail records to Office 365 servers. All historical e-mail is brought over in a post-migration process.

Note   If you have completed loading the users, you can change the DNS records to point to Office 365 services. To determine records that need to change, log in to Office 365 as an administrator, select the domain, and run the Find and Fix Issues operation to show the broken DNS records. Make the changes and you are done with your migration.

Step 12: Configure the Desktop and Mobile Devices

There are different philosophies on when to configure these services. However, unless you want to manually configure these services, you cannot add them until you have changed the MX and Autodiscover records. Desktop services (Outlook) use the Autodiscover record and the Active Directory service control point record to find the exchange server. The mobile device (on older versions of IOS and android software), may need to have the account deleted, then reentered. On the new devices, the configuration is automatic. The newer mobile devices will have a delay, then resync mailbox to Office 365.

Configure Desktop Services

Depending upon the subscription (see Figure 7-48), the user will need to log into Office 365 and download the Office Professional Plus software (located under the gear icon and Office 365 settings). The installation process can be managed by any end user. All that is needed is to log into `prtoal.office.com` and download the new software.

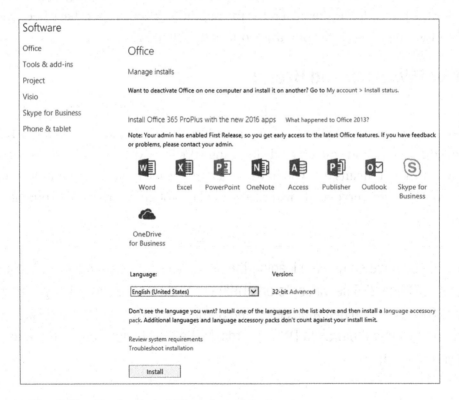

Figure 7-48. *Office Professional Plus download*

Mobile Device Configuration

Office 365 supports different mobile devices. The software can be installed at any time and is user-driven (see Figure 7-49). To install the Office apps on your smartphone, go to the Office 365 web site, log in, select the Software option under Office 365 settings, and install. You will receive a link in the e-mail on where you can download the information to your smartphone and configure the mobile device. The mobile software is also located in the iOS and Android store. This screen is mostly for legacy devices and configuration that do not have a mobile device management configuration.

Figure 7-49. *Adding application support for your smartphone*

Step 13: Configure the External Devices

External devices need to be configured (if there are any devices on your network) to use a different mail server than your Exchange Server instance. There are different ways that you can configure your devices to send e-mail to Office 365, either directly or through an SMTP server in your network. There are four rules that you need to follow when configuring devices to relay e-mail through Office 365:

- The sending device must have a domain name that is verified in the Office 365 tenant.

469

- Sending "on behalf" of someone means you need to create a dedicated "user" in Office 365 and your SMTP relay device will need to log in as that user and have permission to send on your behalf. You must grant send as to this user to access all internal mailboxes. This is completed in the exchange admin center (see Chapter 8)

- Your static IP address of the on-premise firewall (where the e-mail is being relayed from) must be registered as a connector in Office 365.

- The external IP address that is sending to Office 365 (acting as your relay) must be added as a transport rule with the "bypass" spam filter option.

Step 14: Clean Up

The cleanup operation depends on the type of mail system you have migrated to Office 365. If you are using a hosted e-mail system or a non-Exchange e-mail system, you need to contact the software supplier to determine whether there is any special process needed to remove the third-party mail server. Unless the e-mail server is integrated into Microsoft local Active Directory, there is usually no shutdown sequence. The server must be removed from Active Directory.

An Exchange Server must be decommissioned to remove it from your local environment. To remove the Exchange Server, you simply uninstall the server. It seems simple, but to uninstall the server, you need to remove all users and delete the public folders and the attached mail database. To remove an Exchange Server, run the setup wizard and remove the services. This is an iterative process. The wizard walks you through the steps and reboots the server until the Exchange Server instance is uninstalled.

Note   Do not power off the Exchange Server instance once you have migrated to Office 365. Exchange Server must be uninstalled from the Exchange Server setup media. You must uninstall the Exchange Server software.

Final Check List

Office 365 is ready to be used. At this point, verify the following:

1. If you have a desktop version of Office 2010/2013/2016 or 2019, upgrade to the Office 365 subscription version.

2. Check the Office 365 domain setup in the Office 365 admin center to make sure that all DNS entries are green. If you have any errors when you verify the domain (see Figure 7-20) fix those errors before you move forward (see Figure 7-50).

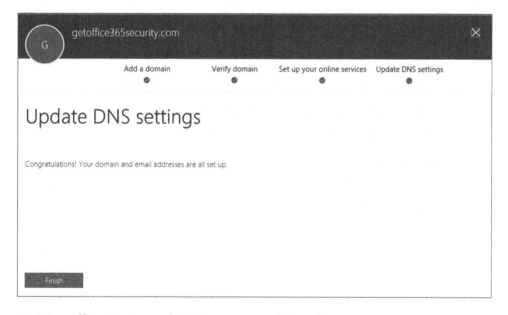

Figure 7-50. *Office 365 records 100 percent validated*

3. Verify that your Office 365 domain is set to Authoritative (see Figure 7-41) and is not shared for e-mail. (This will be set only if you have run a test group.)

4. Verify that you have placed a local DNS record in your on-premises DNS server. You will need to add an Autodiscover cname to your internal DNS that points to `autodiscover.outlook.com`.

5. If you have an on-premise Exchange Server instance and you have migrated to Office 365, set the Autodiscover record to $NULL with the following command. (Note that once it's set, local clients cannot autodiscover the local Exchange Server instance.)

```
Set-ClientAccessServer -Identity "<name>"
-AutoDiscoverServiceInternalUri $NULL
```

6. Extend the 15-day delete hold time to a 30-day delete hold time. Run the PowerShell command.

   a. Extend the 30-day delete for a mailbox:

   ```
   Set-mailbox user@contoso.com -retaindeleteditemsfor 30
   ```

   b. Extend the 30-day delete for the organization:

   ```
   Get-mailbox | Set-mailbox -retaindeleteditemsfor 30
   ```

7. Enable the audit logs on all users' mailboxes. The default logs are kept for 30 days, and this can be extended to multiple years.

```
#Enable Audit Logging
Get-Mailbox -ResultSize Unlimited -Filter {RecipientTypeDetails
-eq "UserMailbox" -or RecipientTypeDetails -eq
"SharedMailbox" -or RecipientTypeDetails -eq "RoomMailbox"
-or RecipientTypeDetails -eq "DiscoveryMailbox"}| Set-Mailbox
-AuditEnabled $true -AuditLogAgeLimit 365 -AuditOwner Create,
HardDelete,MailboxLogin,MoveToDeletedItems,SoftDelete,Update

#Check Status
Get-Mailbox -ResultSize Unlimited | Select Name,
UserPrincipalName, AuditEnabled, AuditLogAgeLimit | Out-Gridview
```

8. Log into the Office 365 admin center, and select the Security & Compliance Center. Under Search & Investigation, select "audit log search" and "enable audit log recording".

9. The default retention policies are not enabled until the archive is enabled. If you enable the archive on a user mailbox, the retention polices begin to execute. For example, the default retention policy is two years. When the retention policy

executes, e-mail is deleted. If you do not want your e-mail to be deleted or moved to an archive, remove the tag in the Exchange admin center, under "Compliance Management" and "Retention tags".

10. Remove any other retention tags you do not want to use in the retention policy.

11. Verify that you have enabled Yammer on your subscription. To enable Yammer, expand the admin center, and then select Yammer. The service should auto-activate and show a green check mark

12. Log in to the OneDrive admin center and set the retention to 1,530 days for deleted files.

13. In the OneDrive administration center, reduce the OneDrive sharing (in the OneDrive admin center) to "Existing External users" to control sharing until you understand the sharing features.

Test Group or Staged Migration

In the early cloud days, there was a lot of work with test groups to train the IT staff. Now test groups are not really used except in unique situations. There are two ways to use test groups: doing a hybrid migration or deploying a few test mailboxes to test processes and then discarding the test group when you move to production. Test groups are nothing more than a stage migration. Stage migrations take a lot of work and should be used only for a limited time and for a small number of users. When we discuss test groups, we mean we are using those users to test our deployment processes. A test group is nothing more than placing a group of users on a different mail server that is separate from the existing organization. A test group does not have access to a common calendar or a common address list (unless a hybrid deployment). It is for these reasons that you want to use test groups for a limited time and with a definite set of objectives. A stage migration is nothing more than a test group.

Note   If the user accounts are POP or IMAP, stage migration is a viable option because there are no common shared resources (like calendars and address lists).

Outlook Client Autodiscover Record Changes

If you are using a test group with an on-premise Exchange Server instance (no hybrid, no Exchange Federation), you will encounter two problems: Autodiscover (for Outlook clients) and the presence of Exchange Server in Active Directory. The workarounds are manual, and you need to edit the registry to enable the clients to find the Office 365 mail server. Once you have deployed, you need to remove these "enhancements" to eliminate a future support problem when using Office 365. If you choose to manually configure Outlook, you still need to make these changes since Outlook will verify the connection via Autodiscover every time it is started.

These are the client steps required to support a test group if there is an on-premise Exchange Server instance. Also, you cannot use Office 2016 as an Outlook client with a test group. The following are the configuration steps:

1. Add the Autodiscover record in the host file, located at
    `<drive:>windows/systems32/drivers/etc`.

    a. Ping `autodiscover.outlook.com`.

    b. Add the Autodiscover record with the address discovered earlier.

    c. Open a command prompt and enter `ping Autodiscover`. This should display the IP address you just entered.

2. Add the two Autodiscover records: `Autodiscover` and `Autodiscover.<yourdomain.com>`.

3. Add the registry fixes to ignore the Exchange Server service control point. The registry entries required to be modified for the clients are listed shortly (see `https://support.microsoft.com/en-us/kb/2612922`).

    a. Navigate to the following registry key that corresponds to your version of Office (12.0 is Office 2007; 15.0 is Office 2013):

        `HKEY_CURRENT_USER\Software\Microsoft\Office\12.0\Outlook\AutoDiscover`

b. Set the following registry names and values. Type in the names that are in the quotes when you create the registry entries:

```
"PreferLocalXML"=dword:1
"ExcludeHttpRedirect"=dword:0
"ExcludeHttpsAutodiscoverDomain"=dword:1
"ExcludeHttpsRootDomain"=dword:1
"ExcludeScpLookup"=dword:1
"ExcludeSrvLookup"=dword:1
"ExcludeSrvRecord"=dword:1
```

4. In the Windows 10 control panel, select the Mail application, then configure the Outlook profile to prompt for a profile.

5. If there is an existing Exchange Server instance, you need to manually configure the Outlook client. Outlook clients (Mac and PCs) require an Autodiscover record. Office 2016 and later cannot be manually configured.

6. Start the Outlook client and create a new profile. In some cases, the client may not start up correctly the first time. Close Outlook and start again.

DNS Troubleshooting

One of the problems associated with the DNS records is figuring out who is managing them. In some cases, this may be a web developer who is no longer in business. You may also have it registered with an e-mail address that you no longer use (or can remember). If you cannot access the DNS server, how do you find the records?

We use http://who.is. This service gives you a good snapshot of the DNS records for the domain you are moving (see Figure 7-51). We use this tool in conjunction with mxtoolbox.com. If you do not have access to the actual DNS zone file before you move, you need to use tools like http://who.is to collect the information before you move the service to a new registrar.

● SOA Record – kamind.net

Name Server	NS97.WORLDNIC.COM
Email	**nanehost**@WORLDNIC.COM
Serial Number	113022613
Refresh	3 hours
Retry	1 hour
Expiry	7 days
Minimum	1 hour

● DNS Records – KAMIND.NET

Record	Type	TTL	Priority	Content
kamind.net	MX	2 hours	0	kamind-net.mail.eo.outlook.com
kamind.net	NS	2 hours		ns97.worldnic.com
kamind.net	NS	2 hours		ns98.worldnic.com
kamind.net	SOA	2 hours		NS97.WORLDNIC.COM. namehost.WORLDNIC.COM. 113022613 10800 3600 604800 3600
kamind.net	TXT	2 hours		v=spf1 include:spf.protection.outlook.com -all

Figure 7-51. *DNS records from who.is for kamind.net*

Onboarding E-mail

After you have loaded the user account to Office 365, you need to copy the e-mail from the current mail servers to Office 365. There are different ways to do this, depending on the method you used for loading users. As an example, if you have an on-premises Exchange Server instance and you enabled DirSync, your only option is to use the Microsoft migration tools. If you do not have an existing Exchange Server instance, you can use different migration tools to move mail to Office 365. The three methods discussed here are PST migration, third-party tool migration, and the Microsoft Office 365 migration tools.

PST Mail Migration to Office 365

PST migration consists of importing the existing PST files into your Office 365 mailbox. A PST export/import is performed at each user's workstation, with data from their version of Outlook. PST migrations are the simplest but should be used as a last resort. When you migrate PST data, you need to export the old mailbox at the root and import the data into Office 365 at the root. If the PST data already exists, then import the data at the level that you want to see the data in Office 365.

Note   If you start a PST migration, you need to complete it. There is no real error checking on data imports or duplicates. If you stop and restart a PST migration, you have duplicate data.

Typical user data in a PST contains all the information in the mailbox, including e-mails, folders and subfolders, calendars, and contacts. To install the calendar and contacts into Office 365, you can either manually copy them over to Office 365 (drag and drop) or overlay the Office 365 calendar and contact information using export and import data commands, specifying the root inbox. Next we cover the two options for this command.

Export Outlook 2010, 2013, or 2016 Mailbox Information

Follow these steps on exporting the PST data into Outlook. If you already have your PST files as an archive, refer to the import. When you export Outlook information into a PST for import into Office 365, you must export the root mailbox.

1. Start Outlook (Outlook 2010 or 2013/2016). Use your on-premises Exchange Server Outlook profile (probably your default profile) for the export of PST mailbox information (see Figure 7-52).

2. In Outlook 2013/2016, click File ➤ Open ➤ Import (this includes file export as well).

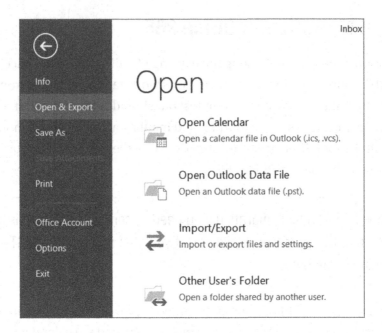

Figure 7-52. *Outlook 2013—exporting files to a PST*

3. Select "Export to a file" and then Outlook Data File (.pst), as shown in Figure 7-53.

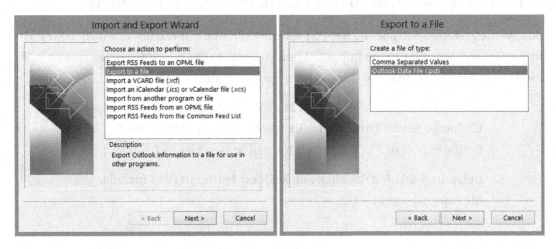

Figure 7-53. *Exporting Outlook files as a PST*

4. Select the mail location to export (normally, you want to select the very top item, the mailbox account) and the export options. Enter a filename and select "Replace duplicates with items exported" (see Figure 7-54).

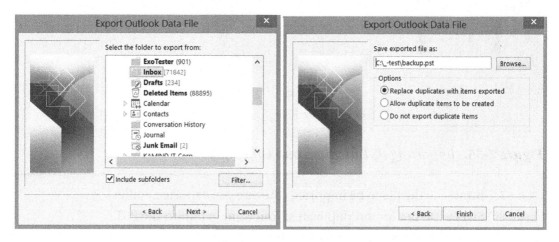

Figure 7-54. *Selecting Outlook mail and file save location*

5. Once you have exported the documents, write down the location where the PST file is located. The next step is to import the PST file.

Import Outlook 2010, 2013, or 2016 Mailbox Information

Follow these steps to import your exported PST e-mail data into your Office 365 e-mail account. This is done by loading the existing mailbox on top of the Office 365 mailbox.

1. Exit Outlook.

2. Sign in to the user's Office 365 account.

3. Start Outlook either with a new profile or with the user's Office 365 profile. (We normally call the new profile O365 to distinguish it.)

4. In Outlook 2010 (or 2013/2016), click File ➤ Open ➤ Import.

5. Select Import from another program or file.

6. Select Outlook Data File (.pst), or it may be Personal Folder File (.pst), as shown in Figure 7-55.

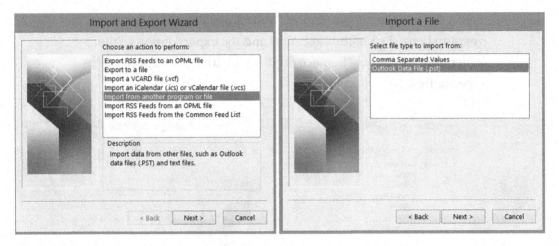

Figure 7-55. *Importing PST archives into Office 365*

7. Browse to the file to be imported (the one you exported earlier).
    Select "Do not import duplicates." You want to import the PST
    folder into the same structure as the export. As an example, if you
    export the PST file as the root mailbox, you need to import it as a
    root mailbox (shown in Figure 7-56). You may import the e-mail
    account to a lower level (for example, if you are importing several
    e-mail accounts into one e-mail account).

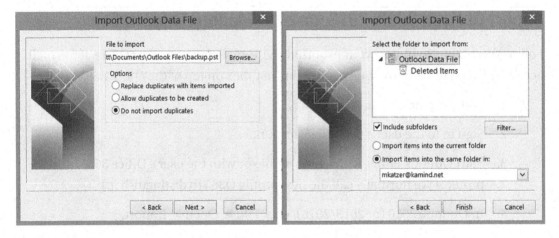

Figure 7-56. *Importing PST archives into Office 365*

The import process uploads the Outlook PST data to the Microsoft Office 365 Exchange Server. Your data will then be replicated down to your Outlook 2010. It is best that you import data using a high-speed data link since the data will travel twice: up to Office 365 and back down to your Outlook local cache.

Migrating E-mail with BitTitan's MigrationWiz

MigrationWiz (`www.migrationwiz.com`) is the tool (see Figure 7-57) that is used for most migrations from either on-premise or another hosted provider to Office 365. The tool is easy to use and allows thousands of mailboxes to move simultaneously.

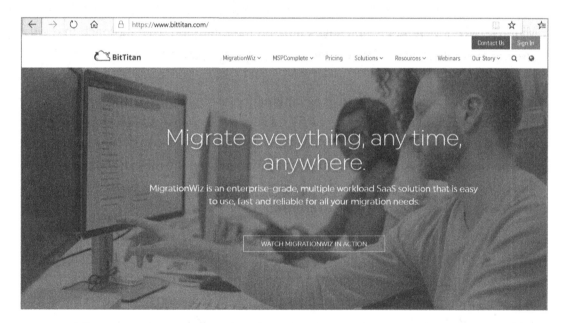

Figure 7-57. *BitTitan: mail and data cloud migration tools (courtesy of BitTitan)*

There are three different migration tools that BitTitan offers: MigrationWiz, DeploymentPro, and User Activation. MigrationWiz is used to move mailboxes to/from Office 365. DeploymentPro is a tool configures the user's Outlook (configures the desktop, the move task, the Outlook cache, etc.) to a new Outlook profile linked to Office 365. User Activation is an end-user tool that integrates MigrationWiz and DeploymentPro for a hands-off migration to Office 365. The tool that you use depends on the migration approach. If you are looking for an automated migration and you have fewer than 25 users, then user activation is the best way to proceed. If you are using any type of SBS server (that has a local Exchange Server), you need to use either User Activation or DeploymentPro/MigrationWiz. These tools patch around the SBS service control point on the desktop. Keep in mind that any time there is an Exchange Server instance, you need to *uninstall* Exchange Server at the end of the migration.

Note   There are two approaches to using BitTitan's tools: using a manual migration approach via MigrationWiz and DeploymentPro or using the User Activation automated tool. If you are migrating a small number of mailboxes, using MigrationWiz or User Activation saves time on the migration. The approach that we are describing here is a manual approach using MigrationWiz.

The migration approach we use is a combination of MigrationWiz and DeploymentPro. If there is an SBS server, we always use DeploymentPro. DeploymentPro configures the desktop and moves the SBS Exchange Server to the side. When we migrate larger accounts of more than 200 or 400 users, it depends on the migration strategy. In some cases, we use a combination of tools, and in others, we use Exchange Federation; it just depends on what you are trying to achieve.

Note   If you are using MigrationWiz with DeploymentPro and you want to upgrade the desktop before you install clients, you need to remove the service control point (e.g., CAS Autodiscover record from the Exchange Server (2007 and 2010) by running the following commands: (1) to retrieve the CAS server identity <name> and (2) to set the CAS server Autodiscover record to $NULL.

(1) `Get-ClientAccessServer`
(2) `Set-ClientAccessServer -Identity "<name>" -`
`AutoDiscoverServiceInternalUri $NULL`

After you have run these commands, the Outlook clients use the DNS Autodiscover records to look up the Office 365 Exchange Server instance.

Using MigrationWiz

In step 9 (earlier in this chapter), we chose a cutover migration. The easiest way to look at a migration is to use a hypothetical situation. In this example, there are ten mailboxes and a Windows server running Exchange. The migration tools that we will use are MigrationWiz and DeploymentPro. MigrationWiz moves the data, and DeploymentPro configures the desktop and sets the default profile. The migration steps using these tools are as follows:

1. Log in to `www.bittian.com` and create a migration account. Confirm your account and select MigrationWiz (see Figure 7-58).

2. Verify that Exchange Server 2007/2010 is set to basic authentication.

3. Configure the permission for the admin user mailbox on Exchange Server.

4. Build the migration project and enter the admin credentials.

5. Load the user for migration.

6. Purchase licenses for migration.

7. (Optional) Select DeploymentPro for desktop configuration changes and send out the Configuration tool.

8. Start the mailbox migration.

9. Retry migration errors.

10. If you are using DeploymentPro, select "cutover" (either manual or scheduled) and cut over the MX records. The migration is completed.

Figure 7-58. *BitTitan: MSP complete - mail and data cloud migration tools*

Using BitTitan tools is a simple process to move mail from an existing service to Office 365 or to use the upload tool to configure and upload the PSTs. Gone are the days where you must import a PST directly into Office 365 (yes, you can do that, and we still do for IMAP migration to pick up calendars and contacts). But in general, if you use the automated tools, life is simpler.

Note   If you are uploading an old PST, it is best to attach the PST to Outlook and then export and create a new PST from the old PST. This will correct the errors in the PST.

Microsoft Mail Migration

MigrationWiz is a third-party tool that you can use to migrate to Office 365. However, there is also the Microsoft Office 365 migration tool. You can use this tool for cutover migration and for Exchange Federation moves to Office 365. The tool is straightforward to use, and you can move user mailboxes to Office 365 or move them back to the on-premises Exchange Server instance.

1. Select Office 365 in the admin center, then select Exchange
    Admin center.

2. Select recipients, then select migration.

3. Select the "+" drop down to see the migration types

4. You will see the screen shown in Figure 7-59. Select Migrate to
    Exchange Online. When a mailbox is migrated, the on-premises
    mailbox is converted to a mail-enabled unit.

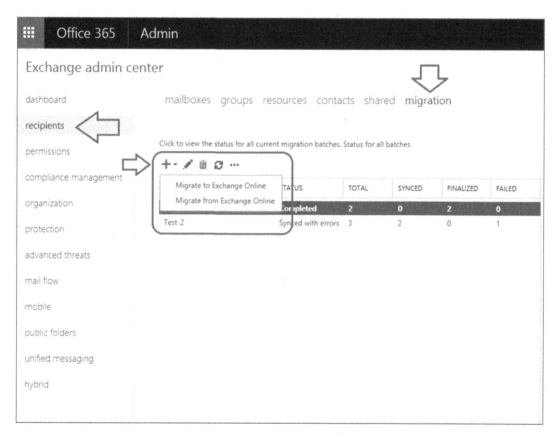

Figure 7-59. *Selecting the Office 365 migration tool*

Your options with the Office 365 tool are limited to Exchange Server 2007 and 2010 and IMAP. POP mail is problematic, since POP e-mail has just e-mail and no folders. Typically, if you are using POP mail, you will most likely use a PST export/import because the POP e-mail is stored locally. We always recommend that you use MigrationWiz as the first option. It is simpler to use. In this example, we are going to use IMAP to import mail from a non–Exchange Server instance, and we need to build a CSV file for the usernames and passwords. To import using IMAP, select the IMAP option (see Figure 7-60).

Note   If you do not have a third-party certificate, do not use the Microsoft mail migration tool; use BitTitan's MigrationWiz.

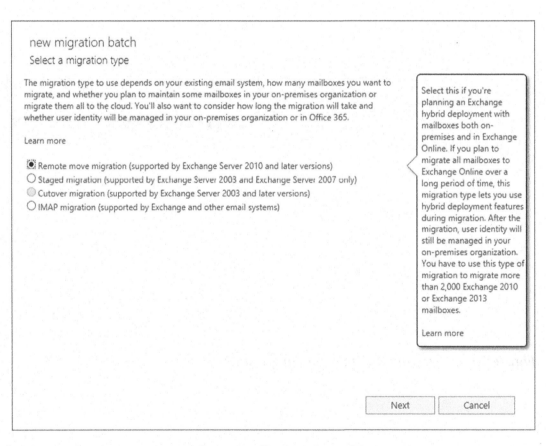

Figure 7-60. *Migrating e-mail using Office 365 e-mail migration*

Provide the credentials to import the user accounts into Office 365, and create a CSV file to load the users from the source server into Office 365 (see Figure 7-61). The wizard assumes that the e-mail address of the source server is the destination e-mail address on Office 365. You need to be a global administrator to use this tool.

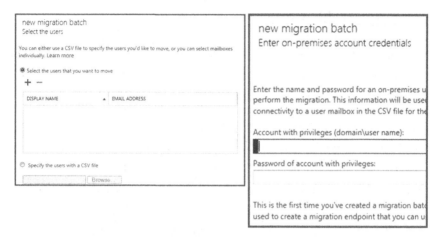

Figure 7-61. *Office 365 e-mail migration*

After you have clicked Run, Office 365 monitors the status and sends you an e-mail when the migration is completed. It lists the batch status (see Figure 7-62).

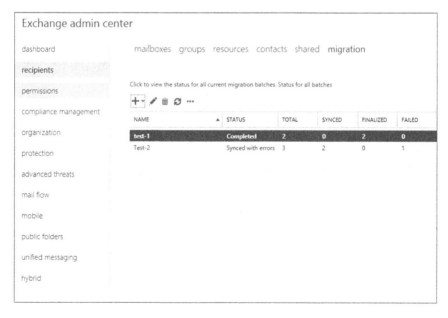

Figure 7-62. *Migration status using Office 365 migration*

After you have started the migrations, the next step is to install PowerShell. In some cases, you may need to install PowerShell early on if you have any problems with domain validation. In most instances, you will use PowerShell under the guidance of the Office 365 support staff.

Configuring Azure AD Connect

Configuring AD Connect is straightforward. The hardest part is the installation of the software on the server and connecting this to Office 365. There are different philosophies for the installation of AD Connect. In our case what we do is the following:

1. Create two new accounts, OnPremSync and OnLineSync. The OnPremSync account needs to be an enterprise admin account, and the OnLineSync account needs to be a global admin account. We create two different accounts because we do not allow the Cloud account (online sync) to be added to the local AD. Likewise we do not allow the onPrem account to be added to the Azure ad. We isolate the accounts for security.

2. Enable Azure AD Connect and download the software to the domain controller (log in to `https://portal.azure.com` and select Azure AD Connect).

3. Install the software using the OnPremSync account. When you install the software, open a command prompt and run as an administrator, then execute the AD Connect download).

4. Configure AD Connect.

5. Check the status of AD Connect in Azure AD Connect Health (see Figure 7-63).

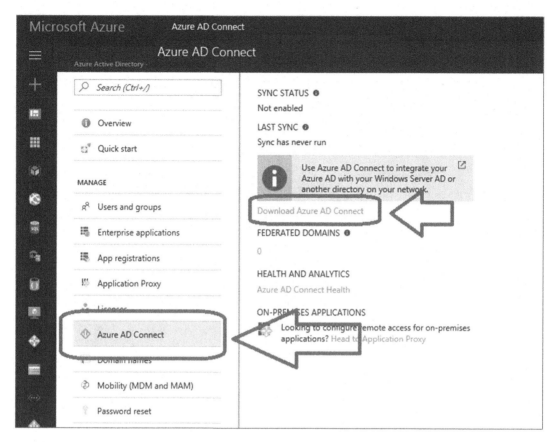

Figure 7-63. *Download Azure AD Connect*

There are multiple ways to download AD Connect. All the approaches use the same download link at `https://downloads.microsoft.com`.

The one area where everyone makes a mistake is not to install the service as an admin (see Figure 7-64) or to log into the system and install using a different account than the OnPremSycn account. The installation process will set up permissions for the account that will be using the service (and the one that installs it (make it the same account). This is extremely important to avoid future problems.

Note   Do not sync the two accounts created. OnPremSync is unique to onPrem, and OnlineSync is used online with no license.

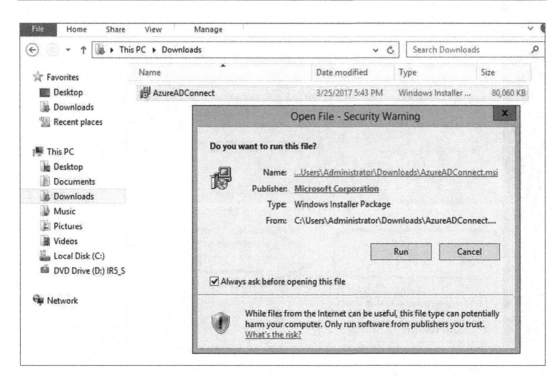

Figure 7-64. *Installing AD Connect as an administrator*

The process to install AD Connect is a two-step process. First you install the connector (run as an administrator or through a command as an administrator), select all the default settings, and leave the sync off. The second step is to start the installed tool and change the configuration. As this point you modify the configuration and set the default settings for your environment. After you run the tool the second time, you fully sync the settings to Office 365. See Figure 7-65 to begin the install of AD Connect (remember to run this tool from an admin prompt and in Figure 7-66, select Express when you start the installation.

Note   Do not sync after running the tool the first time. This will sync the entire AD organizational unit (OU) to Office 365. When you sync, you only want to sync those OU's that are user accounts to Office 365.

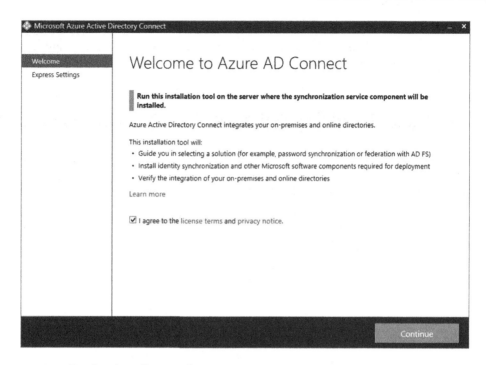

Figure 7-65. *Beginning the configuration steps*

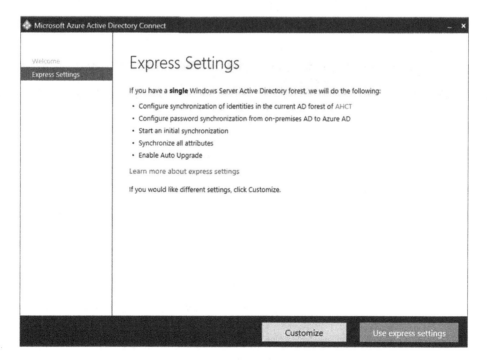

Figure 7-66. *Selecting the Express installation*

Select the Express installation (Figure 7-67) and enter the accounts created for management in Figure 7-68. Unless you have a federated move with exchange server, leave federation off (Figure 7-69).

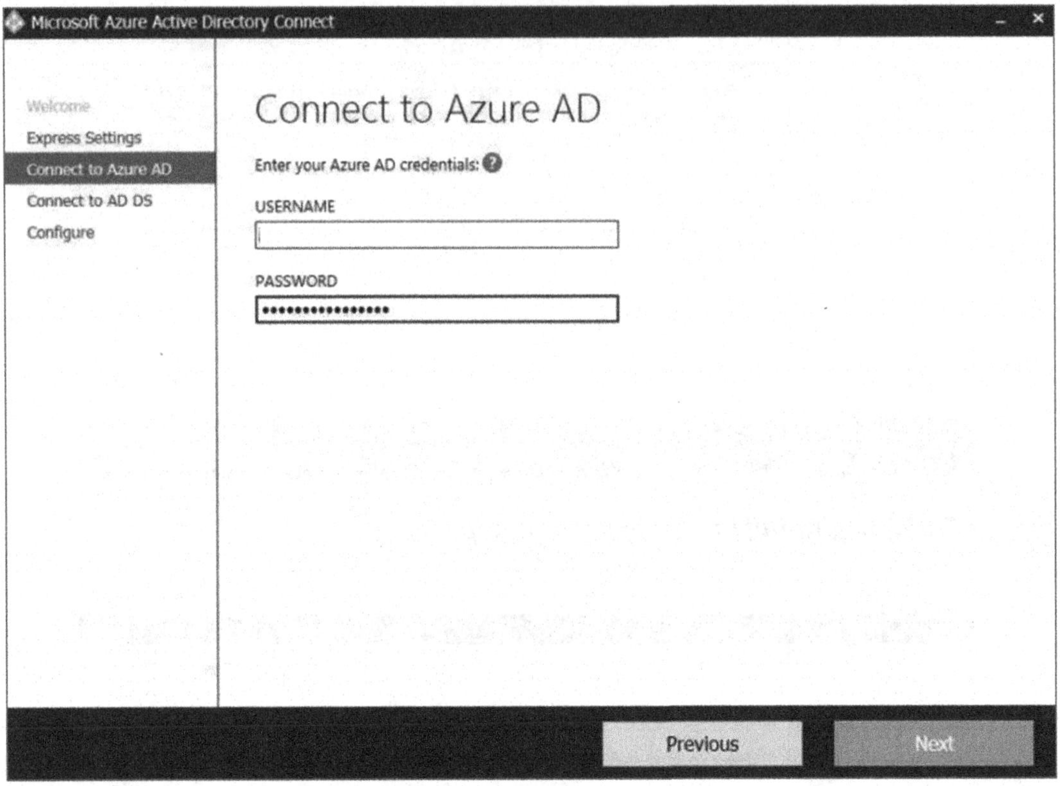

Figure 7-67. *Syncing the Office 365 service*

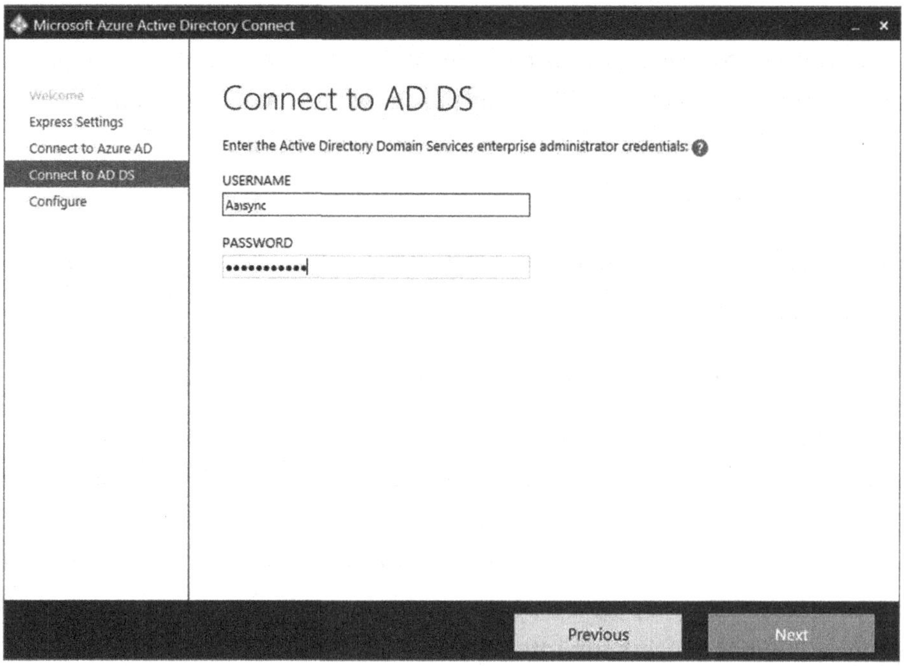

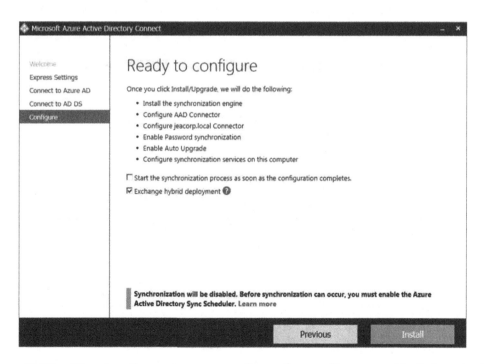

Figure 7-68. *Setting up the local AD Sync (same account as install account)*

Figure 7-69. *Allowing the systems to configure (turn off sync enable federation)*

At this point the base configuration is completed. We do not enable auto sync because we need to configure the on-premise Active Directory sync and the optional features for the AD Connect tool. The next steps are to run AD Connect a second time and set up the optional features. Typically, you set the following:

- Password writeback

- Password hash synchronization

- Exchange hybrid deployment

- OU filtering (so you only sync those accounts that are required)

Just select the AD Connect installed tool on the desktop, and rerun the wizard, select the configuration option, and set the additional parameters required for your operation. The AD Connect tool is linked to Azure, so Microsoft will manage the tool updates. If you do have any alerts on using the tool, make sure you look at the passwords again (remember we use different password for sync admin and sync online accounts). This is usually the problem that users run into in troubleshooting AD Connect issues.

Microsoft is continuously expanding the capabilities of AD Connect. It is expected that Azure directory services will be integrated into the AD Connect tool (See Figure 7-70). After you have completed the installation, you may have additional configurations to complete. Complete the configuration if prompted (see Figure 7-71).

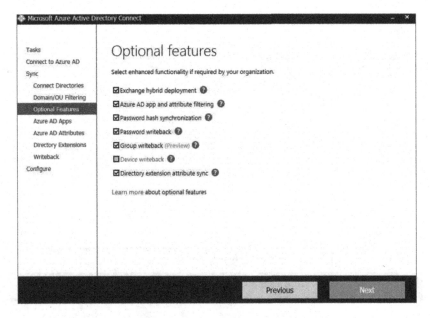

Figure 7-70. *AD Connect configuration options*

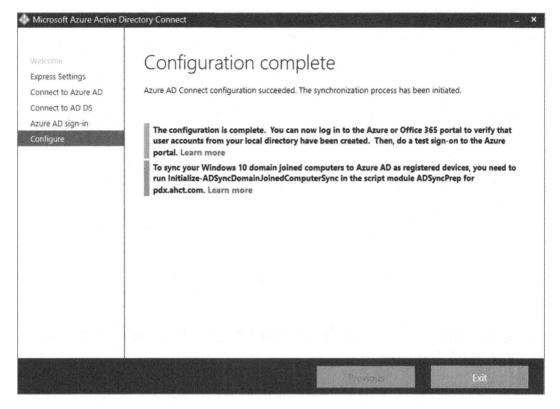

Figure 7-71. *AD Connect final sync notification*

Hybrid Migration with Exchange 2007

In our migration, we talked about the ways to move from the on-premises Exchange Server to Office 365 and turning off your on-premises Exchange Server. There is another option available to all Office 365 users, and that is to run the Exchange Server admin console locally on your Active Directory. Microsoft provides Exchange Server at no charge, if you do not have any mailboxes installed on Exchange Server 2013. If you want to take advantage of this offer (and you are running the Enterprise Office 365 plans), all you need to do is log in to `https://configure.office.com/Scenario.aspx?sid13` and verify your eligibility (see Figure 7-72).

This is important because to use a federation move, you need to be running Exchange 2010 or later. To federate a 2007 server, we deploy Exchange Server 2013 as a mail migration server (requires an Enterprise E3 or E5 license).

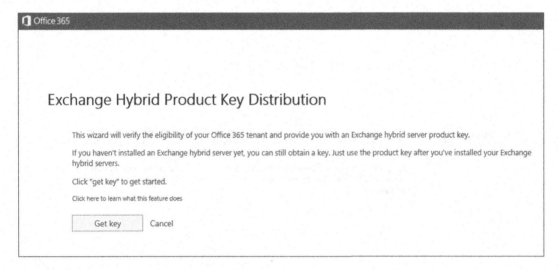

Figure 7-72. Checking the eligibility of Exchange Server 2013

Deploying the Hybrid Configuration Wizard to support Exchange Server 2007 federation move

The Hybrid Configuration Wizard does not need to be deployed on an Exchange Server instance. However, you need to be running Exchange Server 2010 or later. If you are running Exchange Server 2007, then you need to deploy Exchange Server 2013, change the mail flow, and then deploy the Hybrid Configuration Wizard. Exchange 2007 does not support the remote mail move capabilities required to migrate to Office 365. However, Exchange Server 2013 does support them. By joining an Exchange Server 2013 server into an Exchange Server 2007 infrastructure, you can no use the hybrid mail move. To deploy an Exchange Server 2013 server in an Exchange Server 2007 organization, visit the Microsoft Exchange Server Deployment Assistant (see Figure 7-73). Look at the Exchange deployment assistance on upgrading to Exchange Server 2013, and follow that process. Once the upgrade is completed (and the mail flow is running through the Exchange Server 2016 or 2019), you can deploy the Hybrid Configuration Wizard that we discussed earlier in the chapter.

It is highly recommended that you contact a Microsoft Partner to assist you in this process. Hybrid migration is just a different step in the migration process. Exchange Server needs to be up-to-date with all service packs, or the hybrid migration will fail. Once you have compelled the migration, then upgrade the Exchange 2013 server to Exchange Server 2019.

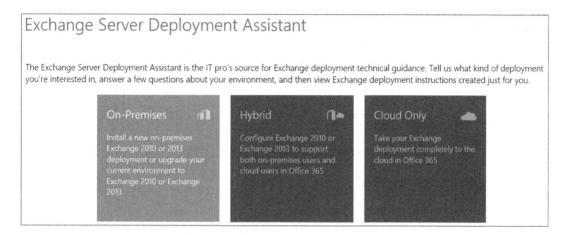

Figure 7-73. *Microsoft Exchange Server Deployment Assistant (courtesy of Microsoft)*

Note   A hybrid migration is a complex migration. If you choose to use a hybrid migration, then follow these additional steps: review the Exchange Server Deployment Assistant (search for this in the search engine), deploy Azure AD Connect on the domain controller, and deploy the Exchange Hybrid Configuration Wizard to move data. If you are using Exchange 2007, you will need to add an Exchange 2013 server into your environment to move to Office 365.

Summary

The focus of this chapter was to migrate to Office 365. Granted this is purpoly out of sequence. In the earlier chapters we talked about security and now migration. This was to help you make the decision on migration to Office 365. There are different ways you can move your business to Office 365; the techniques depend on the size of your organization. Typically, small organizations use cutover migration, and larger organizations use federation migration. Now that you have migrated to Office 365., lets configure the Office 365 and Azure security services to protect what we just deployed.

Reference Links

Office 365 seems simple, but it is complex. There are many different areas to retrieve information about how to migrate to Office 365. The following are the important links for migration.

PowerShell on Microsoft.com

- `https://docs.microsoft.com/en-us/pwoershell`

Onboarding Checking Tool

- `http://fasttrack.office.com`

Office 365 Migration Videos

- `https://docs.microsoft.com/en-us/Office365/index?view=o365-worldwide`

Conversion of On-Site User to Mail-Enabled User

- `http://community.office365.com/en-us/blogs/office_365_community_blog/archive/2011/12/02/convert-exchange-2007-mailboxes-to-mail-enabled-users-after-a-staged-exchange-migration.aspx`

Office 365 Migrating and Managing Your Business in the Cloud—Update

- `www.mattkatzer.com`

CHAPTER 8

Managing Office 365

We have made a lot of progress in securing Office 365. We enabled the audit logs in the Security & Compliance Center, and we completed an initial configuration of Cloud App Security. As part of our MDM deployment, we deployed Azure multifactor authentication, with conditional access support. We also set up data loss prevention policies in the Security & Compliance Center. We placed accounts on legal hold and completed an electronic discovery for a court-ordered subpoena. As part of our discovery process, we set up Microsoft Secure Score and the next-generation Windows Advanced Threat Protection (ATP). The new ATP threat agents combine the latest in machine learning and deep learning. We have made a lot of progress, and we now have a functioning and secure tenant.

Managing our 365 tenant is a different set of problems. We can use our security score to manage Office 365 because it shows how we are doing as administrators. Have we done the correct Office 365 configuration? Have we configured the different 365 services? Are we doing our jobs as administrators and managing our Office 365 company? If we look at the identity management scores, we even have a grade on our accounts. Has our account been configured correctly (see Figure 8-1)?

© Matthew Katzer 2018
M. Katzer, *Securing Office 365*, https://doi.org/10.1007/978-1-4842-4230-8_8

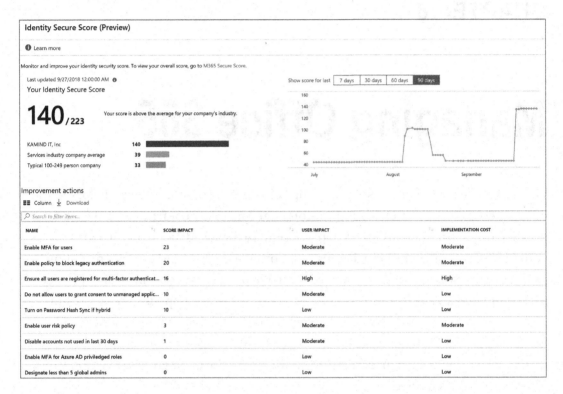

Figure 8-1. *Identity Secure Score*

Office 365 and Azure security and compliance are large topics. There is so much information that the question is where do you start? There are two ways to focus on this problem; first we look at the tactical issues represented by Secure Score, and then we look at the administrative issues of how we manage our Office 365 (and Azure) environment. As an example, our security score was 412/711. As we deployed new tools and solutions, the score drastically changed (Figure 8-2), and our combined Microsoft 365 score is now 1064/1711. At this point, we are going to dive into the administration of Office 365, with a focus on managing the Office 365 tenant and how that impacts the Microsoft Security Score.

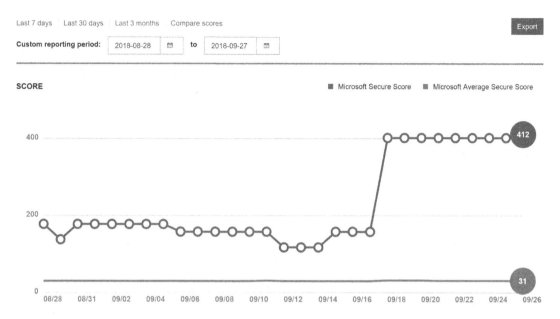

Figure 8-2. *Our tenant security score for Office 365 deployment*

Looking at the score in detail will give us the direction that we need to pursue to be successful with Office 365. We have made a lot of changes since we started make changes in our Office 365 tenant. We started this journey with a score of 31, and now at the end of the book, we are at a score of 412 (see Figure 8-3) – a difference of 381! The scoring gives us an impartial view of how good we are doing.

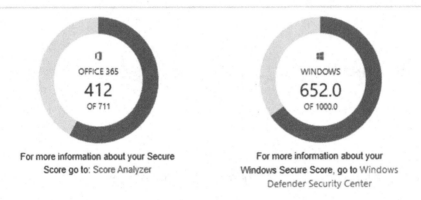

Figure 8-3. *Our tenant security score for Office 365 deployment*

Note   In previous books that I have written, I spent a lot of time on getting the right subscription mix. In this book, the scoring will drive the subscriptions. If you have a low score, you can only increase it by deploying more security functions that are part of higher end subscriptions. You need to change the mindset and manage the 365 tenant by the security score to protect the company.

Our configuration of Office 365 is using the Microsoft 365 E5 subscription. This subscription is the highest security subscription Microsoft supplies. We added an Azure cloud solution provider (CSP) subscription to the mix, and this allows us full access to the Azure security center and services. In the previous chapters, we spent time on the configuration of the different services. In this chapter, we are focusing on the administration functions for Office 365. For example, previous chapters discussed how to secure your business with Office 365. This chapter is focused on the administration of the service in Office 365. Time is money, and as an administrator, you are looking for the simplest way to accomplish a task. This chapter outlines the common tasks that administrators are asked to perform in the administration of Office 365. These tasks include renaming users, adding e-mail aliases, creating shared mailboxes, configuring Teams (Skype for Business), reviewing security logs, and changing the subscription type. There are five different ways to administer Office 365: the Office 365 admin center, PowerShell, third-party cloud-based tools, Azure Active directory services, and Windows Active Directory services. I mention Windows Active Directory services so you will not ignore it, but we will focus very little time on this service. Our use of Active Directory will focus on what you can manage from Office 365 versus what the user can manage from Active Directory.

Office 365 Administration Overview

As an administrator, you'll find that your company needs different components and applications for the different business roles of the employees in your business. Office 365 allows you to add different components to your subscription. In some cases, your business needs will change, and you'll be in a situation where you have too many licenses (or too few). You can easily change your subscription mix. There are three ways to change the license mix. You may purchase directly (via the license portal) or through a Tier 1 or Tier 2 cloud solution provider. The Office 365 admin center (see Figure 8-4) is fully configurable. The dashboard that we set up gives us a snapshot of the different admin centers. There are 15 different centers. Our focus in this chapter is not to look at all of these admin centers but rather to look at the key centers that affect security and compliance of the Office 365 environment.

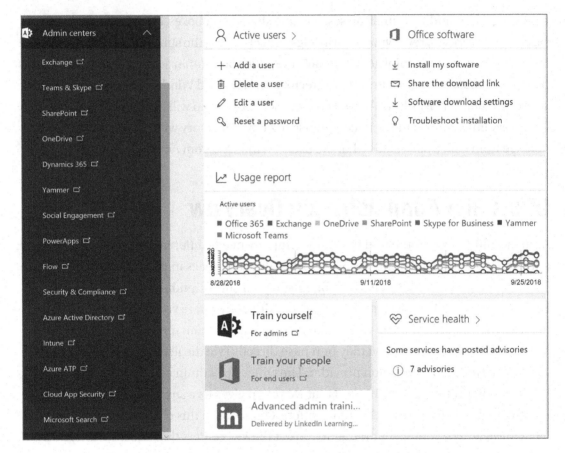

Figure 8-4. *Office 365 admin center*

The global administrator is the first account created when you sign up for Office 365. The global administrator account has full access to all Office 365 resources. You can use the PowerShell environment to configure capabilities, or you can use the graphical interfaces in the various admin centers (Exchange, Skype for Business, or SharePoint) to manage Office 365 capabilities. The only rule to remember is this: to change features using PowerShell, or in the administration graphical interfaces, you must have a license (such as Exchange, Skype for Business, or SharePoint) provisioned to the account that is being used to change that feature. If a global administrator's account tries to change features on a subscription area that the account is not licensed to use, that action will not be permitted. In some cases, the global administrator is denied access to the GUI command options (access to the eDiscovery Center, for instance). Partners with delegated administrator rights do not have a license and cannot access a user's data. You may also see some PowerShell commands fail (with no failure notice) without a license attached to the user.

Note   Only selected Microsoft Partners can offer delegated administrator services to their customers. The global administrator must approve the rights to a Microsoft Partner to act as a delegated administrator. Microsoft Partners that have delegated administration capabilities have earned the right to use this service offering.

A good example is using PowerShell to set up a shared mailbox for a user. If you *do not* have an Exchange license assigned to the global admin account, the Exchange PowerShell scripts will fail when they make a `set-mailbox` call. There are many different commands that you can use to manage Office 365 with PowerShell (see Figure 8-5).

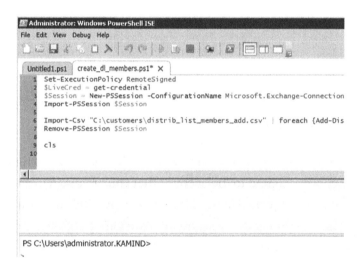

Figure 8-5. *PowerShell command to add members to a distribution list*

For example, you can use PowerShell to administer Office 365, or you can use the GUI interface (see Figure 8-6). Both interfaces provide the same results, but one is much more scalable than the other. There is an additional interface, and that is the Exchange management interface. Over time you will see the new group interface be where you will see change.

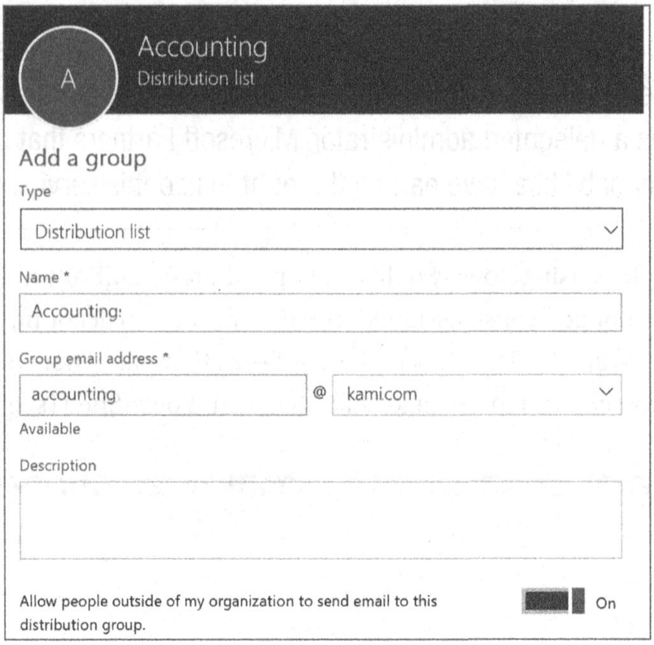

Figure 8-6. New distribution group interface

As an administrator, you will use both interfaces. The only rule to remember is that you must have a license assigned to the account that you are using to grant permissions to the user accounts. The objective of this chapter is to provide you with the tools and capabilities necessary for you to administer your own Office 365 site and provide the best level of service to your organization.

Note   If you have Azure AD Connect enabled, you cannot edit some properties of a user's mailbox, because it's out of the current user's write scope. Those properties in the mailbox are managed by the on-premises Active Directory.

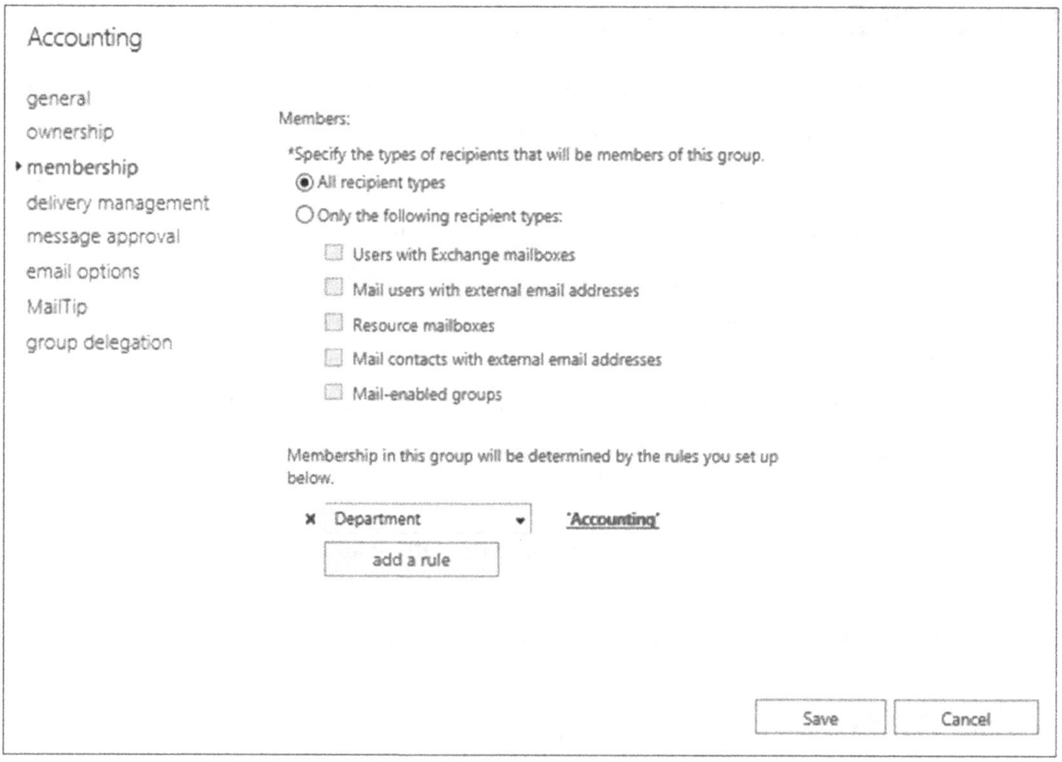

Figure 8-7. *Office 365 legacy group interface to add members to the Accounting group*

Preparing to Administer Office 365

Office 365 is easy to manage if you have configured the service correctly after migration and you have deployed the security services we recommended in this book. You can use the GUI interface or you can manage Office 365 via the PowerShell interface. The choice is up to you. In this chapter, we have assumed that you have configured your Office 365 solution for production, and we use the following checklist to check on your status. This administration chapter assumes that you have completed the necessary configurations in the previous chapters.

Office 365 Configuration Completion Checklist

The completion checklist looks at common areas that are used to prepare your company to use Office 365. Take a moment and verify your configuration of the Office 365 setup with these 13 steps:

1. If you have desktop Office 2013/2016/2019, plan to change your subscription to a version of the Office 365 Pro Plus subscription software. Older versions of Office desktop software (such as Office 2010, 2017, or 2003) are not enhanced, and some cases will not work with Office 365. You want to migrate to Office 365 Pro Plus and no longer use volume licenses or retail versions of Office (it is a support issue).

2. Check the Office 365 domain setup in the Office 365 admin center to make sure that all DNS entries are green. If you have any actions to complete (under the action header), please complete them before you move forward.

3. Verify that your Office 365 domain is set to Authoritative in the Exchange admin center and is not shared for e-mail. (This will be set only if your e-mail domain is split).

4. Verify that you have placed a local DNS record on your on-premises DNS server. You need to add an Autodiscover cname to your internal DNS that points to http://autodiscover.outlook.com.

5. If you have an on-premises Exchange Server and you have migrated to Office 365, set the Autodiscover record to $NULL with the following command (note that, once it's set, local clients cannot autodiscover the local Exchange Server):

   ```
   Set-ClientAccessServer -Identity "<name>" –
   AutoDiscoverServiceInternalUri $NULL
   ```

6. Extend the 14-day delete hold time to a 30-day delete hold time. Run the following PowerShell commands.

   a. Extend the 30-day delete for a mailbox.

      ```
      Set-mailbox user@contoso.com –retaindeleteditemsfor 30
      ```

    b. Extend the 30-day delete for the organization.

```
Get-mailbox | Set-mailbox -retaindeleteditemsfor 30
```

7. Enable the audit logs on all users' mailboxes. The default logs are kept for 30 days and can be extended to multiple years.

```
#Enable Audit Logging
Get-Mailbox -ResultSize Unlimited -Filter
{RecipientTypeDetails -eq "UserMailbox" -or
RecipientTypeDetails -eq "SharedMailbox" -or
RecipientTypeDetails -eq "RoomMailbox" -or
RecipientTypeDetails -eq "DiscoveryMailbox"}|
Set-Mailbox -AuditEnabled $true -AuditLogAgeLimit 365
-AuditOwner Create,HardDelete,MailboxLogin,
MoveToDeletedItems,SoftDelete,Update
```

```
#Check Status
Get-Mailbox -ResultSize Unlimited | Select Name,
UserPrincipalName, AuditEnabled, AuditLogAgeLimit |
Out-Gridview
```

8. Log into the Office 365 admin center, and select the Security & Compliance Center. Under Search & Investigation, select "audit log search" and "enable audit log recording."

9. The default retention policies are not enabled until the archive is enabled. If you enable the archive on a user mailbox, the retention polices begin to execute. For example, the default retention policy is two years. When the retention policy executes, e-mail is deleted. If you do not want your e-mail to be deleted or moved to an archive, remove the tag in the Exchange admin center, under "Compliance Management" and "Retention tags."

10. Remove any other retention tags you do not want to use in the retention policy.

11. Verify that you have enabled Yammer on your subscription. To enable Yammer, expand the admin center, and then select Yammer. The service should auto-activate and show a green check mark.

12. Log in to the OneDrive admin center and set the retention to 1,530 days for deleted files.

13. In the One drive administration center, reduce the OneDrive sharing (in the OneDrive admin center) to "Existing External users" to control sharing until you understand the sharing features.

Office 365 Security Configuration Completion Checklist

The completion check list looks at common areas that are used to prepare your company to use Office 365. Take a moment and verify your configuration of the Office 365 organization.

1. Deploy a Microsoft 365 E5 subscription.

2. Create a log analytics subscription for data logging and configure services.

3. Build out the Azure security center; set the data collection load you want.

4. Deploy Azure threat analytics on the domain controller (on-site or in Azure).

5. Deploy Windows Advanced Threat Protection agents.

6. Deploy MMA agents to all clients and servers.

7. Deploy the commercial ID.

8. Deploy Secure Score and baseline the organization.

9. Deploy Privileged Identity Management.

10. Change all global admin accounts (except one) to security admin and deploy PIM for users to request elevated rights.

11. Deploy Privileged Information Protection.

12. Deploy MFA to all clients.

13. Deploy Azure risk mitigation policies.

14. Deploy Windows 10 update rings.

15. Deploy the Office Pro Plus policy.

16. Deploy Mobile Application Management.

This will give you a good baseline and a secure organization. Once you have done this, the next step is to take a new baseline secure score. This will be your baseline token used to compare the organization. This is your configuration that will be used for success measurements. In our case, we started with a score of 31 and ended with a security score of 136 (see Figure 8-8). Our additional changes has raised this score to 412 - an increase of 381!

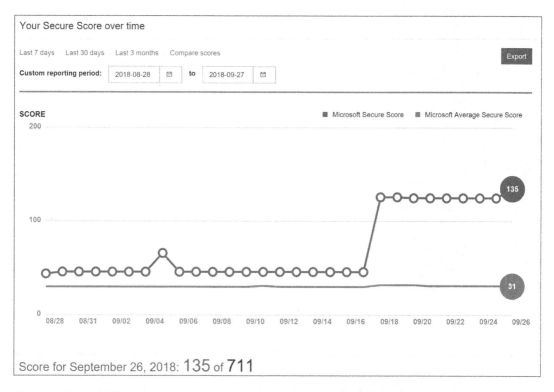

Figure 8-8. *Office 365 security score increase, result of the 16 steps*

Admin Centers

They are on our checklist, so let's visit the admin centers one more time. Office 365, in our example, has multiple admin centers created to support your subscriptions. The standard centers are Office 365, Exchange, Skype for Business, SharePoint, CRM, Power BI, Compliance, Azure AD, and OneDrive for Business. You can reach the admin centers by expanding "Admin centers" (see Figure 8-9).

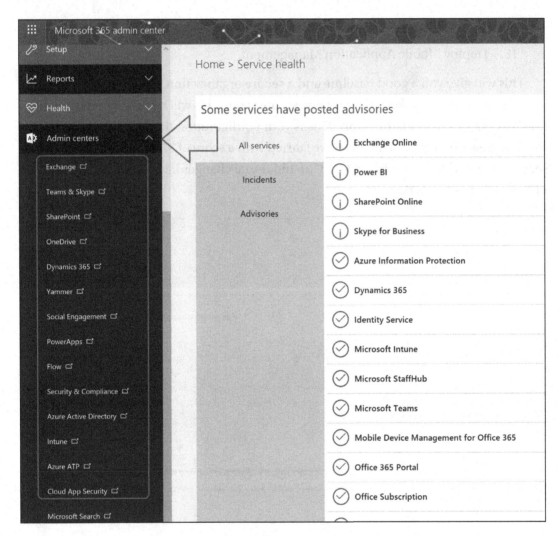

Figure 8-9. *Office 365 admin center view with domains not set up*

In our example, we have a Microsoft 365 E5 subscription, which includes 15 different admin center accesses, including Intune Mobile Device Management and Power BI. Your subscription may have a different number of applications, depending on your licenses and the additional admin centers that are added based on the optional subscriptions. This chapter focuses on the areas of administration in Office 365 for security: Exchange and Skype for Business. The other admin centers (CRM, Power BI SharePoint, Compliance and Data Loss Prevention, and Exchange Online Protection) are beyond the scope of this chapter. I have included the most common questions that you will need to address when managing your Office 365 service.

The Office 365 administration areas that we address in this chapter are Office 365 dashboard, license management, Exchange, and Teams and Teams administration. At the end of this chapter, we will wrap with a discussion on the configuration of PowerShell. This should provide you with all of the tools you need to manage your Office 365 tenant.

Before we start, there are a few navigation rules that you should know when working in the admin center. At any time that you need to get back to the home page in the admin center, click the nine-block grid in the upper-left corner and then click the "A" for administration. This action will always return you to the admin center.

User accounts can be synchronized in two ways in Office 365: through a manual process (single user load/bulk load) or via Azure Active Directory synchronization accounts created through an Active Directory process that can be managed only by on-premise Active Directory tools.

There are different types of administrative accounts on Office 365. The first account created (the first account that was created when you purchased Office 365) is a global administrator account. You can create additional global administrator accounts to manage Office 365. Global administrator accounts do not need a license to perform global administration functions. However, the global administration account does require a license to perform administration functions at the functional level. For example, if you want to configure advanced Exchange services or certain security services, the account you are using must be licensed for the function you're trying to manage. The same is the case with SharePoint. If you do not have a license or if you are running Active Directory synchronization, you cannot configure the functions of the service, only the global access controls for the service. Table 8-1 lists the common Exchange functions that you will use to manage Office 365.

Note   If you are using Azure Active Directory synchronization, Exchange functions are controlled by the on-premises Active Directory. You can find the Azure Active Directory synchronization connector at `https://portal.azure.com`.

Table 8-1. *Exchange Administration Functions*

Task	Description
Exchange administration roles	Reviews the different Exchange roles for managing Office 365.
Default user role	Explains the default user roles and permissions.
Conference Room/Resource Room	Explains how to set up and manage a conference room.
Changing a user name and e-mail address	Changing an e-mail is a two-step process. This is how you change the e-mail address of the user accounts.
Adding a user alias	Adding an alias e-mail or changing the default e-mail address.
Shared mailbox	Explains how to create a shared mailbox for the smartphone or Outlook.
Creating a distribution group	Explains the different Office 365 distribution groups.
Sending e-mail from an alias e-mail address	Allows the user to send an e-mail from a different e-mail address than the user's own e-mail address.
Smartphone management	User configuration options for Exchange.
Troubleshooting: Autodiscover	Desktop configuration to ignore Exchange Server.

Teams allows you to communicate internally without any configuration. The normal configuration is to enable communications with external users (Skype and smartphones). The problem is external communication. The administration topics in Table 8-2 are the configuration changes that are required to address communication across different external domains.

Table 8-2. *Teams Administration Functions*

Task	Description
Setting up Skype for Business	Enabling Teams to communicate with noncompany users
Adding Skype voice and porting phone numbers	Adding Skype voice local and international calling
Configuring dial-in conferencing	Adding dial-in conferencing for Teams users
Communicating with Skype users	Step-by-step instructions to enable Teams to Skype integration
Restricting Teams users' capability	Restricting Teams capabilities in the admin center

In addition to the administration section, we have included an overview and usage section on PowerShell. PowerShell is extremely useful if you must implement unique functions or must repeat a set of tasks multiple times. Office 365 may be completely administered from PowerShell, and our discussion is not a complete list. The objective of this chapter is to show you the various options you can use in managing Office 365.

Office 365 Administration Center

The Office 365 administration consoles are easy to access once the user logs into Office 365. Once you have selected the admin console, select the admin center. The admin center only shows the admin console for the licenses that have been activated for Office 365. For example, if the Teams licenses are not purchased, there is no access to the Teams admin center. The Office 365 admin center is used to administer global functions. These oversee permissions, security groups, domain management, and system health. However, the Office 365 admin center is limited if directory synchronization is enabled. When directory synchronization is enabled, Office 365 acts as a backup to the on-premise Active Directory. In this case, only those functions that are not on the on-premise servers can be modified by Office 365.

Accessing the Office 365 admin center is simple: just log in to Office 365. If you have the permissions, you will land at the main page. Select the Admin dashboard (see Figure 8-10). If your permissions are limited, your menu options will be limited to reflect your privileges. One of the first areas to access is the Licenses area. This is located under the Billing. The Licenses will show you the active license mix in your Office 365 tenant.

Figure 8-10. *Dashboard after logging in as an administrator*

As Microsoft builds out newer releases of Office 365 and reengineers the administrative panel, the biggest change will be the customization of the user experience. As an example, we will have a different experience (similar to the dashboard in Figure 8-11) versus the security administrator, who will have more information about security and less about service tickets.

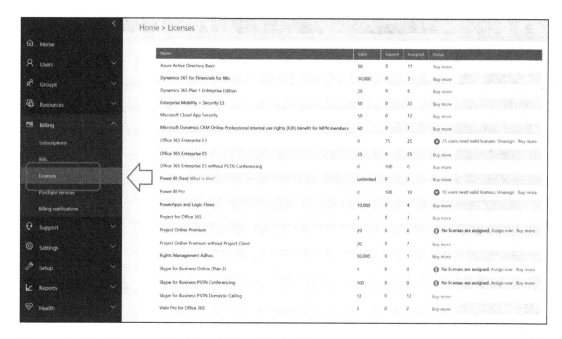

Figure 8-11. *Licenses dashboard, under Billing*

The Office 365 Licenses tab gives you a good overview of the active and expired licenses. Different admin center access is based on the licenses assigned to the user account. Office 365 plans have different admin centers and configuration options.

To access the administration area for other Office 365 features, click Admin and then select the appropriate admin center you want to use (see Figure 8-12).

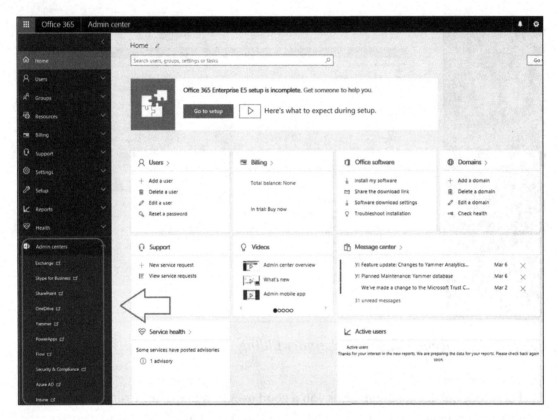

Figure 8-12. *Office 365 admin centers*

The Office 365 admin center is organized into separate admin centers based on your license mix. Administrator access is granted if the license is assigned to the global administrator account (see Figure 8-13). Earlier we discussed the different types of administrators. Different versions of the administration dashboard appear in the previous figures.

Figure 8-13. *Overview of the admin center functions*

The global administrator sees all administrator functions that are licensed and can configure the admin centers, such as Exchange, Skype for Business, SharePoint, Yammer, Compliance, Azure AD, and Intune. Other service centers are added based on the optional subscriptions that were purchased. For example, if you purchased Dynamics CRM and added this to your subscription, you would have access to the Dynamics admin center. Likewise, when we added Windows EMS licenses to our Office 365 tenant, we enabled Azure features for Office 365. Once you have selected the administration dashboard, you can select the different admin centers that you need to configure your Office 365 company.

Note   We review the key administration configuration areas that are important for Office 365 and leave the remaining ones for you to explore. Most of our focus is on the service admin centers.

Administrator Roles

There are different permission structures in Office 365, depending on which console you are given permissions to use. The basic administrator permissions of Office 365 are shown in Figure 8-14. There are five different administrator permissions that may be assigned to user accounts on Office 365. The only account that is assigned global permissions by default is the first account. This account was created when you purchased the service. All other accounts are assigned user-level permissions. Depending on the size of the organization, it may make sense to assign different roles for different job functions.

Office 365 admin roles

Permission	Billing admin	Global admin	Password admin	Service admin	User management admin
View organization and user information	Yes	Yes	Yes	Yes	Yes
Manage support tickets	Yes	Yes	Yes	Yes	Yes
Reset user passwords	No	Yes	Yes; with limitations. This admin can only reset passwords for non-admins.	No	Yes; with limitations. This admin can't reset passwords for billing, global, and service admins.
Perform billing and purchasing operations	Yes	Yes	No	No	No
Create and manage user views	No	Yes	No	No	Yes
Create, edit, and delete users and groups, and manage user licenses	No	Yes	No	No	Yes; with limitations. This admin can't delete a global admin or create other admins.
Manage domains	No	Yes	No	No	No
Manage organization information	No	Yes	No	No	No
Delegate admin roles to others	No	Yes	No	No	No
Use directory synchronization	No	Yes	No	No	No

Figure 8-14. *Office 365 administrative roles (courtesy of Microsoft)*

Microsoft's approach is to provide administration management like on-premise Active Directory. Active Directory Synchronization (using AD Connect) used to "sync" the AD environment to Office 365. The Office 365 (and Azure) permissions are global in design, and the individual admin centers are used to restrict permissions. For example, global administrators have all rights, but to access eDiscovery data, the data needs to be placed in the appropriate Exchange administration permission groups. Smaller companies do not need to have such distributed administration rights and tend to be less granular. Small organizations typically assign three roles: Global administrator, Billing administrator, and Password administrator. There are additional permissions that are assigned based on the additional subscription offerings (see Figure 8-15).

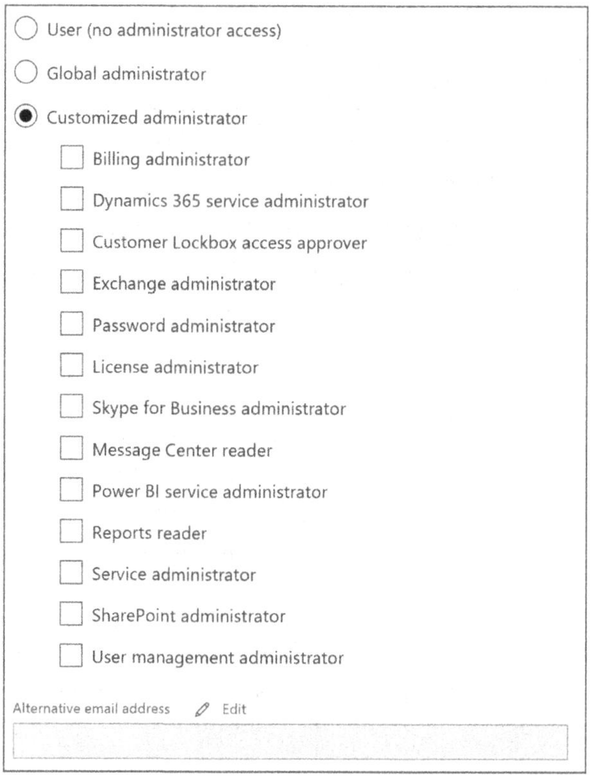

Figure 8-15. *Office 365 administrative roles with additional license roles*

In Figure 8-15, the additional license roles are for Skye for Business, Dynamics 365, and Power BI. In addition to the license roles, there are roles that are granted for the Microsoft Direct and Indirect Cloud solution partners. These additional roles are granted by customers to help manage the Office 365 offering they have purchased from Microsoft.

Step back and look at your company and the different roles you can assign to personnel in your company. Microsoft's security model is to assign the least role possible and to grant basic permissions that are required to complete the job. When you assign roles, verify that you are providing access at the appropriate level needed to execute the administrative task. Table 8-4 has detailed descriptions of the different administrator rights.

Note   Global administrators are assigned all rights by default. A global administrator can grant themselves the rights to read any user's mailbox by simply opening a mailbox other than their own. Business owners are cautioned to grant these rights only to those who need them.

Table 8-3. *Office 365 Role Descriptions*

Role	Description
Global administrator	This is the company administrator. Users in this role have access to everything or the permission to add them to a dedicated role where they do not have permission (such as discovery management).
Billing administrator	Access to all financial transactions. Delegated partners do not have access to this information.
Password administrator	They can reset only passwords of users and other administrators at the same level of permissions.
Service support administrator	This is a limited administration role. Users in this rule can only view the portal and assign support tickets. Typically, users who are assigned this role have a different role assigned to the different subsystems, such as Exchange.
User management administrator	These users can assign licenses and passwords but cannot make changes to other admin accounts that have more privileges than they do.

The typical Office 365 configuration leaves one account (usually the root account—the initial Office 365 account) as a global admin user without any user licenses. Some organizations leave this as a global admin account, and others use it as a user account. Regardless of what you do, the first account is the root account. The root account should never be used as a user account. The root account in Office 365 is the base account that is used to create all the different services that are linked to the Office 365 tenant. As Microsoft has deployed new versions of Office 365, the dependence of the root account has been minimized. We recommend that you do not delete or assign a user to this account.

In the past, the first account was a sacred account, and many Office 365 services depended on this account. Microsoft addressed the dependency of the first account by creating a new internal Office 365 group known as the *company administrators*. All global admins are members of the company administrator group. This group is where the base permissions are assigned in Office 365. This internal account reduces the criticality of using the root account as a user account.

Our approach in setting up Office 365 customers has changed over the years. We always recommend the following configuration for our new Office 365 clients. There are additional measures you can take in the configuration of your Office 365 company. Some of these were discussed in Chapter 7. Our typical configuration for Office 365 includes the following:

- Enable 360-day auditing for all delegated administration and administration access (see the "PowerShell" section).

- Enable the audit logs in the Security & Compliance Center.

- Enable the EMS productivity suite with extended security analytics.

- Deploy Multi-factor authentication on global admin accounts.

- Do not use a global admin account as a personal account.

- Set passwords to never expire (if you have deployed MFA).

- Review the Azure audit logs, Azure sign-in logs, and Office 365 audit logs weekly.

- Download and archive the three logs (mentioned earlier) monthly in case you have a breach. You can also set up the logs for long term storage in Azure.

Our objective is to provide you an overview of the key areas you need to cover on Office 365 as an administrator. To understand the administrator functions better, you need a roadmap as to what to look for.

Note   If you have not configured your domain for Office 365, complete that step before you add user accounts. If you add user accounts and then change the domain, the desktop user configurations will need to change to map to the new IDs and e-mail accounts.

Config: Overview

The Office 365 admin center (see Figure 8-16) is extremely flexible for managing your Office 365 organization. Our first step to managing Office 365 is to make sure you have the correct administrative roles assigned to your IT support staff. The next step is the configuration of the 365 tenant. The basic Office 365 admin center allows you to manage users, groups, support, settings, setup/domains, reports, and health. The additional admin centers are used to manage the unique features to each of your subscription. As an example, if you only purchase Exchange plan 1 (and not other features), then the admin center will only have Exchange and Security & Compliance Center as options.

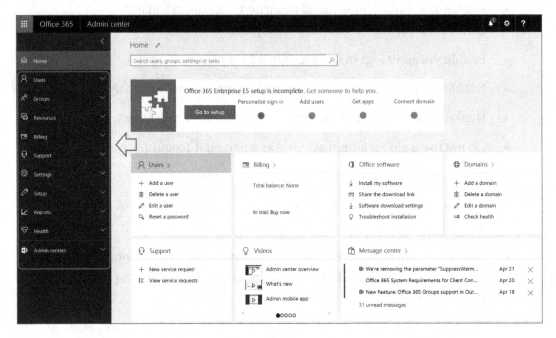

Figure 8-16. *Office 365 admin center*

In previous chapters, we reviewed the Security & Compliance, Azure AD, and EMS/Intune. This chapter, besides covering the Office 365 administration, will also review Exchange, Skype for Business, SharePoint, and OneDrive from an administrator perspective. There may be additional admin centers listed in your Office 365 tenant. These centers appear based on the active license assigned to the Office 365 tenant.

Note   We always recommend that you purchase at least one Microsoft 365 E5 suites and assign it to the first global administrator account created. Your Office 365 tenant will function better.

The configuration sections that follow are organized based on the required configuration order. As an example, to configure users, you need to configure your Office 365 domain and have the appropriate licenses assigned to your tenant. If you have this already configured in your Office 365 account, then use this section to review what you have set up. In our case, when I wrote this chapter, I discovered that the Office 365 domain structure changed, and even though my Office 365 was functioning, the features were having weird hiccups that no one could explain. I discovered that the DNS setup I had was no longer valid and needed to be updated.

Config: Domains

There are no practical limits on the number of domains that can be verified on Office 365. The rules are simple: you need to verify a domain if you want to use the domain in Office 365. Once you verify the domain, you assign the domain different use rights, depending on the licenses that were purchased for your Office 365 service.

There are many reasons to add a secondary domain. This could be to restrict specific services for a segment of users. This allows administrators to restrict services on domains. Adding a domain is straightforward: just add the domain (see Figure 8-17) and enter the necessary record changes in the DNS. When you add the domain, it is easy to follow the wizards; just be careful with the options that you select. We typically use a manual approach when adding DNS records once an Office 365 account is active. To add a domain, follow these steps:

1. Select the Domain sidebar menu option (from the grid, select Admin ➤ Microsoft Admin center ➤ Setup ➤ Domains) and then select "Add a domain."

2. Add the TXT record to your DNS provider.

3. Add the remaining DNS records (if you have not moved your e-mail to Office 365, do not change the MX, SPF, and Autodiscover records).

4. Verify your DNS record and fix any record errors.

5. Verify that you have fully deployed the enterprise mobility cnames.

The migration to Office 365 was covered in Chapter 7. In the previous steps, if you have already cut over to Office 365 or added another domain to Office 365 (the focus of this chapter), then change the MX, SPF, and Autodiscover records.

Figure 8-17. *Office 365 adding a domain*

After you select "Add a domain," enter the records in Office 365 and validate the domain. If the record cannot be validated or is in use by another Office 365 tenant, the domain validation wizard will allow you to send an email transfer request to the owner of the domain you are trying to validate. You can only have one Office 365 tenant per domain.

We started the process of adding the domain to Office 365 (see Figure 8-18). The first step was to verify the domain with the TXT records. Once the DNS verification records was added, we used the Domain wizard to add/validate the complete. When you have successfully added the records, you should see a summary page (see Figure 8-19). If you have errors, the Domain wizard will display the errors so you can resolve them.

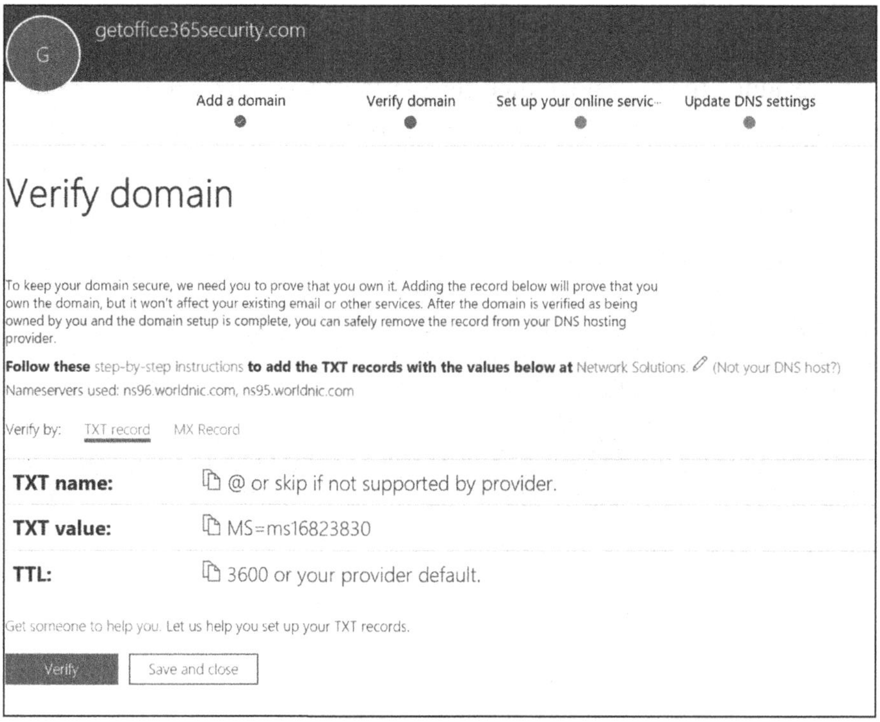

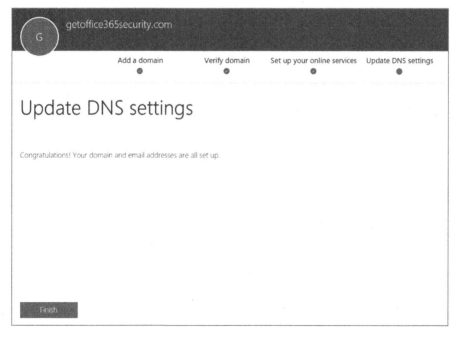

Figure 8-18. *Office 365 verifying the domain in Office 365*

Figure 8-19. *Complete domain adding process for Office 365*

Config: Domain: Troubleshooting

Once you have added the domain, Office 365 constantly verifies your DNS and highlights the invalid DNS records. Fixing the records is easy: just select the domain (see Figure 8-20) and then select Check DNS. If there are any issues present or a configuration that you can't use, Fix Issues is available as an option. Correct these records in your DNS records and verify them until all the records have no errors.

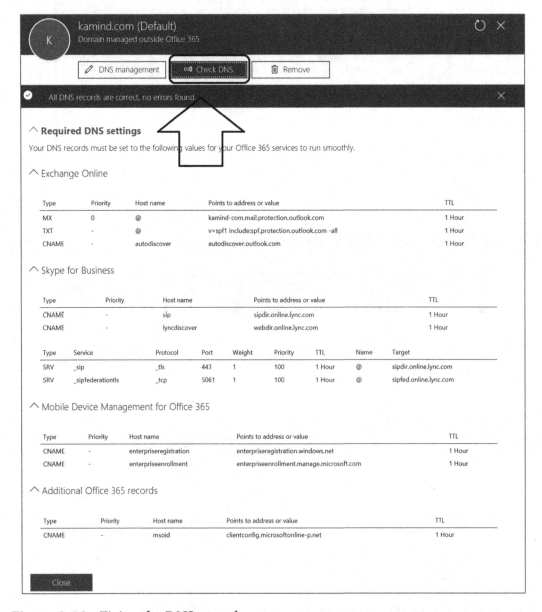

Figure 8-20. *Fixing the DNS records*

Config: Adding/Changing and Decreasing Licenses

There are multiple ways that you can change license numbers in Office 365. Microsoft allows you to change the existing license quantity, add new licenses by purchasing URLs, purchase a volume license key, or purchase licenses from your Microsoft Partner. The question for most users is where to find the simple display that summarizes the license mix. To find out the license mix, select the Products sidebar menu option (from the grid, select Admin ➤ Admin Center ➤ Setup ➤ Products).

You can manage the licenses from the setup portal. What Office 365 does is link the portal into some of the other portals (see Figure 8-21). For instance, the assign function links this to the user assignment. Likewise, the purchase option links you into the subscription adjustments.

If you are using a CSP, you will need to contact your CSP partner or use your partner's configuration portal to adjust the licenses. KAMIND IT's license portal is at `www.kamind.com/license` and requires an Office 365 account to log in. KAMIND IT offers this service at no charge for the license management of Office 365 subscriptions.

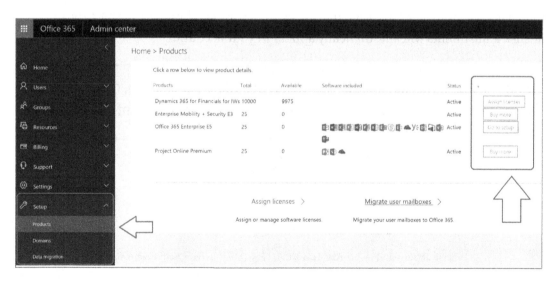

Figure 8-21. *License mix summary with shortcuts*

Reducing licenses is simple in the administration portal (see Figure 8-22); just select the Subscription sidebar menu option (from the grid, select Admin ➤ Admin center ➤ Billing ➤ Subscription) and the subscription that needs the license quantity adjusted. You can reach this same menu from the Products menu.

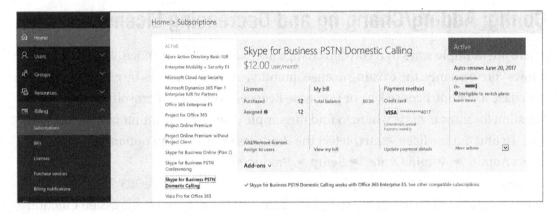

Figure 8-22. *Changing the license quantity*

You can also increase the number of licenses through the same process (described earlier), or you can purchase a volume license key from a reseller. These volume license keys are called *open license* keys. The process of adding licenses is slightly different when you use a reseller to purchase the license. Figure 8-23 shows you the different ways you can activate an open license key from your Microsoft Partner. Open licenses are different than a license from a CSP partner. If licenses were supplied by a CSP partner, these license adjustments will automatically appear in your account.

Note   If your Office 365 is supplied from a CSP (direct or indirect), check with the partner for the best way to change the license quantity. Different partners offer different incentives based on the organization size.

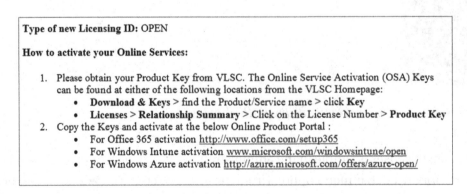

Figure 8-23. *Different types of open subscription activation and links*

When you purchase an open license from a partner, you retrieve the subscription license number from the volume license center (www.microsoft.com/licensing) and select the appropriate link to start the activation process (see Figure 8-24). You must be a global administrator to add the open license key to your Office 365 environment.

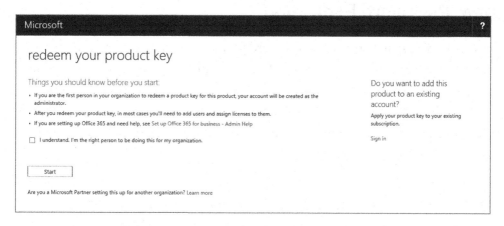

Figure 8-24. *Activating the open license key*

Log in to the Office 365 tenant and follow the wizard to add the new subscription to your environment. If you purchase multiple licenses of the same license type (an E3 Open subscription), all the licenses are pulled together as one license group. It works better if you add each license one at a time to get the correct expiration dates. In Figure 8-25, we are adding 25 licenses. If there were multiple licenses added on the same date, Microsoft gives you the option to group the licenses together for a common renewal date.

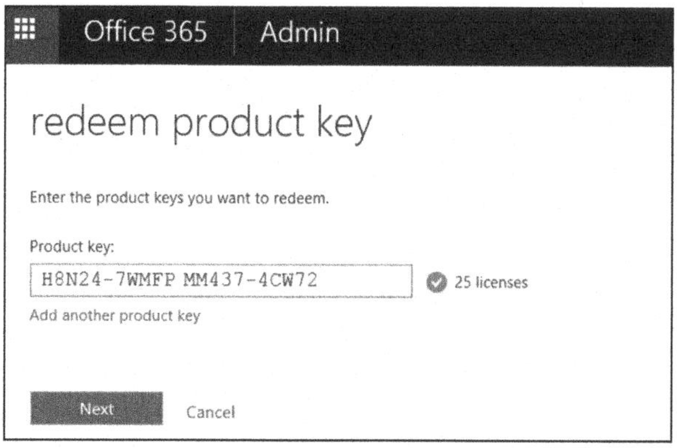

Figure 8-25. *Grouping licenses*

Once you have added the licenses to your Office 365 subscription, the new licenses are updated in your subscription portal. We recommend you always add the licenses before you add users.

Config: Password Expiration

Office 365 allows you to configure a password policy to allow password changes between 14 and 730 days (see Figure 8-26). Typically, a password policy is set to 90-day expiration and with a 14-day warning. To change the password policy, select Security (from the grid, select Admin ➤ Admin center ➤ Settings ➤ Security) and change the parameters for your password reset. In the security area, you also have the master control to turn on/off sharing for the Office 365 tenant.

Note   If you deploy MFA and use the Microsoft Authenticator application (as we discussed in Chapter 5), you can set your passwords to not to expire. This is more secure than changing your password every month.

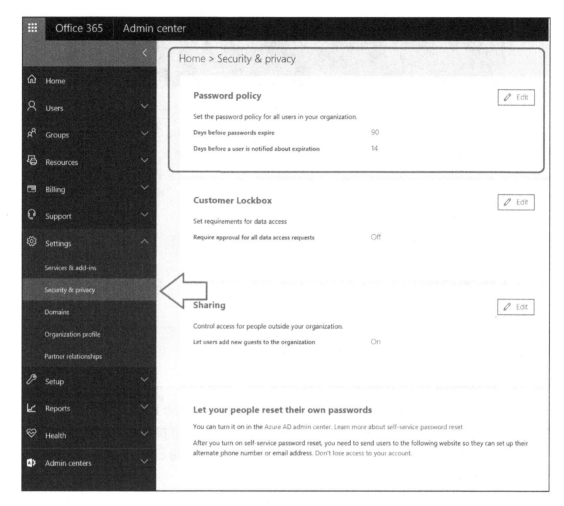

Figure 8-26. *Changing the password policy*

Once you have edited the password option, set the password policy for your organization. We recommend you leave the default (change passwords every 90 days), unless you are planning to enable multifactor authentication. Changing the password is simple: select the new password option and click Save after you make the changes (see Figure 8-27). These changes are global and affect all users.

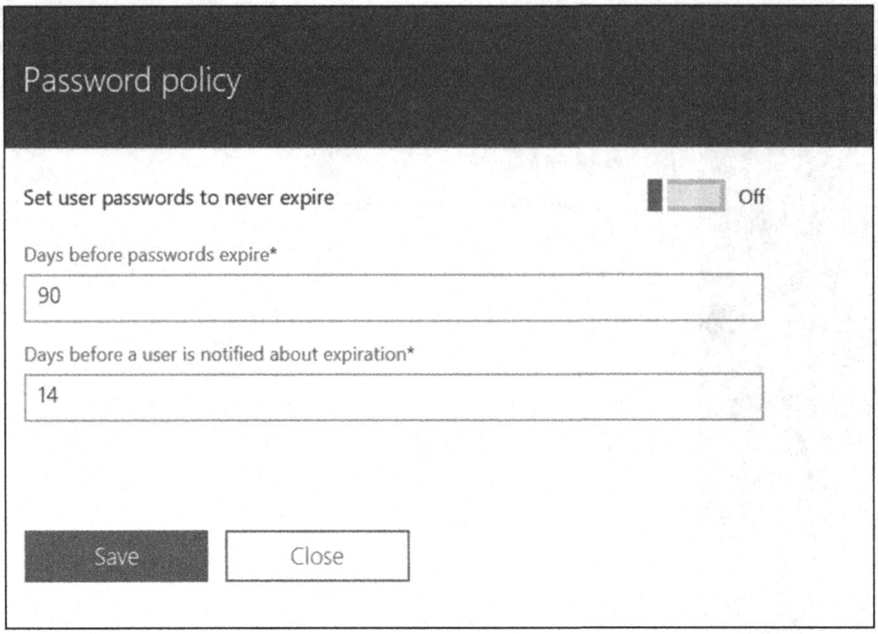

Figure 8-27. *Setting the password option*

Note   If you are setting passwords to never expire, purchase additional security subscriptions to manage your Office 365 tenant and enable multifactor authentication. The best subscription to do this with is to use EMS E5 and enable Azure Identity.

Config: Completing Company Configuration

Before we leave the configuration section, there are some additional areas that need to be changed to support your Office 365 deployment (see Figure 8-28). Let's look in detail at the other functions in Settings (from the grid, select Admin ➤ Admin center ➤ Settings). The Settings area allows you to customize your Office 365 deployment. Settings is where you customize your Office 365 environment and make it unique for your deployment. This section allows you to do the following:

- *Services & Add-ins*: Optional application and features

- *Security & Privacy*: Control external sharing of documents throughout Office 365

- *Domains*: Add/remove domains for new e-mail address

- *Organization Profile*: This section contains information about the company and the organization Office 365 configuration preferences

- *Partner Relationship*: Control partner administration functions

When Microsoft releases a new feature, these features are optional for the organization. To enable the feature, you must actively turn the feature on for deployment. A good example is Microsoft Teams. This is like the third-party product Slack, but Teams is included in your Office 365 subscription. To access Teams, select Admin ➤ Admin Center ➤ Teams & Skype (see Figure 8-29).

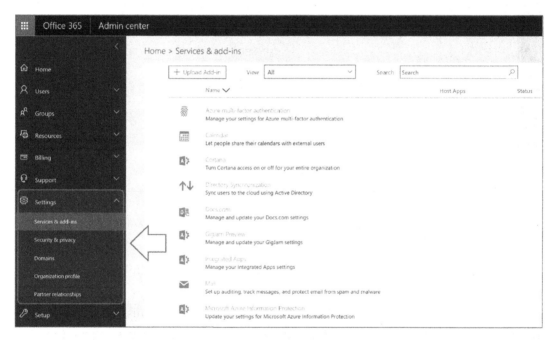

Figure 8-28. *Configuring Office 365 company options*

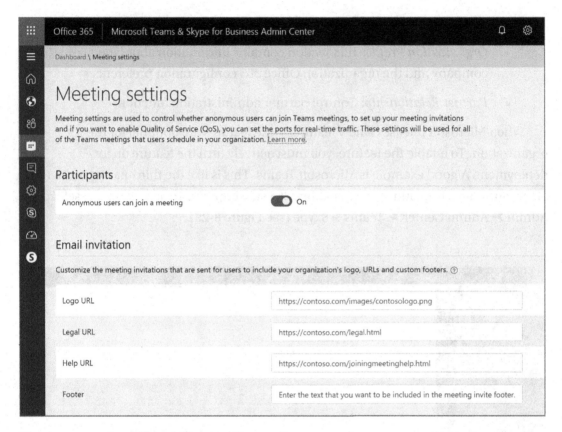

Figure 8-29. *Enabling Office 365 Teams features*

Config: Partner Administrators

"Partner relationships" is where you add a partner as a delegated administrator. These are your trusted advisors. There are two types of delegated administrators: Microsoft and Microsoft Partners. When an Office 365 site is created, no administration rights are granted to any external parties. Microsoft does not have the ability to access user data, unless that right is granted by the account owner. There are two types of partner administrators: delegated administration from a Microsoft cloud advisor and a Microsoft CSP (see Figure 8-30).

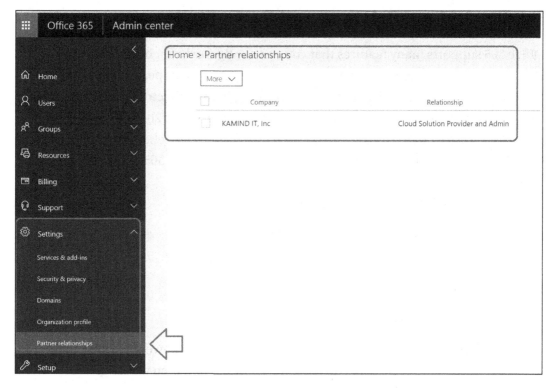

Figure 8-30. *Types of Microsoft cloud partners*

The account owner (global admin) can add (or delete) cloud solution advisors and add (or delete) the CSPs as needed, with some caveats.

- Cloud solution advisors are partner global administrators and need to purchase licenses through Microsoft or a third party. You can add/remove these advisors as needed.

- Cloud solution providers are partner global administrators and provide licenses to Office 365 customers through a partner administrator. You cannot remove these providers unless you have removed the licenses provided by these providers.

CSPs are different from CSAs. For example, KAMIND IT CSP offerings are listed at www.kamind.com/csp. Keep in mind that if you purchase licenses through a CSP, your Microsoft account is managed by the CSP, not Microsoft. If you remove a partner CSP access, you may have breached your agreement with Microsoft.

Config: Adding, Deleting, and Restoring Users

Office 365 supports many features that you can configure through the Office 365 user interface. Some actions (such as setting conference room permissions) are available only using PowerShell. If you are running Active Directory Synchronization (AD Connect), you can use your on-premises Exchange Server 2010/2013/2016/2019 or Active Directory tools to configure services (and sync those changes into the cloud). Our focus in this chapter is on the user configuration of Office 365 using the Office 365 interface.

There are four primary user operations for administration:

- Adding single users via the user interface

- Bulk-adding using a CSV file and the GUI interface

- Deleting users

- Restoring users

If you need to assign user passwords, you need to use the PowerShell commands. Typically, we load the users using the bulk-load options, and then we assign the passwords using PowerShell. If you have an Active Director Connector (AD Connect) running in your on-premises environment, you need to assign passwords using the on-premises Active Directory tools.

Note   Some organizations use Exchange Server Management Console to manage Office 365. This is not needed and causes more problems in managing Office 365. The best tool to use to manage Office 365 connected accounts is the Windows Server Active Directory Administrator Tools.

Users: Adding Office 365 Users via the Office 365 Admin Center

The Office 365 user administration tool can add users only at the Office 365 level. If you have a connected on-premise environment and those users access on-premise resources, you must add the users using the on-premise Active Directory administration tools. The Active Directory Connector enables only specific Active Directory objects to be used in the cloud and is a one-way activity.

Log in as an administrator (at `https://portal.office.com` or `http://portal.microsoft.com`), as shown in Figure 8-31. Click the nine-block grid (at the top left). Next, click Admin ➤ Admin center ➤ Users ➤ Active users. Click "+ Add users" to add a new user.

Figure 8-31. *Adding users to Office 365*

Fill in the information for the user and create the account. The minimum information you need to create a user is the username (first, last), e-mail address, and licenses. There are additional configuration options on user accounts (contacts, password, products, and administration roles) that may be needed. These additional fields are optional. There are four steps to set up a user account.

1. Set up the user name and primary e-mail address.

2. Set the user password.

3. Set the user administration permission (no administrator rights are the default).

4. Assign a license.

These steps are reviewed next.

Step 1: Add User Information and E-mail Address

See Figure 8-32.

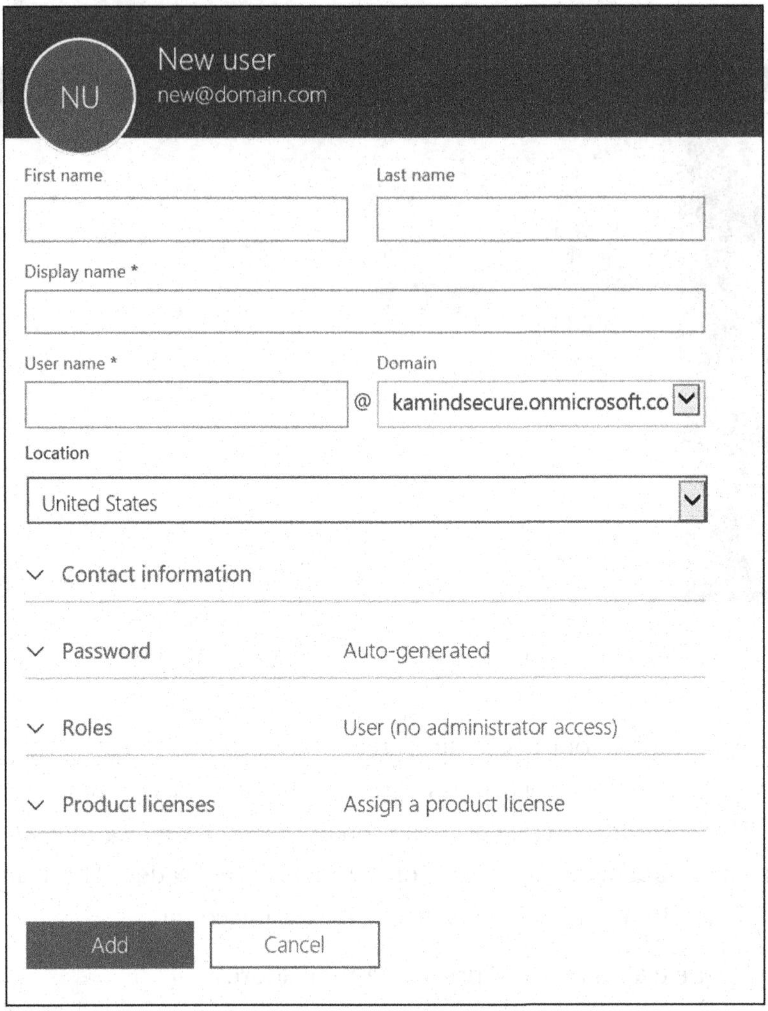

Figure 8-32. *Adding the user information*

Step 2: Add Password Information

It is important that you change the default password policy when you create a new user. There are cases where you need to set the password when the account is created and cases where you need to have the user reset the password. Our recommendation is that you always have the user set their own password (see Figure 8-33).

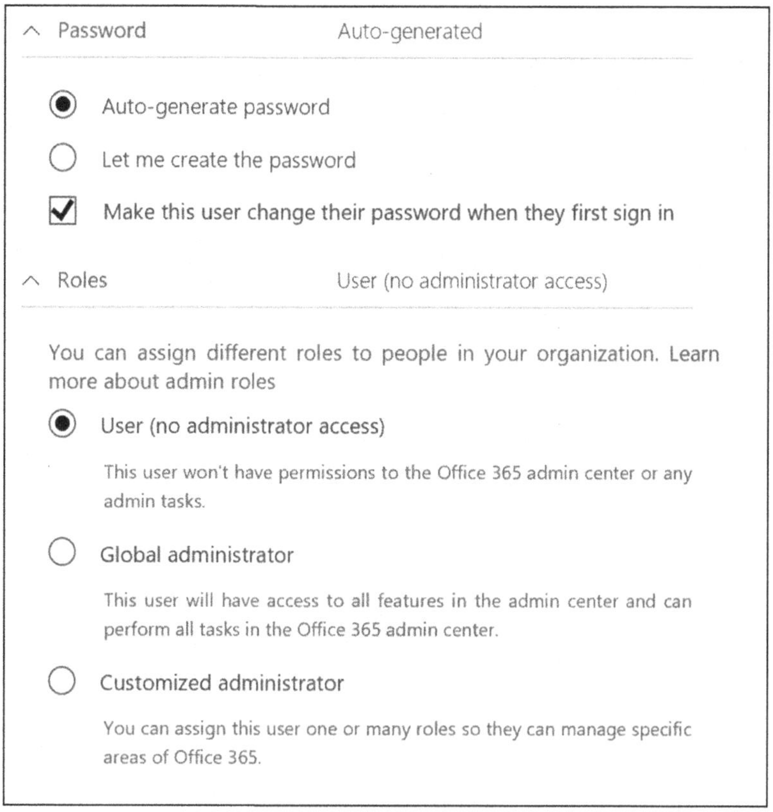

> ∧ Password   Auto-generated
>
>   ⦿ Auto-generate password
>
>   ◯ Let me create the password
>
>   ☑ Make this user change their password when they first sign in
>
> ∧ Roles   User (no administrator access)
>
>   You can assign different roles to people in your organization. Learn
>   more about admin roles
>
>   ⦿ User (no administrator access)
>
>   This user won't have permissions to the Office 365 admin center or any
>   admin tasks.
>
>   ◯ Global administrator
>
>   This user will have access to all features in the admin center and can
>   perform all tasks in the Office 365 admin center.
>
>   ◯ Customized administrator
>
>   You can assign this user one or many roles so they can manage specific
>   areas of Office 365.

Figure 8-33. *Assigning password and setting the administrator role*

Step 3: Assign Administration Roles

When you add a user, you can assign the role for the user (see Figure 8-34). Only global administrators can assign administrator roles. If you assign a user admin rights, you need to supply a mobile phone number in the contacts and an alternate e-mail address (not located in your current Office 365 tenant); otherwise, you cannot create a new account. All administrator users must have a cell phone that receives calls.

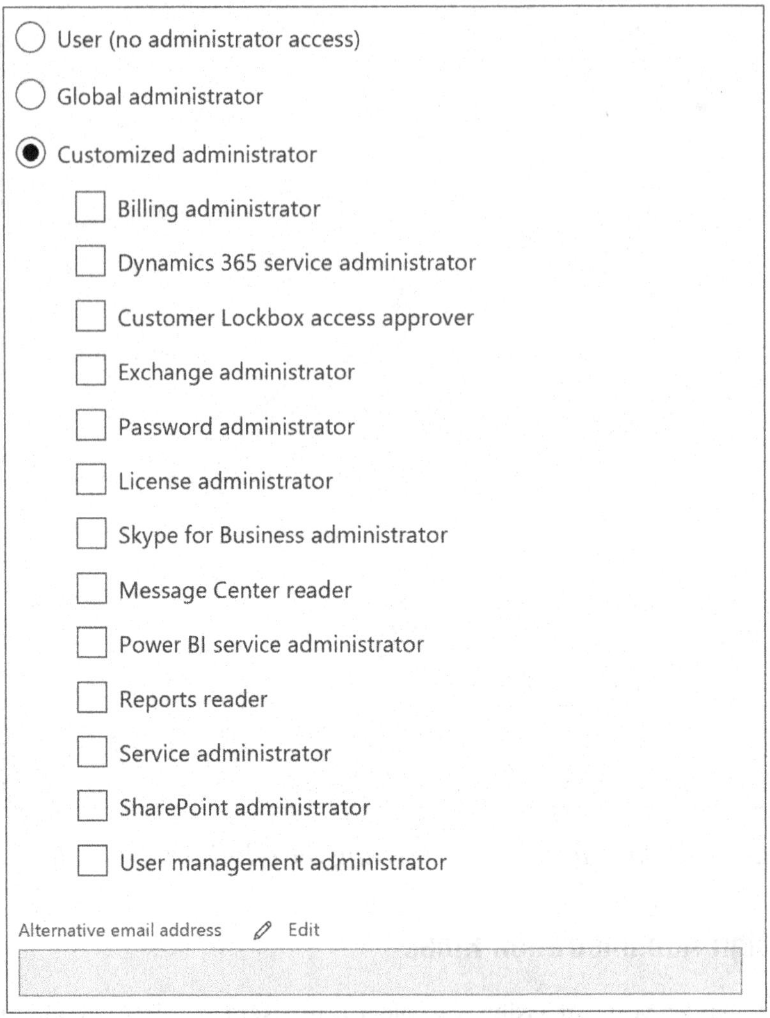

Figure 8-34. *Assigning the admin user*

Step 4: Assign the Licenses to the User

You can assign any valid license to the user. You can also selectivity assign access to the various Office 365 services (see Figure 8-35). Office 365 allows you to enable/disable different services associated with the license. Some organizations do not want to allow users to access services that the help desk cannot support. The global administrators can enable or disable the service on each user account or using PowerShell. Once you have selected the appropriate licenses and other license features, click Save. You have created the user account.

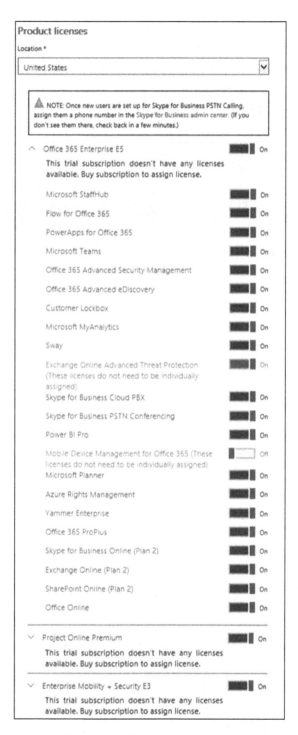

Figure 8-35. *Assigning the license to the user*

In this example, we assigned E5 licenses with the Enterprise Mobility Suite (EMS) and Skype for Business. As an administrator, you can selectively remove access to different licenses. To remove capabilities, just move the option switch to Off.

Users: Changing User Information

You can also change any information about a user. Just select the user and edit the information (see Figure 8-36).

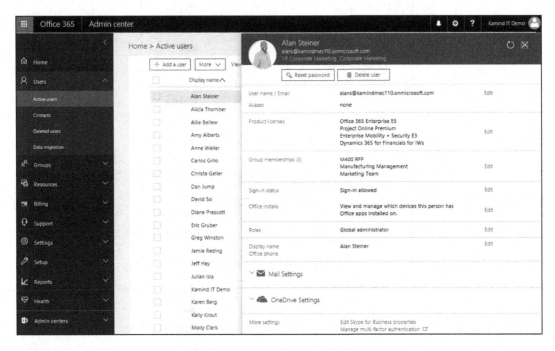

Figure 8-36. *Changing user information*

Users: Deleting

Deleting users is as simple as selecting the user and then selecting Delete (see Figure 8-37). If the "delete user" trashcan icon is not present, then the user is blocked from deletion in Office 365, and you need to use the PowerShell command to remove the user account. A blocked user account usually happens when a user is placed on legal hold or when an account was not deleted properly. To remove users that are on litigation hold, you need to remove the in-place hold or the legacy litigation using PowerShell or the Exchange admin center. Once the in-place or litigation hold is cleaned up, you can delete the user. When you delete an account, we recommend you follow these steps:

1. Remove any legal hold on the account.

2. Disable the archive on the account (if enabled).

3. Remove any e-mail alias assigned to the account (leave only the onmicrosoft.com name and SIP).

4. Set the user account to the onmicrosoft.com name as the primary address.

5. If you do not want to keep e-mail (or move e-mail to another account), then remove all licenses from the account.

6. Delete the account. (If you delete the account, the mail will be deleted!)

Note   Before you remove the user account (as suggested earlier), verify that you have the OneDrive for Business data backed up. Removing the e-mail address may delete the user's OneDrive for Business data. Deleted account data will be retained for 30 days after the account has been deleted or licenses has been removed.

Figure 8-37. *Deleting a user account*

Deleted users can be recovered up to 30 days and are in the Deleted Users folder. If you want to remove the user from the Office 365 Deleted Users folder, run the following PowerShell command to purge the user account. If you have not set up PowerShell, see the "PowerShell" section later in this chapter. These PowerShell examples are code snippets and require the necessary credentials to execute.

PowerShell provides commands to return the list of deleted Office 365 users. This PowerShell command returns all the deleted user accounts in the recycle bin with the GUID for the user.

```
Get-MsolUser -ReturnDeletedUsers
```

Here are the PowerShell commands to remove the user account from the Deleted Users folder using the user e-mail address:

```
Remove-MsolUser -User <such as user@contsto.onmicrosoft.com>
-RemoveFromRecycleBin
```

Users: Restoring

To restore deleted users, select "Users and groups" and then "Deleted users." You can then select the user account you want to restore. Deleted users remain in your Office 365 Deleted Users recycle bin for 30 days, depending on the configuration of Office 365. Figure 8-38 shows the deleted users restoration option. Just select the user and then click Restore. You can only restore users to the same license provisioned to the user account when the account was deleted.

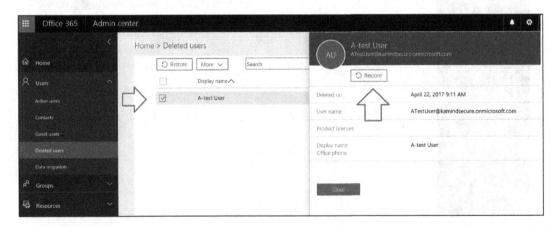

Figure 8-38. *Restoring a deleted user*

After you select the user to restore, Office 365 will confirm the restoration and allow you to set the password as well as decide whether the user should reset the password on login to the Office 365 services.

Note   If you attempt to restore a user and it fails because of the account being managed by a different service, use the `RestoreMsolUser` PowerShell command to restore the user account.

Users: Renaming

Renaming a user display name is a simple process: select the user account from the Office 365 admin center, followed by Actions, and then the property you want to change (see Figure 8-39).

Figure 8-39. *Changing a user's properties*

After you select the user, select the edit function for the area that you want to change. For example, you can select the user name/e-mail address and change the username, add an e-mail alias, and set the domain as the primary login address (see Figure 8-40) of the user.

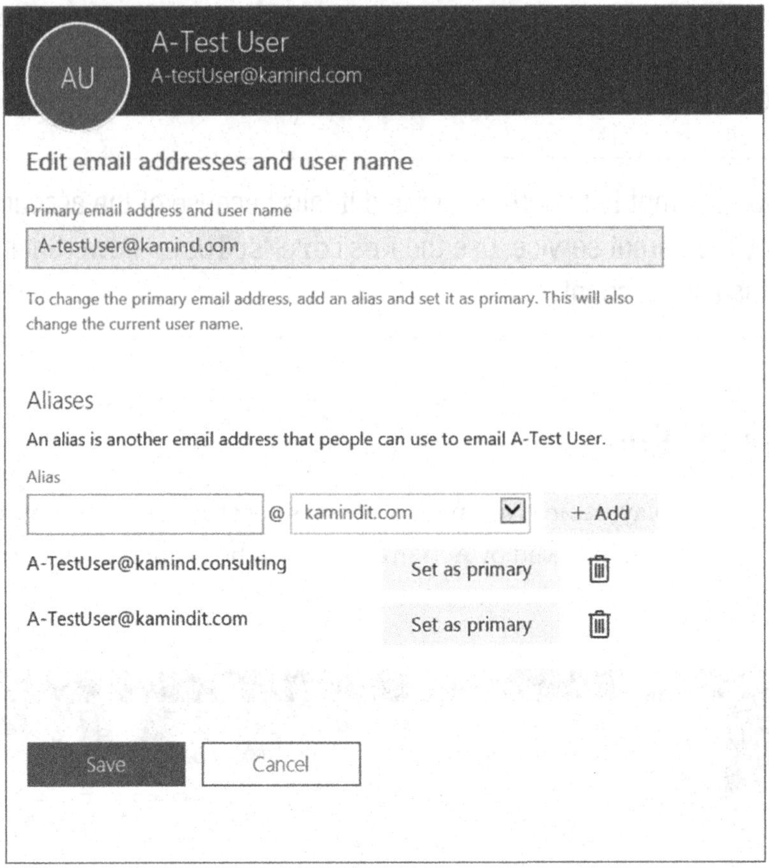

Figure 8-40. *Editing the user e-mail address and login domain*

Note   If you want to change the user e-mail address to a different alias, you can do that when you edit the user account. The e-mail alias will be set only if the alias e-mail address does not exist on any other user account. If the e-mail alias does exist on another user, the change you made will fail.

Config: Groups (Office 365 and Security Groups)

Groups are used to manage permissions globally in Office 365. There are different ways to use security groups. You can use security groups to filter users and administrator permissions (useful in large organizations). You can also use security groups to manage permissions for different services. SharePoint (as an example) can use security groups to grant permissions to various site libraries for users. You can also use SharePoint security permissions to restrict access to different libraries in SharePoint. For example, in large organizations, you can create a security group to isolate users from each other and use security groups to manage access to different federated services (such as Intune and Azure services). There are different ways to use security groups, depending on your business needs. Some organizations use security groups to manage SharePoint services. For example, a SharePoint site is designed and security groups are created to assign permissions to different areas. The global administrator adds accounts to the different security groups, depending on the business requirements. The users added to the security groups inherit the permissions necessary to access the functional areas in SharePoint.

Creating security groups is easy. Sign in as an administrator, and select Groups (select grid, then Admin ➤ Admin Center ➤ Groups ➤ Groups). Click the + to add a new Office 365 group or a security group (see Figure 8-41).

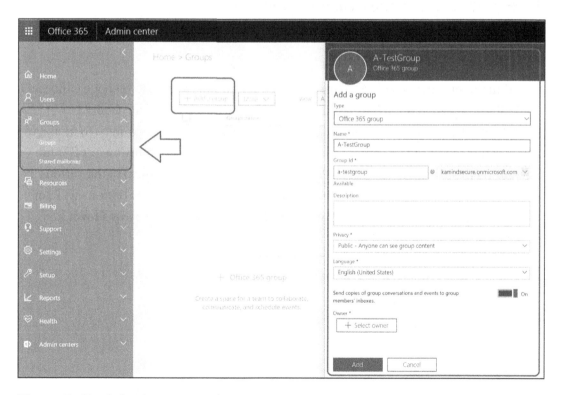

Figure 8-41. *Selecting or creating a new group*

If you're looking to create a different type of group (other than a distribution group), select the type of group from the drop-down (see Figure 8-42) and then follow the same steps for creating a new group.

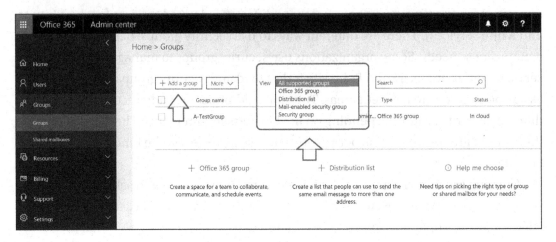

Figure 8-42. *Creating a different type of group*

Config: External Sharing

The administrator uses external sharing to manage external access to manage Office 365. Office 365 is designed for collaboration. As an administrator, you control how SharePoint (aka sites), calendars, and teams are shared. There are two steps to manage collaboration: enabling the service for external users (set the capability on or off) and configuring the local services (SharePoint, Skype for Business account) in the various admin centers. If you disable the global options, then the local service options will not have those external feature options. You should configure the services, as shown in Figure 8-43, for external sharing.

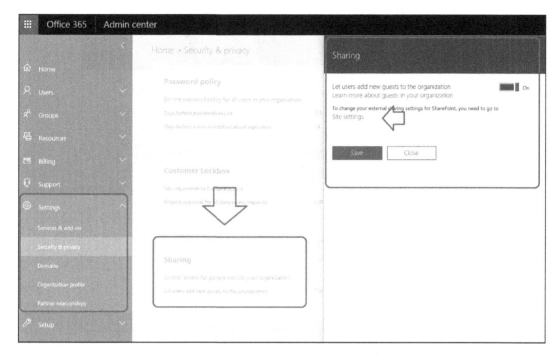

Figure 8-43. *Office 365 admin center: external sharing settings*

Config: External Sharing, Sites

If you select "Site settings," this will give you the necessary controls to manage external sharing for the SharePoint Office 365 SharePoint services and OneDrive for Business. The "sites" sharing controls are used to enable these services for external access. As an administrator, you can choose to define how you externally share. In Figure 8-44, you can see three different models for sharing Office 365 content.

Note Authentication requires that you have an Office 365 Work account or a Microsoft account. A Microsoft account can be any e-mail address. When you create a Microsoft account, you are adding additional security credentials to your e-mail address. To create a Microsoft account, go to `http://account.live.com`.

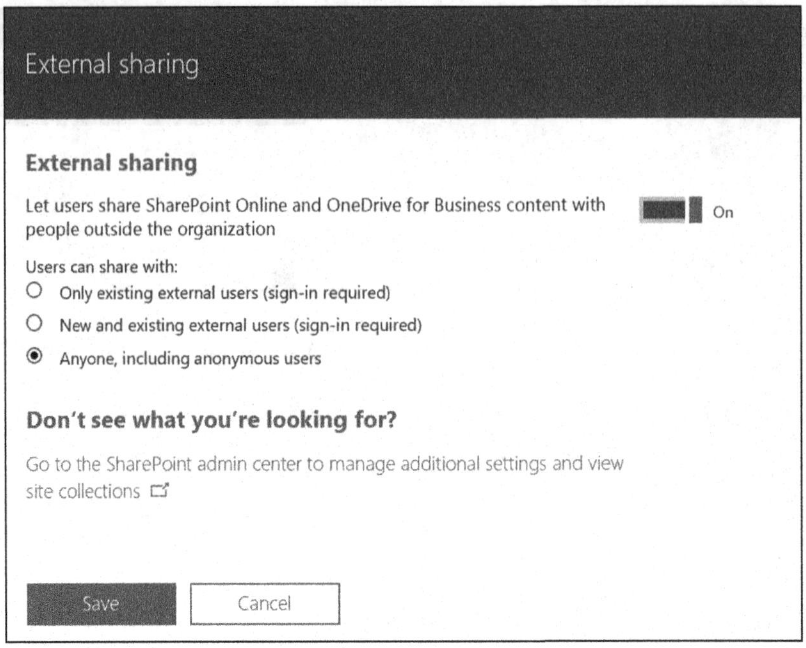

External sharing

External sharing

Let users share SharePoint Online and OneDrive for Business content with people outside the organization   ▮▮▮▮ ▮ On

Users can share with:
○ Only existing external users (sign-in required)
○ New and existing external users (sign-in required)
◉ Anyone, including anonymous users

Don't see what you're looking for?

Go to the SharePoint admin center to manage additional settings and view site collections ⌕

Save   Cancel

Figure 8-44. *Office 365 admin center: external sharing settings*

Once you have set up global sharing, then the next step is to configure the individual sites (see Figure 8-45). Go to the SharePoint admin center (select Grid and then Admin ➤ Admin Center ➤ Admin Centers ➤ SharePoint). When you create a new SharePoint Site, the default sharing is off, and you need to enable sharing. To enable sharing, select the "site" in sharing, then click the Sharing icon, and then define how you want to share the site. If you want to control the OneDrive for Business sharing, select the site that has -my. This is https://kamindsecure-my.sharepoint.com (also known as the OneDrive for Business sites).

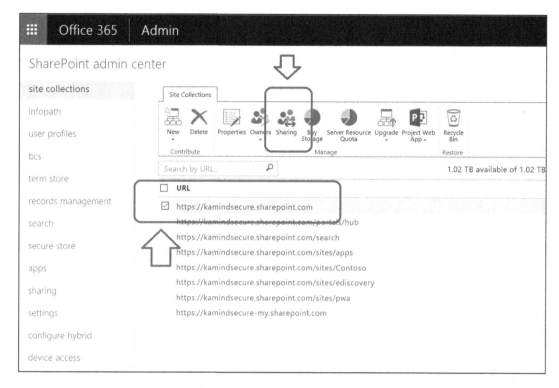

Figure 8-45.   *SharePoint admin center: external sharing settings*

This is how an administrator manages the external access to different sites. Administrators have the permission to set the allowed sharing (with logins, without logins, or disabled altogether). Administrators also can manage the external users that have shared documents (see Figure 8-46).

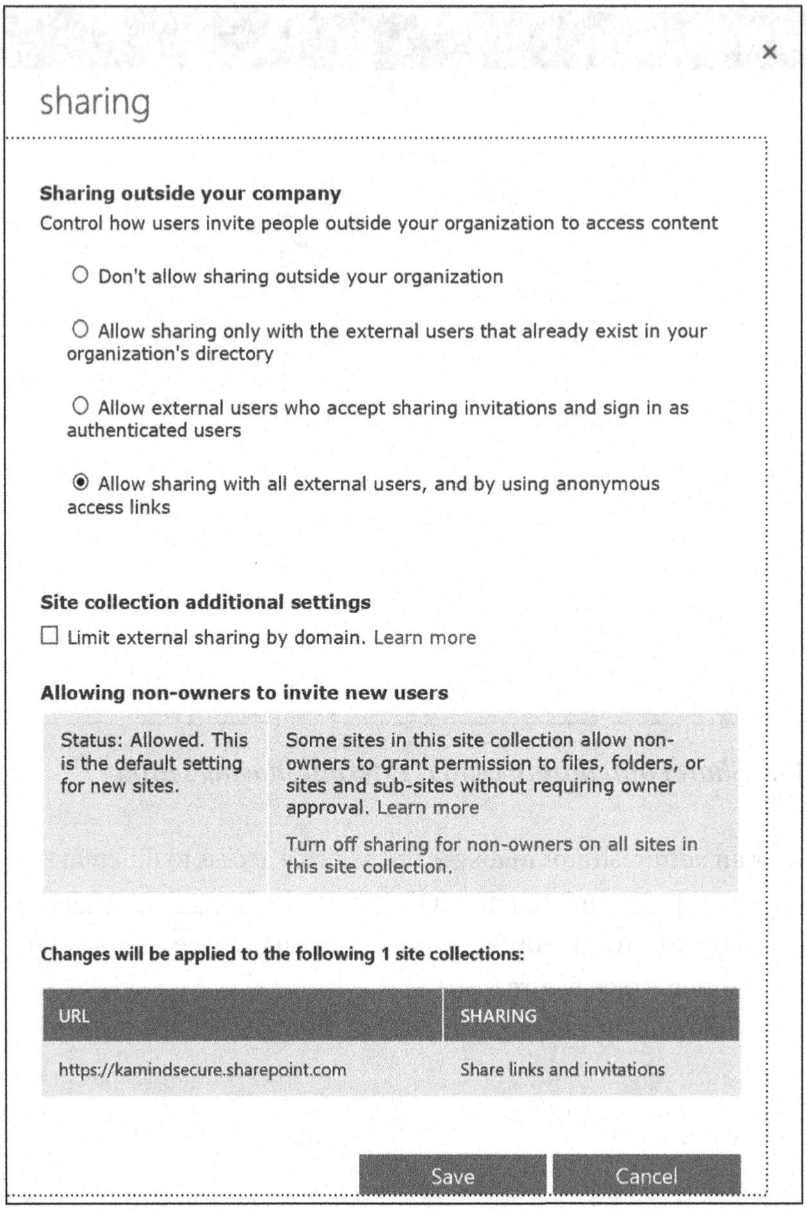

Figure 8-46. *Managing external sharing on SharePoint Site and OneDrive for Business*

Config: External Sharing, Calendar

Administrators can also control the way calendars are shared. For example, you may want to openly share information with external users to see the details in your calendar when you get a meeting invite. Likewise, you may want to restrict the information to free/busy. The settings in Figure 8-47 apply to all users globally, regardless of their individual settings.

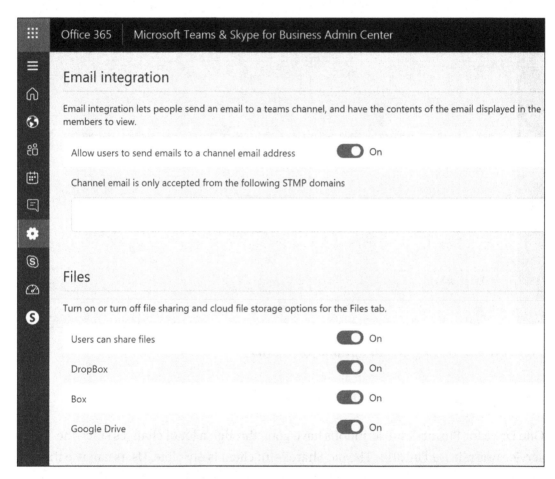

Figure 8-47. *Managing external sharing of calendar for Office 365 users*

Config: External Sharing, Teams

Teams is the business version of Skype. Business users can communicate to other business users by using an e-mail address, if the sharing is enabled in the Office 365 account. Skype users can communicate to Teams users only if the administrator has allowed this option. In both cases, you need to have the e-mail address of the user to speak with them. To set up Teams sharing, go to the Teams admin center (select Grid, then Admin ➤ Admin Center ➤ Admin Centers (at bottom) ➤ Teams & Skype for Business) If you purchased the Teams calling plans, we'll walk you through the configuration steps later in the chapter. The basic sharing configuration (allowing you to speak with other Teams users and Skype users) are controlled, as shown in Figure 8-48.

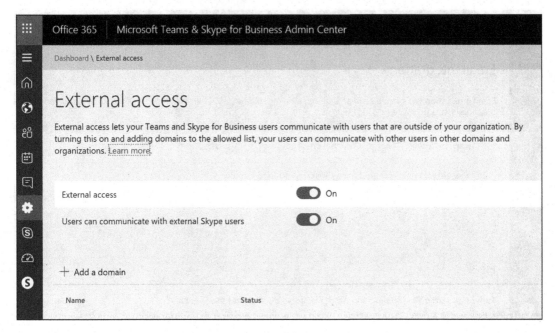

Figure 8-48. *Setting global options for Teams*

Admin Center: OneDrive for Business

One Drive for Business subscriptions have gone through a lot of changes since the service was released in 2014. The old SharePoint client is obsolete. Users can use the same sync client for all OneDrive activities (including SharePoint). The file size limits have changed considerable, and the new sync client can sync up to 100,000 files (see Figure 8-49). If an Office 365 tenant has 5 users or more, the OneDrive for business Plan 2, have unlimited storage, otherwise it is limited to 5TB. OneDrive plans allows you to store files in size up to 15GB in size. There are limitations on file names (see https://support.office.com/en-us/article/invalid-file-names-and-file-types-in-onedrive-onedrive-for-business-and-sharepoint)

OneDrive for Business is available through the following plans.

Service	Office 365 Business	Office 365 Business Essentials	Office 365 Business Premium	Office 365 ProPlus	Office 365 Enterprise E1	Office 365 Enterprise E3	Office 365 Enterprise E5	Office 365 Enterprise F1
OneDrive for Business Plan included	Plan 1	Plan 1	Plan 1	Plan 1	Plan 1	Plan 2	Plan 2	Plan F (formerly Plan K)

Service	SharePoint Online Plan 1	SharePoint Online Plan 2
OneDrive for Business	Yes	Yes

Figure 8-49. *OneDrive for Business limits*

Along with the changes in OneDrive for Business, a new admin center gives visibility into the usage. Administrators can manage OneDrive from either the PowerShell or GUI interface. Figure 8-50 shows the usage reporting available for OneDrive for Business.

Figure 8-50. *OneDrive for Business usage*

The OneDrive for Business administration site has changed. Administrators can select the OneDrive administration (see Figure 8-51). The new admin center will allow you to set the necessary controls on your Office 365 tenant. These controls include sharing, sync, storage size, device access, compliance, and notifications.

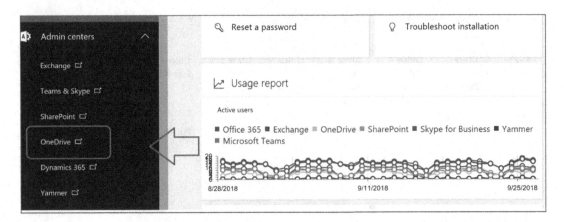

Figure 8-51. *OneDrive for Business usage report*

The approach for OneDrive for Business administration is to enable the service for collaboration. As an administrator, you will need to review the configuration and set up some limits. When we add a new client to us manage services, we have a discussion with the customer about the limits.

Sharing: Do you limit sharing to external companies; if so, what are the limits?

Sync: Do you enable the desktop sync client?

Storage: Set to 5TB limits and 1530-day data retention (see Figure 8-52).

Figure 8-52. *OneDrive for Business with 5TB limits and 1,530-day retention*

Device access: Do you limit this to known IP addresses and deploy policies?

Compliance: What alerts do we set to manage OneDrive activity?

Notifications: How do you communicate to the end user?

These are typically questions that need to be answered by the compliance officer. Data is the company's lifeblood. The Office 365 OneDrive admin center allows you to place strategic controls over the management of the information to prevent data loss in the organization. One of the first questions that is asked is how do you limit external access (see Figure 8-53). The typical follow-up question is how do you limit the devices that can connect to OneDrive for Business.

Figure 8-53. OneDrive for Business sharing

As you look through the OneDrive for Business configuration, refer to the questions that were asked earlier, explore the OneDrive for Business admin center, and set up the configuration to map to your organization. As an example, if you want to control OneDrive for Business for only approved devices, you have the ability to do that with the device access control (see Figure 8-54). OneDrive for Business allows you to do the following

- Limit access from specific IP addresses (lock it to a company's Internet)

- Deploy a policy for Mobile Device Management

OneDrive for Business has the ability to sync files as large as 15MB and as many as 100,000 files. With the size limit of 5TB (and more if you need), there is a lot of flexibility.

Note   OneDrive for Business supports two different deployment plans. Plan 2 is for subscriptions that are E3 or higher. Plan 1 is for all other plans.

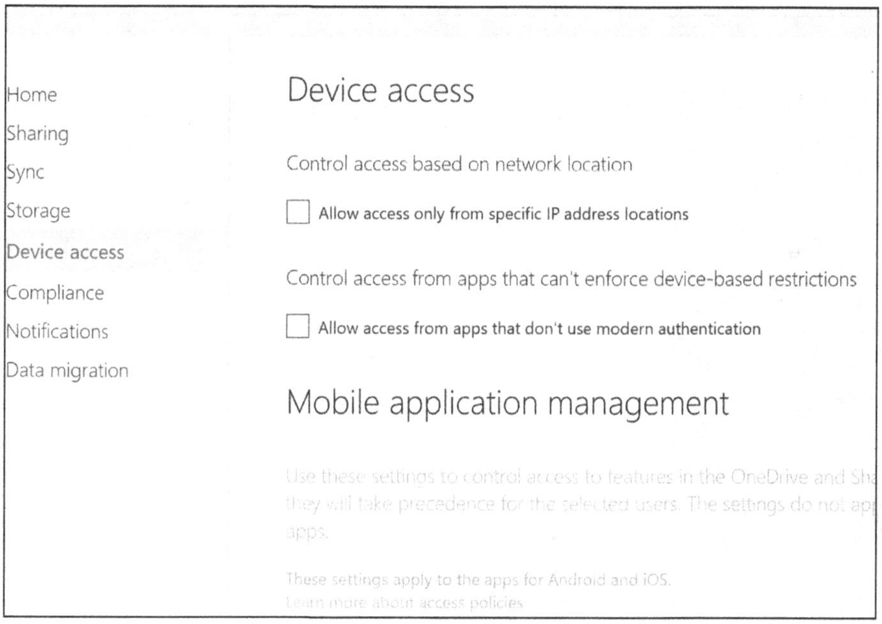

Figure 8-54. *OneDrive for Business device management and mobile policy*

Admin Center: Teams & Skype

Teams (now includes Skype for Business features) is a fully featured communications tool that supports file sharing, web conferencing, voice communications, and many other features (like Skype, but with many more features). Teams integrates into Microsoft Exchange and acts as a phone switch for incoming voice calls. Large organizations use Teams as desktop phone replacements and allow their users to deploy Teams clients on any mobile or desktop device. Teams supports enterprise voice (both people can talk at the same time). There are many different characteristics of Teams; it is a powerful and popular business communication tool, and the data it accesses is encrypted between parties. The Teams phone system services are a $4 to $24 add-on to Enterprise subscriptions in most states.

Note   If you are having trouble with file transfer on Teams clients, download a new version of the Teams client from Office 365 or run an online repair on the Office 2016 installation.

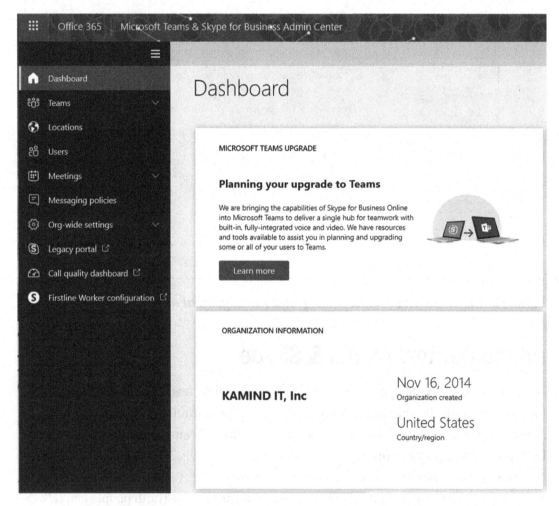

Figure 8-55. *Accessing the Teams administration center*

Teams: Federation

Skye for Business is configured to communicate to external users. To verify the configuration for Skype for Business, select the Teams admin center from the Office 365 dashboard (under the Admin tab) and then select "organization" and "external communications" (see Figure 8-56). Teams federation is enabled, and if the service is not configured within a 12-hour period, submit a service request to Microsoft Online Services. Once the Teams service is provisioned, you are enabled for external communications.

Note   It is recommended that you verify the domain prior to enabling Teams federation. If you enable the `onmicrosoft.com` domain, there may be some service downtime when you switch over to the verified domain.

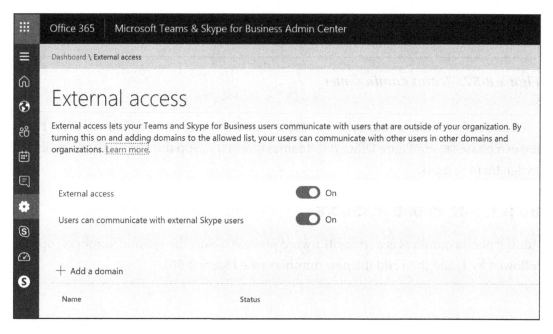

Figure 8-56. *Enabling external communications*

Teams: Voice

Teams supports domestic and international voice. The configuration requires that that you have properly set up and verified the DNS. Teams allows you to port numbers to the service or to generate the necessary numbers for your users (see Figure 8-57). The Teams voice management is in the legacy Skype for Business administration center.

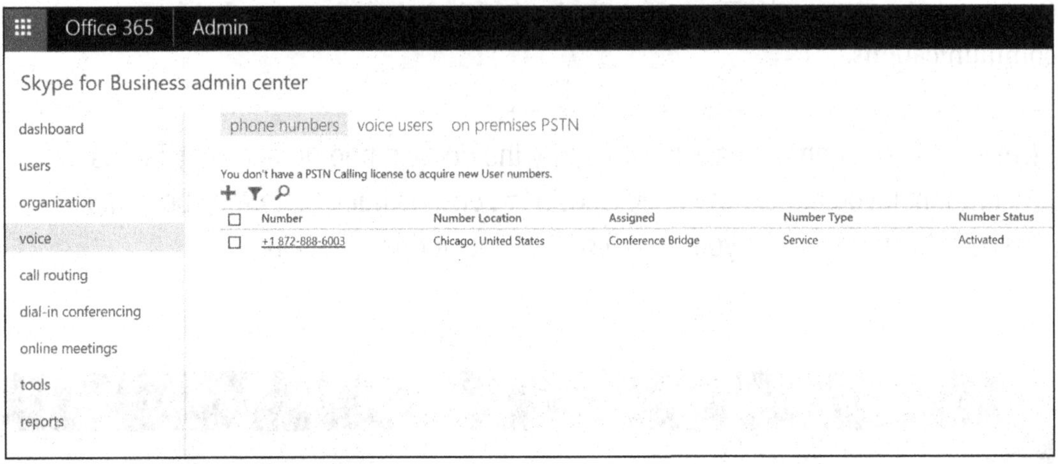

Figure 8-57. *Teams admin center*

The configuration requires that you have properly set up and verified the DNS. There are two phases to configure Office 365 Teams voice. First, add the phone numbers and assign them to users.

Step 1: Add Phone Numbers

Adding phone numbers is a straightforward process. Select the "phone numbers" option, followed by +, and then add the new numbers (see Figure 8-58).

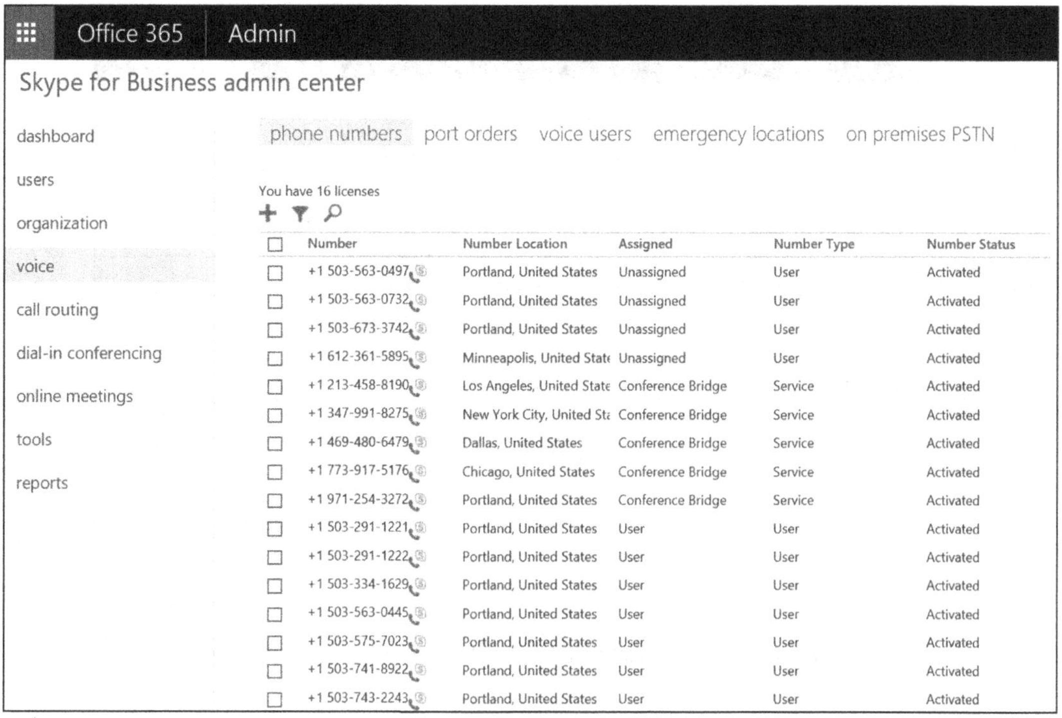

Figure 8-58. *Adding numbers in the Teams (Skype for Business) admin center*

The Teams phones are grouped into two different types: user numbers and service numbers. Select the type of voice link that you need to use for the Office 365 services. You can check your location to see whether a phone number is available (see Figure 8-59). Enter the desired number of phone numbers. Teams will attempt to acquire the phone number that you need.

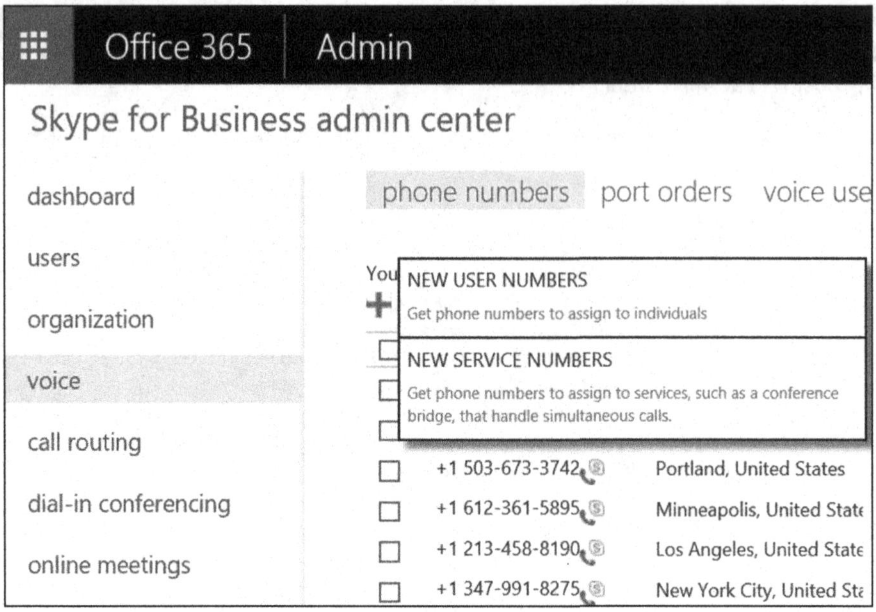

Figure 8-59. Selecting a phone number for Teams (Skype for Business)

The phone numbers are available for only a few minutes. The phone number request is from the telephony service provider. If you do not select the phone numbers, they will be returned to Microsoft for allocation to other users.

Note   Teams voice is a new service. Like any VoIP service, it is best to configure the service to meet the business needs (use the number provided). Once you are ready to transition to the new service, then port the phone numbers. Number porting is not instantaneous.

Step 2: Add an Emergency Response Location

Once you have your phone number, you can set an emergency response location (see Figure 8-60).

Figure 8-60. *Assigning an emergency location*

Step 3: Add Phone Numbers

Once you have your emergency response location set up, the next step is to assign the phone number to the different user accounts. Select the user account (see Figure 8-61) and assign (or remove) one of the phone numbers you allocated from the previous step.

Figure 8-61. *Assigning phone numbers to user for a conference room*

Once you assign the phone number to the user, you have completed the configuration of the Teams voice system. The Save button is enabled if the emergency location has been identified (see Figure 8-62).

Figure 8-62. *Assigning phone numbers in Skype for Business*

Step 4: Verify That Voice Has Been Provisioned

Have your user log out of Teams and then log back in. The "dial paid" will show up once the user logs back in to the service (see Figure 8-63).

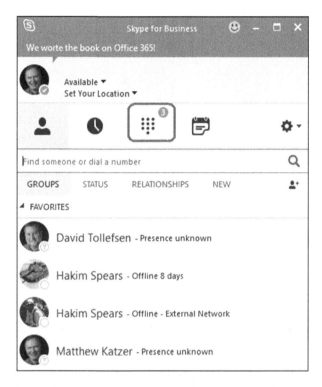

Figure 8-63. *Verifying that the voice number is set up for the user's Skype for Business client*

At this point, you are ready to use the service. There are additional configurations of voice systems that you may want to have the user complete. For example, we let our desk (Skype for Business) and our smartphones ring at the same time. To access the ring options, select Tools ➤ Options (under the gear; see Figure 8-64) and then adjust the time length for the phone to ring.

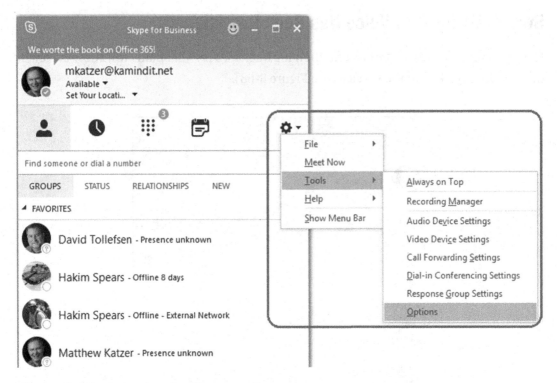

Figure 8-64. *Accessing the Teams options*

We have found that setting the phone number to ring for 35 seconds is about the right amount of time to have the phone ring on our cell phone (and be able to answer the call). You set this option under "Call forwarding" in your Teams client.

Note Make sure that you test the ring delay for voicemail. The default setting, 20 seconds, is too short to ring to a third number; 35 seconds is a better ring delay to launch Teams on your cell phone and to answer the call (see Figure 8-65).

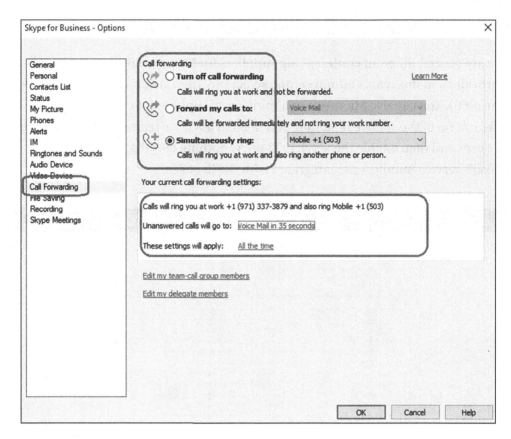

Figure 8-65. *Setting the voice options for 35 seconds*

Step 5: Port the Phone Numbers

After you have tested the service, you are ready to port your phone number to the service. In the Teams admin center, select "Voice" and "Port numbers." This is not an instantaneous process.

Note   Porting phone numbers is interesting. In the Portland (Oregon) area, we have phones that are caught in an artificial rate district. What happens is that you are charged a forwarding fee and your number is locked for transfer. What has worked for us in these cases is to port the number to a cell carrier, wait a month, and then port the number to Skype for Business. Please refer to your state laws on what you can legally do in your state regarding number porting.

Skype for Business: Conferencing Add-on

There are several different conferencing suppliers for Skype for Business. To find all the providers, in the Teams admin center, select the "dial-in conferencing" tab (see Figure 8-66). You can use Microsoft or a third-party supplier (such as InterCall). Configuration of the service is simple: you need to assign a Teams conferencing license to the user and then enable the service. There is nothing else that you need to do. Microsoft service numbers are integrated with the licenses.

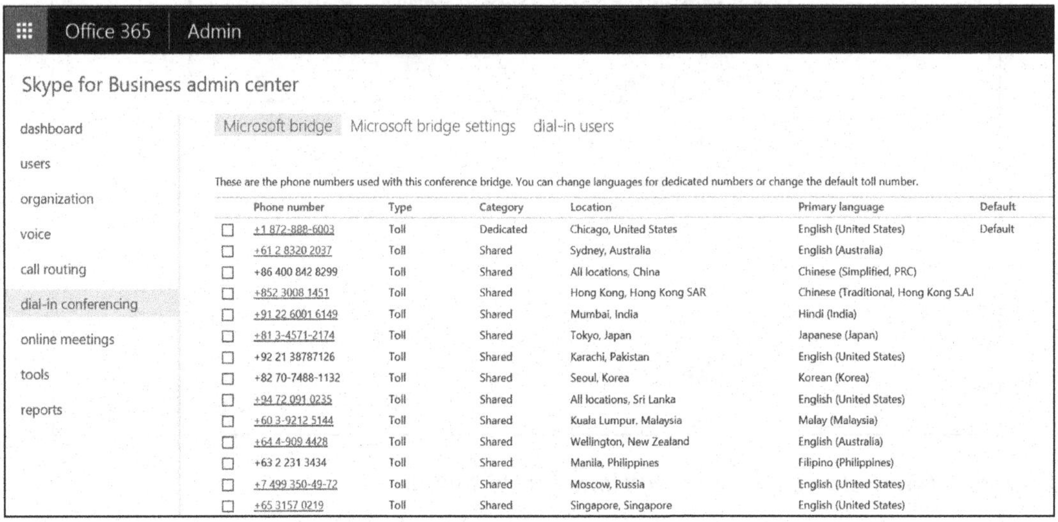

Figure 8-66. *Teams admin center, provider listings*

If you are using a third-party provider, enter the dial-in information for the user account under "dial-in users." Your teleconferencing bridge number is enabled and automatically generated with an Outlook calendar invite if Teams is installed and running on your desktop.

Note   Teams requires that your DNS supplier support service (SRV) records. If your DNS supplier does not support SRV, you need to move your DNS hosting services to a different service.

Admin Center: Exchange

Office 365 administration sites (shown in the admin center) are added based on the licensed purchased. Exchange (e-mail services in Office 365) is a licensed subscription option. The global administrator has access by default, but different administrator access may be disabled if their roles do not permit them access. Role-based permissions are controlled in the Office 365 Exchange admin center (EAC), which is located under Admin ➤ Exchange (see Figure 8-67). All the commands in the following section assume you are operating in the Exchange administration section.

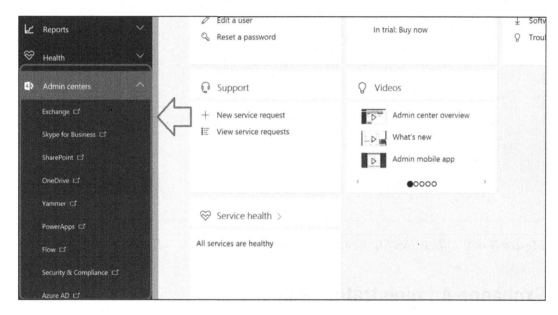

Figure 8-67. *Office 365 admin center*

Select Exchange (under admin centers). This is the location to manage the user account with advanced mail flow and mailbox features (see Figure 8-68). If the account is synced via Active Directory, some of these features need to be managed through the on-premises Active Directory center.

573

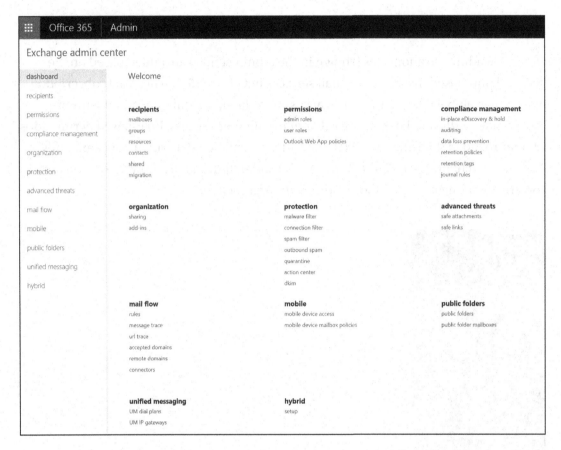

Figure 8-68. *Office 365 Enterprise Exchange admin center (EAC)*

Exchange Administration Roles

The Exchange admin center includes several administration roles. These roles are used to assign various subtasks to users. The Office 365 global administrator is an organization administrator. The global administrator may not have permission in some Exchange roles; however, the global administrator can be added to that role, but that action is audited. In large organizations, the global administrator accounts are controlled and user accounts are modified with administrator permissions based on the job roles. For example, a large company may create a security group of users from one location, and the Exchange administrator is a user in that security group. The Exchange administrator functions are limited to that location, as defined in the security group. This contrasts with a global administrator who has access to all accounts.

Table 8-4. *Exchange Administrator Roles*

Exchange Server Role	Description
AdminAgents	This contains all the administrators in Office 365 and any other users who are added by the admin. This is where the base Exchange administration permissions are granted.
Compliance Management	Users in this role can configure Exchange compliance policies, such as data loss prevention, as well other Exchange policies or compliance issues (see the compliance function in the Exchange admin center).
Discovery Management	This role manages the discovery process. To access discovery information, you must be a member of this role.
Help desk	This manages view-only operations and password resets.
HelpdeskAdmins	Manages the help desk.
Helpdesk Agents	Agent that operates the help desk.
Hygiene Management	Manages the Exchange transport services.
ISVMailboxUsers	Third-party application developer mailbox role.
Organization Management	Allows full access to all user mailboxes for any administrative role except for discovery management.
Recipient Management	Role required to move mailboxes in a hybrid deployment.
Records Management	Users in this role can configure compliance features such as retention tags and policies.
Rim-MailBxAdmins	BlackBerry mailbox access for BlackBerry messaging servers (valid only if the BlackBerry service is enabled on Office 365).
TenantAdmins	Legacy admin role for management of Exchange tenants.
UM Management	Universal messaging management role to integrate necessary functions for Enterprise Voice with Skype for Business.
View-Only Organization Management	View-only privileges for Exchange organization. Users in this role cannot modify any Exchange properties.

In larger organizations, different roles are assigned in Exchange. But in small organizations, there are only two roles that are commonly used: the company administrator role (global admin via the AdminAgents role) and the discovery management role. The global admin does not have access to discovery management unless that role is granted and permission is granted in the discovery SharePoint center.

You can assign any of the administrator roles in Table 8-4 to the user mailbox. Our recommendation for assigning user permissions follows this model:

1. Build a security group for the accounts that will be managed. The user who will manage these accounts should be in the security group.

2. Assign the user Exchange administration permission to the selected account in the newly created security group (see Figure 8-69).

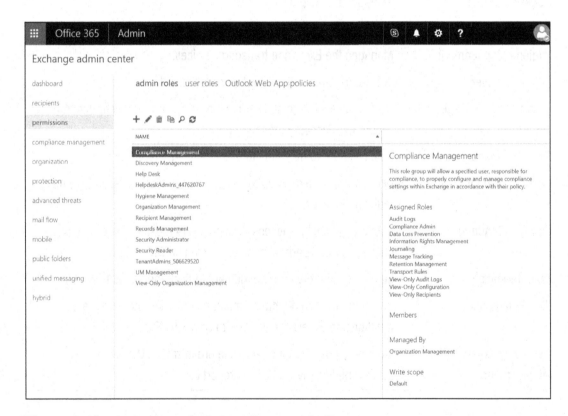

Figure 8-69. *Assigning administrative permissions*

Once you have assigned permission to the user to manage Exchange users, you can create the necessary user roles (if needed) to manage the group.

Default User Role Defined

All users have a default role assigned to them when they are added to Office 365. The default user role defines the characteristics that the user has in accessing the Exchange mail system. For example, Outlook web access is defined as a user role. If you don't want to have users access the web mail, you can remove these privileges. The user roles that you can change are listed in Table 8-5.

Table 8-5. *Default User Role Assignments*

Role Assignment	Description
Contact Information	Allows users to change their personal contact information
Profile Information	Allows users to modify their name
Distribution Groups	Allows users to create distribution groups
Distribution Group Membership	Allows users to modify their distribution group memberships
Base Options	Allows users to modify basic operations associated with their mailboxes
Subscriptions	Allows users to change their e-mail subscription options (such as notification of changes to SharePoint, etc.)
Retention Policies	Allows users to change the retention policies associated with their e-mail account
Text Message	Allows users to change their text message (IM) settings
Marketplace Access	Allows users to change the marketplace access to modify or add remote applications
Team Mailboxes	Allows users to create their own team mailboxes with other users

Either create a new role or modify the existing role, and change the permissions associated with the role. If you modify the default role, you change the role for all users. It is recommended that you create a new role and then apply that role to the user account (or accounts). To create a new role, select Permission ➤ admin roles. Either create a new role (click the +) or modify the existing role (click the pencil icon), as shown in Figure 8-70.

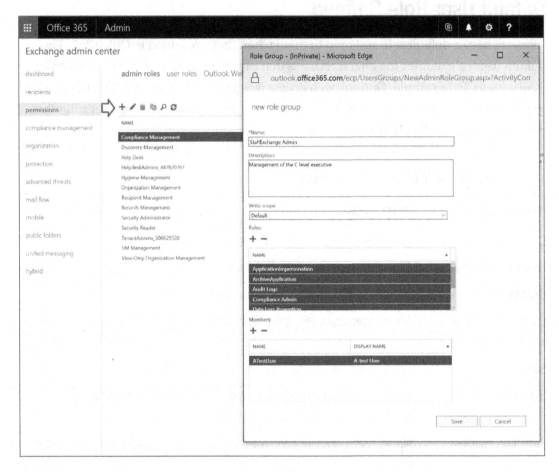

Figure 8-70. *Changing the default user role*

Exchange: Conference Room, Configuration

Office 365 provides a resource called *meeting room*. Meeting rooms are used to control resources that are limited and need to be managed through scheduling. To set up a meeting resource, log in to Office 365 as an administrator and select Admin center ➤ Exchange ➤ Exchange admin center (EAC).

Creating a conference room is simple. After you have selected the EAC, select recipients ➤ mailboxes (in the drop-down dialog box in Figure 8-71), and select "Room mailbox." This sets up the meeting room with a default configuration (if the meeting room is being used, it shows a busy status). There are additional configuration changes that can be made on conference rooms, but there is no GUI interface. These changes would need to be made using PowerShell.

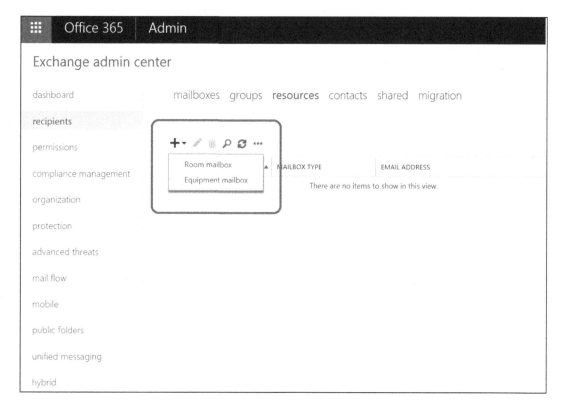

Figure 8-71. *Creating a new conference room*

When you create the meeting room, the first order of business is to assign users that have permission to book the meeting room. These users are called *delegate users*. You have two options on meeting rooms: allow all users to book meeting rooms (default) or allow restricted users to book meeting rooms. Provide the name of the meeting room and select the appropriate option; then click OK (see Figure 8-72).

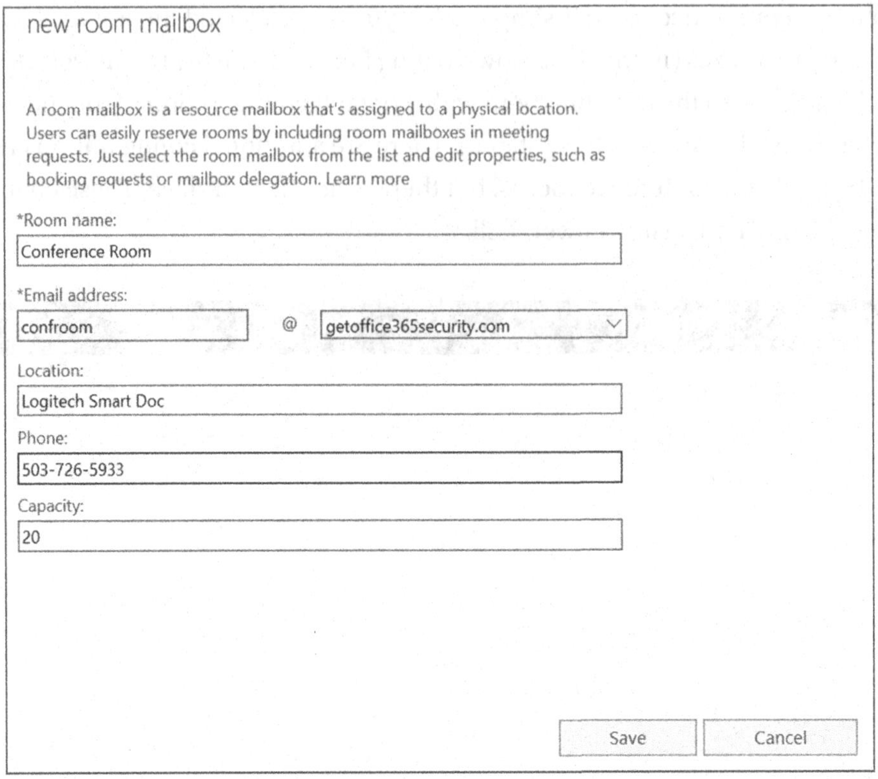

new room mailbox

A room mailbox is a resource mailbox that's assigned to a physical location.
Users can easily reserve rooms by including room mailboxes in meeting
requests. Just select the room mailbox from the list and edit properties, such as
booking requests or mailbox delegation. Learn more

*Room name:

Conference Room

*Email address:

confroom   @   getoffice365security.com

Location:

Logitech Smart Doc

Phone:

503-726-5933

Capacity:

20

Save   Cancel

Figure 8-72.   *Configuring a conference room*

The room is configured with the default setting showing only a busy status. Meeting
rooms are versatile. You can use this function to reserve any type of resource, such as
equipment. Remember, meeting rooms are a single device, and a meeting room resource
manages multiple objects. To use meeting rooms to manage multiple objects, you need
to create a meeting room for each device. After you have created the room, you can
modify the capabilities of the room based on your needs from the Exchange admin
center or from the Office 365 admin center (see Figure 8-73).

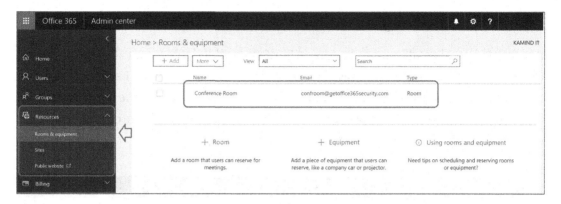

Figure 8-73. *Reviewing conference room characteristics*

Exchange: Conference Room, PowerShell Modification

Conference and resource rooms provide the basic configuration for use, but there are additional configuration options that can be done only using PowerShell. For example, the default configuration hides the meeting status and ownership. If you want to make those available, you need to run the following PowerShell commands.

Set full details of a conference room using PowerShell:

```
Set-CalendarProcessing -Identity ingoodtaste1 -AddOrganizerToSubject $true
-DeleteComments $false -DeleteSubject $false
```

Set limited details of a conference room using PowerShell:

```
Set-MailboxFolderPermission -AccessRights LimitDetails -Identity
```

Note   If you want to approve conference room use, the e-mail address of the "approver" must have fully delegated rights over the conference room resource mailbox.

```
ingoodtaste1:\calendar -User default
```

Exchange: Adding an Alias E-mail Address to a User

It is simple to add an alias e-mail address. Earlier we added the e-mail alias for the main Office 365 admin center. In this case, we are adding the alias from the Exchange admin center. To add an alias, select the user account, click Edit, and select the e-mail address (see Figure 8-74). Enter the new e-mail "alias" address for the user. The domain must be verified in Office 365; otherwise, the alias will not be added.

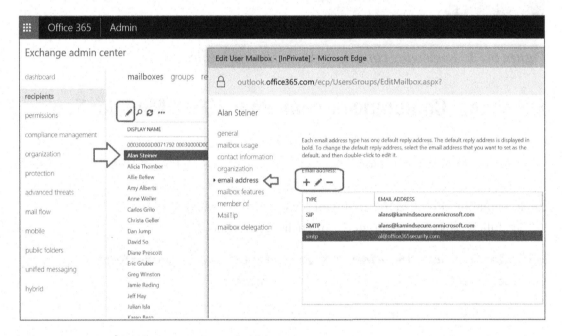

***Figure 8-74.** Adding a new e-mail address to an existing account*

Exchange: Changing a User E-mail Account Primary Domain

Office 365 supports multiple domains and multiple user e-mail aliases per an account. In some cases, an Office 365 organization may need to change to a new domain (e.g., after a company merger or branding change). Making the change for all users is not difficult: all that is required is to verify the domain (set the MX records and Teams records), add the domain to the existing users, and set the reply address to the new e-mail alias. What you cannot do is change the <domain>.onmicrosoft.com account. If you need to change the <domain>.onmicrosoft.com, you must migrate to a new Office 365 organization.

Step 1: Validate the New Domain

Complete a validation for the new domain with the domain intent set to Exchange and Skype for Business. Follow the instructions discussed in Chapter 5 and in this chapter's "Config: Domains" section.

Step 2: Add the User Alias and Set the Reply Address

Add the new e-mail alias to all the users needing a domain change. If a user's primary e-mail address is changing, then select the "Make this the reply address" option. This changes the user's primary login address to the new domain. This step is no different than changing the user's e-mail address to a new address (as discussed earlier).

Note   When the reply e-mail address is changed, the Outlook user is requested to log in with new credentials. Outlook recognizes that the user profile is the same and links the existing Outlook mailbox to the corrected e-mail address.

Exchange: Adding Shared Mailbox

There are two methods for adding a shared Exchange mailbox. The approach you use depends on the capabilities that you want the mailbox to have. If you need to receive information on a mobile device or if you require the mailbox to be an archive for long-term storage, then you need to use a licensed mailbox. If you do not need these features and you want to have access only via Outlook, then the mailbox does not need to have a license. We have outlined the choices in Table 8-6.

Table 8-6. *Shared Mailbox Options*

Approach	Cost (monthly)	Data Size	Capabilities
Shared licensed mailbox	$4–$8	25GB with 25GB or 100GB archive	Can be received on smartphones (active sync support)
Exchange shared mailbox	$0	5GB limit	No active sync

The key decision factor for most users is to receive the information on smartphones. This requirement dictates that you use an Office license rather than a free, shared mailbox.

Exchange: Shared Mailbox, Using with a Smartphone and Outlook

Smartphone devices require an active sync connection. You add a shared mailbox the same way you add a mailbox to Office 365. The only issue is that you must assign delegated rights to the users who want to use the mailbox. This is the same for all user mailboxes. Once a mailbox has been created, you need to assign share rights to the mailbox.

To add a shared mailbox, follow these steps:

1. Purchase an Exchange Plan 1 (or Plan 2) mailbox.

2. Assign a user account to the Exchange e-mail account.

3. Assign user-delegated rights to the mailbox.

In the Exchange admin center, highlight the user account, click Edit (the pencil icon), and then select the e-mail address (see Figure 8-75). Select "mailbox delegation" and then add the user for both Full Access and Send on Behalf. Click OK when done. The mailbox is modified.

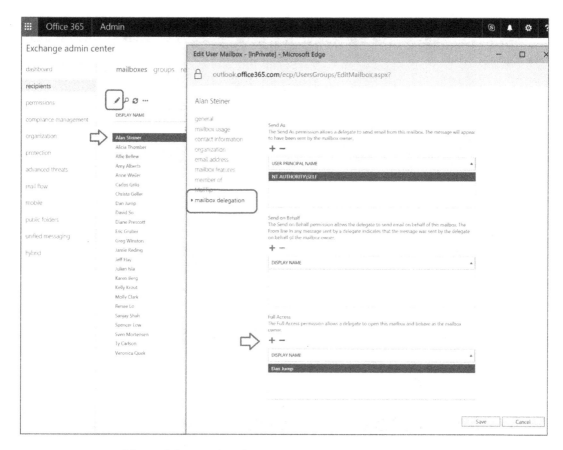

Figure 8-75. *Adding delegated rights to a mailbox*

Exchange: Shared Mailbox, Using Only with Outlook

If you need to add a shared mailbox for use only with Outlook (and you do not want to use a license), you can create a shared mailbox in the Exchange admin center and then add the user as a delegated user to the mailbox.

In the Exchange admin center, click Shared. Create a shared mailbox. In this case, we created a mailbox called CompanyCal (see Figure 8-76). Select the mailbox and then "mailbox delegation." Add the users who will access the shared mailbox. Click OK when completed. The shared mailbox will appear in Outlook for each user added as a delegated user.

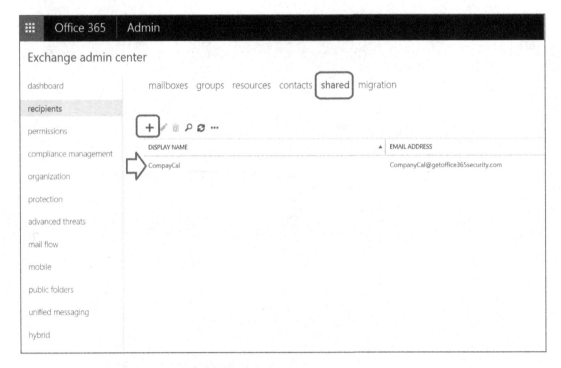

Figure 8-76. *Adding a free shared mailbox*

Exchange: Shared Mailbox, Using PowerShell

In some cases, you need to use PowerShell to set up and configure a shared mailbox. You need to run two PowerShell commands: one to set the permission and the other to set the behavior of the shared mailbox. Once you have modified the shared mailbox, the configuration is updated in the Outlook client at the next login. In this example, Identity is the shared mailbox, and User and Trustee mean the person who has access to the shared mailbox.

Step 1: Add the Recipient Permissions

```
Add-RecipientPermission -Identity user@kamind.com -Trustee trusted@kamind.com
-AccessRights SendAs
```

Step 2: Add Mailbox Access Permissions

```
Add-MailboxPermission -Identity user@kamind.com -User trusted@kamind.com
-AccessRights FullAccess -InheritanceType All
```

Exchange: Adding a Distribution Group

There are three different types of distribution groups: distribution groups, mail-enabled security groups, and dynamic distribution groups. When you add a group (see Figure 8-77), you select a group based on the business role that you want the group to perform.

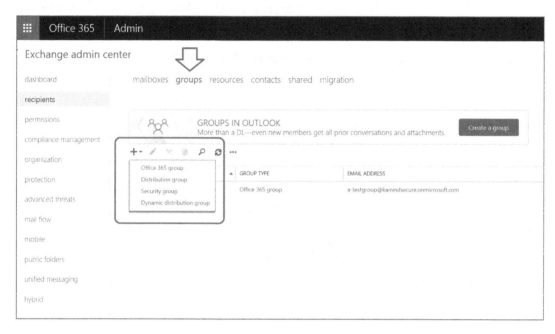

Figure 8-77. *Adding a new group: security, distribution, or Office 365 group*

There are different view types for groups, and the group you use comes down to the management view. In general, security groups are not mail-enabled and are managed externally to the Exchange admin center. Security groups are created in the Office 365 admin center and are managed from Office 365, not the Exchange admin center. Typically, you create a distribution group or Office 365 groups. If you are a large organization, you create a dynamic distribution group.

Table 8-7. *Distribution Group Types*

Group Type	Description
Distribution group	Distribution groups are mail-enabled groups. An e-mail that is sent to the distribution group is sent to all members.
Office 365 group	Automatically created groups are build with the Exchange server mailbox, SharePoint access, and third-party tool access. These are collaboration groups.
Security group	Security groups are groups that are used to grant permissions. In some cases, these may be mail enabled. It is recommended that you do not use mail-enabled security groups.
Dynamic distribution group	This is a distribution group that has a variable number of members based on filters and conditions in Active Directory.

Step 1: Create the Distribution Group

In the Exchange admin center, select "recipients" and "groups" (see Figure 8-78). Verify that the distribution group is being created; otherwise, an Office 365 group is created. Add the group by clicking the + and then select the distribution group to be added.

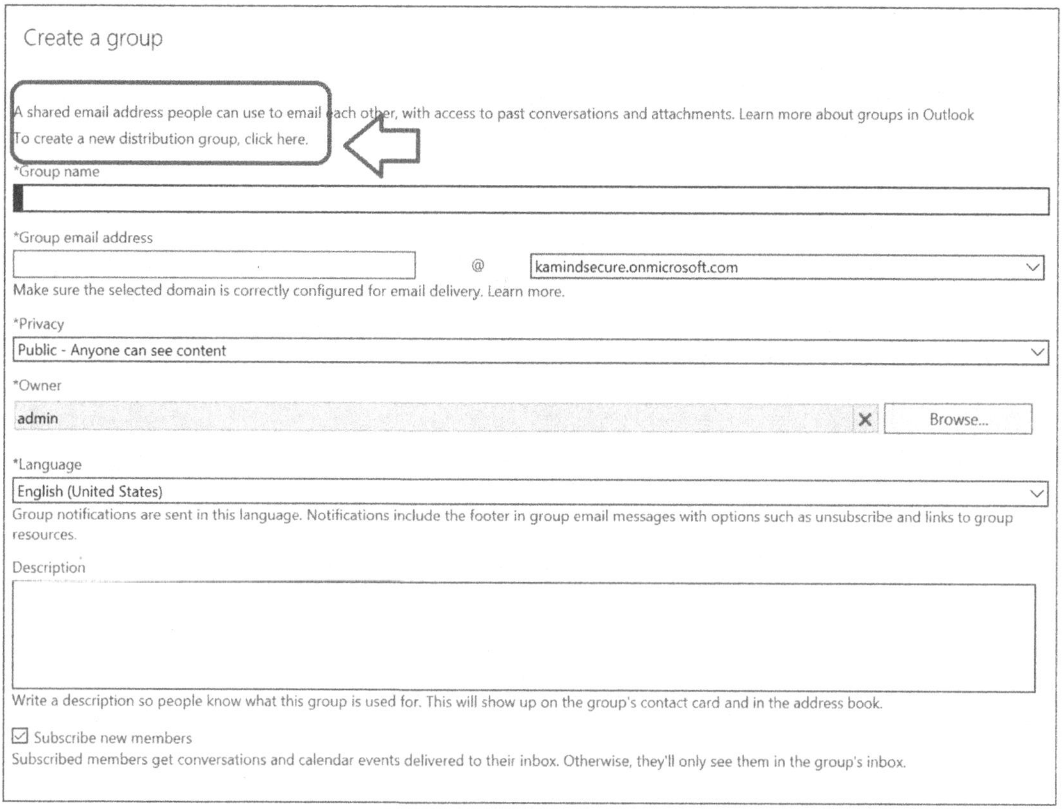

Figure 8-78. *Adding a new distribution group*

Step 2: Define the Distribution Group

Fill in the information about the distribution group. When you first create the group, leave the defaults in place. You must specify an owner of the group and any initial members you want to add (see Figure 8-79).

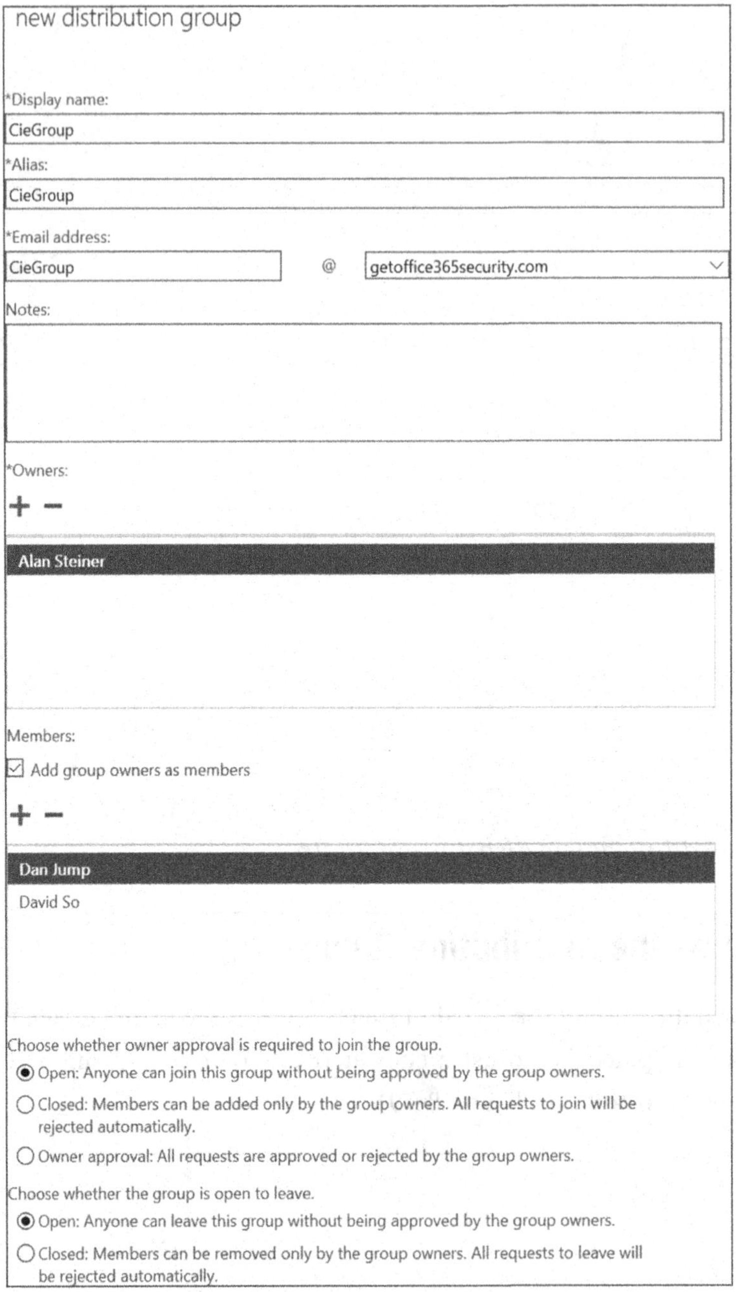

new distribution group

*Display name:

CieGroup

*Alias:

CieGroup

*Email address:

| CieGroup | @ | getoffice365security.com ⌄ |

Notes:

*Owners:

+ −

Alan Steiner

Members:

☑ Add group owners as members

+ −

Dan Jump

David So

Choose whether owner approval is required to join the group.

◉ Open: Anyone can join this group without being approved by the group owners.

○ Closed: Members can be added only by the group owners. All requests to join will be rejected automatically.

○ Owner approval: All requests are approved or rejected by the group owners.

Choose whether the group is open to leave.

◉ Open: Anyone can leave this group without being approved by the group owners.

○ Closed: Members can be removed only by the group owners. All requests to leave will be rejected automatically.

Figure 8-79. *Defining the distribution group*

Step 3: Enable the Group for External Access

After you have created the group and saved it, the group is set up for internal access. If you want to enable the group for external access, you must edit the group and enable the external access options (see Figure 8-80). Select the group, click Edit, and then select the "delivery management" option. This is a two-step process. You must create an internal distribution group (and save it) before you can enable it for external access.

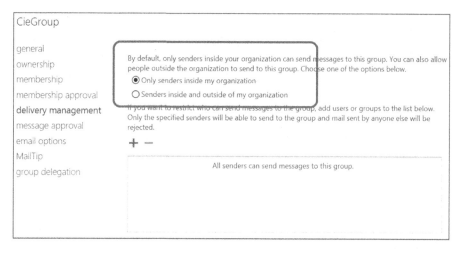

Figure 8-80. *Settings for external delivery*

Exchange: Using Alias to Send to/Receive from E-mail

You may want to use a different e-mail address to send and receive e-mail. Office 365 is designed to allow only one e-mail address to be used: your primary e-mail address. The way to work around this is to use a distribution list and to grant a user account full permission to use that distribution list with PowerShell. Log in to the Office 365 admin center, and on the Admin tab, select Exchange and follow the steps outlined next.

Step 1: Create the Distribution Group

In the Exchange admin center, select Recipients ➤ Groups and click the + to add the distribution group. Use the e-mail alias as the distribution group name.

Step 2: Configure the Group Being Added

Since this is a personal alias, add a description and complete the additional steps for the configuration of the group (see Figure 8-81).

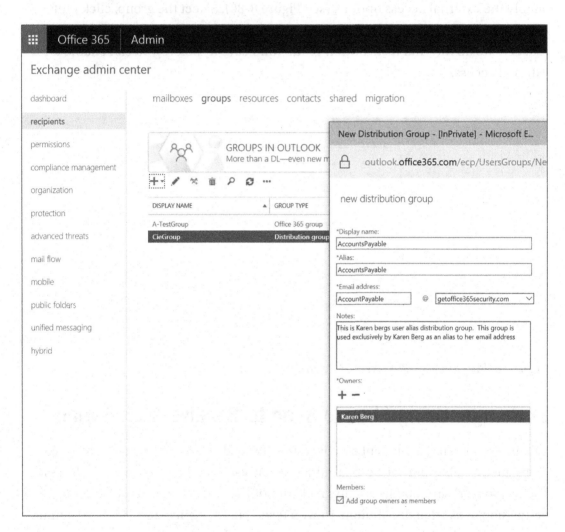

Figure 8-81. *Adding a distribution group*

Add the user and select the membership options. Since this is an e-mail alias (i.e., an internal group), it is recommended that you restrict it to the individual who is using the group (see Figure 8-82).

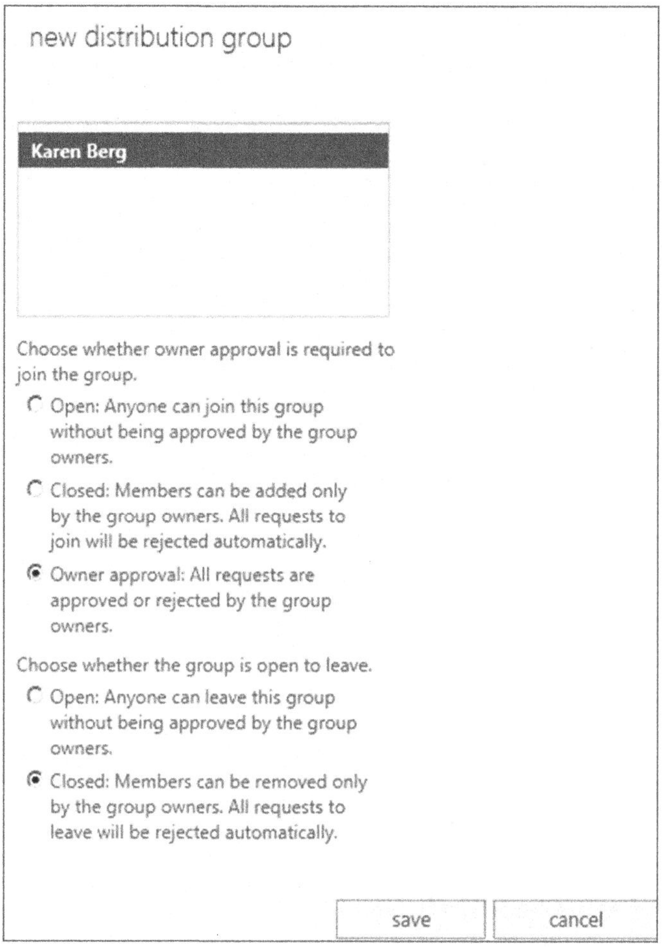

new distribution group

Karen Berg

Choose whether owner approval is required to join the group.

○ Open: Anyone can join this group without being approved by the group owners.

○ Closed: Members can be added only by the group owners. All requests to join will be rejected automatically.

◉ Owner approval: All requests are approved or rejected by the group owners.

Choose whether the group is open to leave.

○ Open: Anyone can leave this group without being approved by the group owners.

◉ Closed: Members can be removed only by the group owners. All requests to leave will be rejected automatically.

save   cancel

Figure 8-82. *Restricting access to the distribution group*

Step 3: Enable the Group for External Access

In the Exchange admin center, select "groups" and then click the pencil icon to edit. Select "delivery management" (see Figure 8-83) and then enable the mail option ("Only senders inside my organization" is the default) and the user for access outside the organization. This is identical to the external distribution groups discussed earlier.

Figure 8-83. *Enabling the group for external access*

Step 4: Grant Permission to the User

The final step is to grant permission to the user. There are two ways to do this: either through PowerShell or by using the Exchange admin center. In the Exchange admin center, select "groups," and then click the pencil icon to edit. Select "group delegation." You need to enter the user account for both Send as and Send on Behalf (see Figure 8-84). Click OK. The user is now able to use the From address in Outlook, or in the Outlook Web App, to send e-mails using the alias e-mail address.

You can also grant permissions using the PowerShell commands for a shared mailbox. In this case, you are using a distribution list and granting full access for its use. Execute the PowerShell command and give access rights to the user mailbox. The shared mailbox PowerShell command is as follows:

```
Add-RecipientPermission -Identity myfakee-mail@domain.com -Trustee
myrealeamil@domain.com -AccessRights SendAs
```

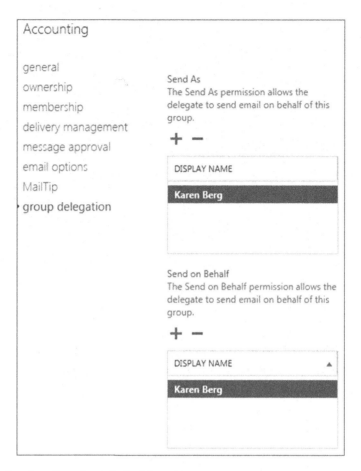

Figure 8-84. *Setting Send on Behalf options*

Step 5: Verify Outlook Configuration

The final step is to send an e-mail from Outlook to verify that you can send a message from an alias (see Figure 8-85). For this to work, you must select the e-mail distribution group you created earlier. In our example, we used Get365. Select Get365 from the group e-mail address book. (If you manually type the e-mail address in, this will fail.) To send an e-mail alias from Outlook, follow these steps:

1. Open Outlook and select From ➤ Other e-mail address (see Figure 8-84).

2. In the From box, select From and find the distribution alias (see Figure 8-85).

3. Click OK to send the e-mail.

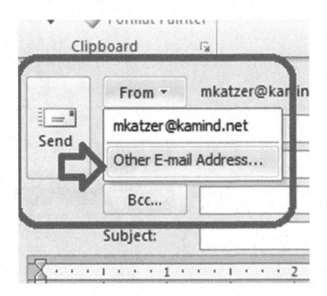

Figure 8-85. *Selecting the From/Other e-mail address*

After selecting "Other E-mail addresses," select the distribution group (see Figure 8-86). You cannot enter the distribution group name in the address bar. The e-mail will not be sent.

Figure 8-86. *Selecting the alias address Get365*

PowerShell

Earlier, we briefly discussed PowerShell and the capabilities that it provides. PowerShell is required for any bulk changes that you need to perform or for special commands that are not part of the Office 365 admin console. Typically, we recommend that if your organization has more than ten accounts, then you may find it more convenient to use PowerShell. The account that you will use for PowerShell management is the global admin user account. The account must have a license in the area that the PowerShell command is executing. For example, if you are using Exchange PowerShell commands, the global admin account must have an Exchange license assigned. If the license is not assigned, then the PowerShell command will fail. The simplest way to install the latest version of PowerShell is to go to `http://docs.microsoft.com/en-us/powershell` (see Figure 8-87) and select the Get Started tab.

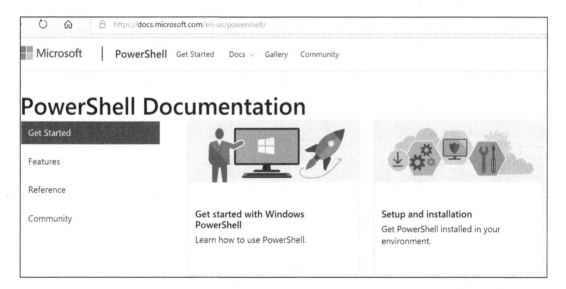

Figure 8-87. *Installing PowerShell for Office 365 (courtesy of Microsoft)*

Note If you have not installed the Microsoft Online Services Sign-In Assistant for IT Professionals RTW, do that now. Go to `www.microsoft.com`, download it, and search for *sign-in services assistant*. PowerShell commands will not work unless the Sign-In Assistant is installed.

The latest version of Azure PowerShell can be downloaded from Microsoft Downloads; see https://docs.microsoft.com/en-us/office365/enterprise/ powershell/manage-office-365-with-office-365-powershell (see Figure 8-88). The PowerShell installation verifies the updates required to support Azure PowerShell. Make sure you download the files and run them as an administrator (right-click and Select "Run as administrator") to make sure the files install correctly.

Figure 8-88. *Installing Office 365 PowerShell from* https://docs.microsoft.com/

Once you have installed Office 365 PowerShell, launch the PowerShell module and enter the following commands:

```
Set-ExecutionPolicy RemoteSigned
$LiveCred = Get-Credential
Import-module msonline
Connect-MSOLService -Credential $LiveCred -Verbose
Get-MsolGroup
```

The result of running these commands should look like Figure 8-89.

Figure 8-89. *Validating PowerShell commands*

You have completed the base PowerShell setup; now use the preceding command to validate the installation. If the command does not work, you have installed the PowerShell GUI incorrectly, there is a lack of permissions, or you have not installed the desktop connector for Office 365. Using PowerShell requires administrative privileges and a license to be assigned to the account that is using PowerShell commands.

PowerShell: Setting Up Teams and SharePoint

There are different versions of PowerShell installations for Teams Online, SharePoint Online, and other Microsoft online services (such as BI and CRM). For those services, you need to install the appropriate Active Directory services. These additional PowerShell modules are available from the Microsoft Download Center (www.microsoft. com/download).

- *Teams PowerShell*: Windows PowerShell module for Teams Online

- *SharePoint PowerShell*: SharePoint Online Management Shell

These additional commands are described in the following sections. Before you can use the commands, you must download and install the PowerShell extensions.

PowerShell: Using the Standard Header for Microsoft Online Services and Exchange

PowerShell can be complex for any user. When using PowerShell with Office 365 and Exchange, you need to use a standard PowerShell header. This standard header allows you to connect directly to the Office 365 administration interface and make the necessary changes. However, if you do not set up the commands correctly with the remote interface execution parameters, the PowerShell command will fail. The only issue is that the user account that you log in to (for Office 365) must have a license assigned to it. The licensed user can only execute the PowerShell commands for Office 365 that the user admin account is licensed to use; otherwise, it will fail.

We use a standard PowerShell interface, which allows the command to run in a PowerShell command prompt, or the integrated systems editor (ISE). The standard command interface (or PowerShell header) can be invoked with this script:

```
Set-ExecutionPolicy RemoteSigned
$LiveCred = Get-Credential
Import-module msonline
Connect-MSOLService -Credential $LiveCred -Verbose

$Session = New-PSSession -ConfigurationName Microsoft.Exchange-
ConnectionUri https://ps.outlook.com/powershell/ -Credential $LiveCred
-Authentication Basic -AllowRedirection

Import-PSSession $Session -Allow Clobber

# Insert Other Power shell commands before remove PSSession
#*********
# PowerShell Commands go here
#*********

#Clean up and close the session
Remove-PSSession $Session
```

Once you have verified the functionality of the header script, you are ready to make the necessary changes in Office 365. This section of the administration maintenance manual lists the type of problems encountered and the PowerShell solution. All that is needed for the user to execute these commands is to use an account—with global administrator rights—that is licensed with an appropriate subscription (such as Exchange, SharePoint, etc.).

PowerShell: Not Remotely Sign Error

The first time you run PowerShell, you may get the error "not remotely signed." To correct this error, you need to enable PowerShell on your system.

1. Start Windows PowerShell as an administrator by right-clicking the Windows PowerShell shortcut and selecting "Run as administrator."

2. The WinRM service is configured for manual startup by default. You must change the startup type to Automatic and start the service on each computer that you want to work with. At the PowerShell prompt, you can verify that the WinRM service is running using the following command:

    ```
    get-service winrm
    ```

    The value of the Status property in the output should be Running.

    a. If the value is not running, you can start the service from the command prompt:

        ```
        sc config winrm start= auto
        ```

        ```
        start winrm
        ```

    b. To configure Windows PowerShell for remoting, type the following command:

        ```
        Enable-PSRemoting -force
        ```

Mail flow should resume in the next two to four hours.

PowerShell: Winmail.dat Problem

Let's say the e-mail is being sent externally to users in an RTF MIME format, and the users cannot read the e-mail and see a `winmail.dat` file. The `winmail.dat` file appears on the client e-mail because Outlook (on the sender) is not installed correctly or there is another Outlook add-in (on the sender) that is preventing the e-mail from being converted to text. To resolve this issue, either disable the Outlook add-ins (on the sending device) or uninstall and reinstall Office 2007/2010.

If this fails, then as a last resort you can force Office 365 Exchange Server to send only pure-text e-mail. This command forces the e-mails to be sent out in a pure-text format:

```
Set-MailContact <ExternalE-mailAddress or GUID> -UseMapiRichTextFormat Never
```

Verify that the mail format was applied:

```
Get-MailContact | Select <ExternalE-mailAddress or GUID> | Select
UseMapiRichTextFormat
```

These commands will only display the user e-mail address if it supports RTF format; otherwise, it will display other options.

PowerShell: Enable Audit

The `Audit` command turns on full tracking for any access to a mailbox. To change the audit state on a mailbox, run this command:

```
Set-Mailbox <Identity> -AuditEnabled $true
```

Set multiple mailboxes for audit:

```
$UserMailboxes = Get-mailbox -Filter {(RecipientTypeDetails -eq
'UserMailbox')}
$UserMailboxes | ForEach {Set-Mailbox $_.Identity -AuditEnabled $true}
```

PowerShell: Verification of Audit Logs

Run the following command to verify the audit log configuration and the time limit configuration. Administrator audit logs are on by default; mailbox logs are off by default. Audit logs are enabled for 15 days.

```
Get-AdminAuditLogConfig
```

PowerShell: Mailbox Audit Log search

To perform an audit log search in PowerShell, use the following command (it requires that auditing be enabled on the mailbox in question):

```
New-mailboxAuditLogSearch -Mailboxes user@domain.com -Startdate 1/1/2010
-EndDate 12/31/2013 -StatusMailRecipients manager@domain.com
```

PowerShell: Passwords Forever

Passwords can be set from the user interface. However, when you reset a password, all passwords revert to the 90-day password reset.

```
Get-MSOLUser | Set-MsolUser -PasswordNeverExpires $true
```

Note   If the user's password is reset, the policy changes back to 90 days. If you want the forever policy applied, you need to set it again with PowerShell and every time you reset a password. The Office 365 interface allows passwords to be fixed for up to 720 days.

PowerShell: Get Mailbox Statistics

This command retrieves all the usage data about the user:

```
Get-Mailbox | Get-MailboxStatistics | Select-Object DisplayName,
StorageLimitStatus,TotalItemSize
```

PowerShell: Enable Litigation Hold–No Notice

There are different legal holds—with notice and without notice. This command places a mailbox on legal hold with no notice given to the end user:

```
Get-Mailbox -ResultSize unlimited | Set-mailbox -LitigationHoldEnabled
$true
```

PowerShell: Review Permission Assigned to a Mailbox

This command retrieves all the permission information about the user:

```
Get-MailboxPermission -Identity user@domain.com
```

PowerShell: Review the Management Role Assignment to a User Account

This command retrieves all the permissions assigned to different roles in Office 365:

```
Get-ManagementRoleAssignment- -Enabled $True -Delegating $True
```

PowerShell: Display All Mailbox Forwarders

The following commands retrieve information about the mailbox forwarders and allow you to turn them on or off.

Display all mailbox forwarders:

```
Get-Mailbox | Where {$_.ForwardingSMTPAddress -ne $null} | Select Name,
ForwardingSMTPAddress, DeliverToMailboxAndForward
```

Turn off all mailbox forwarders:

```
Get-Mailbox | Where {$_.ForwardingAddress -ne $null} | Set-Mailbox
-ForwardingAddress $null
```

Turn off a single mailbox forwarder:

```
Set-Mailbox <e-mailaddress> -ForwardingSmtpAddress $null
```

PowerShell: Change Mailbox Permissions

The mailbox permission command is useful; you can use this on any e-mail-enabled item (such as distribution groups):

```
Add-MailboxPermission -Identity public@kamind.com -User john@kamind.com
-AccessRights FullAccess -InheritanceTypeAll -Confirm:$false
```

```
Add-RecipientPermission -Identity public@kamind.com -Trustee rajk@kamind.
com -AccessRights SendAs
```

PowerShell: Change the User Principal Name on a User Account

After you configure ADDConnect, you may run into a situation where the user account name has not synced correctly to Office 365. This is usually because the e-mail address is not set up in the on-premises Active Directory or the UPN is missing in the root of the Active Directory. If you have corrected the on-premises AD and the user's principal name has not changed, then run the following PowerShell command:

```
Set-MSOLUser -UserPrincipalName user@domain.onmicrosoft.com
-NewUserPrincipalName user@domain.com
```

Note   The Office 365 account has the Active Directory from the on-premise server. Make sure you check the configuration of the Active Directory to make sure that the user's e-mail address is in the correct field and the UPN is set for the AD login. If you need to execute this command, there is a configuration problem in the local Active Directory.

PowerShell: Assign License to a User Account

After you have directory-synced an account, there may be a need to bulk-assign licenses via PowerShell. To complete this, you need to execute the following two PowerShell commands. There are additional PowerShell commands that you also need to run to retrieve the subscription SKUs to use this command. The license types must be active.

```
Set-MSOLUser -UserPrincipalName user@domain.com -UsageLocation US
Set-MSOLUserLicense -UserPrincipalName user@domain.com -AddLicenses
{tenantid}:ENTERPRISEPACK
```

PowerShell: Purging Users in the Delete Bin

There are cases where you need to remove users that have been deleted in Office 365. A deleted user is retained in Office 365 for 30 days, which allows you to easily restore the user account to the same subscription that the account had prior to deletion. If you need to delete all user data, use these PowerShell commands to perform this action:

```
#Get a list fousers in the RecyleBin
Get-MsolUser -ReturnDeletedUsers

#Purge all users from RecyleBin
Get-MsolUser -ReturnDeletedUsers | Remove-MsolUser -RemoveFromRecycleBin
-force
#Purge a user from the RecyleBin
Remove-MsolUser -UserPrincipalName testmatt@testmatt.com
-RemoveFromRecycleBin -force
#Restore a user from the recycle bin
Restore-MsolUser -UserPrincipalName testmatt@testmatt.com
```

PowerShell: Bypass Spam Filtering for E-mail

Allow all mail to be sent to a mailbox without filtering e-mail by using Exchange Spam Confidence Level (SCL) for e-mail processing. This command accepts all incoming e-mail that is processed by Office 365 Exchange Transport server role.

```
Set-ContentFilteringConfig -Bypassedrecipients public@kamind.com
```

PowerShell: Extend the Purges Folder to Greater Than 14 Days

E-mail in Office 365 is deleted from the Purges folder after 14 days, once the user has selected the item in the Delete folder. You can extend this to 30 days with the following commands.

- Extend 30-day delete for a mailbox:

  ```
  Set-mailbox user@contoso.com -retaindeleteditemsfor 30
  ```

- Extend 30-day delete for the organization:

  ```
  Get-mailbox | Set-mailbox -retaindeleteditemsfor 30
  ```

PowerShell: Meeting Room Configuration

To make meeting rooms more useful, you need to add additional user information about the meeting room. The only way to add these capabilities is to use PowerShell to extend the meeting room options. This example uses the "ingoodtaste1" meeting room.

Set the conference room to show "limited details–free & busy":

```
Set-MailboxFolderPermission -AccessRights LimitDetails -Identity
ingoodtaste1:\calendar -User default
```

Troubleshooting: Autodiscover

Autodiscover allows an Outlook client (including your laptop and your smartphone) to discover the location of the Office 365 Exchange e-mail server and to automatically connect to that server (see Figure 8-90). You need to insert the Autodiscover record in the external DNS and the internal DNS. Both records should point to outlook.com.

Type	Priority	Host name	Points to address	TTL
CNAME	-	autodiscover	autodiscover.outlook.com	1 Hour

Figure 8-90. *Autodiscover record value*

Note   Outlook clients (Mac and PC) use Autodiscover to find the mail server. Smartphones use the MX records.

The Autodiscover process is outlined in Figure 8-91. When an internal client looks up an Autodiscover record, it first determines the Autodiscover record through Active Directory. If the client is external, it looks up the Autodiscover record from the DNS.

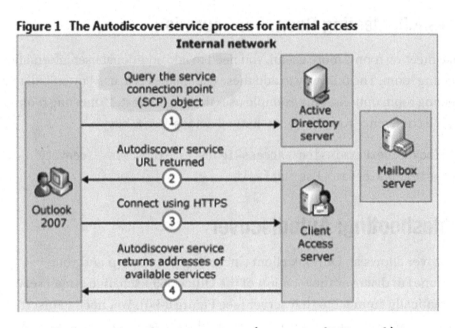

Figure 8-91. Exchange Autodiscover process (courtesy of Microsoft)

If you are on-site and you are trying to connect to the Office 365 Exchange Server, the Outlook client uses the Exchange Service Control Point connection object to attach to the local Exchange Server and bypass the external Autodiscover lookup. If you have chosen not to use Microsoft migration tools, you need to block the local clients from finding the on-site Exchange Server in the Autodiscover process or convert the mailboxes to a mail-enabled user (MEU). The registry entries that must be modified for clients are listed next (see `https://support.microsoft.com/en-us/kb/2612922`).

1. Navigate to the following registry key:

    `HKEY_CURRENT_USER\Software\Microsoft\Office\12.0\Outlook\`
    `AutoDiscover`

2. Set the following values:

    `"PreferLocalXML"=dword:1`
    `"ExcludeHttpRedirect"=dword:0`
    `"ExcludeHttpsAutodiscoverDomain"=dword:1`
    `"ExcludeHttpsRootDomain"=dword:1`
    `"ExcludeScpLookup"=dword:1`
    `"ExcludeSrvLookup"=dword:1`
    `"ExcludeSrvRecord"=dword:1`

Summary

Office 365 administration is a large topic, and many books could be written to cover this topic. The objective here was to provide you with an overview of how to administer Office 365. I wanted to provide you with exposure to the new tools and techniques so that you can see how easy it is to manage and secure Office 365. As you begin to work with Office 365, you can revisit the "PowerShell" section. Office 365 is about productivity and management of company resources.

References

There is a lot of information about Office 365 on the Web; the issue is finding the right site. The information contained in this chapter is a combination of my experience doing deployments and of support information published by third parties.

Installing PowerShell for Teams Online with Office 365

- www.microsoft.com/en-us/download/details.aspx?id=39366

Installing PowerShell for SharePoint Online with Office 365

- www.microsoft.com/en-us/download/details.aspx?id=35588

Introduction to SharePoint Online with PowerShell

- http://office.microsoft.com/en-us/sharepoint-help/
  introduction-to-the-sharepoint-online-management-shell-
  HA102915057.aspx

Microsoft Online Services Sign-In Assistant for IT Professionals RTW

- www.microsoft.com/en-us/download/details.aspx?id=28177

PowerShell Tools Site

- http://powershell.office.com

Office 365 Service Level Permissions

- http://community.office365.com/en-us/wikis/manage/535.aspx

PowerShell for Office 365

- https://docs.microsoft.com/en-us/office365/enterprise/
  powershell/manage-office-365-with-office-365-powershell

Glossary

The following terms are mentioned in this book.

A record: Part of the Domain Name System (DNS). Normally, it returns a 32-bit IPv4 address.

AAAA record: Part of the Domain Name System (DNS). Normally, it returns a 128-bit IPv6 address.

AAD Connect: Tool that allows you to link an on-premises (or Azure) Active Directory service to Office 365. This allows seamless integration to Office 365 resources, such as password reset and password synchronization.

Active Directory (AD): Database designed to store information about your Microsoft network environment, including users, groups, passwords, user contact information, and network configuration. It is normally replicated across your network.

AD FS: Active Directory Federation Services. This tool extends Active Directory to off-premises applications and systems (outside the firewall). AD FS allows single sign-on.

alias: An e-mail address that points to another e-mail address. People outside the system can e-mail to an alias address. You can have as many alias addresses as you want in Office 365.

app: A component of Office 365 business subscriptions. Apps have a single-purpose focus.

app store: An application-marketing place where applications may be purchased to extended Office 365. Apps may be added on a per-user or a company basis in Office 365.

© Matthew Katzer 2018
M. Katzer, *Securing Office 365*, https://doi.org/10.1007/978-1-4842-4230-8

autodiscover: Part of the Domain Name System (DNS). Autodiscover describes the name (IP address) of the location that a program such as Outlook can find the Exchange Server for a given e-mail account. Implemented as a CNAME record, it may have to be implemented on a DNS local server, as well as at the domain registrar. For Office 365, the initial Exchange Server address is `autodiscover.outlook.com`.

Azure: The Microsoft cloud platform that manages all computing activities for Microsoft. Office 365 and other third-party public clouds are cloud applications that are hosted in Azure.

BPOS: Business Productivity Online Standard Suite (the previous name and version of Office 365).

BYOD: Bring your own device. The user brings their own mobile device and connects it the work e-mail client using an MDM or MAM solution.

browser: Web browser, such as Internet Explorer, Firefox, Chrome, or Safari.

CISO: Chief information security officer.

cloud: Any off-premises remote servers connected by a network and hosted on the internet. Examples include Hotmail, Google Docs, Azure and Office 365.

Cloud App Discovery: An Azure service (part of Enterprise Mobility Suite) that deploys an agent on the user's desktop to determine the applications being used. This tool is useful in determining which applications need to be included as a shared resource across Office 365 users.

cloud backup: A third-party service that backs up e-mail, OneDrive for Business, and SharePoint documents to a cloud service for recovery to Office 365.

Cloud PBX: The Skype for Business phone service that may or may not be integrated into a company's office communications systems (or PBX). Cloud PBX may be deployed in hybrid or stand-alone mode in Office 365.

cloud solution provider: A Microsoft cloud partner that offers cloud solutions that include Office 365 for its customers. A CSP bills Office 365 services on behalf of its customers.

CNAME record: Part of the Domain Name System (DNS). The alias of one name to another.

coexistence: A type of migration, where the mail flow (via the MX record) remains through the original e-mail server as test groups are migrated to Office 365. Mail flow is redirected to Office 365 at the end of the migration.

compliance: A set of business policies that allows businesses to operate and meet local, state, federal, and international regulations on information sharing and business operations.

content type: Defines the attributes of a SharePoint list item, a document, or a folder. There is a content type per site collection. It could be considered as a "collection of columns for reuse" in other lists or document libraries. Content types are inherited.

core business software: The software that is the heart of the business. This could be the point-of-sale software for a retail store or the order-tracking system for a warehouse. This is the software that runs the business.

CSP: See *cloud solution provider*.

cutover: A type of migration, where the mail flow (via the MX record) is redirected to Office 365 for the entire organization at one time.

data loss prevention: A machine learning process that reviews all business communications based on a set of rules that can permit or block information to third parties. DLP is used to prevent the distribution of information to users outside of an organization.

Delve: A machine-learning tool that looks at all of the users' business documents and organizes them in a way that is relevant to what is trending with users.

DirSync: Allows an Active Directory instance to be synchronized to another Active Directory instance. In the Office 365 world, an on-premises Active Directory is synchronized (now including passwords) to the Office 365 Active Directory for your tenant. This has been replaced by AAD Connect.

distribution groups: Lists of e-mail addresses. E-mailing to a distribution group (previously called a distribution list) sends the e-mail to each user in the group. A distribution group can be for internal e-mail only or available to the outside world.

DLP: See *data loss prevention*.

DNS: Domain Name System; also the protocol used by the Domain Name System. Used to look up additional information (or translate) a name to an IP address.

document: A Word, Excel, PowerPoint, or other type of file within a SharePoint document library. A document may have independent permissions.

document library: A set of documents within a SharePoint site. In many ways, a document library is a specialized list that contains the document and associated metadata. A document library is separate from a page but usually is displayed on a page. When you select and display a specific document library, the page ribbon shows actions that can be performed in the document library or the folders and documents within it, such as setting permissions or deleting an item. A document library may contain folders and documents.

document set: A feature in SharePoint Server 2013 that enables an organization to manage a single deliverable, or work product, that can include multiple documents or files. A document set is a special kind of folder that combines unique document set attributes—the attributes and behavior of folders and documents—and provides a user interface (UI), metadata, and object model elements to help manage all aspects of the work product.

domain name: Often referred to as "custom" or "vanity" domains, this is the name of an organization on the Internet, used for its e-mail and web site. A domain name is maintained (and reported to the rest of the world) by a domain registrar. Examples of domain names are `kamind.net`, `microsoft.com`, and `getoffice365now.com`.

domain registrar: An organization that maintains your domain information; example are eNom, Network Solutions, and GoDaddy. See also DNS.

EBS: Essential Business Server.

e-mail migration: The process of moving existing (historical) e-mail to a new e-mail service.

EMS: See Enterprise Mobility Suite.

Enterprise Mobility Suite: A suite of software from Microsoft that helps to manage and monitor user identity (access to cloud resources) and information rights (how those resources are used).

Essential Business Server: A configured three-server solution (Exchange, SharePoint, Systems Center) for companies with 75 to 400 employees. Microsoft canceled this offering on March 4, 2010. One of the factors was the cost per employee, as compared with the Microsoft cloud offering.

Exchange Federation: A mechanism for trust between Exchange servers.

Exchange Federation remote mailbox move: A form of e-mail migration between federated Exchange servers. In Office 365, this is normally between an on-premises Exchange server and the Office 365 Exchange server(s) of your tenant.

Exchange Online Protection (EOP): A Microsoft service that filters incoming e-mail for spam and viruses. Formerly known as Forefront Online Protection for Exchange (FOPE), this service is included in the hosted Exchange area of Office 365. Several controls can be used to customize the service.

Exchange public folders: A method of sharing information within an organization, using Exchange Server as the database. Contrast this with SharePoint.

Exchange Server: A Microsoft services software product that receives, stores, and forwards e-mail (and other information, such as calendars, contacts, and folders) for an organization. A user typically sees the e-mail, calendar, and contacts through a client, such as Outlook, or through a web browser. Hosted Exchange servers are maintained by an external service, such as Office 365.

.exe file: Executable file. These cannot be stored (directly) in SharePoint; use a .zip file.

external contacts: Contact information about people outside an organization.

FastTrack: A service that speeds the onboarding and education of Office 365 customers on Office 365.

firewall: An appliance that monitors and inspects Internet traffic according to a set of rules that filer or block Internet communication and protects local computer resources from public (Internet) access.

folder: Similar to a folder on your PC and part of a SharePoint document library. Folders may have independent permissions. A folder contains documents.

FTP: File Transfer Protocol. When implemented by an FTP server, it is a method used to share files. There are security and usability issues. See SharePoint as an alternative.

governance: A set of business polices governing an organization's actions. Governance can be internally driven or regulation driven.

hybrid coexistence: A type of migration. In the Office 365 context, an organization's e-mail can be stored in the organization's on-premises Exchange Server or the Office 365–hosted Exchange Server for the tenant. After establishing Exchange Federation, an administrator can move users' e-mail boxes to and from the cloud.

immutability: The attribute of not being able to be changed. The preservation of data in its original form is "immutable" (cannot be changed) and is kept in a form that is electronically discoverable.

Intune: A device management tool that manages the company's computing assets (phones, tables, laptops, Macs, or PCs). Intune is used to manage mobility devices' access to company business information.

IP address: Internet Protocol address. This is the numeric address of a device or service.

KAMIND IT: IT cloud advisors (see `www.kamind.com`).

legal hold: An action that is placed on a mailbox to meet compliance requirements for future discovery and searching.

list: A set of items within a SharePoint site. You can think of a list as a bunch of rows and columns with a data value potentially at the intersection, like a spreadsheet. There are specialized lists that have special properties. A list is distinct from a page but usually is displayed on a page. When you select and display a specific list, the page ribbon shows actions that can be performed on the list or items in it, such as setting permissions or deleting an item. Special list types include Task List and Calendar List.

Lync: See Skype for Business.

mail flow: How a particular piece of e-mail flows from the sender to the receiver. See also *MX record*.

MAM: See *Mobile Application Management*.

MDM: See *Mobile Device Management*.

metadata: Additional data stored about/with a SharePoint item; for example, the date and author of a document. This data is searchable.

Microsoft domain name: The prefix for `.onmicrosoft.com`. This is also the basis of your SharePoint site; for `xxx.onmicrosoft.com`, the SharePoint site is `xxx.sharepoint.com`. This cannot be changed, nor can it be moved between different Office 365 plans.

Microsoft online services: Services provided by Microsoft, including Office 365 and Windows Intune.

migration: Copying data (typically e-mail, calendar entries, and contacts) from your existing environment to Office 365.

Mobile Application Management: Links the mobile applications (like Microsoft Office applications) to Office 365 and Azure for application management. A MAM enrolled device protects company data and allows the company to remove the data from the device remotely without erasing the device.

Mobile Device Management: Links the mobile devices to Office 365 and Azure for hardware management. An MDM enrolled device protects company data and allows the company to remove the data from the device remotely.

MX record: Part of the Domain Name System (DNS). An MX record tells the outside world the location of your mail service (name or IP address).

Office 365: The brand for the collection of Microsoft cloud services. Office 365 includes hosted Exchange e-mail, Lync Enterprise voice, SharePoint, and several software options. It is generally considered to be software-as-a-service.

Office 365 ProPlus: The current version of Office Professional, currently Office 2013. This is the full Office product and can be installed on up to five devices (under the same login), such as your work desktop, a laptop, a Mac, and a home computer.

Office 365 Wave 14: A version first released in July 2012.

Office 365 Wave 15: A version first released in March 2013.

off-premises: Often used as a synonym for *cloud*, this actually denotes hardware devices and software that are located outside of your company location (off-site).

on-premises: This generally refers to equipment, computing resources, or people who are located at a company location (as opposed to at home or on the road).

on-site: People or equipment that is located at a company location (as opposed to at home or on the road). Usually a synonym for on-premises.

OneDrive: The consumer version of OneDrive for Business. OneDrive is a file sync tool and does not incorporate version control or business data mining.

OneDrive for Business: Stores business documents in a structure manner that allows full searching and access using the Office 365 machine learning tools. The OneDrive for Business configuration maintains a version history of up to 500 copies of a document.

OneNote: A note-taking tool that allows any form of communications to be recorded in a business document called a *notebook*. Business communications include voice, typed and transcribed notes, pictures, and links to other business communications.

Outlook profile: Read by the Outlook client and contains the e-mail accounts that are to be included in this execution of Outlook.

OWA: Outlook Web App.

page: What you see with your web browser. You can have multiple pages within a site. Generally, a site presents a default page that users will think of as "the site."

permissions: The "who can do it" aspect of SharePoint. Permissions are set on a site, list, document library, and so forth. Permission levels include None, Read, View, Contribute (Read and Write), and more. A particular user must have "permission" to do that activity on that item, for example, the ability to update the item.

pilot/test group: A group of users who are to be migrated. The first pilot/test group should include both raving fans and naysayers, and it should be designed to test a combination of user needs to ferret out issues early in a migration.

POP mail: Post Office Protocol mail. POP is a protocol (method) of transferring e-mail from an e-mail server to an e-mail client. In a practical sense, each e-mail client receives its own copy of the e-mail. The effect is that you must frequently delete an e-mail from each client after it has been received. Contrast this with Exchange Server, where e-mail is stored on the server and the protocol allows an action (such as deletion or movement to a folder) on an e-mail to be reflected immediately on Exchange Server.

Power BI: Organizes information contained in one or more spreadsheets in a visual manner to speed business decisions.

PST export/import: A PST file (the file extension for an Outlook personal information store file) stores e-mail on your computer. It can contain archived e-mails or current POP mail. Export is a process in Outlook that copies e-mail from a mailbox to a PST format file. In the context of Office 365, PST Import is the Outlook process that copies a PST file to the Office 365–hosted Exchange Server. It is a method of e-mail migration.

PSTN: Public Switch Termination Network. This is your traditional wired phone systems for homes or business.

push install: An automated installation that is set up by IT to push updates to the desktop, with no user interaction. Software updates are pushed and automatically installed.

S4B: See Skype for Business.

security group: A security group is a type of Active Directory object that can be used to grant permissions in SharePoint.

selective wipe: A security process where Intune (part of EMS) selectively wipes business information from a mobile device. This feature is part of a MAM and/or MDM deployment. .

SharePoint: Microsoft's document storage and content management tool. SharePoint was first released in 2001. Originally, SharePoint was used as an enterprise's on-premises intranet. SharePoint is fundamentally a web server that presents web pages to your browser (Internet Explorer, Firefox, Chrome, Safari, etc.). The SharePoint data (structure, permissions, sites, your documents, etc.) is hosted on SQL Server, which is maintained by Microsoft within its secure environment.

single sign-on: Lets users log in to an organization's computing resources with a single ID, using Active Directory Federation Services (AD FS).

single-user identity: A service provided by EMS that allows Office 365 to manage third-party credentials such as Google Docs, Salesforce.com, and other cloud offerings using the users Office 365 credentials. This allows a single user login for all resources.

site: A collection of SharePoint "apps" and web parts (components), such as document libraries, lists, tasks, blogs, pictures, templates, and text that are presented to a user at a particular URL as a page. A site is within a particular site collection. An example is a project site.

site collection: A collection of SharePoint sites. With the Enterprise plan, you may have multiple site collections within your tenant. Site collections have sets of properties that are the same for all sites within a site collection; they may be different between site collections.

site contents: The contents of a SharePoint site. The site contents page shows lists, libraries, and other apps and subsites that are associated with this site. This page is a helpful reference to your site structure. Access to this screen appears as a link on a site page or as a drop-down choice under the "gear" icon at the top right of the screen. Only items that you have permission to see will show.

Skype for Business: A communications client tool included in Office 365 that supports text, voice, and video communication with a whiteboard, shared programs, PowerPoint, shared monitors, and polls to one or more people. It can be used for planned or ad hoc meetings, person-to-person communication, and remote support.

SPF record: Part of the Domain Name System (DNS). Sender Policy Framework is an e-mail system to help prevent e-mail spam. The SPF record (normally implemented as a TXT record) describes which hosts are allowed to send from the domain. In Office 365, the sender is `spf.protection.outlook.com` for your domain.

SRV record: Part of the Domain Name System (DNS). An SRV record describes the location (protocol and port) for a given service at a host. Office 365 Lync requires two SRV records for correct implementation.

SSO: Single sign-on provides a single sign-on to an organization's computing resources, using Active Directory Federation Services (AD FS).

subsite: A SharePoint subsite is simply a site under (within) a site. You can nest sites until you confuse yourself.

SWAY: An Office 365 application that allows you to express your ideas across any device. SWAY is future replacement to PowerPoint for presentations and is included Office 365 business subscription with the Office component.

Teams: A software application that allows users to collaborate in a self-managed environment on Office 365.

tenant: Your Office 365 account, including hosted Exchange, Lync, SharePoint, and Office 365 Active Directory. The first account that you create when you first purchase Office 365 is the "owner" of your tenant. This account should be an admin account, not a person. This account does not normally require an Office 365 license. Relating to SharePoint, all of your site collections are within your tenant. You can have any number of domains within your tenant (with e-mail accounts), but you will have only one root SharePoint URL: `https://xxxx.sharepoint.com`.

TXT record: Part of the Domain Name System (DNS). A TXT record can contain any type of text. See *SPF record*. For Office 365, a TXT record is also used to prove domain ownership. (A specific TXT record is added by the domain registrar for your domain.)

two-factor authentication (2FA): Part of EMS that manages access to Office 365 and Azure information resources. 2FA uses two parts of the security rule that includes something you know (knowledge), something you have (device), and something you are (bio). Typical 2FA uses a smartphone with a PIN that changes and a password to grant access to computing resources.

URL: Universal resource locator. The specific universal address for a web page, a URL is essentially a specific location within a domain within the World Wide Web. (This doesn't necessarily mean you can see it from anywhere; there can be security restrictions.) Examples are `https://kamindit.sharepoint.com`.

virtualization: A server or desktop operating system running on a virtual host. The server or desktop operating systems are running in a hardware-agnostic mode because the hardware services are supplied by the virtual host.

web part: SharePoint components that can be inserted into a page (part of a site). Web parts are powerful and can interact with other sites and data outside of SharePoint.

web site: A SharePoint web site is a specialized site collection that can be seen by the outside world (public-facing) through a standard URL (such as `www.kamind.com`). You may have only one web site within a tenant.

www record: Part of the Domain Name System (DNS). It provides the name or IP address of a web server for a given domain name.

Yammer: A business communication tool where the business information is owned by the company that allows users to express and share information in an unstructured manner. Yammer is sometimes referred to as the internal Facebook of the business. Yammer information is data mined by Delve for the internal use of the company.

Index

A

Admin center, 62, 504
Administer global functions, 515
Administration center
    administrator roles, 519
    billing administrator, 522
    configuration
        administration roles, 541–542
        company options, 534–536
        deleting users, 544
        domains, 525
        external sharing, 550
        grouping licenses, 531
        license, assigning, 542, 543
        license quantity, changing, 530
        multifactor authentication (*see*
            Multifactor authentication)
        open license key activation, 531
        open subscription activation and
            links, 530
        password expiration, 532
        password information, 540–541
        renaming user, 547
        restore deleted users, 546
        security groups, 549
        troubleshooting, domain, 528
        user information and E-mail
            address, 540
        user information, changing, 544

functions, 519
global administrator, 522
licenses dashboard, 517
logging administrator, 516–517
new Office 365, 518
One Drive for Business (*see* One Drive
    for Business)
partner administrators, 536–537
password administrator, 522
service support administrator, 522
Skype for Business (*see* Skype for
    Business (S4B))
user management administrator, 522
Administrator roles, 519
Advanced Threat Protection
    (ATP), 27, 374, 499
Advance query strings (AQS), 401
Alias e-mail address
    adding distribution group, 592
    distribution group, creation, 591
    grant permissions, 594–595
    group for external access,
        enabling, 594
    Outlook, 595–596
    restricting access, distribution
        group, 593
Autodiscover, 607–608
Azure Active Directory, 231–232, 252, 279,
    309, 323

© Matthew Katzer 2018
M. Katzer, *Securing Office 365*, https://doi.org/10.1007/978-1-4842-4230-8

N

O

T

Printed in the United States
By Bookmasters